FLYING FORTRESS

FLYING FORTRESS

The Illustrated Biography of the B-17s and the Men Who Flew Them

EDWARD JABLONSKI

ECHO POINT BOOKS & MEDIA, LLC

Published by Echo Point Books & Media
Brattleboro, Vermont
www.EchoPointBooks.com

ISBN: 978-1-62654-904-3

Cover Image: *B-17s Over Europe* by David Ray
Courtesy of National Archives (6425779)

Cover Design by Adrienne Núñez,
Echo Point Books & Media

Editorial and proofreading assistance by Christine Schultz,
Echo Point Books & Media

For DAVID

*It was just that on some nights the air
became sick and there was an unspoken
contagion of spiritual dread, and we were
little boys again, lost in the dark.*
ERNIE PYLE

One picture is worth a thousand words.

CONTENTS

BALLAD OF THE BLOODY CENTURY

FESTUNG EUROPA

SUPERFORTRESS

SUPPLEMENT

PREFACE

The pretty German girl pedaled her bicycle to the side of the street. She heard the roar of a speeding truck approaching from behind; it was probably a military vehicle and the wiser course was to get well out of its way.

Safely at the curb she stopped, turned to watch and froze in horror. Just a few feet above the street she saw not a truck but an enormous four-engined aircraft bearing down on her. Black, deadly snouts of machine guns projected from various positions in the plane's massive body, its upper part a mottled brown and its underside an indeterminate light blue. Near one wingtip she could see a white, five-pointed star—the insignia of the American air forces. As fascinated as she was frightened the *Fräulein* recognized it as an American bomber.

The enemy plane overtook her in seconds, and as it passed by, she saw the men in the side gun positions waving at her. Although the two gun barrels in the round turret underneath the belly of the plane pointed directly at her, there was no gunfire as the plane thundered over. And, though she could not hear them, other members of the crew whistled at her.

She watched, shaken and at the same time curious, as the big plane reached the square where the two churches stood, their twin spires jutting above the flight path of the bomber. With its engines trailing a black wisp of smoke, the wounded craft merely banked gracefully, one wing almost scraping the cobbled street, and flew between the two steeples. As suddenly as it had appeared from one distance, the great aircraft hurtled into another, leaving behind a perplexed, shocked girl bicyclist. "Little Willie" was taking the *Autobahn* route home to England.

"Little Willie" was a Boeing B-17 Flying Fortress, piloted by Bernard M. Dopko of Old Forge, Pennsylvania; their destination: Station 136, Knettishall Airdrome, England, home base of the 388 Bombardment Group (H). Struck by flak over Berlin, with the supercharger on one engine out of commission, and a runaway propeller on another, "Little Willie" plunged out of the group formation. German fighters swept in for the kill. As tail gunner Robert M. Haydon, Jr.

drove them off, Dopko pointed the plane toward the earth to shake off the fighters. When bombardier William Kelly shouted, "Look out, Dop, you're going to run into the curb!" Dopko leveled out and they were now fifty feet above the ground on the outskirts of Berlin.

As far as the Group was concerned "Little Willie" was officially "missing in action." The runaway engine was threatening to wrench off the wing, the other engine was useless, the tail was badly damaged and the radio was out completely. Feathering the windmilling propeller, Dopko was able to remain airborne, but barely, and pointed toward England. With only two engines it was impossible to gain altitude, but that was protection from fighter attack. Across Germany and Holland the B-17 never exceeded a hundred feet in altitude; over the English Channel they were down to ten. At this level one of the dead engines came back to life and "Little Willie" climbed to 5000 feet and easily made Knettishall. The Flying Fortress had brought its crew home again.

This is not strictly a military history, but rather the "biography" of a single aircraft, the legendary Boeing B-17 Flying Fortress, from its inception as the ill-fated Model 299, through its evolutionary modifications and ultimate development as the B-29 Superfortress. While historical content is inevitable and as accurate as I could make it, the emphasis is upon the men who flew in the B-17 and not a little upon the lore the plane inspired.

Officially the B-17 was listed on the Air Force procurement tables as a "heavy" bombardment airplane; its mission: strategic bombardment accomplished with precision during daylight hours over long distances. Stated in another way, the Flying Fortress was a long-range heavy bomber whose function in time of war was daylight precision strategic bombardment. It is interesting to note how misunderstood and controversial a concept this is, even today. While it made good sense in wartime to fly over enemy cities and bomb them, that was not the purpose of strategic bombardment. Targets, and especially populated areas, were not bombed at random; there was careful selection of targets and the mission of the heavy bombers was to destroy the enemy's facilities for making war, to make it impossible for him to fight by denying him weapons, machines, and fuel.

This concept has been called by one German writer "wasteful, inhumane, and ineffective." The implication is that a war waged otherwise would be humane and not wasteful. The effectiveness of the heavy strategic bombardment program in Europe was attested to in the death of the *Luftwaffe* which was destroyed in the air and on the ground and in the denial of fuel to the Nazi war machine. No better exemplification of this may be suggested than the absence of air opposition to the Normandy landings on June 6, 1944. In the Pacific the dropping of two atomic bombs made the already planned invasion of the Japanese home islands unnecessary. Just how many lives were spared because of this we shall never know (some estimate about two million). Thus would it appear that Hiroshima and Nagasaki, despite the terrible personal tragedies they brought, were less "wasteful, inhumane, and ineffective" than it has become almost fashionable to believe. The aim was not retaliation but prevention. There are no degrees of death: a .30-caliber bullet is no more merciful than an atomic blast. The victim—man, woman, or child—is equally dead.

And, it might be remembered, that there would never have been a Hiroshima had there been no Pearl Harbor.

xii

This is not interjected as a means of justification but only as a statement of fact. Another is that the high command of the U. S. Air Force, in wartime, was not dedicated to saving the lives of enemy civilians but to keeping its own losses down while doing its job. In modern war the innocent suffer with the guilty; there is no sharp distinction between soldier and civilian. The latter supplies the former with the means.

The job of the men flying in the Boeing B-17 was to strike at military targets. They did this with courage and skill and their stories are little known. They hated their job, they knew fear, dread, and death. Whatever their varied backgrounds they shared a hatred of war and love for their plane. Many continue to recall the Flying Fortress as "the best plane of the war," capable of absorbing unbelievable punishment and still bring them home. In their darker moments they believed they could cling to this plane and it would bring them home. With wings punctured and ablaze, tail surfaces shredded, with chunks of its graceful body gouged out by cannon fire, flak, or mid-air collision, the B-17 brought them home. With an almost human will to live this great plane, shattered and torn beyond the limits of flyability, carried them to safety and, for some, to life itself.

Watching one of these giant aircraft, like some living thing, clawing at the air in a vain attempt to remain aloft or at least in momentary level flight, was an awesome sight. The life and death struggle of so large a thing had its further poignance: there were ten men inside, some dead perhaps, some wounded, some not even so much as scratched, but at that moment all their lives had reached a crisis in that single plane, heaving and smoking in a freezing, hostile sky.

Defining the valor of these men, and many will insist, of this plane, is a difficult task. After more than two decades it is possible for the men to look back upon the "work" they were engaged in during the Second World War with some detachment. Whatever the arguments of the adherents to the opposite view, it is unquestionable that the men in the heavy bombers—B-17s as well as B-24s, and the B-29s—made victory possible. They shortened the war. They paid a heavy price. They were young when it all began and, if they lived, they were old when it ended. They had, and have, no illusions about the glamour of the "wild blue yonder." And because they "worked" in the air—five or six miles above the earth—they placed themselves in double jeopardy. They had not only all the risks that the ground troops encountered, but had to contend with the element of the air in between. There was no friendly earth to burrow into when the shooting became rough. And there were times when you could not even have the satisfaction of shooting back at those who were shooting at you. It all became a tragic demonstration of the laws of chance as you continued on through the puffs of black antiaircraft smoke. Would it be that the speed of your B-17 and its altitude would chance to be in the particular path which would intersect the path of a projectile which was shot up, more or less at random, and end it all there? Despite this they went out day after day, some came back, some cracked and some gave up. But most of them believed in what they were doing and completed the job.

Today these men recall their war experiences with some dread; it is difficult for them to believe that once they endured such adventures. They would not want to relive them; and not one of them—of the several dozen I interviewed for this book—could be called a "war lover." They hated their work, but they knew they had to do all they could to stop the man who had got them their job. And they did in the most devastating demonstration of modern warfare ever known. Neither they, nor we, nor anyone else can afford to have further demonstrations of strategic bombardment. Its application in the Second World War was only the beginning—even at Hiroshima.

There is another, almost ineffable, sentiment shared by these men: they loved their plane. Ex-crew members continue to this day to recall the B-17 with a mingling of devotion, gratitude, and *mystique*.

The more objective, professional, military evaluation supports their beliefs. Lieutenant General Ira C. Eaker, pioneer of the Air Force's strategic bombardment program during its critical period, said, "The B-17, I think, was the best combat airplane ever built. It combined in perfect balance, the right engine, the right wing and the right control surfaces. The B-17 was a bit more rugged than the B-24. It could ditch better because of the low wing and it could sustain more battle damage. You wouldn't believe they could stay in the air."

General Curtis E. LeMay, Chief of Staff of the Air Force and an outstanding air leader during the Second World War, told me that "the Air Force kind of grew up with the B-17. It was as tough an airplane as was ever built. It was a good honest plane to fly—a pilot's airplane. It did everything we asked it to do, and did it well."

"By far the best bomber we had in the war," is the opinion of General Carl A. Spaatz, who commanded all air operations of the U. S. Air Force in Europe. "I'd rather have the B-17 than any other. The B-29? That was another plane—and another war."

E.J.

NOTE

Proper military historians will discover, perhaps to their consternation, that contrary to correct military usage, I have not capitalized operation code names. The term TORCH therefore, will become "Torch." The use of Roman numerals (VIII Bomber Command) will be avoided. Such proper usage, I feel, can make a book look like a coded message. I leave its distinctive look to more formal histories.

During the period this book covers the United States Air Force passed through various reorganizations and consequently so did its name—United States Army Air Corps, GHQ Air Force, Army Air Forces, etc. Unless the distinction is important, the term "Air Force" will be employed throughout, although the Air Force as such did not materialize until 1947. Whatever it was properly called, it was still the same organization of young American men flying American aircraft.

Finally, although a long list of acknowledgments may be found in the Supplement, special mention should be made of the Air Force's excellent Book Program under the direction of Lieutenant Colonel Gene Guerny. A superb sense of history is responsible for the Air Force's many remarkable archives, photo collections, and other source materials so readily available to writers, historians and scholars. Everything right in this book must be attributed to the aid and cooperation of the Air Force, the nature of which never interfered with any of my own opinions, however militarily wayward. The contribution of my editor, Harold Kuebler, at every stage of this book's production is beyond mere praise. The care and attention to details, his splendid suggestions, his wide knowledge of the subject and his genuine interest did more for this book than I can ever fully acknowledge. It was at all times a most gratifying collaboration.

E. J.

PRELUDE

The greatest battle plane of its time, and perhaps of all time, was conceived aboard a battleship—its mother was an unknown necessity and its father a sailor. As it is with most happy illegitimacies, the birth occurred before the advent of the necessity which would come to be known as World War II. Had this birth not happened, the course of recent history might have been tragically different.

In the spring of 1928 Clairmont L. Egtvedt, then a vice-president of the Boeing Aircraft Company, called on Rear Admiral Joseph M. Reeves aboard the Navy aircraft carrier *Langley*, docked off North Island in San Diego Bay. Egtvedt had flown down from Boeing's headquarters in Seattle to talk with Reeves, who commanded the Navy's air fleet, about the latest development in Boeing's series of little F4B shipboard fighters. In the course of their talks the two men touched upon the subject of the battleship versus the airplane, a controversy which had not been settled despite the efforts of Brigadier General William Mitchell seven years before. Though Mitchell's bombers had, indeed, sunk the "unsinkable" German battleship *Ostfriesland* in 1921, the Navy rejected the results of the experiment as inconclusive because the setting hardly simulated actual battle conditions. The battleship, as well as all the others sunk in the tests, was neither manned nor maneuvering. But there was no denying that it had gone to the bottom.

An Army-Navy Board, with General John J. Pershing at the head, found on evaluating the results of the tests that the battleship would continue as "the bulwark of the nation's sea defenses," though it recommended that aircraft car-

A Boeing F4B-1, early shipboard fighter leaving the deck of the Langley.

riers be developed as auxiliary vessels. There was a slight nod in the direction of the air, when the Board conceded that land-based aircraft might very well have "important strategic and tactical qualities in operations of coast defense."

The function of the little shipboard fighters was to harass any attacking fleet once it had been found by the wide ranging patrol planes, the lumbering flying boats. The best that these planes could do would be to drop its load of four 230-pound bombs (or its equivalent) and return to base for more. An entire squadron of fighters, each plane carrying a single 500-pound bomb, could barely dent a battleship and could hardly equal a single battleship in fire power. With a battery of 16-inch guns and a firing range of twenty miles or so, the battleship was a most formidable defensive as well as offensive weapon.

"The airplane," Admiral Reeves told Egtvedt, "is not a dreadnought. No airplane now flying can even be compared with a battleship."

Not even the Army Air Corps with its heavy bombers could match that. Under the provisions of the Air Corps Act of 1926 the Air Service was transformed into the Air Corps and fell under control of the Army's General Staff. Comprised mainly of conservative ground traditionalists, the General Staff believed that the proper function of air power was as a servant to the ground forces. They failed, or refused, to recognize the full implications of the terms "air power" and "air force," which had been suggested merely during the Great War and demonstrated by Mitchell's declarations and denunciations.

The challenge to Egtvedt was a complex one. Not only would he have to overcome the inertia of the services, but there was an even more formidable problem: how to design, let alone build, an airplane comparable to a battleship?

Boeing F2B-1s lined up on the Langley.

Giantism in aircraft design proved only to be spectacular in appearance; performance was another thing. The 1920 Barling bomber, a triplane with a wing-span of 120 feet and six engines to power it, barely attained a speed of 90 mph and on a clear, calm day might just make a flight of 300 miles. Provided, that is, it were not encumbered by a payload.

There were other, even more subtle, problems. The nation, in 1928, was reaching the climax of its Jazz Age joyride and its mood hardly encompassed the purchase of weapons of war. This was reflected in an isolationist Congress which proceeded to scuttle the League of Nations and to cut itself off from Europe. The "War to End All Wars" was over and America, secure in a splendid two ocean isolation, could lavish its adulation upon "Lucky Lindy," without at all being aware what it was that the young pilot had proved.

When he returned to Seattle, therefore, Egtvedt carried with him the germ of an idea, a challenge, that he would have to set aside while he confronted more immediate problems. Coincidentally, the answer to the challenge lay in a series of developments that Boeing undertook at this point.

Patently the future of an aircraft manufacturer in 1928 did not lay in focusing on military planes. Under the impetus of the Lindbergh flight aviation once again captured the public imagination as it had during the Great War and shortly after; there was a quickening of interest in commercial aviation also. With this in mind Clair Egtvedt and Edward Hubbard, airline pioneer and founder of Boeing Air Transport, decided to work up a design for an all-metal monoplane for commercial use. As a mail and cargo transport it would be more efficiently rugged than the fabric-covered planes; if it were fitted with a thick

Clairmont Egtvedt.

wing of cantilevered construction it would not only have strength but would be unencumbered by drag-producing external supports such as struts and wires. It was agreed to use a smooth stressed-skin metal covering in place of the corrugated type of "skin" of the then operational Ford transports.

Charles N. Montieth was engineer in charge of the project to produce the Boeing Model 200, which emerged as the Monomail and flew for the first time in May 1930. The Monomail, called "the first modern air transport," was a cleanly designed low-wing monoplane with quite innovational features such as a retractable landing gear, the bridge-like interior structure of the wing, the employment of "drag-ring" cowling to lessen the wind resistance of the Pratt & Whitney "Hornet" engine. The pilot, however, was provided with an open cockpit.

A second Monomail (Model 221), was constructed along similar lines but with provision for six passengers in addition to cargo space. Subsequent models (the 221A) were modified for transcontinental mail and passenger service. The one major obstacle to a full exploitation of the inherent performance of the Monomail was the fact that it had appeared before the advent of the controllable pitch propeller. Since take-off and climb required low pitch and cruising high pitch, the Monomail with its single pitch propeller was never able to show what it could do. By the time the new propeller had been developed the Monomail was rendered obsolescent by multiengine designs. Despite this, the ideas in aircraft design and structure introduced by the plane were to have far-reaching effects.

The Monomail, the first modern air transport.

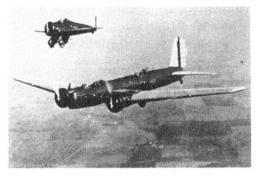

In the foreground: the Y1B-9A and, behind it, the first modern pursuit, the Y1P-26.

Boeing 247.

One of the first was a military adaptation of the design. Even before the Monomail had flown, drawings for the Boeing Model 214, a bomber, were prepared by John Sanders in January 1930. By April of 1931 the B-9, as the Army Air Corps designated it, was ready for its test flight. Though Boeing's concept had been encouraged by the Air Corps, financing the design and construction devolved upon the Boeing Company. The test flights in June proved that the B-9 could fly 85 miles an hour faster than the Army's Keystone bomber, then much in use, and could, in fact, overtake the most modern pursuit planes of the day. The B-9 not only revolutionized bomber design but also that of the fighter plane. Tests on the wing at Wright Field proved that it was one of the finest ever designed, but some "bugs" remained. The engines vibrated excessively and the long slender fuselage of the plane had a tendency to twist in flight. These could easily be fixed, but the Glenn L. Martin Company, whose earlier design lost out to the B-9 in the competitions, had submitted yet another plane. The Martin B-10 was the result and would become the backbone of the Air Corps' bombardment arm for the ensuing decade.

Disappointed in the loss of what might have been a good contract, Boeing turned to yet another plane inspired by its Monomail concept. A return to the commercial design, the Model 247 was designed to carry ten passengers, including a crew consisting of pilot, co-pilot, and stewardess. Project engineer was

xxi

Frank Canney and Robert Minshall served as co-ordinator; their efforts, plus those of greater anonymity, resulted in a plane which revolutionized the design of commercial aircraft. For William Boeing it won the coveted Guggenheim Medal for "successful pioneering and achievement in aircraft manufacture and air transportation."

Like the original Monomail, the performance of the Boeing 247 was restricted until the introduction of hydraulically controlled Hamilton-Standard propellers. Such improvements, which included also rubber de-icer "boots," were worked into the Boeing 247D, converted into a racer for Roscoe Turner, who flew it in the MacRobertson Race from England to Australia in 1934. The earlier drag rings were replaced by more efficient NACA (National Advisory Committee for Aeronautics) cowlings. With such refinements the 247D was capable of a top speed of 200 mph and a cruising speed of 189 mph. Practically overnight it made all other contemporary airliners obsolete.

The stage was set for the next evolutionary step. Clairmont Egtvedt was subconsciously searching for a flying dreadnought; the Monomail, the B-9 and the Model 247 had each contributed a giant step toward a yet not clearly defined goal. Boeing had within its reach the ability to produce an aircraft which was dynamically beautiful, efficient, capable of outperforming all other planes in its class, it could carry great loads at high altitudes over long distances and it was structurally rugged.

In 1934, Boeing was fully ready for the next step; it remained only for the Air Corps to initiate it.

THE FLYING FORTRESSES

Declared to be the largest land plane
ever built in America, this 15-ton
flying fortress, built by the Boeing
Airplane Company under Army specifications
today was ready to test its wings . . .

RICHARD L. WILLIAMS
Seattle Times
July 17, 1935

1. Project 299

The standard attitude toward bombardment aviation during the latter 1920s and well into the '30s was as stated in Captain Rowan A. Greer's paper, *International Aerial Regulations*. Published as Air Service Information Circular 566, the paper reflected both the military and civilian point of view especially when it said that "such a thing as aerial bombardment merely for the purpose of indiscriminate terrorizing of a civilian population or wantonly destroying private property not of a military character could not be countenanced by any of the civilized nations of the world." This was, of course, a commendable attitude, provided the other "civilized nations of the world" subscribed to it also. "At present," Greer pointed out, "there are really no rules or laws as to aerial bombardment other than those that a consideration of humanity itself would dictate. Thus, even conceding that war is a merciless thing that knows only force [its] object always is to destroy the enemy's army or resources . . ."

With all the benefits of hindsight (World War I hardly scratched the surface of air power) we now have, it would be unfair to criticize this honestly, even naïvely, held point of view. That wars could be fought according to rules, when the very function of war—to take, and to kill while taking—canceled out all need for rules, seems now an antiquated idea. Modern war, with World War II, became total war without neutral civilians. If the object of war is to "destroy the enemy's army" and "resources," then the blindness of the War Department at the time to

3

the employment of strategic bombardment aircraft is obvious. If the army of the enemy is denied resources, whether it be ammunition, fuel, lubrication, weapons, or tools—which it will be if the resources are destroyed by aircraft which are neither confined to water nor by national boundaries—then the function of strategic bombardment is a most important one.

This was the doctrine preached by many of the younger airmen at the time, among them Henry H. Arnold, Carl A. Spaatz, George C. Kenney, Hugh J. Knerr, and others. They were not intent on killing helpless civilians or destroying cities, but they did advocate the use of large, high performance (fast, heavy load), high flying aircraft which could knock out an enemy's will to fight. Of course, in theory at least, both the ground and navy forces would seem to be relegated to lesser roles in the nation's defense. Actually this was not the purpose of the Air Corps' hopes for a heavy bombardment program. There were those who advocated an independent air force, in agreement with the doctrines of General William Mitchell, but even more were interested in exploiting the full impact of air power in the nation's defense. It was the inability of the War Department, the General Staff, the Army, and even Air Corps senior officers, to grasp the importance of the concept of strategic air power that disgruntled the more imaginative and more progressive airmen.

In the late spring of 1933 the Air Corps held command and staff exercises to test the efficacy of a General Headquarters Air Force under simulated wartime conditions. Under the command of Brigadier General Oscar Westover the GHQ Air Force (Provisional) concentrated the bulk of the Army Air Corps on the west coast. The problem was to repel an "enemy" overseas invasion. Apparently successful, the maneuvers elicited several valuable observations in Westover's report. The concept of a GHQ Air Force to control combat aviation was regarded as sound, although reconnaissance and bombardment were to be the major functions. In his report Westover said, "During these exercises, observation aviation appeared woefully obsolete in performance, as did pursuit aviation in speed characteristics." The new bombers outperformed both. "Bombardment aviation has defensive fire power of such quantity and effectiveness as to warrant the belief that with its modern speeds it may be capable of effectively accomplishing its assigned mission without support," he noted. What with modern devices, formation flying and other means of defense, General Westover concluded that "no known agency can frustrate the accomplishment of a bombardment mission."

Thus was the thinking of the General Staff turned toward the encouragement of bombardment aircraft that might also be employed in reconnaissance.

By July 1933 the Matériel Division at Wright Field undertook an engineering study to determine whether or not an aircraft capable of carrying a bomb load of a ton over a distance of 5000 miles could be built. Such a plane would "reinforce Hawaii, Panama and Alaska without the use of intermediate servicing facilities" and its tactical mission was to destroy distant land and naval targets. Thus was initiated the Air Corps' "Project A," which was submitted to the General Staff for approval. By Lincoln's Birthday, 1934, a budget for the development of a long-range bomber was approved and on May 12 negotiations with Martin and Boeing were authorized for preliminary designs and engineering data.

Clairmont Egtvedt's dream of a flying dreadnought was beginning to come true. By June of the same year the Air Corps awarded Boeing preliminary contracts under the terms of "Project A." Because the undertaking was experimental

4

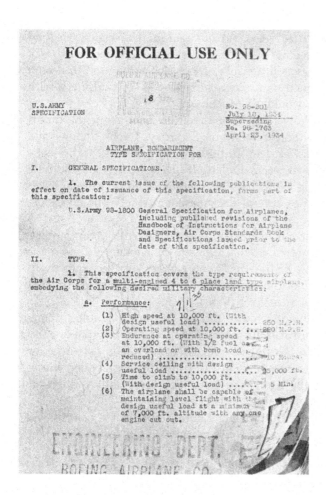

First page of the original booklet containing the Type Specification which initiated the B-17 design.

only one plane was to be built (with the possibility of future orders if it proved worthy) and was designated the XBLR-1 (Experimental Bomber, Long Range Model 1), later simply XB-15.

As visualized by Boeing designers the bomber would be the largest aircraft built in the United States with a wingspan of 149 feet and a fuselage measuring 87 feet 7 inches. When finally completed late in 1937, the XB-15 proved to be conceived on a scale too ambitious for the power plants then available. Under-powered as it was, it could not attain a speed of more than 190 mph and high fuel consumption greatly limited its range. The XB-15 appeared before its time.

Even while Boeing concentrated on the problems posed by "Project A," a circular from Wright Field arrived at the Engineering Department on August 8, 1934. In it were specifications for the hoped for next production (as differenti-ated from the experimental) bomber. Boeing, along with several other manu-facturers, was invited to submit bids for such a plane. The approved design— "a multiengined" aircraft capable of carrying a ton of bombs at more than 200 miles an hour over a distance of two thousand miles—would win the firm an order for as many as 220 planes. The prototype for such a plane was to be ready for tests within a year.

When the U. S. Army specification came in twenty-four-year-old engineer

5

Edward Curtis Wells was just three years out of Stanford University. He had worked on the design of the tail section of the 247. Boeing, having decided to risk its own capital on the new plane, voted the sum of $275,000 to be used to design and construct the bomber. Assigned as project engineer was E. G. Emery with Wells as his assistant; the plane would be Model 299.

"I happened to be placed on Project 299," Wells recalls, "just about the time I planned to be married. We had the ceremony on Saturday; I took Sunday and Monday off." On Tuesday, Wells was deep in preliminary work on the project—within three weeks the basic design was complete. By December when the bulk of the blueprints was ready, young Wells had been promoted to project engineer. Details of the 299 were assigned to several designer-engineers; Wells chose the fuselage as his special job.

Around this time all the concepts were combined: Egtvedt's flying dreadnought, the ideas which had resulted in the all-metal monoplane 247 and the final touch from the still a-borning XB-15: the "multi-engines" of the Army specification were interpreted as four, not the traditional two. The 299, though smaller, bore a striking family resemblance to the XB-15.

With all its facilities, practically, devoted to the 299, Boeing was able to complete the plane by July 1935. Word had already appeared in the newspapers of a "mystery ship" at Boeing Field in Seattle. Keeping the giant plane (at this time the 299 was the largest landplane ever built in the United States) under wraps, Boeing prepared the plane for the Air Corps tests. The field had by this time narrowed down to Boeing, Douglas, and Martin.

The 299 flew for the first time, with test pilot Leslie Tower at the controls, on July 28, 1935. Legend has it that one Seattle newspaperman, on seeing the plane for the first time, exclaimed, "Why it's a flying fortress!"

It was a beautifully designed, streamlined, gleaming giant of a plane. The wings spread to more than a hundred and three feet; the cylindrical fuselage stretched almost sixty-nine feet from turret to tail. Immediately striking was the array of four giant Pratt & Whitney engines protruding from the wing, each with a three-bladed, eleven and a half foot in diameter, propeller. In the nose, a complex of plastic and steel stripping, was a gun position—another bulged from the rear of the cabin, yet another underneath the fuselage and two more on either side of the fuselage. These five gun emplacements won the 299 the name of Flying Fortress. So did the size, as has been suggested. One of the main wheels was almost as tall as a man and the elevator spanned thirty-three feet—three feet more than the wingspan of the Boeing F4B-4 fighter.

To prevent damage by wind to the tail surfaces, the elevators were locked in position when the plane was on the ground. Before taking off the pilot unlocked the tail surfaces by releasing a spring lock in the cockpit. It was just another innovation introduced into the design of the 299.

Following a period of factory testing the plane was flown on August 20, 1935, to Wright Field for Air Corps evaluation testing. With Tower were his assistant, and co-pilot, Louis Wait, Henry Igo of Pratt & Whitney to look after the engines, and C. W. Benton, to serve as mechanic. The more than 2000-mile flight from Boeing Field in Seattle to Wright Field, in Dayton, Ohio, was made in nine hours, non-stop, at an average speed of 232 mph, breaking all previous records for the distance. The average altitude was 12,000 feet and much of the way was flown on the autopilot.

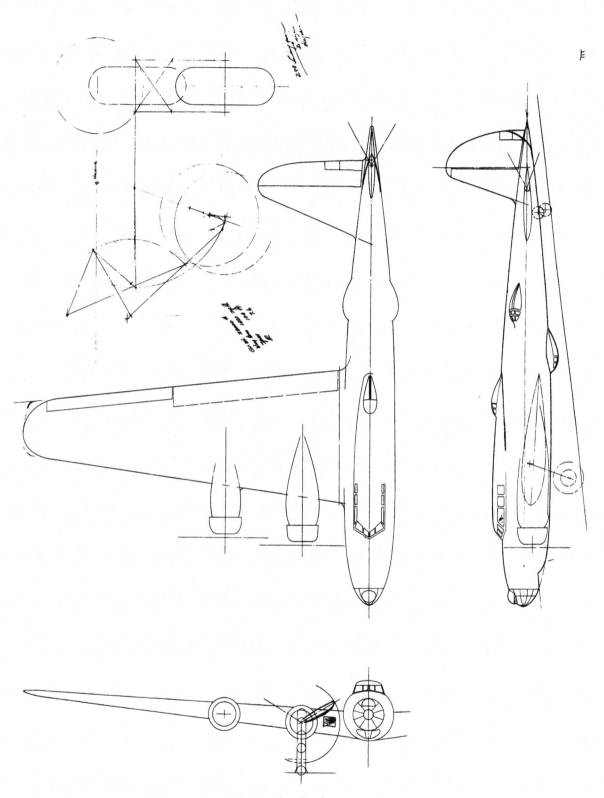

Early design sketches of the B-17 drawn during the development of Project 299.

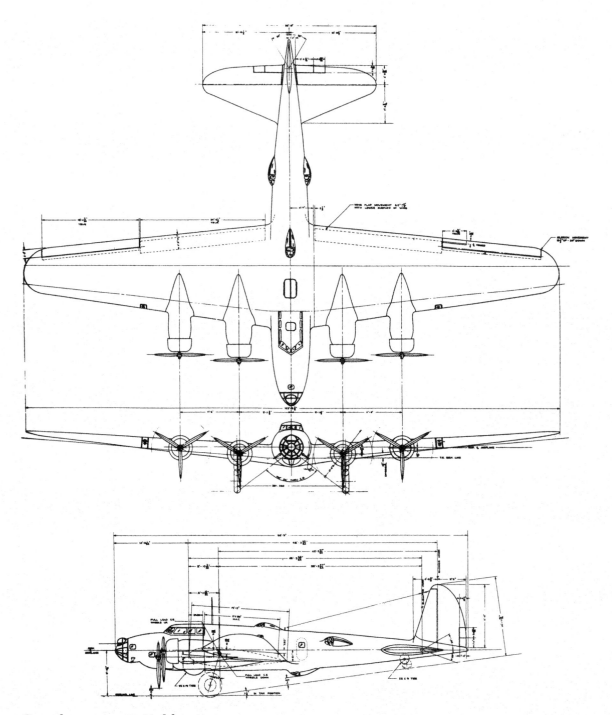

General arrangement, Model 299.

8

The "Mystery Ship," Boeing Model 299, sees the light of day in Seattle.

When the 299 touched down at Wright Field, Tower and the crew were met by Egtvedt and Wells who informed them that they had made such good time that the Air Corps officials did not expect them to arrive for another two hours. The men were exhilarated by their flight and Tower, especially, was loud in the praises of the smooth flying characteristics of the 299.

Preliminary evaluations began when the Air Corps assigned Lieutenant Donald Putt to the plane as project test pilot. Only two other planes, the Martin 146 and the Douglas DB-1, were entered in the competition and each of these was powered by two engines. Preliminary test results were excellent; in fact, the 299 surpassed all the Army specifications for speed, climb, range, and load carrying requirements. Advocates of the strategic bombardment concept recognized the plane as a realization of the plane they had been seeking for years. Then something went wrong.

Major Ployer P. Hill, chief of Wright Field's Flight Testing Section, was to undertake the final phase of the evaluations. On October 30, 1935, Hill sat in the pilot's seat ready for take-off. Putt was to his right, in the co-pilot's seat, and Tower stood behind them to observe. The 299, which the Army was practically ready to designate the XB-17, warmed up and taxied down the field. The four engines roared as the plane began the take-off run, smoothly it rose into the air,

9

The first Flying Fortress on an early flight; Mount Rainier looms in the background.

began to climb—then for some reason stalled, turned on one wing and plunged to the ground. The great plane burst into flame.

When the first of the rescue crew arrived at the scene of the crash, Putt, Igo, and Benton had staggered out of the burning fuselage, but Hill and Tower were still trapped inside. While Captain Leonard Harman attended to the three men, First Lieutenant Robert K. Giovannoli leaped onto the burning wing and was able to pull Tower out through a cabin window. Boeing's test pilot was obviously seriously injured. Giovannoli snatched up a blanket from the ambulance, put it over his head, and returned to the now fiercely blazing plane. Major Hill's foot was jammed in the wreckage. With a penknife, Giovannoli cut away his shoe and pulled him free of the plane. Everyone who had been on the plane, as well as Giovannoli, was badly burned. (For his part in the rescue, Giovannoli was to be given the Cheney Award, but was himself killed in a plane crash before he received it.)

Major Hill never regained consciousness and died later in the afternoon. Leslie Tower, although for a time seemed to be on the way to recovery, died a few days later. To many it seemed that along with these men, Project 299 had died also.

An investigation revealed the cause of the crash. No one had remembered to unlock the tail surfaces before the take-off and, once the plane was airborne, there was no way to control it. Tower attempted to reach the unlocking levers but it had been too late. The official report on the accident emphasized that the crash could not be attributed "to structural failure; to malfunctioning or failure of any of the four engines or propellers; to the action of the automatic pilot because it was not in operation at the time of the crash; to any faulty structural or aerodynamic design of this airplane nor to any undesirable or adverse flying or handling qualities of the airplane."

10

The end of Model 299, Wright Field, Ohio, October 30, 1935.   *Test pilot Leslie Tower.*

While the plane itself was exonerated, the crash furnished fuel for those who would want to see the Air Corps' vision of a powerful fleet of strategic bombers go up in smoke. Perhaps it was true, as it had been hinted even before the crash of the 299, that it was simply "too much airplane for one pilot to handle," or even two. Even with such fine pilots as Tower, Hill, and Putt in the cockpit, the plane had proved too much. To the non-airman the fact that the plane itself had been cleared meant little. The important fact was that it had crashed and killed two men. The presence of four engines was enough to stagger anyone who found the inside of his automobile hood a great mystery.

The airmen who had seen the 299 perform were enthusiastic despite the accident and continued to argue for it. In place of the 185 aircraft authorized by the budget, the Air Corps recommended instead the purchase of 65 B-17s (as the plane would eventually be designated). That was before the crash of the 299, however.

The General Staff, thereupon, authorized production contracts in January 1937 for only thirteen Y1B-17s and 133 twin-engined Douglas B-18s. Part of this could be attributed to the demands of economy for it seemed to make sense that a lot of cheaper planes would be a wiser purchase than a few costly ones. Secretary of War Harry H. Woodring was an advocate of this policy and U. S. Army Chief of Staff General Malin Craig favored the use of aviation for close support of ground forces. Proponents of the strategic concept knew they would have to bide their time.

The YB-17s (the "Y" prefix indicated that the planes were undergoing service testing before, if ever, they were to be purchased in larger orders) differed from the prototype 299 only in the engines. In place of the Pratt & Whitneys, Wright 1820s were installed which increased the horsepower per engine from 750 to 850.

11

The Army's service test aircraft, the Y1B-17, virtually the same as the Model 299 except for the new engines, Wright Cyclones and the single leg landing gear strut.

Slighter changes were introduced into the landing gear (from double to single leg) and in the armament systems.

But bad luck seemed to plague the hopeful Air Corps and its plans for a powerful striking force. The first of the Y1B-17s was ready for flight on December 2, 1936; to test and try out the planes as they came off the assembly lines the Air Corps had sent Captain Stanley Umstead to Boeing Field. On December 7, after a flight, Umstead brought the plane in for a landing. In attempting to brake the heavy bomber, he applied pressure upon the brake too forcefully causing the steel and bronze to heat up and fuse. Aircraft number AC 36-149 snapped over and skidded for eighty yards right into the middle of a Congressional investigation. There was serious consideration given to abandoning the plane, but nothing came of it except to place everyone concerned with the development of the strategic bombardment program on the alert. Any further incident would certainly lose them the Boeing Flying Fortress.

By August 5, 1937, a dozen Y1B-17s were delivered to Langley Field, Virginia, for use by the 2nd Bombardment Group commanded by Lieutenant Colonel Robert C. Olds. The thirteenth plane ordered on the same contract was delivered to the Matériel Division, Wright Field, for experimental testing. Another contract was already drawn authorizing the purchase of another plane (Y1B-17A) as a structural or static test airplane; it was similar to the previous planes produced, but without installations. During the static tests it was to be destroyed on the ground in an attempt to learn how much stress the plane could take before it disintegrated.

One further mishap—this time with a happy ending—would cancel out the need for the static tests.

The Wright R-1820 "Cyclone" engine which powered all of the Flying Fortresses which followed the Model 299.

The 2nd Group, which at the time constituted the entire heavy bombardment strength of the U. S. Army Air Corps, launched a campaign to demonstrate the excellence of the B-17. "We were a careful bunch of fliers in those days," recalls Robert F. Travis, then a second lieutenant and later a brigadier general in World War II, "and each crew was hand-picked. We knew if a YB was crashed we could probably say goodbye to the nation's bomber program." To prevent future pilot error the 2nd Group devised a pilot's check list, a device listing all the actions of the pilot and co-pilot in preparing the plane for take-off, flight, before and after landing. While the B-17 was not "too much airplane" for any one man, the complexities of its operation were too much for any one memory. This plus other precautions, besides a well-thought-out campaign of history-making flights, worked, for the YBs flew more than 9000 hours totaling a distance of 1,800,000 miles (equivalent to 72 times around the earth at the equator) without serious accident.

Meanwhile the thirteenth YB, the static test plane, was undergoing a long range test. Heavily loaded with instruments and piloted by Lieutenant William Bentley the plane arrived over Langley Field in the summer of 1938 during a storm. Bentley found himself inside a thunderhead which flipped the plane on its back. By the time he was able to bring the plane under control, Bentley, and plane, had spun down through the overcast. A plane of the B-17's size and weight was not designed to be flown upside down or spun, so Bentley was not a little amazed to see the wings still attached. Upon landing it was found that although the wings were bent and some rivets popped, the plane was intact. In addition, the recording instruments had registered all the stresses through which the plane (AC 36-161) had gone. It had taken more than even the most severe critic could demand.

It was decided then that the static test plane would be converted into a flying model, equipped with turbo-superchargers for the engines to study the possibilities of high-altitude performance. In order to achieve accuracy, the plane would have to attack by daylight; to be as safe as possible from enemy antiaircraft guns, it would also have to fly in the sub-stratosphere.

Step by step the principles that would change the face of war, and more terribly, the face of Europe, came into being.

2. Milestones and Millstones

For a long time the proponents of a separate Air Force, one that would be co-equal with the Navy and Army and subservient to neither, raised their voices to no avail. The only one that seemed to be heard, finally, was the irritating one of Billy Mitchell. Although he regarded the Army's General Staff as incompetent and uninformed on matters pertaining to military aviation, he chose as his special target the more hide-bound traditionalists of the Navy.

Flamboyant, inconsistent, but almost always correct in his vision, Mitchell vocalized himself into a court-martial. He was found guilty of bringing "discredit upon the military service" and suspended from duty for five years. Mitchell countered by resigning from the service, but died before he ever saw his views vindicated. What he had not been able to accomplish as an outspokenly combative advocate of air power, he was at least able to initiate as the victim of his own enthusiasms and the blindness of others.

The germ of the idea of an independent air arm was planted by Mitchell even in the minds of the most conservative military thinkers. In time, following several studies by various committees and boards, a board headed by former Secretary of

15

War Newton D. Baker, recommended the reorganization of the Air Corps into a General Headquarters Air Force to exist along with the Air Corps and Observation Corps. The GHQ Air Force was visualized as the strategic arm of the Air Corps. In actuality, this was a subtle means of appearing to establish an independent air force without actually doing it. It would pacify the exponents of a separate air force and at the same time keep aviation under control of the General Staff.

Still, the GHQ Air Force was a small step in the direction toward which Mitchell pointed. It placed control of the air striking force under an air officer who could work more or less (mostly less) independently of ground control.

On the other hand, the creation of a GHQ Air Force in 1935 actually muddied up the picture. The chain of command and responsibility were complicated beyond definition. Major General Frank M. Andrews was placed at the head of the GHQ Air Force; Major General Oscar Westover was named Chief of the Air Corps. It was the responsibility of the former to organize, train, and operate the air force in his command and would report to the Chief of Staff in peacetime; in wartime he would report to the commander of the field forces. The Chief of the Air Corps would concern himself with individual training, procurement, and supply. However, the administrative control of all Air Corps bases remained, as before, in the hands of the Army corps area commanders. Thus authority was divided among the three heads and frequently no one actually knew who was in charge. Though Andrews was in charge of the combat force, for example, he had no voice in the decisions effecting their training, nor in the kind of equipment with which they would be trained. While both Andrews and Westover agreed that the duality of command would best be ignored in favor of a single chain of command, neither would agree to the priority.

Despite the disagreement and confusion the very fact of the existence of the GHQ Air Force did make possible the further exploration of the doctrine of strategic bombardment and the development of the heavy bomber.

Tucked away under the Second Wing of the GHQ Air Force at Langley Field, Virginia, was the little 2nd Bombardment Group to which was allocated the first dozen B-17s. Under command of Lieutenant Colonel Robert C. Olds, the 2nd Bomb Group's mission was to devise a system of training and to develop the B-17 as a strategic weapon. One of the plane's missions would be coastal defense.

Characterizing this period, it might be noted, was a definite paucity of funds for national defense and a consequent rivalry between the Navy, which hoped to build up a powerful battle fleet based upon the battleship, and the Army, which had its heart set upon a large Regular Army. It was understood that the GHQ Air Force was on hand to spring into immediate action should either coast be attacked, but only in support of the first line of defense, the Navy. The Army would take over, should any enemy penetrate the coasts and would, in turn, employ the GHQ Air Force's tactical units as it saw fit. But the Navy was jealous of its water and the Army of its land—as if there was no sky over either.

When the 2nd Group's B-17s took to the sky it was in the form of non-aggressive demonstration of the Fortresses' performance as a record-breaking aircraft. The military possibilities were, of course, implied. The year 1938 opened auspiciously when Colonel Olds piloting a YB broke the east to west transcontinental record by making the flight in 12 hours, 50 minutes; he then turned around and broke the west to east record, averaging 245 mph in 10 hours, 46 minutes.

Flight officers who took part in the historic Good Will Mission to Buenos Aires.

More spectacular was the epochal Good Will Mission flight from Langley to Buenos Aires, Argentina, which followed not long after. Under the command of Olds, the six planes took off from Langley Field on February 15. In charge of the other five planes were Major Vincent J. Meloy, Captain Neil B. Harding, Major Caleb V. Haynes, Captain Archibald Y. Smith, and Major Harold George—all of whom were to contribute to Air Force history during World War II.

Take-off began at 9:00 A.M. Five and three-quarters hours later the Fortresses landed at Miami. The navigator of each plane plotted the course of his own plane, for generally the planes were out of sight of each other, and kept in touch by radio. Before landing the six planes would rendezvous over a chosen spot. It might be noted that one of the B-17 navigators was a young officer by the name of Curtis Emerson LeMay. He had just transferred from pursuit aviation and because he had not yet acquired sufficient flying time on multiengined aircraft served as a navigator on the flight and not as a pilot. Other men making the same flight included Cornelius W. Cousland who would be the first commander of the historic 97th Bombardment Group of World War II, Robert B. Williams, who would in 1943 lead the First Bombardment Wing on a mission to Schweinfurt,

17

John A. Samford, who would serve as Chief of Staff of the 8th Air Force and others. Of the airplane commanders, Major George was principal lecturer on strategic bombardment at the Air Corps' Tactical School and Captain Harding would serve as CO of the celebrated "Bloody" 100th Bombardment Group.

Though conscious of their historic mission, these men had no conception of the wider implications of their flight nor of what the future held for them. Their immediate aim was to carry out the problem at hand and to accomplish it without incident, particularly of the kind that might in any way prejudice the future of the heavy bombers.

After a short layover in Miami, during which the planes were carefully inspected and the fuel supply replenished, Colonel Olds took off on the longest leg of the trip to Lima, Peru. Except for the necessity to fly over an equatorial storm, the 2695 mile flight, completed in 15 hours and 32 minutes, was without incident. Colonel Olds was the first to set his Boeing down on the Pan American-Grace Airways runway. During the seven-hour layover, Pan American's engineers serviced the B-17s while the crews were welcomed, made speeches, and cemented Pan American relations. It was learned that the propellers of the ship commanded by Major Meloy required adjustments so that when the other five Fortresses took off for Santiago, Chile (because of the weather conditions it was decided to land there before heading for Buenos Aires), Meloy remained behind. But when they arrived over Santiago, it was found that the weather had cleared up somewhat so Olds chose to continue on to their destination. Swinging to the east, the five ships began a 21,000 foot ascent that would bring them safely over the rugged peaks of the Andes jutting up between Chile and Argentina. As they dropped down over the far side of the mountains all communications with Group headquarters at Langley Field were cut off until relays could be established through Buenos Aires. Just a little over twelve hours after they had left Lima the five B-17s touched down in Buenos Aires.

Some time later, Meloy took off to rejoin the rest of the flight only to arrive over Buenos Aires at the height of a *pontero* (an Andean tornado). He circled over the city for an hour and, despite this delay, had made the 6000 mile flight from Lima to Buenos Aires in a record time of 11 hours, five minutes.

The Good Will Mission of the 2nd Bombardment Group was climaxed when the men appeared at the inauguration of the new president of Argentina, Dr. Roberto M. Ortiz.

The return trip to Langley Field, via the Panama Canal, was almost as trouble free as the flight out. The Fortress commanded by Captain Smith broke through the concrete cover of a gas pit while it was being towed for refueling. Raising the twenty-two ton B-17 out of the break delayed Smith's take-off for five hours. There was further trouble with the plane's starter but Smith eventually caught up with the rest of the flight at Lima.

There were no additional delays or problems and the flight of six B-17s set off for Albrook Field in the Panama Canal Zone. At nearby France Field the Fortresses were serviced, demonstrating that Panama's facilities were capable of handling such large aircraft. The flight from Panama to Langley was made in a single hop, proving that Panama could be reinforced by air very easily should it come under siege.

On Sunday, February 27, 1938, the six B-17s came in for smooth landings at Langley Field, where they were greeted by a crowd of five thousand. Major

General Andrews greeted the crews with congratulatory messages (including President Franklin D. Roosevelt's, "Well done!") and the statement, "You have added another accomplishment to the long roll of Things the Army Does Besides Fight." Also on hand were Secretary of War Woodring and Army Chief of Staff Craig.

Colonel Olds and his crews, numbering forty-eight, had covered some 12,000 miles without serious accident and with consistently well functioning equipment; the men and the machines had proved themselves. This flight was the most important one since the then Lieutenant Colonel Henry H. Arnold led a mission of Martin B-10 bombers from Washington to Alaska and return in the summer of 1934. However, the flight of the 2nd Bombardment Group was the longest up to that time, an achievement which was duly recognized when the Group was awarded the Mackay Trophy on November 7, 1939.

Three days after the ceremonies, the 2nd Group again boarded their Flying Fortresses and took off on another South American Good Will tour, this time to Brazil. Seven planes, with Major General Delos C. Emmons, now commander of the GHQ Air Force, as flight commander and with Colonel Olds as squadron commander, made the 12,000 mile round trip flight to Rio de Janeiro. They arrived in time to take part in the observance of the fiftieth anniversary of the Republic of Brazil. As with the first Good Will Mission, the second was trouble-free and strategically, as well as politically, significant.

The B-17s were not, obviously, "too much airplane for one man"; they could carry heavy loads over great distances and at near stratospheric altitudes. Pilots found that the B-17 was truly a pilot's airplane and that controlling the big plane posed no great problems. As quickly as they became familiar with the plane, the pilots set out to see what it could do.

During the celebration of the thirtieth anniversary of the Air Corps (late July–early August 1939), B-17s were flown to break several national, as well as international, records for speed, payload and altitude. Also taking part in these celebrations was the true ancestor of the B-17, as well as the B-29, B-19, and all other very heavy bombardment aircraft, the XB-15. Though conceived before the B-17 as the "Project A" experimental aircraft, the XB-15 was not completed and ready to fly until 1937. Too massive—35 tons—for the engines then available, "Old Grandpappy," as the XB-15 was affectionately called, was unable to reach speeds comparable with other contemporary aircraft. But it was capable of lifting heavy loads and flying vast distances. In the former category it won international honors during the anniversary celebrations in the summer of 1939. And earlier in the year (February 1939) the XB-15 flew a mercy mission to Chile, carrying medical supplies and food to the victims of a devastating earthquake. The XB-15 was a "one-of-a-kind" aircraft and while it was never to go into production (the planes it inspired quickly outperformed it), it did see service during World War II, as the XC-105, a cargo and personnel transport.

Also completed in time for the Air Corps celebrations was the latest Fortress, the B-17B (the "Y" now being dropped on completion of the service tests). With Colonel Stanley Umstead and Lieutenant Colonel Leonard F. Harman piloting, the B-17B took off from Seattle and landed in New York 9 hours and 14 minutes later, setting a new record for an aircraft in its class and averaging 265 mph.

While all this history was being written, all was not perfectly serene behind

"Old Grandpappy," the XB-15, first of the very heavy bombers.

the scenes however. As early as May 1938 the men in the B-17s were confronted with two typical problems. One of the most formidable was contained in a memo from the Adjutant General to Louis A. Johnson, assistant Secretary of War. It read in part: "The Chief of the Air Corps [General Oscar Westover] has been informed that the experimentation and development for the fiscal years 1939–40 will be restricted to that class of aviation designed for the close-in support of ground troops and for the production of that type of aircraft such as medium and light aircraft, pursuit and other light aircraft." The death knell of the heavy bombardment concept was ringing. The note emphasized that "No military requirement exists for the procurement of experimental pressure bombers in the fiscal year 1939 or the fiscal year 1940, of the size and type described [four engine bombardment aircraft]." Thus there were no orders for the B-17 nor for any other heavy bomber in 1938, the lag which was to be felt in "fiscal" and almost fatal 1941.

The 2nd Bombardment Group found itself afflicted with yet another, even more devious, millstone that same May 1938. As a test of the skill of the B-17 navigators the GHQ Air Force dispatched three Fortresses out to sea with the mission of "intercepting" the Italian liner *Rex*. With Colonel Olds in the lead plane and Lieutenant LeMay as navigator, the trio of B-17s actually succeeded in locating the tiny dot on the ocean while the *Rex* was still over 700 miles from American shores. Swooping down, Olds dropped a message on the ship's deck and, elated over the performance of his men and the Boeings, returned to Langley Field. Not only had they proved their navigational abilities, but also that they could intercept an invasion force at sea before it was close enough to do damage.

"Somebody in the Navy apparently got in quick touch with somebody on the General Staff," General Arnold later wrote of the incident, "and in less time than it takes to tell about it, the War Department had sent down an order limiting all activities of the Army Air Corps to within a hundred miles from the shore line of the United States." Curiously, and perhaps significantly, this order was never put on paper but was issued verbally by General Craig to Colonel Carl Spaatz.

The Navy, ever-protective of its ocean, maintained that its job was to meet an invader beyond the one-hundred-mile limit. It would find any possible invader —the Air Corps could help destroy this enemy provided that it stayed on its side of the line of demarcation. In time of war, however, the Army and Navy were expected to work together and all limitations would be regarded as merely theoretical. But, with the issuance of the hundred-mile limitation, the Air Corps found itself with a mission for which it could not train its men. Flying over water, out of sight of land, required practice for all crew members. Thus did the Army-Navy stalemate continue.

Yet another stalemate directly affecting the heavy bomber program was one of an even greater gravity, for it almost led to the cancellation of further manufacturing of the B-17. The Boeing Company had used its own funds to build the first B-17 (the Model 299) and had received comparatively small orders instead of the promised large orders. Up to the order which came in just prior to the decision not to order any heavy bombers for 1939–40 there existed only thirteen Y1B-17s, one Y1B-17A, and an order for thirty-nine B-17Bs. Original price quotations had anticipated orders in lots running from 25 to 220. Boeing found itself building aircraft on which it was losing money.

The Second Bombardment Group intercepts the Rex.

It fell to James P. Murray, Boeing's Washington representative, to contend with the assorted forces he was to encounter in the old Munitions Building. It was a frustrating assignment for, to begin with, as Murray now recalls, Secretary of War Woodring "was a bullheaded sort of a man" and Woodring was determined to get a lot of airplanes for his money. Unfortunately, their quality seemed to be of little consequence for Woodring was most interested in numbers.

Even more directly concerned was his next in command, Louis Johnson, who, according to the Air Corps Act, was charged with the responsibility of the procurement of matériel for the Army. The Secretary of War and the Assistant Secretary had their own disagreements which eventually led to White House intervention in 1939. But, in the meantime, anyone having to deal with the office of the War Secretary found himself in the center of interoffice bickerings in addition to all his other problems.

Actually Johnson himself was in favor of using heavy bombers rather than the more limited mediums, but he too was most concerned with economy. Aligned against him with his chief was Army Chief of Staff Craig, a stanch advocate of the employment of aircraft in support of ground forces.

In its anxiety to save its heavy bomber program the Air Corps adopted the role of the tough bargainer. According to the original contracts Boeing could charge $205,000 per B-17, but the Air Corps insisted that that was too high a figure. About the time that the B-17 contracts were to be renegotiated a tragic accident contributed to a shift of command. General Oscar Westover was killed when his plane crashed during a tour of duty and Henry H. ("Hap") Arnold was appointed Chief of the Air Corps; his assistant was General George H. Brett. It was with the latter that James Murray was forced to haggle.

Brett maintained that a per plane price which the Air Corps would accept would have to be $198,000 "and not a dime more." This shocked Murray, who tried to explain that at the current order placement Boeing would lose even on the authorized $205,000 figure. Attempting to meet Brett's figure could very well mean ruin for Boeing. Brett grew angrier and more insistent. "If we could only get a little cooperation from Boeing," he snapped at Murray, "maybe we could do a little business."

His Irish up, Murray responded with, "If we could only get a little cooperation from the Air Corps . . ."

But he got no further for Brett ordered him out of the office. He was also informed by the general that he was not to attempt to deal with anyone at Wright Field's Matériel Division.

"Well, then," Murray shot out on his way to the door, "can I get to see 'Hap' Arnold?"

"You can see Jesus Christ, for all I care," the livid Brett answered.

Arnold was most concerned with the heavy bomber program and hoped there was some means of not only saving it but also of developing it further. He had found a powerful ally in President Roosevelt who, despite the rulings affecting the future of the heavy bombers into 1939–40, had begun to plan for an expansion of the American air arm in September 1938. He had been quick to recognize the weight of the German *Luftwaffe* in forcing the appeasement at Munich.

Having seen that the economic conservatism of the Secretary of War might be eventually swept away by the course of events, and choosing to set aside tem-

James P. Murray.   P. G. Johnson of the Boeing Company.

porarily the problem of the Navy's hundred-mile limit, it worried Arnold that yet another small war had erupted.

"What's the trouble between you and George?" he asked Murray as soon as they were able to meet after the altercation in Brett's office. Arnold listened sympathetically as Murray outlined the problems of cost, orders, and personalities. His only comment was, "You've just got to get that figure under 205." There was no display of temper, no demands, no flare-ups but merely an appraisal of the situation as it stood. Promising to see what he could do, Murray then called Philip Johnson, president of Boeing, in Seattle. "We just can't afford it," Johnson told him, "stick to the 205."

The B-17Cs were already under construction (the order was for thirty-eight) and the time drew near for exercising the option for the next order, if any. The War Department's Johnson (Louis) called Murray in order to arrange for further discussion, but no solution was found. Rather than drop the whole thing Boeing agreed to extend the option period for an additional thirty days in hopes that the extra time might make agreement possible. Arnold himself escorted Murray to Louis Johnson's office; the latter was willing to raise Brett's offer another thousand dollars—it now appeared that the War Department was willing to pay $199,000 for a B-17. In vain did Murray try to convey the importance of the higher figure to Boeing and the company's future; he tried to explain the implications of building the big planes in small dribbles. Whereupon Louis Johnson turned to Arnold and said, "Take this man out of here and don't bring him back till he can talk our language."

So Murray was ushered out of another high office. There seemed to be little future for Boeing in building the Flying Fortress. It was not a time of national emergency for the country, but if Boeing was to meet the demands of the Air

Wellwood Beall.

Corps and War Department it could easily develop into an emergency for the Boeing Company. But no one, except perhaps Arnold and a few men in the GHQ Air Force, was willing to view that side of the argument. Soon, however, Roosevelt would declare a state of national emergency, though many believed that the United States was safe from all European involvement. Boeing could of course contribute to national preparedness by some other means and without risking the life of its company.

Still Murray had given his word that the option would be extended a month. He was joined in Washington by Boeing's Johnson (Philip) to draft a note to that effect for the Air Corps. Johnson, like Murray, was discouraged and quite angry over the treatment they had received. It struck him as ironic that the extension would bring the new date to April 1, 1940.

"April Fool's Day!" he exclaimed. "That's a laugh, but I'll be damned if I'll put that date on any contract." He preferred to add a few days to the option just to avoid using the April 1 date. Even so, the drawing up of the promised memo was misinterpreted by Brett, who had not been informed that he was to receive it. He encountered Murray in a hallway one day. "I see," he remarked, "that you have delivered your ultimatum."

24

The B-17 of 1939.

Boeing was now ready to drop the B-17 and the tension around the city of Washington with its eyes on Europe did not help to ease the situation. Again Arnold felt compelled to call Boeing officials to bring them together with representatives from the Air Corps Matériel Division. Wellwood Beall and Murray were on hand for Boeing. Arnold, because of a previous appointment, could not be present but wisely he chose Carl Spaatz to be there among those who appeared for the Air Corps. It was Spaatz who tried to impress everyone there at that meeting of the importance of it. "We've got to get together," he told them, "or it will mean the end of the heavy bomber program."

He was not aware that Boeing, too, was just about at that point also.

Beall outlined the problem as fully as possible, eliminating those interjected by the clash of personalities. Spaatz, poised, alert, wise and quick to get to the point, listened and asked, "What can you take off in order to lower the price?"

Here was an idea that had not occurred to anyone before. The long meeting lengthened and as it did it was agreed that it would be possible to remove the electrically controlled cowl flaps, the external bomb racks and yet another feature. Despite this, it meant that Boeing's rock-bottom price of $205,000 went down to $202,500—still some dollars away from the $199,000 that the War Department demanded.

In the meantime General Arnold had returned from his appointment. Spaatz vanished into his chief's office with the newly adjusted figures. He returned to inform the by now exhausted gathering that the option for the B-17Ds would be exercised at the figure they had agreed upon. It was the final decision that saved the heavy bombardment program of the Air Corps.

There was one other decision made in 1939 which was to have a profound effect upon the program: on September 1 Hitler unleashed his panzers and Stukas against Poland. The Second World War had begun.

3. Fortress I

The combat debut of the Flying Fortress was a premature tragedy of errors.

Under the terms of the Lend-Lease Bill (H.R. 1776) it became possible for the British to procure much needed war materials from the United States in their lonely stand against the seemingly invincible German forces. By late June 1940, Britain had lost its most powerful ally, France, less than a year after the war had begun. Italy, in the meantime, had declared war on France and Britain and the rest of the world watched and waited, expecting the badly mauled British to give up. But when the Battle of Britain began, on July 10, 1940, the courageous and scrappy British were led by the resolute Winston Churchill; a brilliantly mad Adolf Hitler planned for the coming, he was certain, invasion of England.

Roosevelt and his advisers recognized the full implications of the moment: if Britain went down, the United States would be next. "There is absolutely no doubt in the mind of a very overwhelming number of Americans," Roosevelt said during a press conference, "that the best immediate defense of the United States is the success of Great Britain defending itself; and that, therefore, quite

26

aside from our historic and current interest in the survival of Democracy in the world as a whole, it is equally important from a selfish point of view and of American defense that we should do everything possible to help the British Empire to defend itself."

Among the dissenting voices raised, one of the many who did not belong among the "very overwhelming number of Americans," was that of Charles A. Lindbergh. He had seen, under the auspices of Field Marshal Hermann Göring, the might of the *Luftwaffe* and did not feel that the British could possibly win. And he warned further that "we cannot win this war for England, regardless how much assistance we extend."

Despite this and other objections the Lend-Lease Bill was passed on March 11, 1941, empowering the President to manufacture, sell, lend, transfer, lease, or trade any war materials "to the government of any country whose defense the President deems vital for the defense of the United States." The beleaguered Churchill hailed it as "an inspiring act of faith . . . the most unsordid act in the history of any nation." The way was clear for the United States to begin supplying the British with other than old destroyers and guns from the First World War.

When the RAF requested a number of B-17s, the Air Corps agreed to send the first twenty of an order for thirty-eight of the new B-17Cs. This model was

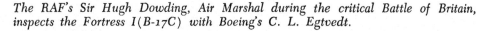

The RAF's Sir Hugh Dowding, Air Marshal during the critical Battle of Britain, inspects the Fortress I(B-17C) with Boeing's C. L. Egtvedt.

identical to the B-17B except that the bulging side blisters were replaced by flat, paneled gun positions and, under the fuselage, a "bathtub" type of gun position was installed to protect the vulnerable tail. More protective armor was added around crew stations and six .50-caliber and one .30-caliber machine guns completed the offensive-defensive equipment. The B-17C could carry a maximum of eight 600-pound bombs.

Misled by the planes' reputation as "flying fortresses," the RAF proceeded to employ the B-17s as if they had already been battle proven. Although a more potent model was already under procurement—the B-17E—as result of the studies made by Air Corps observers who had gone to Europe, the British did not seem particularly interested in hearing that the B-17Cs were suitable only for training. Short of matériel, fighting with their backs literally to the wall, the English found cautionary advice rather superfluous. Their Spitfires and Hurricanes, and their superb pilots, had accomplished miracles in the Battle of Britain, and Bomber Command almost nightly sent the Stirlings, Halifaxes, and Wellingtons into the strategic, industry-laden, Ruhr Valley. The possession of the formidable high altitude, precision bombardment B-17s meant they had one more powerful means of striking back at the Axis.

It was in May 1941 that the first B-17Cs, which the British labeled "Fortress I," were flown from Langley Field to Wright Field to be refitted with self-sealing fuel tanks and otherwise modified to British specifications and ferried over the Atlantic to West Raynham for use by No. 90 Squadron.

"I was in England when the planes arrived," an Air Force officer was later to recall. "We explained to the British our doctrine for the use of the planes. We told them that the crews had to be well trained, that a crew should drop two hundred practice bombs before attacking a real target; that the planes were designed to fly in formation for protective purposes and that by using them as trainers, trained crews could be ready to operate the new, properly equipped Fortresses when we delivered them. For some reason, which only the British understand, they decided to use the planes offensively."

He watched the entire operation get off to a bad beginning when the very first Fortress I set down on the runway at West Raynham. It ran off the concrete, a landing gear leg collapsed and it never flew again. "While it sat there it was cannibalized—a part taken off here and a part there, until the ship was picked clean as a Thanksgiving turkey."

On the eighth of July three of the Fortresses were sent out on a trial mission to bomb the naval barracks at Wilhelmshaven. Engine trouble forced one of the planes to attack a secondary target; the other two, bombing from an excessive altitude of 30,000 feet, failed to hit anything and, when attacked by German fighters, found themselves in the embarrassing situation of being unable to return fire because the guns had frozen.

The first official raid was aimed at the French naval installation at Brest where the troublesome German battle cruiser *Gneisenau* was berthed. The date was July 24, 1941; equipped with the Sperry rather than with the jealously guarded Norden bombsight which was claimed to be so accurate that it was supposed to be capable of putting the bombs in a pickle barrel, the Fortresses dropped their bombs from 30,000 feet and missed, although strikes were claimed. German fighters swarmed in to attack the small formation and although all B-17s returned to England, one was so badly shot up that it literally fell apart when it landed.

That made two down; a third was "burned from pure carelessness. Numbers 4, 5, 6, were flying in formation over Narvik, Norway, when they were set upon by Nazi fighters. All of them were lost. One apparently landed intact in Norway and probably gave the Germans their first look at the American bombsight.

"Number 7 took a gallant American to his death. Lieutenant Bradley was testing equipment in the upper reaches of turbulent air currents and fast-forming ice when something happened. The sole survivor was the squadron medico.

"Number 8 was turned over to the RAF experimental laboratories and continued its career as a guinea pig.

"Number 9 dove out of the clouds one day at about a thousand feet and continued straight into the ground."

By September the British decided to discontinue daylight raids. After twenty-two missions, eighteen planes had aborted (that is, turned back because of mechanical trouble or bad weather) and two bombed secondary targets of the total of thirty-nine planes dispatched. Only about half of the sorties resulted in the bombing of primary targets. It was not an impressive percentile showing. Besides in the brief period from May to September, eight of the twenty Fortresses had been destroyed or lost. The survivors of the experiment were turned over to Coastal Command in October for use in reconnaissance and sub hunting.

The failure of the Fortress I, for whatever reasons, served only to assure the British of the truth they had learned from the Battle of Britain: that daylight, high altitude, precision bombardment was fruitless and costly. The RAF had torn the *Luftwaffe* to shreds when it attempted to bomb England during the day. Even the most accurate bombsight was next to useless when a bomber had to contend with flak and the fighters. Since the Fortresses were able to operate over distances beyond fighter range they were without fighter cover during the most critical phase of the mission; consequently they easily succumbed to concentrated fighter attacks by very skilled and victory-certain pilots.

"Flying Targets" the British dubbed the Fortress I and Herr Joseph Goebbels gleefully referred to them as "Flying Coffins."

Overlooked during the steady run of bad luck and argument was the fact that, as reported in the British publication *The Aeroplane*, "Lavish praise is showered on the Fortresses by their crews. The pilots like their flying qualities and the gunners their armament." One pilot, on returning from the unfortunate raid on Brest, reported that "these Fortresses are wonderful aircraft—perfectly maneuverable, steady as a battleship, and incredibly efficient. We thank you in America," he concluded in a broadcast from England, "for these bombers."

But No. 90 Squadron returned to its Stirlings and the long-awaited battle test of the Flying Fortress had seemed to prove the inapplicability of its popular name. Air Corps observers, however, continued to object and reported that the British had overloaded the planes (the bomb capacity was actually less than that of British bombers), that they had tried to bomb from too great an altitude, that failures in the modified oxygen and heating systems had impaired crew efficiency, that the crews were appallingly undertrained. It was obvious that the armament needed to be increased and methods devised to keep it from freezing at altitude. Another problem was that of heavy frost on the windows, which interfered with the pilot's vision, not to mention that of the gunners.

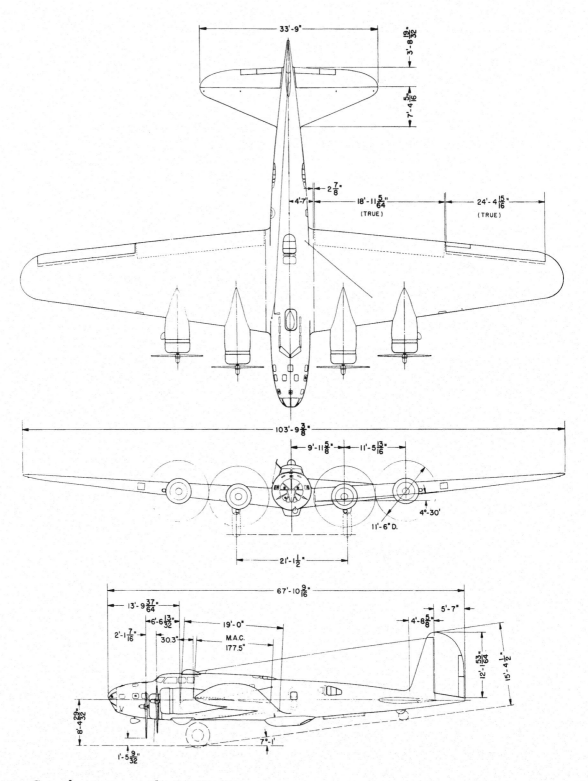

General arrangement, the B-17D.

30

One leading British writer on aviation, Peter Masefield, went so far as to suggest that the B-17 was not suited to European combat and that the American aircraft industry would do better to drop it and turn to building the new Lancaster for night bombardment. But the U. S. Air Corps stuck to its guns and defended its hard-bought B-17, its concept of daylight bombing and strategic bombardment. The British experience proved the need for improvement in defensive gunnery, the need for operating the Fortresses in considerable numbers (the RAF sent them out in flights of three or four) so that interlacing patterns of fire could contribute to maximum defense. Equally obvious was the need for intensive crew training. Because each crew would have to operate as a tightly knit unit, its training would have to be oriented accordingly. The ten men (although at this time the crew consisted of nine) would have to learn to trust each other and to be able to anticipate one another's reactions to combat situations.

These were some of the valuable lessons learned from the British use of the B-17 in combat. The cost was high and the end was not yet in sight, for the argument about basic principles of strategic bombardment was not yet settled and would, in fact, continue even after the British and Americans became Allies. Although Britian's Chief of Bomber Command, Air Marshal Sir Arthur T. Harris, had written enthusiastically to General Arnold that he believed the B-17 to be "a very fine airplane," relations between the USAAF and the RAF were

The B-17D, identical to the C but modified after the operational lessons learned from the Fortress I. Alterations included self-sealing fuel tanks, more armor protection for the crew, increased armament and cowl flaps for controlled engine cooling. In the Pacific, tail guns were added by slicing off the tail.

strained. The argument never reached the point of bitterness for it was one over theories among professionals. Each respected the other's opinion, but was certain his own was the correct one. Despite official and unofficial criticism and suggestions, the Air Corps stood firm behind its Flying Fortress and all the ideas based upon its employment and refused to abandon it. It was Arnold who best summed up the entire fiasco when he said, "The British never gave the Flying Fortress a chance . . ."

31

4. Big Bird

The first B-17s, from the Model 299 through the Model D, were not built for war. Initially designed for a defensive role, they were to prove lacking in fire power and thus not able to defend themselves under heavy attack. The five to seven guns, some of them of a rather meager .30 caliber, may have looked impressive in photographs but were less than impressive when under attack by fighter planes designed in nations more devoted to war than the United States.

Long before Pearl Harbor, however, statesmen and military leaders were practically certain that war was inevitable for the U.S. and began planning accordingly. Despite criticism from certain quarters, the nation was tooled for defense and, if necessary, offense.

At Boeing, Edward Wells and his staff had greatly modified the B-17 design into the first "offensive" Flying Fortress, the B-17E. Its most striking exterior difference from the previous model was in the large, swooping, dorsal fin which increased the area of the vertical tail surfaces. The horizontal area was increased also—the span of the elevator was lengthened by ten feet (the Ds had mea-

Sketches tracing the evolution of the B-17's new, and enlarged, dorsal fin and rudder and facilities for the "stinger" in the tail.

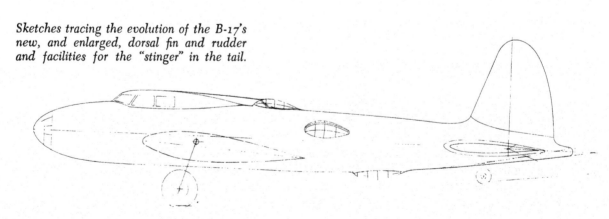

32

Edward C. Wells, chief of the B-17 design team, studies modifications which will make the Flying Fortress an offensive aircraft.

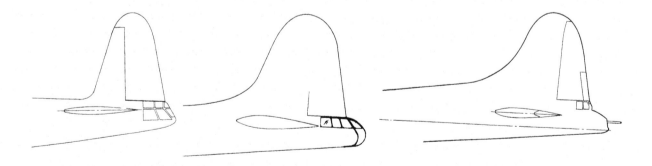

sured 33'9" and the E spanned 43 feet). The result was greater stability in flight, especially important for high-altitude bombardment.

The fuselage of the E was six feet longer than that of the D to accommodate yet another characteristic innovation—the twin .50-caliber "stinger" in the tail. Twin fifties were also installed in a power turret in the top of the fuselage just aft of the pilots' compartment; in the bottom of the waist section, aft of the radio compartment, another twin fifties protruded from the ball turret into which the belly gunner curled during operations. Originally this was a remote-control periscopic turret which did not prove successful and was replaced by the Sperry turret. In the nose the bombardier or navigator, when not occupied with their primary assignments or when the plane was under fighter attack, could operate the hand-operated guns which were placed in socket-like flexible gun mounts in the Plexiglas nose and small side windows on either side of the fuselage. In the waist, as on all models of the B-17, were two .50-caliber machine guns (one to a side). A removable window in the radio operator's compartment provided a station for an additional gun in the top of the fuselage in later models.

The B-17E was seven tons heavier and 40 per cent faster than the original Model 299—weighing 33,279 pounds empty and capable of a top speed of 318 mph. The Es were the first Fortresses to be sent to the Pacific to replace the destroyed or battle-weary Cs and Ds, and the first to be sent to England for use by the 8th Air Force. In the meantime, Boeing had already begun work on a Very Heavy Bomber (Model 345) which would fly as the XB-29 just a few months after the last of the B-17Es was delivered. Forty-five Es were shipped to the RAF for use by Coastal Command in August 1942 and were known as the "Fortress IIA."

Anticipating the need for great numbers of Flying Fortresses, the Air Force initiated a production pool late in the summer of 1941, at least four months before the attack on Pearl Harbor. This remarkably cooperative arrangement combined the efforts of the Boeing Company with those of the Douglas Aircraft Company and the Vega Aircraft Company (a subsidiary of Lockheed) to mass-produce Flying Fortresses. Beginning with the Model F the three companies jointly turned out B-17s to keep up with the demands of the Air Force. Boeing's blueprints and Boeing-designed tools were supplied to Douglas and Vega so that, except for very minor differences, the planes were identical.

The subsequent model, the F, was actually an improved E and could hardly be distinguished from the E except for the more elongated Plexiglas nose. This slight change improved the bombardier's range of vision and gave him more working room. Other modifications were internal, mainly, and numbered into the hundreds. Such improvements as the installation of "Tokyo" tanks in the wings extended the range; broad "paddle" propellers made a higher operating ceiling possible; more protective armament was also added and the landing gear was strengthened to support the additional weight. Nineteen B-17Fs—designated "Fortress II"—were sent to the RAF's Coastal Command.

Battle testing demonstrated that even the "offensive" Flying Fortress needed more fire power in the nose. Until fighters could be developed which were capable of providing cover to and from targets, the B-17s were forced to rely upon large formations for concentrated fire power. Once the "Little Friends" (as the fighters were called by bomber crews) had to leave the formations, the German fighters swarmed in for the attack. The enemy pilots quickly learned

34

Looking down on the first wartime B-17, the Model E, clearly showing details of control surfaces. Different textures are discernible because ailerons and elevators were fabric covered. Trimming tab1 on left aileron only, though on both elevators. Egg-shaped window in radio operator's compartment was removable. Narrow black strips on leading edges of wing and horizontal stabilizers are rubber de-icer boots.

The B-17E with the new ball turret.

35

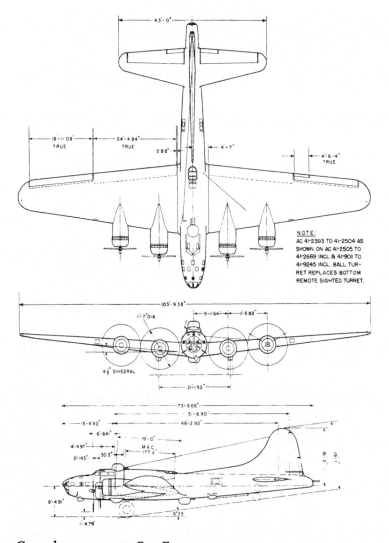

General arrangement, B-17E.

(some from B-17s which had landed intact in enemy territory or from experience) that the Flying Fortress was vulnerable to head-on attacks.

Until the long-range fighter arrived, the Air Force hoped to do something about it. In August 1942 an Air Force Board headed by Brigadier General Alfred J. Lyon submitted the suggestion that some B-17s be converted into "destroyer escort" aircraft—a kind of superfighter. Instead of carrying bombs, these planes would be heavily armed and well supplied with ammunition and scattered through the formations. Outwardly they would appear to be the same as the other planes on the mission and would thus, it was hoped, deceive the attackers.

Vega converted a B-17F into the XB-40, armed with no less than fourteen .50-caliber machine guns and carrying twice the number of rounds of ammunition generally carried in the Fortress. In the nose, almost directly beneath the bombardier's position, a twin fifty power operated turret was installed to meet the

36

head-on attack problem. With its bristling armament, additional rounds of ammunition, extra armor protection as well as the new "chin" turret, the B-40 emerged as an imposing challenge to the German fighters. An additional thirteen B-17Fs were converted by Vega into YB-40s and placed in service in May 1943. It was soon learned that once the bombers dropped their bomb loads, they left the heavily laden B-40s behind in their dash for home. The idea was abandoned after a couple of months.

But the chin turret was retained for the later Fs and became standard equipment on the B-17G, the last of the Flying Fortresses. The first G was delivered on September 4, 1943, and the last on April 13, 1945—less than a month before Germany surrendered unconditionally to the Allies. The RAF received 85 B-17Gs ("Fortress III"), some of which were used by Coastal Command and others by Bomber Command. The latter employed them in night bomber missions as decoys and for dropping "window" (metal strips which jammed and confused enemy radar).

Except for the chin turret, the G was the same plane as the F out of which it developed. The "offensive" Fortresses were the most extensively built of all the B-17s. A total of 512 Es were produced, 3400 Fs, and 8680 Gs. These were the Flying Fortresses of wartime newspaper headlines, possibly the most celebrated, best known and widely publicized aircraft of World War II. Loved (the term is used advisedly) by their crews, respected (but not held in awe) by the enemy, the Flying Fortresses became legendary and accumulated lore and myth as would any folk hero. It was called by many titles, suggesting some of the postwar mystique that would grow up around the plane—such as "Queen of the Skies," for example. Pilots sometimes referred to it sardonically as "The Glory Wagon," in acknowledgment of the wide publicity it was given. Crews devised colorful names for individual planes, some of them as unprintable as the designs painted on the noses were suggestive. This practice shocked "the folks back home" and some even protested over the vulgarity of the names and sexuality of the insignia. Possibly the most commonly used name for the B-17 was the affectionate recognition of the increased size of the empennage—a classic in innocent ribaldry, "Big Assed Bird."

The lore and majestic aspect of the B-17 in flight, plus its favoritism among newspapermen, tended to obscure the role of other aircraft, such as the Consolidated B-24 "Liberator," which was equally effective and possibly a little more potent. It lacked, however, the ability to absorb punishment that the B-17 could take—and it was not as beautiful a plane.

"Although the B-17 looked like a humpback hawk when its wheels were down and taxiing on the ground," Harry H. Crosby, a former navigator and now a professor at Boston University, said recently, "in the air it was a slender, beautiful silhouette . . ." This deadly silhouette was to become a familiar one during the long war years; without it, those years might have stretched even longer.

In looking back on the inception of the B-17 and its implications, namely the encouragement of the development of the B-24 and the B-29, as well as the employment of the Flying Fortresses in strategic bombardment, especially in the costly campaigns against oil installations, General Carl A. Spaatz succinctly expressed the professional's tribute when he said, "Without the B-17 we might have lost the war."

THE OTHER FORTRESSES

A B-17G modified to carry JB-2 jet bombs under the wings. These were American adaptations of German Buzz bombs.

The Boeing B-17H was a modified B-17G used by the Army Air Forces for long-range air-sea rescue duties. Equipped with a large air-borne powered lifeboat, which contained emergency rations, sails, water and radio equipment, the B-17Hs were used during war years to patrol areas at sea where aerial traffic was heaviest and ditchings were to be expected because of battle damage. Similar Flying Fortresses, known as PB-1s, were used by the United States Navy and United States Coast Guard for similar long-range rescue duties.

This is a Boeing PB-1W, one of a number of B-17Gs ordered by the Navy as specially fitted with early warning radar for search purposes. These planes had sealed bomb bays and extra internal fuel tanks for longer range.

The Boeing XB-38, a B-17E fitted with liquid-cooled Allison engines in place of the regular Wright "Cyclones." This was the only one built, for the Allisons were needed on the Lockheed P-38 and other planes. Experimentation with this plane was prematurely ended when it caught fire and burned.

The B-17F in battle paint; external bomb racks have been installed under the wings.

A Navy B-17F—a Boeing PB-1 used in antisubmarine spotting and experimentation.

The XB-40, experimental "escort-fighter" converted from a Boeing-built B-17F by Vega. Though its heavy armament made it too slow to keep up with bombing formations, and therefore unsuitable for its mission, it was the first of the B-17s with a "chin turret."

FROM THE LAND
OF THE RISING SUN

There's a large number of planes
coming in from the north, three degrees east . . .

PVT. GEORGE ELLIOT, JR.
Opana Outpost
7 December 1941

5. "Climb Mount Niitaka"

Tragic ironies inevitably emerge from great calamities, creating the brief anecdotal footnotes to history, the lesser dramatic touches that all but overshadow the greater event.

Such an encounter, a mere incident in an hour of dramatic happenings, joined the lives of Staff Sergeant Charles M. Judd of the U. S. Army Air Forces stationed at Hickam Field, Honolulu, and Lieutenant Fusata Iida of the Japanese Naval Air Force. At almost the precise moment that Sergeant Judd was engaged in an argument with his friend, Sergeant Max Butterfield, Lieutenant Iida was at the head of his squadron of Zero-Sen (fighters) flying toward Oahu.

For weeks the talk at Hickam had centered on the speculation of a possible Japanese attack in the Pacific. On the way to the mess hall that morning Judd maintained that the Japanese Air Force would prove to be no match for the American Air Forces, not to mention the British and Dutch fighting forces also in the Pacific. "The Japs," he said, "are lousy pilots and they fly lousy planes." Butterfield suggested that perhaps everything about the Japanese air forces was not known and reserved judgment. But Judd was firm and said he was ready to back up his statements with an authoritative article, "Japanese Air Power," in the September (1941) issue of *Aviation* magazine. An important point that the author made was that all of Japan's first rank military aircraft was obsolete or

43

Japanese planes line up on carrier decks before taking off on December 7, 1941.

obsolescent. The article did not mention the Zero-Sen which Lieutenant Iida deftly guided toward Pearl Harbor.

"Japan," Judd had read, "if engaged in a great air war would crumble like a house of cards . . ." He invited Butterfield to meet him in his barracks so that he could read the article for himself. By the time Butterfield arrived at Judd's barracks an hour or two later, Judd was dead with a Japanese bullet through his head, the result of a strafing attack by a Zero. His life and that of Iida's had converged and ended for both. The Japanese squadron leader's Zero was a burning wreckage where it plunged to earth between two American hangars.

From the Land of the Rising Sun, with sudden unexpectedness, had come one of the most brilliantly executed air strikes of all time. Aside from its moral implications, the attack was a breath-taking military coup accomplished at great cost to the unprepared Americans and little cost to the Japanese.

"The Hawaiian Operation" was the idea of Admiral Isoroku Yamamoto, Commander-in-Chief of the Combined Fleet, as the opening stroke in a wider expansion of its so-called Greater East Asia Co-prosperity Sphere, an impressive phrase for Japan's plan for the conquest of Southeast Asia. It was Yamamoto's plan to wipe out the American Pacific fleet, particularly the aircraft carriers, at Pearl Harbor while co-ordinated attacks upon Malaya and the Philippines further upset the balance. The Pearl Harbor blow would prevent the reinforcement of American, British, and Dutch positions in the Southwest Pacific.

When it appeared that negotiations in Washington between Secretary of State Cordell Hull and the special envoy from Japan, Saburo Kurusu and Ambassador Kichisaburo Nomura, were getting anything but the results for which the Japanese hoped, the decision was made to execute the "Hawaiian Operation."

As early as November 22, 1941, a Japanese fleet assembled in the Kurile Islands north of Japan. Commanding a thirty-two-ship task force, which included

44

six aircraft carriers, Vice-Admiral Chiuchi Nagumo set the operation in fateful motion on receiving Yamamoto's radio signal, *"Niitaka Yama Nabora"* ("Climb Mount Niitaka"). The date was December 2, 1941. By December 7 (December 8 in Japan and in the Philippines, to the west of the international date line), the task force had approached to within 200 miles of the Hawaiian Islands. At 6:00 A.M. the first wave of planes took off the carrier *Akagi*; within minutes almost two hundred aircraft—horizontal bombers, dive bombers, torpedo bombers, and fighters—of the first wave thundered toward an unsuspecting Pearl Harbor. A few minutes after seven the "blips" of this formation were discovered on a radar screen by Sergeant Joseph Lockard and Private George Elliot. When they reported this to their headquarters they were informed that it was a flight of B-17s which had set out from Hamilton Field, California, the day before and were due in at Hickam Field, the bomber base, within an hour.

Before that hour was up, at 7:55 A.M., the first bomb hit the battleship *Arizona* in Pearl Harbor. The primary targets were the neatly lined up ships of the Pacific fleet; almost equally important were Army and Navy aircraft distributed around the various bases on Oahu. As torpedo-bombers hurtled at the ships in the harbor, dive bombers attacked the fighter base, Wheeler Field, and the heavy bomber base, Hickam.

At the height of the attack, men in the control tower at Hickam were astonished to hear the calm tones of an American voice requesting landing instructions.

A dozen new B-17s, just completing the first leg of a flight from California to

A Mitsubishi Type 97 torpedo bomber, which was known as the "Kate" by Americans; these planes attacked the ships in Pearl Harbor.

Type 99 dive bombers in flight en route to Pearl Harbor; twenty-five of these so-called "Vals" were in the first attacking wave.

Clark Field in the Philippines, approached Hickam and were anxious to land. The crews had been aloft for about fourteen hours, the fuel supply was low and the men were tired. Fatigue was forgotten, however, as the crews peered out of the windows for their first glimpse of romantic Hawaii. Though occasionally obscured by cloud, a bright sun illuminated the islands and water below. It was clear that they were to be given a warm welcome, for the sky seemed filled with small, obviously private planes (for they were certainly not American Air Force or Navy planes), as a kind of honorary escort.

Major Richard H. Carmichael, leading the first flight of six Fortresses, arrived during the attack by the first wave. Because of the great number of planes cluttering up the sky and the ominous columns of smoke rising from Hickam, he decided to seek a better haven. He eased the Fortress up and turned toward Bellows Field only to find it too was in the same condition. Turning north he flew up to the short fighter strip at Haleiwa and put the plane down there. Another plane followed him into the field, landing safely.

Back at Hickam, Lieutenant Frank Bostrom, also of Carmichael's flight, was instructed to land from "east to west" and that the field was under attack by "unidentified aircraft." Confused ground fire converged on the B-17, so Bostrom pulled it up into a cloud bank for temporary safety while he tried to decide on the next move. This was settled for him by the fuel gauges. When he approached Hickam again he was informed to stay away by the tower. Whereupon Bostrom selected a nearby golf course to set down in. This was an amazing feat, for the course was hardly large enough for so heavy a plane. Bostrom was to contribute

46

A Japanese photograph of Wheeler Field, the pursuit base near Pearl Harbor. The burning fighters are to the right of the lines of fighters not yet attacked.

further to history when he piloted the B-17 which took General Douglas Mac-Arthur and his party out of the Philippines.

The remaining three Fortresses of Carmichael's flight, which happened to arrive during a brief lull between the second and first wave of attackers, landed intact at Hickam Field and were quickly pushed under cover.

Shortly after, the second flight, commanded by Major Truman Landon, appeared over the field. Lieutenant Bruce Allen brought his ship into a scene of chaos. Three more B-17s of the flight also landed without incident and then, around 8:40 A.M., the second wave struck. Lieutenant Karl T. Barthelmess landed safely although "escorted" by several small planes. The plane flown by Captain Raymond Swenson was similarly escorted and under fire; the B-17 was shot in half on the runway. Zeros pounced in and shot up the men as they ran from the wreckage, killing Flight Surgeon William R. Shick.

Lieutenant Robert Richards, whose plane would have been the last of the flight to land, pulled away from Hickam. The fighters sprayed the Fortress, severely wounding two crew members. It might be said here that none of the B-17s which had come in from the mainland were armed and could not in any way defend themselves. Richards brought the big bomber down on the tiny runway at Bellows Field; there was no time to seek out an easier landing spot, for the wounded men required quick medical attention.

Just as abruptly as the attack had begun, it ended. By 10:00 o'clock it was all over, the Japanese returned to their carriers leaving behind a scene of chaotic dismay. The once powerful Pacific fleet was a shattered, burning wreckage;

47

"Unidentified aircraft" (probably "Vals") seen over the wing of one of the B-17s which arrived from California over Clark Field during the attack.

hundreds of planes were destroyed, some of them shot down by the superior Zeros. Over two thousand Americans were dead, and as many were wounded. Control of the strategic Pacific area had shifted into the hands of the Japanese.

The cost to the Japanese was a mere forty-nine planes, one submarine and a few midget submarines. Their only failure was an accidental one. Although they had succeeded in sinking or disabling eight battleships, they found no aircraft carriers berthed at Pearl Harbor. The carriers and their escorts were maneuvering in mid-Pacific and were spared. Within six months after Pearl Harbor, the significance of this chance absence would be realized at Midway.

Another aspect of the plan for a co-ordinated attack on American installations went awry, but, tragically, this made little difference in the final results. Inclement weather forced the postponement of the take-off of the land planes based on Formosa. The projected targets lay just two hours' flying time to the south on the island Luzon in the Philippines. The mission would aim at wiping out the fighters based at Iba Field and the heavy bombers at Clark Field, the main striking force of the Far East Air Force under command of Major General Lewis H. Brereton, air commander of General MacArthur's army in the Philippines.

The 19th Bombardment Group (H) was based at Clark Field. In September, 1941, the group's 14th Squadron, commanded by Major Emmett C. O'Donnell, Jr., had completed a spectacular trans-Pacific flight to Clark; this was followed by another flight in October, when two squadrons, led by Group Commander Lieutenant Colonel Eugene L. Eubank, flew from California via Hawaii, Midway, Wake, Port Moresby (New Guinea), Darwin (Australia), and finally Clark Field, to the north of Manila. These units were to be reinforced by the flights

48

which had been caught at Pearl Harbor. On December 8 there were thirty-five B-17s based in the Philippines. Of these, two squadrons remained at Clark with a total of nineteen Fortresses; two squadrons had gone down to Del Monte, Mindanao, with the other sixteen B-17s.

What actually occurred at Clark Field is still contended and conjectural. Depending upon the military authority one chooses to believe, varying and conflicting accounts tend to confuse the issue. Whatever occurred in the first few disordered hours after the Japanese struck at Pearl Harbor, the fact remains that a full nine hours after that practically every B-17 at Clark Field was destroyed on the ground.

The first news of the attack on Pearl Harbor was received at Clark Field around three o'clock in the morning; a half hour later radar picked up some air activity to the west of Iba, a fighter base. Almost immediately a squadron of P-40s took off but no interception took place. All units were placed upon combat alert.

According to the plan "Rainbow 5," an attack on bases on Formosa was to follow a definite show of Japanese hostility. When he heard of the outbreak of war, General Brereton from his headquarters at Nielson ordered preparations for the strike on Formosa to begin. When he reported at MacArthur's headquarters at Fort Santiago, he informed Brigadier General Richard K. Sutherland, Chief of Staff, of his plan for operations on Japanese installations on Formosa and wished to have authority to do so.

Although Brereton hoped to bomb targets in Takao Harbor, Formosa, he had no recent maps or aerial photographs to base the mission on. It was likely that enemy shipping as well as warships would be in Takao so that, even with meager

Robert Richards' B-17 at Bellows Field, a fighter base.

The battleship Arizona *burning in Pearl Harbor.*

preparations, there was a chance of hitting something. Brereton also ordered three B-17s prepared for reconnaissance flights in order to be able to base future actions on up-to-the-minute intelligence.

Such actions never took place. It is this aspect of the early morning confusion on Luzon which has never been resolved. Brereton maintains that he recommended the bombing of military targets on Formosa; MacArthur maintained that he knew of no such recommendation. The man between, Sutherland, later recollected something about a plan to bomb Formosa, but more vividly recalled Brereton's insistence upon getting reconnaissance photos first. Sutherland also made an even greater issue over the fact that not all of the B-17s were sent down to Del Monte, as—he maintains—they were ordered. In short, if they hadn't been kept at Clark Field, they would not have been destroyed. None of which really clears up the question of why the B-17s did not strike Formosa.

There is a political consideration, a subtle fine point, which restrained MacArthur. The Philippine Islands, an American protected commonwealth, was not technically at war with Japan. If the Americans, using the Philippines as a base for attacks against the Japanese, went to war prematurely, it would involve a still neutral nation.

Whatever the reasons, no order was issued to bomb-up the B-17s even though, hours before, the United States and Japan were at war. Hoping to avoid a repetition of the destruction at Pearl Harbor, Major David Gibbs, operations officer of the 19th Bombardment Group and in charge during the absence of Colonel Eubank (then at Brereton's headquarters), ordered all of the flyable B-17s into the air. Word had come that Japanese planes were approaching and while the P-40s rose to meet them, the B-17s were ordered to patrol the waters around Luzon until ordered to return to Clark.

When Eubank returned to Clark he ordered the B-17s back to prepare for

Hickam Field after the Japanese left on December 7, 1941. A new B-17E is in the foreground; behind: a B-17D.

the as yet not authorized photo mission to Formosa (three planes) and to get the rest of the planes ready for an attack. The Fortresses returned to the field to fuel up and to take on 100-pound and 300-pound bombs. Plans were initiated to prepare the B-17s at Del Monte for offensive action. The noon hour was approaching while the men at Clark Field worked feverishly. The three B-17s began to taxi out to begin taking off on the photo mission.

These three planes were destroyed by the first bombs to hit Clark Field. High-altitude bombers began to drop their bombs some time after noon upon the two squadrons of B-17s lined up on the field. The attackers came in waves, the vertical bombers were followed by dive bombers, in turn followed by fighters strafing the field. American fighters attempting to intercept the Japanese planes were destroyed before they left the ground. Four or five P-40s managed to get into the air, however, to engage the Zeros. From another field at Del Carmen, obsolete P-35s were put into service against the faster, more maneuverable Zeros.

Once again, when the Japanese planes returned to their bases, they left behind a scene which could only be described as a shambles. The dead lay sprawled among the burning wreckage of buildings and planes. The only Fortress that had not been hit was one which, because of generator trouble, did not take off on the morning alert. When the rest of the planes had returned, it was taken up by Lieutenant John W. Carpenter. When he came back to Clark he saw what he thought was a thunder shower over the field; it was the smoke rising from the fires caused by the accurate Japanese bombing. Carpenter was attacked by a dozen or more Japanese fighters but he eluded them by racing for cloud cover. When his fuel supply began to run low he returned to Clark Field and the desolation there. A hundred dead lay about the field, over two hundred wounded were being tended to and on Clark Field, the most important air base in the Philippines, not one flyable aircraft remained.

51

Alexander, the Swoose.

6. Improvised War

When the Japanese warlords agreed that war with the United States and Great Britain was inevitable, Admiral Isoroku Yamamoto promised Premier Fumimaro Konoye that with the tactics he had in mind he would "run wild" and bring Japan "an uninterrupted succession of victories . . ."

And he did. Despite a feeling of resentment toward the United States, Yamamoto did not welcome the idea of a war with a great industrial nation. He realized that a long war would give the United States time to bring its tremendous potential for manufacturing war materials to bear and then despite the early victories Japan would have to face forces of unimaginable impact. The younger warriors, inspired by what would be the initial triumphs of stealth and surprise, might soon come to believe the myth of their own invincibility. Few were willing to listen to Yamamoto's cautionary statement in which he said, "should the war be prolonged for two or three years, I have no confidence in our ultimate victory."

But, immediately following the Pacific attacks, even the prudently shrewd Yamamoto must have experienced a secret hope that, despite his reservations, perhaps the ultimate was not beyond his grasp. The U. S. Pacific fleet lay smoldering in Pearl Harbor, the Hawaiian Air Force was a shattered remnant and, after the "Little Pearl Harbor" at Clark Field, the only striking force remaining in the entire Pacific area was half of the 19th Bombardment Group and a few obsolescent pursuit planes.

Japanese assault forces moved in rapidly to exploit their stunning blows; their troops began to invade Malaya and Thailand. Three days after Pearl Harbor their once-despised air fleets proceeded to sink the newly arrived British battleship *Prince of Wales* and the cruiser *Repulse* which had been dispatched from Singapore in search of the Japanese fleet. The way was now clear for a drive toward Singapore.

To protect their lines of communication into the East Indies, with their rich oil and mineral deposits, the Japanese had to cripple or wipe out the U.S. forces in the Philippines. After all but erasing Clark and Iba Fields from the battle maps, the Japanese attacked the naval base at Cavite and drove the American Asiatic fleet out of the Philippines. MacArthur was left on Luzon with practically no air cover and no naval support. The Japanese were ready to launch amphibious assaults on northern Luzon.

At Clark Field desperate and ingenious salvage work put three or four of the riddled B-17s into operational condition. To these were added the Fortresses which had been at Del Monte, six hundred miles to the south and still out of the range of the Zeros from Formosa and still undetected. By December 9 reconnaissance missions were being undertaken by the 19th Group; limited loads of bombs were carried just in case. For safety's sake the planes were kept off the field until after dark.

On December 10 a large Japanese convoy was spotted in the vicinity of Vigan. Five B-17s were bombed-up with twenty 100-pounders and dispatched on the first American bombardment mission of World War II. Led by Major Cecil E. Combs (the other pilots were Lieutenants Elliot Vandevanter, Walter R. Ford, Morris H. Shedd, and Sig R. Young), the flight attacked from 12,000 feet. All dropped their bombs except Vandevanter, who had to bring his ship down to a dangerous level at 7000 feet before his bombardier could get the bomb rack to operate. Some hits were thought to have been made and it was believed that a transport was sinking when the Fortresses headed back for Clark. There had been no fighter opposition, but antiaircraft fire had put a hole through the wing of Vandevanter's plane.

In the meantime, several B-17s from Major Emmett O'Donnell's 14th Squadron had come up from Del Monte. O'Donnell had come in to Clark early in the morning and was followed later by the others. Of the six planes that appeared over the field, only three were permitted to land because of an air raid alert. The three B-17s that landed were piloted by Lieutenants G. R. Montgomery and George E. Schaetzel, and Captain Colin P. Kelly.

O'Donnell was the first who was ready so took off for Vigan north of Clark Field. Bomb-rack trouble forced him to make five runs over the targets, a cruiser and destroyer, before he could drop the eight 600-pound bombs he carried. No hits were observed and O'Donnell returned to Clark to refuel. Captain E. L. Parsel, who had taken off shortly after O'Donnell, came in over Vigan and dropped several bombs; one at least hit a transport.

While he was still out a red alert interrupted the loading of the three remaining B-17s. They were ordered into the air immediately; Montgomery carried a single 600-pound bomb, Kelly three and Schaetzel a full load of eight. As Montgomery headed for Vigan, Schaetzel and Kelly set out for Aparri, where Japanese landing parties and shipping were located.

Montgomery released his one bomb on the transports off Vigan, but to no effect and returned to Clark to take on another bomb load. Armed with twenty 100-pound bombs, he took off again to follow Schaetzel and Kelly to Aparri. He saw neither of their Fortresses and proceeded to bomb the beach and left, certain that one ship was afire in the bay. Back over Clark, Montgomery was ordered to continue on to Del Monte. Night was falling by this time and the B-17 ran into rough weather. Before long it was obvious that they had missed Del Monte and that their fuel supply was low. Montgomery ditched the plane in a heavy downpour four miles offshore; though the Fortress sank all crew members safely got to shore.

Captain Colin P. Kelly, Jr.

Schaetzel had come in over Aparri at 25,000 feet and bombed through the clouds. The B-17 was attacked by Zeros which Schaetzel shook off by diving the plane back into the clouds. In the fight, however, all the ammunition had been expended and the B-17 badly shot up. One engine was out, an oil leak streaked the nacelle and the tail section was in tatters. Miraculously no one aboard the plane was hit. Schaetzel managed to bring the crippled plane into San Marcelino, a field which lay between Clark and Del Monte.

Kelly had proceeded northward after taking off from Clark and from 20,000 feet he and the crew observed to their left the landing operations under way at Vigan. They continued on to Aparri in search of an aircraft carrier which had been reported there. In the landing area below them they could see six small vessels, probably cruisers, moving about and about five miles out from Aparri a great ship, a battleship they thought, firing at the proposed landing area on the beach. Still flying north they continued out to sea in search of the carrier. Finding no sign of it, they turned back toward the Aparri beach head; there was no doubt as to their "target of opportunity"—the big battleship off the tip of Luzon.

Coming over Aparri at 22,000 feet, they were spotted by the cruisers which began evasively twisting and turning and to toss up flak. The battleship, however, remained obliviously on course moving parallel to the beach line.

Kelly turned the Fortress into a bomb run and control of the plane was in the hands of bombardier Sergeant Meyer Levin. One after the other, the three

54

The Mitsubishi Zero-Sen, an A6M2 Model 11, the type of Zero fighter which originally saw service in China in 1940. The excellent performance of this plane was noted by General Claire L. Chennault, commander of the American Volunteer Group in China, who tried to warn others of the plane's qualities but to no avail. Later, after the Pearl Harbor attack, in which later models were employed, Chennault's warnings proved only too true. Zero in the photo was captured in China and rests on a Flying Tiger base; directly behind it is a Curtiss P-40 decorated with characteristic Flying Tiger shark design.

600-pound bombs lurched out of the bomb bay and Levin shouted, "Bombs away!" It was a signal for Kelly to take control again and he pointed the bomber inland, banking so that the crew could watch the bombs hurtling toward the sea. One fell short of the big ship, a second landed in the water almost adjacent, and the third struck the aft turret. A tremendous explosion convulsed the great vessel and it was quickly enveloped in thick black smoke. The men were certain they could see an oil slick on the water's surface, but because of the smoke, could not determine the actual damage to the ship.

Suddenly Japanese fighters converged on the B-17, made a few tentative passes and flew off. Kelly turned the plane toward Clark. Then flying his Zero at 18,000 feet was Saburo Sakai, who with his group had left the vicinity of Clark Field where no suitable targets had been found and were returning to the Aparri area to cover the landings. Peering down he was startled to see the rings form around the big ship below, indicating that it was under bombardment. Four thousand feet above him he saw a lone B-17 speeding toward Clark Field.

The Zeros climbed for the attack and about fifty miles away from Clark they overtook the plane. Because of altitude they could not thrust and parry but had to line up to come in at the bomber singly. (The Zero did not handle well in higher altitudes and tended to skid out of control.) The giantism of the Fortress—their first—and its speed at first threw the attackers off, but they soon learned that an attack from its vulnerable rear was the best method of approach.

The Zero pilots marveled at the great amount of punishment the Fortress could absorb, although during the initial attacks a good deal of damage had been done. The instrument panel splintered and disintegrated before Kelly's eyes, Pfc. Robert Altman was wounded, an explosive bullet decapitated waist-gunner Technical Sergeant William J. Delehanty and another caused the oxygen tanks in the radio compartment to blow up. Kelly's plane, a B-17C, was not equipped with self-sealing wing tanks and soon the left wing was smoking; another burst of fire set the bomb bay aflame. A spurt from yet another Zero's guns cut the cables which controlled the elevators.

In the smoke-filled cockpit, Kelly and his co-pilot struggled to keep the plane in level flight. Kelly ordered the crew to bail out. As observers watched from Clark Field they counted the parachutes blossoming under the stricken plane now rapidly losing altitude. From the rear compartment plummeted Staff Sergeant James E. Hokyard, Pfc. Willard L. Money, and the wounded Altman, whose scalp was bleeding. In the forward section navigator Joe M. Bean and Meyer Levin had some trouble opening the emergency hatch, but in a moment Levin had dropped through and, as he fell, Bean could see co-pilot Lieutenant Donald D. Robins preparing to leave by the top escape hatch. Kelly continued to hold the plane in more or less level flight making it possible for them to clear the plane safely.

At Clark the count had reached six parachutes which meant only two men remained. A second later the plane blew up. When the wreckage of Kelly's B-17 was found strewn along a dirt road to the west of Mount Arayat, Kelly's body was found nearby. His chute had not opened.

When the surviving crew was questioned later, word was flashed out that they had accounted for no less than the battleship *Haruna*. To a nation starved for triumph amidst an unrelenting series of humiliating disasters, the news was electrifying. Colin Kelly was hailed as the first great hero of World War II and the sinking of the *Haruna* a magnificent victory, the first step on the long road back. The stateside press took up the story and splashed it across the front pages.

The fact is that the ship which was attacked was neither the *Haruna* (no ship of its class took part in the Aparri invasion; it was probably the heavy cruiser *Ashigari*), nor was it sunk. That the ultimate military achievement of Kelly and his crew was exaggerated by no means detracts from his personal heroism. The fact of his death was not amplified. To save the lives of his crew, Kelly had chosen to remain with the Fortress beyond that point at which he could also save himself. His was the first B-17 lost in combat.

Missions like Kelly's, Schaetzel's, and Montgomery's were typical of the disorganized and seemingly unplanned early attempts at striking back at the Japanese. Planes were patched together and the men were fatigued and overworked. As for theories of strategic bombardment, all were disregarded in the desperation of just being able to strike back. If one or two or three B-17s could be dispatched with a small load of bombs it was regarded as a worthy effort; a formation of six was a major striking force. There was no fighter cover, for the pursuits were also in disrepair, the pilots weary and both were outmatched by the Japanese. Still, they went out and were shot down, most of them, and even succeeded in shooting down the Zeros. But it was a hopeless battle.

Four days after the Kelly exploit word came through that the Japanese were establishing a bridgehead at Legaspi on southern Luzon. With their landings at Aparri and Vigan practically secure it was clear that with another at Legaspi, the Japanese would be able to close in on MacArthur from north and south, pushing him onto the Bataan peninsula.

To harass the Legaspi landings, six B-17s were readied for a mission from Del Monte on December 14; the war was now one week old. Del Monte was now the main heavy bomber base in the Philippines—in the entire Pacific. Lead-

Hewitt T. Wheless visiting the Boeing plant in Seattle after his return from the Pacific.

ing the mission of six bombers, Lieutenant James T. Connally began his take-off —a tire blew and his B-17 would not be able to get off the ground for hours. Taking over, Lieutenant Lee B. Coats led the rest of the B-17s north toward Legaspi. He was forced to turn back when the plane developed engine trouble; afflicted likewise was the plane piloted by Lieutenant Walter Ford. Both returned to Del Monte.

And then there were three. The still-functioning B-17s were flown by Lieutenants Jack Adams, Elliot Vandevanter, and Hewitt T. Wheless. About halfway to the target they ran into murky weather where Wheless separated from the other planes in the overcast and because an engine stopped functioning. He brought the ship down to 10,000 feet and the motor kicked in again.

Adams and Vandevanter continued on to Legaspi. From 20,000 feet they saw a beach swarming with troops and a bay blackened with transports and other shipping. Adams released his bombs first and almost instantly was attacked by a flight of Zeros. He pushed the B-17 into a cloud bank 10,000 feet below, but the six little fighters followed. Two men were wounded in the first sweep, one, radio operator Pfc. Anthony E. Jumia, Jr., seriously, and two engines were knocked out. Though they believed they had shot down three of the attackers the other three continued darting in and around the B-17 with guns blazing. Losing altitude, Adams knew he would have to set the plane down. Hoping to make a landing on the beach on the island of Masbate, just south of Luzon, he brought the wheezing plane down through the clouds. Unfortunately, there was no smooth beach at that point, but Adams did see a rice paddy beyond the beach line and headed for that. Skillfully he brought the Fortress in on its belly. The Zeros buzzed in angrily and strafed Adams and the crew, assisting the wounded, as they ran from the plane. The plane would not burn (later Adams burned it to keep it from falling into Japanese hands), so the Zeros pulled away. With the

57

help of Filipino guerrillas Adams and the rest of the crew were able to reach a small nearby settlement where they left Jumia in a hospital. The rest eventually made their way back to Del Monte, but not before serving in the field artillery and infantry in the last ditch defense of the Philippines.

Vandevanter, on the same mission to Legaspi, made three runs over the target, dropped his bombs and returned to Del Monte without incident.

When Wheless appeared over Legaspi, following the attacks of Adams and Vandevanter, the sky was aswarm with enraged Zeros. Just as he brought the B-17 out of the clouds to begin a bomb run on six transports eighteen Zeros bounced down upon the Fortress. Four fighters began firing at the bomber, two took positions on either side of the Fortress and the other two attacked from the rear. Waist gunners Sergeant Russell Brown and Corporal W. W. Williams flamed the two side Zeros, but during the attack radio operator Pfc. W. G. Killin was fatally wounded.

Once the eight 600-pound bombs left the ship Wheless was able to kick rudder to take evasive action and also to give the side gunners a crack at the Zeros on the B-17's tail. One burst into flame and careened off.

Both Brown and Williams were hurt badly enough to be unable to man their guns; Sergeant John Gootee, whose right hand was mangled, took over the waist positions and continued firing with his left hand. Navigator Lieutenant W. F. Meenaugh and bombardier Sergeant R. W. Schlotte left the nose of the plane to give a hand in the waist. Killin's gun had been put out of commission by the same burst that killed him and the two waist guns were jammed. The radio had been destroyed and the oxygen system was out; the main wheels were flat and the tail wheel was completely shot away.

Wheless had more immediate problems. A number of control cables were shot out, making control difficult, No. 1 engine was dead and they had come down to three thousand feet. A stream of gasoline sprayed out of the right wing fuel tank which had been punctured; this not only increased the fire hazard but also very rapidly depleted their supply of fuel. They would never make it back to Del Monte and, as it grew dark and rain began falling, Wheless began looking for a place to land.

He pointed the ship toward a small landing field he knew about at Cagayan, just about twenty miles northwest of Del Monte. The heaving, struggling Fortress had already begun its descent on the strip before Wheless saw that the Cagayan field was covered with barricades.

There was no choice. Wheless lowered the gear, flat tires and all, and continued in. After plowing through the barricades and rolling for two hundred yards, after which the brakes locked, the Fortress stood on its nose for a moment, teetered and then fell back on its tail. The shaken crew crawled out of the plane. Later they counted well over a thousand bullet holes in the Fortress. They never knew what, if anything, their mission to Legaspi had accomplished.

Of the original thirty-five B-17s that had been in the Philippines when war came, only fourteen remained at Del Monte, six hundred miles south of Clark Field. With the Japanese pouring onto Luzon and with rumors that they would soon be coming to Mindanao, it was obvious that if these few Fortresses were to be preserved for future combat they would have to be based beyond the range of Japanese aircraft. Once the Japanese were on Luzon, Del Monte would no longer be safe.

58

It was decided then that the Far East Air Force should be evacuated to Australia. Beginning on December 17 the first B-17s began moving to Batchelor Field near Darwin—a flight of 1500 miles. On December 19 Del Monte was vigorously attacked from the air for the first time. The B-17s, luckily well camouflaged, escaped damage. By Christmas Eve all of the B-17s were in Australia where they would be safe, for a time at least, from Japanese air attacks and where they could receive sorely needed maintenance. From Australia, and later Java, these few Flying Fortresses were practically the only offensive weapons against the Japanese. The great distances they had to cover in order to reach their targets necessitated staging fields in between, such as Del Monte, for servicing and fuel. The hope was, however trifling the effects of their missions against overwhelming Japanese forces, just to hold the line until much needed—and promised—replacements arrived.

The first mission out of Australia took place on December 22 for which all of nine B-17s were in condition to make the long trip to Davao to bomb Japanese shipping. Led by Captain Cecil Combs (the other pilots were Lee B. Coats, James T. Connally, Walter Ford, Henry Godman, D. M. Keiser, Elmer Parsel, Earl Tash, and Edward C. Teats), the flight took off for Mindanao. They made the long flight without interception and appeared over Davao just as the sky was darkening with approaching evening and a storm. Though the area was overcast they bombed through whatever openings they could find, hitting the dock areas and sinking a tanker.

Speeding away from Davao the nine planes turned toward Del Monte, hoping that when they arrived they would be greeted by Americans. Del Monte was still in American hands they found and by morning six of the nine planes were ready for another mission (facilities were so limited at the base that these were all that could be handled). Combs had been ordered on another mission to Lingayen Gulf where eighty Japanese transports were reported to be. As soon as six planes were ready Combs decided they would take off, but his engines began to act up and he had to withdraw; the other five B-17s took off. Then Coats' engines developed trouble and he was forced to turn back. Knowing the limited capacities at Del Monte, he elected to continue on back to Batchelor. The four remaining planes (Keiser, Parsel, Tash, and Teats) continued up to Lingayen. In the dark Teats discovered that a Japanese plane had hitched on to his tail and, though it did not attempt to fire on them, it did follow. The B-17 was loaded with gas and bombs so Teats was unable to maneuver it into a firing position; instead he climbed above the intruder and turned toward the ocean so that the direction of their flight would not be revealed. Finally the Japanese plane gave up the chase.

Despite getting off course, Teats' plane arrived over the target first and saw that Lingayen Gulf was dotted with Japanese transports, cruisers, destroyers, and landing craft. Heavy fire rained down on the Americans inland, who were able to return only a feeble fraction of what was being thrown at them. It was an impressive and discouraging sight. Teats dropped his bombs and headed for home. The other three B-17s came over later and did the same. There was no antiaircraft fire and though Zeros darted up at them they were not hit. After landing at a Dutch airfield in the Moluccas, the three crews returned to Batchelor on Christmas Eve after flying almost 5000 miles to drop their light bomb loads.

59

Cannibalism: battle damaged B-17s are worked over by ground crewmen to salvage usable parts for less damaged bombers. Patched-up Fortresses were the rule, rather than the exception, during the early phases of the war in both the Pacific as well as Europe.

On Christmas Day Lieutenants George E. Schaetzel and Alvin Mueller brought their Fortresses over Davao from Batchelor in order to bomb a Japanese airdrome. Antiaircraft hit both ships, knocking out an engine in Schaetzel's B-17 and killing a gunner, Sergeant J. L. Cannon. They were then attacked by Zeros and Messerschmitts. Mueller, in remaining behind to help protect Schaetzel's now slower plane, was subjected to repeated attacks so that his plane literally became a sieve. The gunners on both B-17s returned the fire and managed to beat off the attackers.

Schaetzel and Mueller still had over a thousand miles to go before they could land at Batchelor Field. But they made it and after they landed in the afternoon of Christmas Day and had sent their wounded to the hospital and Combs began to arrange for Cannon's burial, the status report made up that day read: "3 B-17s in commission here; 1 at Del Monte, status unknown; 7 out of commission here."

New planes—B-17Es which the 7th Bombardment Group, Pearl Harbor refugees had—began to trickle in. But long flights at maximum performance and limited maintenance took its toll.

Of the original Clark Field B-17s, only one would survive, and that single ship was a patchwork from a half dozen others. It became one of the most celebrated planes of the war as *Alexander, the Swoose*, a name bestowed upon it by one of its first pilots Weldon H. Smith. Basically a B-17D, *The Swoose*, according to the popular song of the time was "half swan and half goose" because of its salvage background. *The Swoose*, and its various other parts while still on their original B-17s, was used in the frantic bombing missions out of Batchelor Field and later Java until the Japanese overran that island also. When some newer and tougher Model Es arrived to replace the battle worn Ds, *The Swoose* was eventually requisitioned by Lieutenant General George H. Brett (the same Brett who had tossed Boeing's James Murray out of his office a few years before). Brett was then in command of the U. S. Army Forces in Australia and had lost

Part of The Swoose *crew: Marvin McAdams, Harry Schreiber, Frank Kurtz, Harold Varner, and Aubrey Fox. The first pilot of the plane was Henry C. Godman; another was Weldon H. Smith, who named the plane. The Air Force serial number was 40-3097.*

Lieutenant General George H. Brett in the pilot's seat in The Swoose.

his command plane when the Japanese ravaged the airfield at Broome, Australia.

As a command plane, *The Swoose* remained in service long after it might have been scrapped. Even so, the sturdy ship continued to log an average of 150 hours a month in the air. In his official capacity Brett was required to travel around a good deal, particularly between New Guinea and Australia. Getting around Australia, with its great barren stretches and vast distances, was in itself a problem. Brett's pilot was Captain Frank Kurtz, one-time Olympic champion, whose original Fortress was destroyed on the ground at Clark Field on December 8.

The Swoose, consequently, ferried some Very Important People. On one flight from Darwin to Cloncurry, a distance of about 800 miles south and east into the Australian interior, the plane was loaded with high brass. Besides Brett there were Brigadier General Ralph Royce, Brigadier General William F. Marquat, Brigadier General Edwin S. Perrin, Lieutenant Colonel Samuel E. Anderson and, as described by one of the crew, "a big lanky guy from Texas," Congressman Lyndon B. Johnson, then on active duty as a Navy lieutenant commander. In all, about sixteen passengers were crowded into *The Swoose,* including also Australian officers and newspapermen.

When they arrived over Cloncurry, navigator Harry Schreiber was surprised to find that it wasn't there. A highly skilled navigator, Schreiber found that the octant he had used was not functioning properly. In a word, they—and all those important men—were lost.

Schreiber informed Kurtz of their predicament and while radio operator Sergeant Aubrey Fox tried fruitlessly to get a fix on any radio station that might lead them to a city, Kurtz began flying in a box-search pattern, hoping that they might find Cloncurry. Behind him he carried a heavy load of worried officers, one of whom naturally took to pacing up and down. From time to time he would poke his head into the cockpit to ask about their position and the fuel

The Swoose *after its forced landing near Carris Brook Farm, forty miles southeast of Winton, Australia. Lieutenant Commander Lyndon B. Johnson (second from left) sips coffee sent out to the grounded plane by S. H. Taylor, owner of the farm. It was later learned that* The Swoose *had got lost because, no longer a combat aircraft, its steel plates protecting the pilots had been removed. No one, however, thought to compensate the compasses, which were then completely off. The group of men under the wing are trying to figure out where they are.*

supply. This was distraction enough for Kurtz and co-pilot Marvin McAdams, now engaged in trying to find a place to land, but the movement of the general through the plane threw off the balance and they would have to adjust the trim tabs to keep in level flight.

As their fuel indicators hovered dangerously near the empty mark, Kurtz picked out a couple of buildings below them. If they piled up at least there would be people around to help them. He chose what appeared to be the softest spot in the rough terrain and pointed *The Swoose* down.

The pacing general continued with his exercise until he was collared by Sergeant Harold Varner (who was known as "The Hostess") and lectured him on the danger of the pacing. Rank aside, the sergeant informed the general that Kurtz had enough to think about besides twirling the trimming wheel. "Now," Varner growled, "get back there and sit down!" He guided the general into the rear of the plane and sat him down on the toilet near the tail wheel well.

Shortly after, Kurtz set the plane down with a jolt on the rocky ground—it was a perfect three-point landing. As their landing run continued, Kurtz could sense that the wheels were sinking into the soft earth. By applying throttles he eased it along until they reached firmer ground. With a sigh of relief he glanced at McAdams and both were able to relax as the engines sputtered to a stop.

Australian sheep ranchers began to gather around *The Swoose* as the passengers began to jump out. Lieutenant Commander Johnson promptly began making friends with the Australians, shook hands and, as Varner put it, "pretty soon he

62

Suzy-Q at Boeing Field after returning from the Pacific. Note absence of belly turret. Indian head insignia was marking of the 93rd Bombardment Squadron to which the plane belonged and which Felix Hardison, the pilot of the Suzy-Q commanded.

knows all their first names and they're telling him why there ought to be a high tariff on wool, and there's no question he swung that county for Johnson before we left."

When Brett was relieved of his command in the Pacific (because of his inability to get along with MacArthur and especially MacArthur's chief of staff, Sutherland), he took *The Swoose* with him to his Caribbean Defense Command. In the summer of 1942, with Kurtz at the controls, *The Swoose* made the flight from Australia to Washington, D.C. in the record time of thirty-six hours. (This last surviving aircraft from Emmett O'Donnell's 14th Squadron, 19th Bombardment Group (H), now rests in the Smithsonian Institution's National Air Museum.)

Another "celebrity" from the 19th Group was the *Suzy-Q*, one of the newer B-17Es. It had been flown to the Pacific by Captain Felix Hardison over the South American-African-Indian ferry route to the Pacific and landed at the Singosari air base in Java in February 1942. The *Suzy-Q* (Hardison's wife Priscilla was nicknamed "Suzy") acquired a reputation as "the fightingest Fortress of the war" in almost a year's battle service. It was also believed to be a charmed ship, for no crew member suffered so much as an injury while flying in the *Suzy-Q*. "Air Force men in the Southwest Pacific," *Yank* correspondent Howard Maier reported, "are inclined to think that the Suzy-Q has sunk more ships and killed more Japs than any other plane of ours in the entire war . . . The Suzy-Q has been hit a countless number of times, engines have been knocked out and replaced; she has slugged it out with Zero fighters in superior numbers and made forced landings. But always she comes up off the ground to fight back again and again . . . she has become something of a legend."

A new B-17E was a most welcome addition to the depleted 19th Bomb Group's forces and the *Suzy-Q* had barely landed when it was scheduled to take off with five other B-17s to bomb shipping in the Macassar Straits. With its formidable tail-stinger the *Suzy-Q* presented quite a problem to the Zeros. On the other hand, it soon became obvious that the remote-control ventral turret would not do. It was operated by a man in the plane via a complicated system

63

Suzy *and its crew: Coleman Stripling, Felix Hardison, William Bost-
wick, John Geckeler, John Irons, Orville Wright Kiger, and Durward
Fesmire.*

of mirrors which confused the gunner. No one is known to have hit an enemy
plane with this system, replaced by the Sperry ball-turret, which enabled the
gunner to curl up inside the gun position and see what he shot at. The remote-
control turret was removed from the *Suzy-Q,* which upped its speed a little,
but also made the plane a bit more vulnerable to attack from below. In time,
the *Suzy-Q* was used mainly on night missions when fighter opposition was
negligible or nonexistent.

Hardison and his crew arrived in Java just in time for the bitterly demoralizing
last ditch stand. The Japanese were "running wild" through the Netherlands
East Indies in a massive, seemingly inexorable amphibious blitzkrieg. By January 2, 1942, when the *Suzy-Q* took off from the runway at Boeing Field in
Seattle on its flight to the Pacific, Manila was occupied by the Japanese; Hong
Kong had surrendered on Christmas Day. The seas and harbors within bombing
range of the 19th Group were filled with targets, only there were never really
enough planes to cover them with real patterns. The *Suzy-Q* went out time
after time to attack transports and other ships, but never to any decisive purpose
beyond that of the doubtful pleasure of killing. Even this did not stop the
Japanese, who were now beginning to strike at Australia. On February 19 about
a hundred planes (the number is uncertain), bombers and Zeros, appeared over
Darwin and all but wiped it off the face of the earth in a raid that the Australians came to refer to as the Coventry of Australia.

Allied fighters were outnumbered and outperformed by the Zeros. In Java,
for example, the Dutch used obsolete Brewster "Buffalos" which were no match

64

for the Japanese aircraft. American squadrons were equipped with Curtiss P-40s, which could contend better with the Zero, but were not as maneuverable. They were, in addition, too few in number and poorly serviced because of the shortage of parts.

When it became necessary to leave Java evacuation began in earnest by February 27. On this day the *Langley,* on which the B-17 had been conceived, was speeding toward Java with a deck load of thirty-two P-40s and was sunk. The still flyable B-17s were pressed into service to evacuate American personnel from Java to the city of Broome on the northwest coast of Australia. The *Suzy-Q* flew on a last futile mission to drop bombs on a Japanese convoy before returning to the Dutch base to pick up as many Americans as possible before taking off for Broome.

As they pulled away from the airdrome the place blew up under them as the Dutch detonated the mines which had been placed under the runways, ready for the inevitable day when the enemy would arrive. Great fires filled the air over Java with black, oily smoke as the *Suzy-Q* raced for Broome.

The small frontier town was choked with refugees, Dutch civilians, women and children from Java as well as military personnel. Most of these were American for the Dutch remained in Java to continue fighting—as did some American field artillerymen. Broome was an undefended town facing the ocean, its outer boundaries limited by the vast arid Australian desert. Its tiny airfield could barely cope with the number of planes that came and went and with others that were parked on the field. There were B-17s, B-24s, LB-30s (the export version of the B-24) and several other planes. In the harbor there were ships as well as Navy PBYs, the large Consolidated flying boats. And throughout the town there was desperation, fear, and confusion.

On March 3 nine Zeros swooped down and wreaked havoc. A Liberator taking off with the most seriously wounded just about the time the Zeros attacked, crashed burning into the bay; at least a dozen flying boats, some carrying Dutch women and children, were left burning in the bay also. Another B-24 (General Brett's command ship before he took over *The Swoose*) was destroyed on the ground as were other planes, including two B-17Es. The crowded dock areas were mercilessly strafed; the only return fire was from a hand-held .30-caliber machine gun which was fired by one of the Dutch soldiers until the heated barrel scorched his hands to the bone. Among the dead were over forty Dutch civilians (mostly women and children) and twenty American airmen, among them one of the men who had served as a bombardier on the *Suzy-Q.* The plane itself had left Broome some hours before to get it out of attack range and to prepare the men for reorganization of the 19th Group.

Morale was low. They were tired and their planes were worn and abused beyond limits. "Right then the safety margins of peace in a heavy bomber operation disappeared," Edward Teats later observed. "We found out a lot about those big Fortresses we hadn't known. We discovered we could take off from any field we could land in. We took off and landed no matter what the wind direction was. We operated at maximum most the time. We threw the book away . . ."

The men of the shattered 19th and 7th Groups, dispirited, fatigued and without hope, could not help but wonder what was in store for them next. Painfully and at great cost and for what appeared to be minimal results, they had heroically made it up as they went along. It was no way to run a war.

Take-off at Midway.

7. Turning Tide

With the seemingly inconquerable Japanese forces pouring down through the Southwest Pacific it would only be a matter of time before the sorely besieged Philippines must fall.

The Japanese advances were based primarily on air power. After a build-up of strength at a given base the planes would set out to overcome the consistently inferior Allied air opposition at the next attack point. A heavily screened amphibious assault would be sent out and as soon as the newly taken area was under Japanese control, the airfields would be repaired and forces would be gathered for the next attack. Fanning out, the Japanese invested the strategic bases at Rabaul in Northern New Britain and Bougainville in the Solomon Islands.

Practically all of the resistance in the Philippines had been crushed except for MacArthur's depleted troops, now pinched onto the narrow Bataan peninsula of Luzon. Lieutenant General Masaharu Homma's 14th Army was sent in at Lingayen Gulf to decide the issue.

To prevent his capture, and thus enable the Japanese to enjoy more than a military victory, MacArthur was ordered out of the Philippines. He was reluctant and for a time refused but a Presidential order could not be ignored and MacArthur finally prepared to evacuate. Major General Jonathan Wainwright was left behind to fight the losing battle.

MacArthur, his wife and infant son, and members of his staff boarded four PT boats at Corregidor for a dash south to Mindanao. At Del Monte they were to be picked up by four B-17s and taken to Australia. When MacArthur's party arrived at Mindanao they were met by Major General William F. Sharp who informed them that the expected B-17s had not yet arrived. On the following day, however, one lone Flying Fortress fluttered into Del Monte field. MacArthur was visibly shocked.

That the plane had flown at all was only because it had somehow been able to in defiance of all the laws of aerodynamics. Like *The Swoose* it was a thing of scraps and patches (where aluminum could not be found patches were made from empty tin cans) and looked anything but shipshape. Worse was to come: down from the cockpit bounced what must have seemed to MacArthur an infant who claimed to be the wreck's pilot. The rest of the raffish crew piled out and

66

Lieutenant Harl Pease, Jr.

MacArthur waited, hoping perhaps that the pilot's father would also emerge and calm his trepidations.

Lieutenant Harl Pease, the B-17's pilot, though barely in his twenties was one of the best of the 19th Group. He reported that all four of the promised B-17s had left Australia, but two had turned back with engine trouble, the third had pancaked into the bay near Buka just a few miles away. His plane, Pease conceded, could be in better condition. The superchargers weren't really functioning, thanks to the overusage and parts shortage, and with the hydraulic system leaking there were no brakes. Both Pease and the plane were veterans of the Philippine and Java campaigns and one, at least, looked it.

MacArthur was livid. He muttered something about the condition of the plane and an "inexperienced boy" and ordered blistering messages to be sent to Brett in Australia and to General George C. Marshall in Washington. "The best three planes in the United States or Hawaii," he told Marshall, "should be made available with completely adequate experienced crews." He made it plain that making such a trip in the plane supplied, not to mention the child who was supposed to fly it, "would amount to consigning the whole party to death . . ."

Thus rejected, Pease and the B-17 loaded up with a number of airmen—who trusted both—and took off for Australia. Luckily they encountered neither bad weather nor Zeros, for the dangerously overburdened plane, unescorted as it was, could not have survived either. Even so, they were critically low on fuel as they approached Batchelor Field. Pease brought the plane in for a good landing and just as he was pulling into a hardstand, the engines quit—they were out of gas.

Brett, now off to a bad start with MacArthur, managed to find four new B-17Es with mature pilots and sent them off to Del Monte. MacArthur, his family and immediate staff, were placed aboard Captain William Monay's B-17 which then refused to start. What with the Japanese closing in and what appeared to be a B-17 fiasco, the atmosphere was charged with tension. The party was transferred to the Fortress piloted by Frank Bostrom (who had so skillfully set down a B-17 in a golf course at Pearl Harbor). Except for a few trying

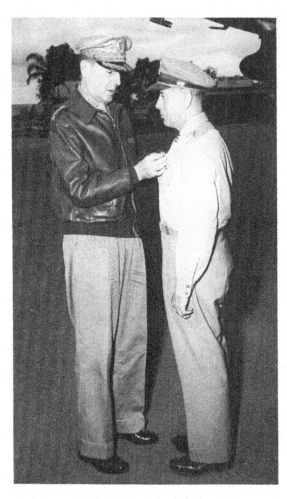

General Douglas MacArthur, commander of the Southwest Pacific Theater, decorates Lieutenant General George C. Kenney with the Distinguished Service Medal at Amberley Field, near Brisbane, Australia.

moments during take-off, when the B-17 dipped a little at the end of the runway, the evacuation was carried out without further incident.

MacArthur, having had his fill of airplanes, wanted to continue his journey by train. His medical adviser, Major Charles Morhouse, advised him that the 800-mile trip from Batchelor to Alice Springs across the desert might prove fatal to MacArthur's son, Arthur. The general turned again to the 19th Group. On the following day, with Zeros approaching Batchelor Field, MacArthur's party again boarded a B-17, this one piloted by Major Richard H. Carmichael (who set his plane down on a tiny fighter runway at Pearl Harbor), and flew to Alice Springs. There MacArthur made his famous statement: "The President of the United States ordered me to break through the Japanese lines and proceed from Corregidor to Australia for the purpose, as I understand it, of organizing the American offensive against Japan, a primary object of which is the relief of the Philippines. I came through and I shall return."

He was to keep his word, of course, but the road was to be a long and bitter one. As for the "primary object," it would not come in time. The decision had already been made that Germany was the most formidable enemy and all possible resources would be turned toward the European Theater of Operations. A de-

68

The Bataan, *General Douglas MacArthur's specially converted B-17E flying head-quarters. Only the single .50-caliber gun in the nose and twin fifties in the tail were retained of the armament; the other turrets, bomb racks and armor plate were removed to make way for all the facilities of a command plane. The converted aircraft was designated an XC-108.*

laying action would be carried on in the Pacific until the Germans were defeated after which all the might of the Allies would be concentrated on Japan.

Reinforcements, supplies, and other necessities for the Pacific came through with irregular paucity for the next few months because of the ETO priority and the long lines of communication. Bataan fell less than a month after Mac-Arthur broke through and Corregidor, the stubborn Rock, held out until May 6, 1942.

The sole bright light in all the gloom of this period was the stirringly courageous, though militarily inconclusive, attack on the Japanese home islands by carrier-launched B-25 "Mitchell" medium bombers led by Lieutenant Colonel James H. Doolittle on April 18. A stimulating morale booster if nothing else (all the planes were lost though most crews managed to survive), this remarkable feat was the first in a series of events that were to prove the mettle of the "soft, decadent democracies." The lazy, sleeping giant that had worried Yamamoto was beginning to stir, and the purely defensive phase of the Pacific war was shifting.

By mid-April the Japanese had established bases in the New Guinea-New Britain-Solomon Islands area, which put them in position to strike out at all of Melanesia and Australia itself. The forces available to the Allies, however eager for battle, were hardly adequate for effective defense against major enemy concentrations—and large-scale offensive actions were inconceivable.

Unknown to the Japanese their code had been broken by American intelligence and their moves were known in advance by the Allies. Consequently, when the Japanese launched their Port Moresby invasion force, a fleet of some seventy ships including the aircraft carriers *Shokaku, Zuikaku,* and *Shoho,* Rear Admiral Frank J. Fletcher was ready for it in the Coral Sea. If the Japanese could take Port Moresby, they would not only be able to shut down a major Allied air base, an air threat to their bases at Rabaul and Kavieng, but would themselves have a jumping-off place for their proposed Australian campaign.

The Battle of the Coral Sea was the first in history in which two naval forces fought without exchanging a shot. All of the battle was done in the air. B-17s

69

from the 19th Group and B-26s from the 22nd Group (Medium) were alerted for reconnaissance and bombardment. The climax came on May 7–8, 1942, when the air fleets of the opposing forces met.

Navy dive bombers and torpedo planes from the U.S. carriers *Yorktown* and *Lexington* sank the *Shoho*, the first carrier loss for the Japanese. A furious counterattack by Japanese aircraft, however, so badly damaged the *Lexington* that it was eventually sunk by an American destroyer. The *Yorktown* was also damaged as were the Japanese carriers *Shokaku* and *Zuikaku*. The latter, while not sunk, were so badly mauled that they required a two-month layover for repairs, which would have further repercussions in June.

By May 9 the Battle of the Coral Sea was over. Each side had lost a carrier as well as other smaller ships and planes. In the lesser sense, that is, tactically, the Japanese had won, for the *Shoho* was not an even trade for the *Lexington*, a larger more powerful carrier. Strategically, however, it was a victory for the Allies. They had stopped a Japanese invasion armada for the first time since Pearl Harbor. Both sides issued exaggerated claims after the smoke had cleared, neither at the time realizing the greater significance of the encounter. Even Hitler, who fancied himself a military genius, offered an evaluation when he crowed: "After this new defeat the United States warships will hardly dare to face the Japanese fleet again, since any United States warship which accepts action with the Japanese naval forces is as good as lost."

Yamamoto hoped, even believed, that this might be true. Already, in fact before the Port Moresby Invasion Force had been unleashed, an even more spectacular plan was in motion. As long as the American Pacific fleet, particularly its carriers, was permitted to exist, Japanese operations in the Pacific would be challenged. It was Yamamoto's idea, therefore, to lure out the American fleet, destroy it and perhaps bring about a negotiation for peace in the Pacific. He planned to do this by staging a double blow, one at the Aleutians, close to the American homeland as a diversionary strike, and the other at Midway, one of the few Pacific bases still in American hands. Certain that this would bring out the remnants of the American naval forces Yamamoto assembled a massive task force to finish off what was left of it. The date was set for some time in June; surprise and large numbers would secure certain victory.

Once again however, the Americans had some idea of Yamamoto's next move. It was learned that the Aleutian operation would get under way first to bring out the American forces. On the following day carrier planes under the command of Nagumo, veteran of Pearl Harbor, would begin the attack on Midway; the invasion force would then follow. Yamamoto would lay in wait with the great main force of the Imperial Japanese Fleet to annihilate the Americans as they came out to counterattack.

Despite the losses sustained in the Coral Sea battle, and the unavailability of the two damaged carriers, Yamamoto was able to launch a great armada of two hundred ships, the carriers of which held seven hundred aircraft. The Americans were outnumbered heavily: the Japanese had six carriers, for example, to the Americans' three. No American battleships were available; the Japanese had eleven. All that Admiral Chester W. Nimitz had in his favor was the elimination of the element of surprise, thanks to the breaking of the Japanese code, and the Navy and Marine pilots, especially, who valiantly decided the outcome of the Battle of Midway.

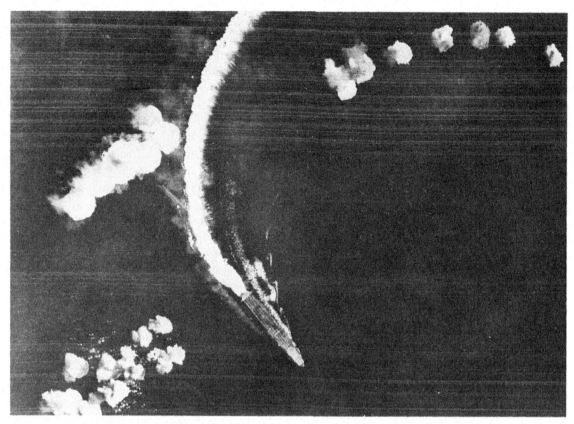

A Japanese aircraft carrier, believed to be the Akagi *seen from a B-17 at 20,000 feet during the Battle of Midway. High altitude attacks on moving targets were proved unsuccessful at Midway; though several attacks were made by the B-17s none was able to hit a Japanese ship. It was later sunk by Navy torpedo planes.*

On the morning of June 3, 1942, Japanese forces were sighted several hundred miles southwest of Midway on an easterly course. Late in the afternoon they were attacked by a squadron of B-17s from the 7th Air Force under command of Lieutenant Colonel Walter C. Sweeney. Although claims were made, no actual hits were scored. The next day Japanese aircraft bombed Midway causing much damage but took heavy losses. Army, Navy, and Marine planes based on Midway flew out to attack the Japanese fleet.

At this point, American carriers were in position to take part in the engagement. From the *Hornet* rose Torpedo Squadron 8, without fighter protection or dive bomber support, to attack a force of four Japanese carriers. All fifteen of their antiquated "Devastators" were shot down and only one pilot, Ensign George H. Gay, Jr., survived. Tragically, despite the sacrifice, no hits were scored.

About an hour later, torpedo squadrons from the *Yorktown* and *Enterprise* attacked the Japanese carriers, also suffering heavy losses, but managing to hit two of the carriers. The dive bombers from the *Enterprise* appeared over the *Akagi,* whose decks were crowded with planes which had returned for fuel. Explosions amidst these planes turned the deck into a roaring mass of flames. Other planes struck the *Kaga* and *Soryu* savagely and in a few moments three of the finest of Japan's aircraft carrier force were a molten shambles. They could neither launch nor receive their planes. The *Kaga* exploded and sank that same day, the burning *Soryu* was administered the *coup de grâce* by the American submarine *Nautilus* and the Japanese themselves sank the *Akagi*. The *Hiryu*, had, meanwhile, escaped serious damage, but that carrier also was doomed by planes on the way from the *Enterprise*. But Japanese planes from the *Hiryu* were to write the finish to the career of the *Yorktown* first.

The sinking of the *Yorktown* on June 7 closed the Battle of Midway. Although he knew better Yamamoto sent a message to his by now dispersed forces claiming "The enemy fleet has been practically destroyed and is retiring eastward." American losses were high—over three hundred men were dead, 150 planes were shot down, including two B-17s, the destroyer *Hammann* was sunk and the *Yorktown* was lost.

But the Japanese had lost no fewer than four aircraft carriers and with them hundreds of their first-line aircraft and most experienced pilots. The heavy cruiser *Mikuma* was sunk, several ships were damaged and casualties ran into the thousands. Yamamoto had stopped running wild.

With MacArthur in Australia planning the road back into the Philippines, with the Japanese turned back in the Coral Sea, thus leaving Port Moresby open as an allied air base and Australia safe from invasion and, finally, with the battle of Midway over, there remained one more decision to be made that would complete the command situation on the Southwest Pacific. The ABDA Command (the letters stood for the allies involved: America, Britain, the Dutch, and Australians) had not worked out for various reasons, among them such problems as the language barrier and nationalism besides the shortage of supplies, machines, and men. General Sir Archibald Wavell, Supreme Allied Commander in the Southwest Pacific, had no other recourse but to close up the ABDA Command and get out of Java; Brereton was shunted off to India with some of the pieces of the 7th Bombardment Group—one LB-30 and five battle-scarred B-17s. Brett, Wavell's Deputy Commander, remained in Australia and he was quickly at loggerheads with MacArthur and particularly the general's chief of staff, Sutherland.

The final decision was made when Major General George C. Kenney was appointed to command MacArthur's air arm. As outspoken as he was capable, Kenney quickly won over MacArthur if not his staff as he whipped into the reorganization of the tattered Allied Air Forces (later the 5th Air Force). One of his first acts was to inform MacArthur's chief of staff, Sutherland, that as the most competent airman in the area he (Kenney) would run the Air Forces in the Pacific and would not be told how to run his "air show" (Kenney's term) by anyone, whatever their position. Their argument became heated and Sutherland did not rescind an order to which Kenney had objected until the latter insisted that they thrash it out in the presence of MacArthur. This practically put Kenney into the deposed Brett's shoes except that MacArthur took a liking to the belligerent airman. But MacArthur's staff found him too unorthodox, even reckless, and rarely failed to let the opportunity pass by to remind the general, if they could.

Kenney believed that his primary mission, once he had put his forces into shape, was "to take out the Jap air strength until we owned the air over New Guinea. That there was no use talking about playing across the street until we got the Nips off of our front lawn." He quickly antagonized a number of his peers by going to bat for his "kids," the youngsters who flew the planes that fought the battles. He tangled with the Services of Supply when he uncovered a colonel "whose passion for paper work effectually stopped the issuing of supplies" and who firmly believed that "it was about time these combat units learned how to do their paper work properly." Much needed supplies, therefore, were not sent to the combat zones because a requisition form was not made out properly. Kenney decided then and there that the pompous little colonel was obviously suffering from "overwork and fatigue through tropical service" and shipped him home. His successor was informed that he would fill the needs of the kids whatever the state of the forms. Kenney also swooped down upon the rear echelon bases, closed them up and pushed them up farther into northern Australia, closer to the fighting zones where it would not take so long to move supplies to the men who needed them.

His swashbuckling style greatly pleased the patrician Douglas MacArthur, who frequently referred to Kenney as a "buccaneer." The rapport between these two very different men was to produce remarkable results. Kenney did not find it always a simple job, but he did have a fine ally in MacArthur. Each became sensitive to the other's moods, respected and understood each other.

One day Kenney walked into MacArthur's office, obviously in a bad humor. "What's the matter, George," MacArthur inquired, "have you run out of coffee?"

"I've got troubles, General," Kenney told him. "Five of them."

"What are they?"

"First, there's your goddam staff; second, the SOS [supply]; third, the Navy; fourth, the weather. The Japs are in fifth place."

One of Kenney's first "shows" was a strike on the Vunakanau airdrome near Rabaul, New Britain, and timed to keep the Japanese busy while the Marines began landing on Guadalcanal in the Solomons. Also striking directly against the Solomons from New Hebrides was Colonel LaVerne G. Saunders' 11th Bombardment Group of the 7th Air Force. For this attack Kenney hoped to get twenty B-17s of the 19th Group. After months of pitifully small strikes the promise of so impressive a showing was a morale booster for the group and all were eager to take part.

It was on the mission to Rabaul that a tragic sequel was written to MacArthur's encounter with "the inexperienced boy," Harl Pease.

Now a captain, Pease had flown a reconnaissance mission on the day before the "big show" was to take place and returned to the 19th's base at Mareeba, Australia, with one engine out. Neither he nor his crew wanted to miss the strike at Vunakanau so they worked through most of the night putting another plane, which was declared unserviceable for combat, into flying condition (unlike their own plane it did have all four engines). By late evening they had the B-17 functioning and took off for Port Moresby to join the 19th Group; one engine was missing badly but they saw to it that their plane was loaded with bombs. They managed then to get about three hours of sleep before the group took off.

The distance from Port Moresby to the Vunakanau airdrome was only 550 miles, which presented little problem for the long-range craft except that jutting up between was the Owen Stanley Mountains of New Guinea, a 12,000 foot barrier. Extra fuel was required to get over the mountains or, if you were in

Loading up for a mission against Japanese positions in the Philippines.

A typical jungle landing strip of the 49th Fighter Group near Port Moresby, New Guinea. The planes are Curtiss P-40 "Warhawks."

trouble and could not reach altitude, to go around them. Pease's B-17 had no electrical fuel-transfer pump so before take-off he and his crew dug up a hand-pump. Pumping the fuel from the bomb-bay tanks would be a tedious and dangerous job, especially if the plane were under attack.

As the 19th Group, led by Colonel Richard Carmichael, approached Rabaul, about thirty Zeros whirred down on the formation—which had dwindled down to eighteen planes. The fighters came in from the side of the formation in which Pease was flying. The faulty engine had already stopped functioning and Pease had feathered the propeller. Instead of turning back for Port Moresby, which he could have, he continued toward the target. About 150 Japanese bombers were caught on the ground and at least half were destroyed by the bombardment, which set gasoline fires and caused ammunition to detonate.

After Pease had released his bombs the formation was attacked by another wave of Zeros which concentrated upon the crippled Fortress. The bomb-bay tank was set afire and was seen to drop into the sea—then the B-17 itself also burst into flame and plunged into the Pacific.

General MacArthur approved of Kenney's recommendation that Harl Pease, the boy with whom he had refused to fly out of the Philippines, be given the Medal of Honor for his mission to Vunakanau. His was the only plane lost on that raid.

His first shows out of the way, Kenney very quickly devised or encouraged unorthodox methods of warfare. Among them were the "para-frag" bomb, skip-bombing, "Kenney Cocktails," and a commerce destroyer. The para-frag was a bomb released at low altitude over Japanese installations dangling from small parachutes. By the time they detonated the low-flying plane which had dropped them was out of danger of being blown up by its own bomb. These bombs could be dropped with great precision on parked aircraft, or other targets. The "Kenney Cocktail" was an adaptation of the general purpose bomb and the incendiary which, when it detonated, blew streamers of burning white phosphorous over a radius of 150 feet. These were effective against parked aircraft as well as antiaircraft installations.

Skip-bombing was low-level attack, employing any plane from a B-17 to a

74

P-38, at mast level or tree top level against shipping and enemy installations. Bombs would be bounced into the sides of ships in the manner that a stone can be thrown to skip along the surface of a pond. To facilitate this form of attack, Kenney entrusted Major Paul I. ("Pappy") Gunn with the job of developing a "commerce destroyer." North American B-25 "Mitchells" were fitted out with four .50-caliber machine guns in the nose, two on each side of the fuselage and, with the two in the top turret, could bring ten forward firing guns to bear in any low-level attack.

The Japanese, who suffered terribly from these devices, objected to these methods (even after the rape of Singapore and the Bataan death march) and characterized Kenney as a "beast" who employed "new and fiendish methods of warfare"; he was, Tokyo Rose insisted, the leader of "a gang of gangsters from a gangster-ridden country."

The skip-bombing techniques were developed mainly by Kenney's one-time aide, Major William G. Benn, commander of the newly organized 64th Squadron of the 43rd Bombardment Group. Kenney proposed to take some of the burden off the 19th Group, which had taken the brunt of the early fighting in the Philippines and Java. When he first heard of the 43rd, Kenney found that "all they had left was a flag and a couple of guys to hold it up." They had run out of planes and their men had been scattered all over Australia doing everything but flying.

It was then that Kenney reactivated the 43rd Group and ordered the dispersed personnel brought together and fitted out with B-17s. One of the best-known crews of the 43rd was called "The Eager Beavers" because of its willingness to take on all sorts of assignments. The pilot of the Fortress was Captain Jay Zeamer who had a fixed .50-caliber machine gun installed on the fuselage just below his cockpit so that he too might now and then have a shot at the Japanese.

On June 16, 1943, the crew volunteered to photograph the Buka airstrip near Bougainville in the Solomon Islands. When they were about ten miles from Buka, the unescorted B-17 was attacked by twenty Zeros.

They were too close to their objective to abandon the mission so the men in the B-17 prepared to meet the attack. In the nose, Lieutenant Joseph R. Sarnoski, the bombardier, knocked out the first Zero which was hurtling in head-on; from the top turret, Sergeant John J. Able set another aflame with a short burst.

On the Leyte air strip, after the return to the Philippines. Major Richard I. Bong, American Ace of Aces and P-38 pilot with Lieutenant General George C. Kenney on the right and Colonel David W. Hutchison, commander of the 308th Bombardment Wing (H), in the center.

75

Major Jay Zeamer.   *Lieutenant Joseph R. Sarnoski.*

But the interceptors were scoring hits also. At 28,000 feet their main oxygen line was severed and Zeamer dived the plane down into a more breathable atmosphere. The Zeros tenaciously clung to the plane. As he pulled out, Zeamer pointed the B-17 at a Zero and pulled his gun's trigger and shot it out of the sky. Immediately after, another Zero made a head-on pass. A 20-mm shell exploded in the bombardier's compartment, flinging Sarnoski into the passageway beneath the pilots' compartment. Zeamer, in the meantime, had been struck in the legs so that co-pilot John Britton had to control the rudder while Zeamer otherwise piloted the plane.

"I'm all right," Sarnoski assured them, "don't worry about me." He then crawled back into the smoking bombardier's compartment. He shot off another burst stopping another Zero which began spiraling down. Sarnoski then collapsed, dead from a stomach wound

This battle went on for forty minutes during which the Buka airstrip was photographed and five Zeros were shot down. But "The Eager Beavers" were in a tough spot. Sarnoski was dead; their radio was shot away and radio operator William Vaughan was wounded, the co-pilot was wounded and out, the navigator Ruby Johnston was wounded—and Zeamer himself had fainted from loss of blood. The only men who had escaped injury were tail gunner "Pudge" Pugh and the photographer, William Kendrick. Top turret gunner Able was hurt but still on his feet. But there were no brakes, no flap control, no radio, no compass— and no pilots.

Though he had never flown a B-17 before, John Able took a position between Zeamer and Britton and calling upon whatever he had learned when he rode up front on previous missions and instinct, he piloted that B-17. He steadied the control column and kept the sun to their back so that the plane was headed in the general direction of their base at Dobodura, New Guinea, 600 miles away.

Whenever Zeamer regained consciousness, he would assist and instruct Able in the flying and navigation. Zeamer had been wounded through the arms and legs; one leg was broken and he could only use one arm. Britton was still out.

A Japanese transport burns offshore while a supply dump goes up in flames inland after B-17s bombed Guadalcanal.

After almost three hours, familiar landmarks appeared in the water below them. When they arrived over Cape Endiaidere they knew they were only twenty-five miles from the field. Both Zeamer and Britton had revived by this time and felt they could take over to try landing the plane. While Britton applied his feet to the rudder pedals, Zeamer guided the plane down with his one good hand. There was no time for a correct landing pattern as they hurriedly brought in the B-17 before they might lapse into unconsciousness again.

All they could see was the runway before them as they rushed in. They had not even checked for wind direction and brought the plane in with the wind and used up all of the 7000-foot runway before the plane stopped rolling.

The five wounded men were removed from the plane and it was then that Pugh, still dazed by the experience, looked up at the wind cone. It pointed in

After Guadalcanal, with its excellent Henderson Field, was taken in the Solomons, the next objective became Bougainville in the north. A B-17 on the way to Buka airfield passes over an active volcano.

the same direction as the B-17. That couldn't possibly be right so he stormed into the control tower demanding to know why the wind sock was pointed in the wrong direction.

Gently he was assured it would be fixed, for no one wished to discuss this with the obviously distraught and tense Pugh. He, along with the rest of the crew, was awarded a Distinguished Flying Cross. Sarnoski received, posthumously, the Medal of Honor; Zeamer, who recovered also received the Medal of Honor.

The 43rd Bombardment Group was probably the last in the Pacific to fly B-17s, for the Fortresses were being shipped to the European Theater almost as quickly as they emerged from the factory. But the B-17Es and Fs continued in service with the 5th as well as the 7th, 10th, 11th, and 13th Air Forces in the Pacific even after the arrival of the Consolidated B-24 "Liberators."

Like the old B-17s, the 19th Bomb Group was finally retired and sent home, what was left of it, in the summer of 1942. It would return later in the war as a Very Heavy group equipped with B-29s. Until it converted to B-24s, the 43rd Group fought the Japanese from New Guinea with the B-17.

William H. Schiffer, a crew chief then in the 43rd, recalls some of the confusion of their initial missions. On one they took off to discover later that, instead of .50-caliber ammunition, their ammunition boxes were full of Army manuals. Flying out of Australia had its natural hazards for, as Schiffer watched one day, a kangaroo hopped out onto the runway in front of a B-17 taking off. The bomb-loaded plane struck the kangaroo, flipped over on its back and exploded killing everyone aboard.

Schiffer found that the "Zero was a good plane, but it burned easily. And the

Nakajima 97 float plane—it was a shame to shoot it down. It 'was slow and not very maneuverable—like Lindbergh going past."

Schiffer had the distinction of shooting down three Zeros by accident. During an air battle his top turret guns jammed and in his disgust and anger Schiffer began pounding on the breech. Suddenly the gun began firing on its own—and continued firing until the belt was empty. Just at that moment a Zero plunged in to attack and dived into the fusillade, burst into flame and gracefully rolled over. It collided with another Zero diving in for the Fortress and the resultant explosion enveloped yet another Zero. All three went down blazing.

The 43rd Bombardment Group distinguished itself in the battle of the Bismarck Sea (March 1943) in which practically an entire Japanese convoy was wiped out by Kenney's bombers, fighters, and commerce destroyers. For this the 43rd was awarded the Distinguished Unit Citation. It was Kenney's belief that "little bits of ribbon" as a sign of recognition would bolster morale. For months they had been virtually ignored, it seemed, by all concerned, from their own replacement centers to the home front. Such remarkable exploits as those of Kelly, Pease, or Zeamer were quickly broadcast and fittingly. But without fighter cover, without proper maintenance, the "kids" soon proved that even the unique became typical and commonplace.

The wording of a citation recommending a decoration is a curious mingling of military objectivity and understated pride. Word for word, the following is such a request which arrived at General Kenney's headquarters in June, 1943.

"1. Under the provisions of AR 600-45, War Department, Washington, D.C., dated 8 August, 1932 as amended, it is recommended that Staff Sergeant WILLIAM H. SCHIFFER, 20249494, 64th Bombardment Squadron (H), 43rd Bombardment Group (H), be awarded the Silver Star for gallantry in action over Finschhafen, New Guinea, on 31 May 1943.

"2. Sergeant Schiffer was the side gunner on a B-17 type aircraft, which started on an armed reconnaissance of the north and south side of New Britain on the afternoon of May 31, 1943. When about twenty miles southeast of Finschhafen, New Guinea, at 4000 feet, this aircraft was attacked by 16 Zeros, which came out of cloud cover directly in front of the plane. This aircraft started evasive action immediately by going into a light low haze and dropping the bombs and the bomb bay tank. Approximately five minutes later as the aircraft came out of the haze, enemy aircraft, which went under the haze, attacked from below rendering the lower turret, the radio equipment, oxygen system, hydraulic system and No. 3 engine inopperative and damaging the control surfaces, and the right landing gear, and putting cannon holes thru two cylinders of number two engine causing it to throw oil badly, and severing some gas lines. For the next thirty minutes of this engagement this aircraft was forced to fly at such a low altitude that it was impossible for the Zeros to attack the unprotected belly of the plane. While barely clearing the tops of the foothills near Finschhafen seeking cloud cover, the enemy aircraft made individual and simultaneous attacks from all possible angles. That altitude during the attack was extremely difficult to hold because of evasive maneuvering and loss of power because of damaged engines. After approximately thirty-five minutes of combat, this aircraft escaped by following scattered cloud cover out at sea. Although three members of the crew were wounded in the first few minutes, thus decreasing the

A Fortress of the 43rd Group after a crash-landing on the beach in New Guinea.

efficiency of the crew, five Zeros were definitely destroyed and were seen to crash, another was last seen going down as the aircraft entered cloud cover, and in several other instances tracers were seen to enter the attacking planes. After interception had been broken off, the pilot and crew elected to bring the damaged plane, if possible, back to its base, although the oil and gas from broken lines was being blown onto the fuselage, and number two engine was smoking badly threatening to envelop the plane in flames. Although wounded, this Sergeant remained at his gun in spite of overwhelming fire power and definitely removed one enemy aircraft from its service against the allied forces of the Southwest Pacific area. And his act of electing to try to bring the aircraft back without regard to personal safety shows gallantry in its highest sense."

It was signed by Lieutenant Henry W. Evans, co-pilot of the plane; the pilot was Captain Ealon S. Hocutt.

Shortly after the Battle of the Bismarck Sea, Kenney left for Washington to "squawk to 'Hap' Arnold about getting more airplanes." He wanted more B-17s, more fighters for cover and more replacement parts. He was told by Arnold that he could have no more B-17s, but Kenney was not easily dissuaded or discouraged and continued to "squawk" until finally President Roosevelt made it clear that no more B-17s were to be shipped to the Pacific.

"Eaker wants them," he was told.

ACTION OF THE TIGER

In peace there's nothing so becomes a man
As modest stillness and humility;
But when the blast of war blows in our ears,
Then imitate the action of the tiger:

❋ ❋ ❋

Be copy now to men of grosser blood,
And teach them how to war!

HENRY V

"Pinetree."

8. O Mistress Mine!

Great Britain had stood defiantly and gloriously alone against the Nazi onslaught until the United States itself was forced by the Pearl Harbor attack into the Second World War. Three days after that event, Germany and Italy declared war on the United States. The high command readily agreed that the European enemy was the first requiring attention—a decision made and agreed to as early as late December at the "Arcadia" conference in Washington for which Prime Minister Winston Churchill came to the United States. A delaying action would be the keynote in the Pacific while the Axis was given priority.

The tiny island of Great Britain would become with the hoped for arrival of the 8th Air Force, one great, crowded, mass of airdromes. Onto it would assemble the mightiest air armadas in history with the purpose of bringing to the Germans, leaders as well as the led, the full terrible and furious meaning of modern war, which they themselves had unleashed.

Even before the Japanese struck, American officers had been sent to England to study air combat firsthand. The outnumbered RAF proved itself more than a match for the *Luftwaffe*, thanks to the indomitable young pilots and their Hurricanes and Spitfires. The Americans hoped to glean information that might be used in the future design of American aircraft, in the selection of the necessary equipment and in projecting appropriations.

The theoreticians were somewhat disturbed to learn that the Battle of Britain and the London blitz had not contributed much to the cause of strategic bombardment. Losses on both sides had been high and results not very impressive during the daylight raids. The RAF devastated the German bomber formations and

83

those that got through did not cripple British industry or its fighting forces as much as had been hoped. And instead of demoralizing the British, the Germans only succeeded in rallying them to a stubborn resistance. And the Nazis were to pay heavily for such raids as that upon Coventry which the British would never forget.

The RAF carried the war into the Ruhr Valley, where most of the German heavy industries were located, at night. This eliminated the precision aspect of the bombing and meant that the cities in the vicinity of the heavy industries included in the area under attack were also destroyed.

Among the first American observers to go to England was Colonel Carl Spaatz, whose prolonged stay coincided with the Battle of Britain (July–October 1940) and the ensuing London blitz (September 1940–May 1941). It had not at that time been decided, but in time Spaatz would return to England to command the American air forces in Europe. His canny perceptiveness and an unusual ability to see through detail into the core of a matter won the British over; Spaatz in turn was impressed with their quiet efficiency and fighting qualities. His wry sense of humor delighted the British. They freely revealed their secrets to Spaatz in an amazing show of confidence. On one visit to an English air base Spaatz was asked to sign the guest register and caused momentary consternation when, in the space marked Occupation, he wrote in a single word: *Spy.*

Spaatz and other American officers studied the British techniques and reported on the feasibility of their employment in conjunction with American military doctrine. The importance of radar was noted; though no secret, the Germans paid heavily because they failed to recognize its full potential as both a defensive as well as offensive device. When they did not bother to destroy radar stations along the eastern coast of Britain before the Battle of Britain began, the Germans themselves practically decided the outcome of the battle.

As for battle planes, the British believed in short-range fighters of great speed, maneuverability, and heavy fire power; the bomber should be able to carry heavy loads over long distances—speed was of secondary consideration. The restricted range of the fighters, however, precluded their serving as escort for the bombers. This problem was alleviated in the British doctrine of night bombing. The Americans were committed to and trained for daylight precision bombardment and found themselves in disagreement with the British in this area. Arnold, on one of his visits, observed that he thought "the British still have a lot to learn about bombing. But who am I to question the experiences of the RAF in two years of bombing in a real war?"

RAF pilots who had bombed Germany told Arnold that the evasive action required over target areas rendered the use of a precision bombsight such as the Norden or Sperry useless. In attempting to dodge the aggressive German fighters, or to fly in an unpredictable path to throw off antiaircraft guns, the plane would never remain in the sustained level flight necessary to the proper use of the bombsight. About the only point on which there was agreement was in the training of a bomber crew; both the British and the Americans saw the benefits of preparing the crew as a unit in order to produce an effective and, it was hoped, efficiently operating team, each member of which was familiar with the abilities as well as the personalities of every other member. Ideally this would make for a perfectly balanced combat unit if all things were equal—which they rarely were.

When war came to the United States, unprepared as it was, the continuity of the relationships with the British simply went on as before. The sole difference lay in the fact of American participation; the passive role was over.

Colonel Ira C. Eaker, who had served as a special observer with the RAF in 1941, returned as a Brigadier General the following year to set up the 8th Bomber Command. He was ordered by General Arnold "to make the necessary preparation to insure competent and aggressive command and direction of our bomber units in England."

Eaker arrived in England with an advance detachment of six other Air Force officers on February 20, 1942. Before one American bomber could take off from an English base to bomb Germany it would be necessary to suffer the complexities of establishing airdromes, arranging for accommodations for crews, ground echelons, supplies—all problems implied in the term "logistics." The planes had to be brought to England, a place found for them, they would have to be serviced and—no doubt—repaired. Thousands of men would be required to fly them, fight in them, maintain them. It was no simple problem confronting Eaker and his small detachment.

They had arrived at a low ebb in British fortunes. Rommel in Africa denied them the promised victory in Libya, the German ships *Scharnhorst*, *Gneisenau*, and *Prinz Eugen* escaped right under their noses from Brest through the English Channel and by the middle of the month, the "Gibraltar of the Pacific," Singapore, had fallen.

Although Eaker proceeded with his arrangements with the British, he would be somewhat handicapped. The necessity for supplying the Pacific momentarily set aside the plan for thrusting the major Allied effort against Germany as the predominant member of the Axis, first. The so called operation "Task Force BR," the build-up of American forces in the British Isles, was third on the priority list which would cause some delay in the shipment of planes and men to Britain. Eaker also found that he was confronted with the imposing staff of Major General James E. Chaney, in command of all American Army forces in Europe at the time.

Eaker found it difficult in facing these thirty-five men (only four of whom were air officers) to convince them that the air forces would play an important role in that theater of operations. He found some members "definitely antagonistic to air forces and Air effort." He found the staff afflicted with "a complete inflexibility of mind" on the subject of the air forces. "They are unalterably opposed to an Army Air Forces in Britain. They say that they are perfectly able to handle this in addition to their other duties and such an organization would make them merely rubber stamps. They consider that function their primary mission here and are not willing to surrender it."

In time this problem was solved with the decision to launch operation "Bolero" (the code name given to the transfer of American forces from the United States to England) in preparation for the proposed "Roundup"—the plan for the invasion of France in April 1943. General Dwight D. Eisenhower replaced General Chaney as Commanding General, European Theater of Operations. Eisenhower's flexibility, appreciation of air power and personal liking for General Spaatz who would command the air forces in Europe smoothed the way for Eaker.

The British from the beginning were gracious and helpful, placing their facilities, experience, and personnel at the disposal of Eaker and his staff. The RAF

"Pinetree," High Wycombe—the one time girl's school which served as the head-quarters for the 8th Air Force during World War II.

hosts, despite adversity and austerity, made the long weeks of exasperating paper work and preparation simpler and more pleasant than it easily might have been. One of the very first acts of hospitality was to set up Eaker and his staff in a former girl's boarding school at High Wycombe in Buckinghamshire about thirty miles from London and less than five miles from RAF Bomber Command headquarters. It was here that "Pinetree," headquarters for the 8th Bomber Command, would be established and housed for the duration.

The story is told (it is probably apocryphal) that on the first night that the newly arrived 8th Bomber Command settled at "Pinetree," the duty officer was plagued by the ringing of bells. On investigation it was learned that each bedroom, still dainty and feminine and little changed from the time when it had been occupied by schoolgirls, had little cards affixed to the walls (in anticipation of girlish distress) which stated: *"Ring twice for mistress."*

An important decision to make was the choice of the site for the American airdromes, which were supplied by the RAF. It was to lie, finally, in East Anglia to the north of London. Construction costs and development for American occupancy would be undertaken by the British. While modifications would be necessary to suit these airdromes to American use, General Eaker chose to build the American system around that of the British. This would simplify communications and operations in the cooperative effort. Besides the British had the experience.

The only serious remaining disagreement was theoretical; the British continued to discourage the American plans for using the B-17s and B-24s in daylight precision bombardment. General concepts were identical in regard to the application of strategic bombardment to destroy the German war machine—it was only in the tactical area that the differences arose.

British officers continued to raise objections to the B-17. They were certain that losses would be terrible and when they inspected a B-17E for the first time,

86

Brigadier General Ira C. Eaker with an English friend.

were definite in condemning the bomber for European operations because "(1) defensive fire power is too weak to afford reasonable protection, the tail-gun position is too cramped and the belly turret so awkward as to be useless" and "(2), the 4,000-pound bombs cannot be installed and bomb loads in any case are small unless the bomb-bay fuel tanks are removed at the expense of range."

The Americans, however, maintained that strategic targets could best be annihilated by large formations of bombers in level flight from high altitude. This would prove most effective in the destruction of the target and the least wasteful of civilian life. By day, navigation would be more true and the location of targets more precise. Despite the discouraging attitude of the British the 8th Bomber Command continued with its plans, helped by the RAF as usual.

In June, Eaker wrote to General Spaatz that the British "in whose theater we have been understudying and operating for the past five months, have co-operated one hundred per cent in every regard. They have lent us personnel when we had none, and have furnished us clerical and administrative staffs; they have furnished us liaison officers for Intelligence, Operations, and Supply; they have furnished us transportation; they have housed and fed our people, and they have answered promptly and willingly all our requisitions: in addition they have made available to us for study their most secret devices and documents. We are extremely proud of the relations we have been able to establish between our British Allies and ourselves . . ."

My Gal Sal down on an ice-cap in Greenland after a forced landing on the North Atlantic route to England. The crew was rescued by Bernt Balchen.

Control tower of a typical English base; this was the home of the 381st Bombardment Group (Station 167), Ridgewell, Essex County.

But up to this time there was still no tactical American unit based in England. As part of the build-up for "Roundup" the hope was that by April 1943 there would be twenty-one heavy bombardment groups in addition to medium, fighter, observation groups—a total of sixty-nine—based in England. At the same time American ground troops were to begin concentrating for the blow across the Channel. As it turned out, "Roundup" gave way to "Torch" (the North African invasion), which would have its effect upon the hopefully budding 8th Bomber Command.

The 97th Bombardment Group (H) was selected as the first B-17 unit to take part in "Bolero." This group was to be accompanied by the 1st Pursuit and the 31st Pursuit Groups on the flight to England via Presque Isle (Maine), Goose Bay (Labrador), Ireland, and finally England. There was a delay in the beginning of the movement when the 97th Group was hurriedly alerted and flown out to the West Coast pending the outcome of the Battle of Midway. Once that had been decided, the 97th was permitted to return to Maine for the movement across the North Atlantic. Ground echelons were to travel by ship through waters rendered hazardous by German U-boats.

The air movement was to begin for England on June 23, 1942, touching down at specially constructed bases en route for fuel and maintenance. It was accomplished with unusual lack of incident; the accident rate, which was expected to reach 10 per cent, hovered around 4 per cent. Flights were arranged so that the pursuit planes, which were not equipped with navigation instruments, would follow the bombers across. The low loss percentage was gratifying in the light of the fact that the crews had had so little experience flying over wide stretches of water. There were forced landings on ice-caps, skids into the mud on primitive bases, and some planes that simply disappeared, but considering the large numbers involved, the transatlantic flights were accomplished with remarkable skill by the green crews.

Obviously, however, it would be a while before General Eaker's 8th Bomber Command would be ready to test its long-held doctrines of strategic bombardment. The bitter English winter suddenly turned into spring and the hot summer had arrived and it seemed that the only visible accomplishment was a pile of paper, in triplicate. Then, on July 1, 1942, a B-17E, serial number 19085, gracefully roared into the field at Prestwick, England. There it joined the lone B-24 which had arrived some time before. By July 4 a notation was made in the 8th's table of equipment: *Arrival of aircraft: 1 B-17E. Total: 1.*

Summer had come and the swallow was late, but the infant 8th Bomber Command of the young 8th Air Force was beginning to stir.

9. This Scepter'd Isle

On August 15, 1942, twenty-four crews of the 97th Bombardment Group, under command of Colonel Frank A. Armstrong, Jr., were declared "available for combat." Since a group was comprised of four squadrons (of about twelve B-17s each), this meant that half the Group was ready for the first mission. As the build-up continued and more men and planes arrived from the United States, the crews were occupied with training missions and in time grew bored and restless.

Before the first mission actually took place, an incident occurred that demonstrated the durability of the B-17 and the tenacity as well as naïve valor of the young men who flew it. On a high altitude training mission (crews were not yet very familiar with the use of oxygen and formation flying) at 32,000 feet a pilot found himself inexplicably afflicted with trouble when his No. 4 engine "ran away." It was uncontrollable from the cockpit and as it raced faster and faster threatened to heat to the point of fusing the metals and causing a fire.

"I feathered the prop," the pilot reported, "and when it came into full-feather position we saw that one of the blades had broken off. I rang the alarm bell as a safety precaution and put the plane into a glide. At 30,000 feet the No. 3 engine blew up and caught fire. I rang the alarm bell again and ordered the men to bail out."

With Numbers 3 and 4 engines out, there was no power on the right side, starboard, of the plane. When the plane was in serious trouble it was the tradition that the pilot, like the captain of a ship, leave last. He would stay at the controls to keep the plane in level flight; centrifugal forces in a gyrating aircraft pinned aircrews inside the fuselage so that they were unable to move and consequently went down to their death even if unwounded. Once the other crew members escaped, the pilot of the two-engined B-17 surveyed the situation.

"I started the plane down in a circle to the left, keeping the two good engines down. By the time I reached 14,000 feet, fire had spread all the way back to the ailerons, over to No. 4 engine and all along the side of the fuselage. At 12,000 feet the No. 2 engine sputtered, backfired, and then quit.

"This made me sort of mad.

"Up till then I'd been too scared to do anything. I looked over at the No. 3 engine. It was hanging over the side of the wing, held by a few cables. The oil tank was visible and on fire.

"I started to get out of my seat to bail out, but the wings were still on and I thought I'd try to get it down.

"Control was nearly impossible, since the bottom of the right wing had been blown off, and a piece of cowling had knocked off the vertical fin. I broke through the cloud layer at 9000 feet and looked for a field. It was a heavily wooded area, but I spotted a pasture about 800 feet long. I circled the end of it, losing altitude, and as the tires had been destroyed by fire, I came in with a wheel-up landing.

"The entire right side of the ship was in flames by this time. I started to leave the ship. The place where I had landed was the rifle range of a British Rifle Brigade. About five hundred of them were there, and as I came out they came running up, about a dozen of them with fire extinguishers. Though the gas tanks were leaking we managed to get the fire out." It was only the prelude to the drama to come.

When the 97th Group was alerted for a mission eighteen crews of the two dozen available were to ready themselves for the first 8th Air Force mission from England. Targets had been chosen and the operational wheels set into motion.

General Eaker had begun to define the mission of the Bomber Command in his notes made at the time as follows, "First the factories, sheds, docks, and ports in which the enemy builds his submarines and from which he launches his submarine efforts. Next, his aircraft factories and other key munitions-manufacturing establishments. Third, his lines of communication. A subsidiary purpose of our early bombing operations will be to determine our capacity to destroy pinpoint targets by daylight precision bombing and our ability to beat off fighter opposition and to evade antiaircraft opposition."

The practice missions over England quickly revealed many of the weaknesses in the training of the bomber crews, particularly in formation flying and gunnery (one gunner, Sergeant Allie Moszyk of the 414th Squadron never fired a gun until his first mission). Part of this may be attributed to the rush with which tactical units were dispatched to the combat zones because of civilian criticism.

Practice missions also afforded the crews a chance to work out rendezvous with RAF's fighters which would function as protection against the *Luftwaffe* until enough American fighters had arrived to attend to what would be their primary mission.

The 97th Group was initially alerted on August 9, but—and this too would prove characteristic—poor weather conditions over the target scrubbed the mission. By August 16 the weather cleared and the mission was called again. By this time the crews were quite jumpy.

The good weather held on August 17 and 8th Bomber Command was definitely slated for Mission No. 1. The target was to be the Sotteville railroad marshaling yards near Rouen, France. It was an important traffic center for the shipment of supplies and personnel for the Germans; the yards contained, according to reconnaissance photos, great numbers of freight cars besides being the site of a repair depot for locomotives and rolling stock. It was just across the English Channel, south of East Anglia, and well within range of the Spitfires which would escort the B-17s. Of the eighteen Fortresses participating in the raid, six were to be dispatched as a diversionary force along the French coast to bring out the *Luftwaffe* and to lure the German fighters away from the vicinity of Rouen.

At 1526 hours (3:26 P.M.) the first B-17 took off from Polebrook leading the first flight of six; in it was the 97th's commander, Colonel Frank A. Armstrong, Jr. The second flight followed on schedule led by the "Yankee Doodle" in which General Eaker flew as an observer. By 1539 hours all twelve of the B-17s scheduled for the Rouen raid were airborne. So far no hitch.

Four squadrons of RAF Spitfires joined them to furnish fighter cover to the target; five squadrons were scheduled to rendezvous later to provide withdrawal support.

The two flights of Fortresses approached Rouen at 23,000 feet; visibility was excellent. There was a little antiaircraft fire, but the green crews performed very well as they loosed their bombs at the target. Though it was a rather large target, the bomb patterns were good considering that the crews were experiencing their first combat mission. About half the bombs fell directly into the target area. Siding tracks were damaged, rail cars were destroyed, damaged or knocked off the tracks and a workshop received a direct hit.

The attacking force was too small, actually, to do more than token damage, but the showing was good and the Germans would have a rail problem in the Rouen area for a while (it never proved to be as long as the Allies hoped, however).

Besides the flak (German: *Flieger Abwehr Kanonen*), a few Messerschmitts came in for a few half-hearted attacks at the formation. They were, apparently, respectful of the new Flying Fortresses and the darting little Spitfires. In the encounter, two Spitfires were shot down and claims were made for two Messerschmitts. The only casualties among the bomber crews were a bombardier and a navigator of the diversionary force who were in the nose of a Fortress which flew through a flock of pigeons.

The men at Polebrook anxiously awaited the outcome of Mission No. 1. Shortly before 7:00 P.M. tiny specks were discerned in the distance and when they materialized into B-17s, all twelve had returned intact. The first plane settled down precisely at 1900 hours and soon the combat crews were surrounded by an elated mob of welcomers, from privates up to generals. Mission No. 1, for all its embryonic scale, was a success.

By a curious coincidence, just the day before the London *Times* had published an article by American bomber critic Peter Masefield in which he stated, reflecting obviously the official British opinion, "American heavy bombers—the latest Fortresses and Liberators—are fine flying machines, but not suited for bombing in Europe. Their bomb loads are small, their armour and armament are not up to the standard now found necessary and their speeds are low."

By the time General Arnold wired General Spaatz for his views on the Masefield comments, the Rouen raid had obviated any need for a defensive reply.

The Supermarine Spitfire Mark VB. Wingspan was 36 feet, 10 inches, length of fuselage 32 feet, 8 inches. Powered by a Rolls-Royce engine, its top speed was 400 mph, range 480 miles, and ceiling 40,000 feet. Small projection over cockpit bubble is a rear-view mirror.

Spaatz did inform the office of the Adjutant General in the War Department that the bombing of Rouen had exceeded by far all previous high-altitude attacks in the European theater and, he added, he would not exchange the B-17 for any British bomber then in production.

General Eaker, on his part and based upon firsthand observations, had some practical comments to make for the future. These were to have a familiar ring as time went on: tighter formations for protection from fighters, improved navigation (for it would be unlikely that all targets would be as easy to find as the Sotteville marshaling yards), split second timing in meeting the fighter escort, the training of bombardiers would have to be improved and there was the old one—better gunnery training.

Air Marshal Sir Arthur T. Harris, General Eaker's British counterpart, wired him the day after Mission No. 1: CONGRATULATIONS FROM ALL RANKS OF BOMBER COMMAND ON THE HIGHLY SUCCESSFUL COMPLETION OF THE FIRST ALL AMERICAN RAID BY THE BIG FELLOWS ON GERMAN OCCUPIED TERRITORY IN EUROPE. YANKEE DOODLE CERTAINLY WENT TO TOWN AND CAN STICK ANOTHER WELL-DESERVED FEATHER IN HIS CAP.

Eaker was pleased with all the elation about him, but he viewed it with typical caution. "The raid went according to plan," he said, "and we are well satisfied with the day's work." But he was to add, "One swallow doesn't make a summer."

When he was called upon by his British guests at a dinner at High Wycombe to make a speech, he was equally characteristic when he simply said, "We won't do much talking until we've done more fighting. When we leave, I hope you'll be glad we came. Thank you."

As if to underscore the American theoretical point of view based upon the B-17, the Fortresses continued for several days to be dispatched with amazing immunity from the *Luftwaffe* and even flak. For a while, that is.

On August 19 (Mission No. 2), twenty-four B-17s took off (twenty-two actually bombed) the German airdrome at Abbeville to keep the German Air Force pinned down and otherwise occupied while the ground troops struck at Dieppe. Under pressure from Stalin for a second front which would relieve the Russians, a combined force of British and Canadian troops attempted to break through German coastal defenses at Dieppe; it was a tragic operation for half the force was killed or wounded, a terrible price.

Because Stalin's rather primitive military mentality could not fathom the point of heavy bombardment of targets within Germany, he continued to insist upon a land invasion of France. Wars were won on the ground, not in the air. The wily Russian even suggested that the British were afraid to fight the Germans. The Dieppe raid disproved this (as if proof were required) and it also proved that the time was not yet for "Roundup." Winston Churchill himself flew to Moscow to inform Marshal Stalin of the premature attempt at invasion.

All twenty-two of the B-17s which had bombed Abbeville returned safely to

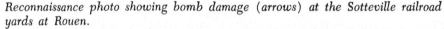

Reconnaissance photo showing bomb damage (arrows) at the Sotteville railroad yards at Rouen.

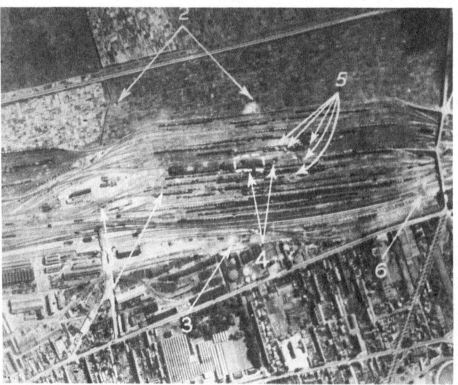

The Messerschmitt Bf 109, more popularly referred to as the Me-109, Germany's first effective combat fighter plane. Wing span was 32 feet, 6½ inches; fuselage length: 29 feet, 4 inches. Top speed was 400 mph, range 570 miles and ceiling 37,000 feet.

England again with a mission accomplished to their credit—and without loss.

It was not until Mission No. 4 that they were to experience a real taste of fighter opposition. A small formation of twelve B-17s were dispatched toward the Dutch coast to bomb the docks near Rotterdam. Things were not going well; three Fortresses had been forced to turn back with mechanical troubles and the Fortresses were sixteen minutes late for rendezvous with their Spitfire escort. Consequently, the fighters were low on fuel and could not accompany the bombers all the way to Rotterdam. Just as the nine unescorted B-17s approached the Dutch coast a recall, abandoning the mission, came in from 8th Bomber Command.

The formation had begun to wheel about for the return flight when they were jumped by over twenty Focke-Wulf 190s and Messerschmitt 109s. The running battle lasted for twenty minutes and, while the Fortresses were able to present a formidable mass of fire to bear (two enemy fighters were shot down, five probables were claimed and six were damaged), without the Spitfires to help, it was a tough battle. Five FW-190s pounced upon a single Fortress which lagged behind the main force and one of them succeeded in firing a 20-mm cannon shell into the cockpit. Both the pilot, Lieutenant Starks, and the co-pilot, Lieutenant Walter, were wounded, the latter so seriously that he died later—the first combat casualty from a B-17 crew of the 8th Air Force.

The pilot's hands were so badly burned that he was unable to control the aircraft so that the bombardier (who had washed out of cadet school), Lieutenant Sconiers, came into the cockpit and flew the plane on two engines back to England and crash-landed it on the first RAF base they could find. The plane was damaged, Lieutenant Walter was dead, but the Fortresses had proved they could hold out against a large formation of German fighters.

On September 5, the 97th returned to Rouen accompanied by B-17s from the newly operational 301st Bombardment Group. Though the bombing was fairly good, some spillage resulted, unfortunately, in the deaths of 140 civilians and the wounding of scores of others. On the following day the B-17s again appeared over occupied France, this time to attack the Avions Potez aircraft factory at Meaulte. With the 301st Group employed as a diversionary force to attack a German airdrome, the 97th Group and the freshly operational 92nd Group set out to bomb Meaulte. Of the forty-one bombers dispatched, thirty-three succeeded in reaching the target despite constant fighter opposition. Both groups lost one plane each—the first combat losses for the 8th in the war.

Over Flasselles, as one bomber went down, four parachutes were seen to open. The other B-17 was observed headed for the British coast with five fighters on its tail. It was in trouble and heading for the water. British Air-Sea Rescue launches raced out to the approximate area where the plane would land, but no trace of the B-17, piloted by Leigh E. Stewart of the 92nd's 327th Squadron, was ever found.

Clearly fighter opposition was getting stronger and more daring. The German planes were decorated with yellow noses and undersides, they were members of Göring's personal fighter squadrons made up of the finest fighter pilots of the *Luftwaffe*. Based at Abbeville, they were known as the "Abbeville Kids." They were tough, courageous and aggressive, and greatly respected by the British and, now, the American airmen.

During this period claims for German aircraft destroyed were quite high—something the more experienced British viewed with a doubting eye. Optimism and morale ran high and no one was inclined to discourage either.

But the weather would not be as considerate. Only two additional missions were flown in September thanks to poor weather conditions and on October 2, there was a return to Meaulte and a reminder of what persistent fighter opposition could mean,·although there were no losses. Crews continued to be optimistic and even a little cocky. They had no idea that the battle of Lille was only a week away.

Lille, the great industrial center in northern France, was the home of the Compagnie de Fives-Lille, a steel works, and the locomotive and freight car factory, Ateliers d'Hellemes—a most attractive complex of targets within fighter escort range. The impressiveness of the Lille strike was not its target, but the fact that it was the first (and as it eventuated, the last for about six months) truly strategic mission worthy of the name.

For this first full-scale attack 108 heavy bombers were dispatched to Lille, the primary target. Of these, twenty-four were B-24 Liberators, flown by the 93rd Bombardment Group on its first mission. Only sixty-nine planes succeeded in bombing Lille, however, for there were a large number of "aborts," no less than thirty-three planes which returned to their bases because of mechanical failures. Other planes attacked alternative targets and some the last-resort target—the Saint-Omer airdrome. It was not, in fact, an impressive demonstration of strategic bombardment despite the size of the attacking force. But it was not a failure,

The Focke-Wulf 190, one of the finest fighters of World War II. In its early operations the FW 190 proved itself more than a match for the Spitfire (later developments of the British fighter, however, changed that). The span was 34 feet, 5½ inches, fuselage length 29 feet. Top speed was around 400 mph, range 525 miles, and ceiling 37,500 feet.

taking into consideration the greenness of some of the crews as well as one other important factor.

That day the *Luftwaffe* was at its most aggressive up to that time and the Lille mission was the first great aerial battle in which the 8th Air Force engaged. Three B-17s and one B-24 were shot down; of the former, one managed to get away from the coast of France and successfully ditched in the English Channel, the first plane whose crew was rescued by the RAF-Royal Navy's active Air-Sea Rescue Service.

As described in the history of the 92nd Group, "Fighter attacks were exceptionally severe . . ." which accounted for the surprising number of claims. The approach, it was noted, was from "six o'clock" (from the tail) and slightly below. In the heated encounters several gunners were certain they had accounted for a great number of German planes. According to the initial reports it would have amounted to no less than forty-eight destroyed (not taking into account the "probables" and "damaged"), but postwar research brought the actual number down to two.

With sixty-nine aircraft, armed with as many as a dozen guns each, and with 828 nervous, frightened, or excited gunners shooting at everything that flew in the sky, it was inevitable that claims for that day would be exaggerated. This was especially true when several gunners from different planes shot at the same FW-190 or Me-109; if a plane went down as many as a dozen gunners might claim the same plane. Also, air combat was an instantaneous thing; planes closed at each other at what was then tremendous speeds—if the B-17 was making 250 mph and the FW-190 400 mph, the planes approached one another at more than 600 mph. It was impossible to get off more than a quick burst at the enemy plane. In this instance, most attacks were made from the rear; even so the speeds were tremendous and the actual encounters brief.

In addition there were thirty-six Lockheed P-38s flying escort for the B-17s for the first time in company with 120 Spitfires. An estimate of the German fighters was around sixty. Three hundred aircraft, therefore, were engaged in the melee in the vicinity of Lille. That the reports of it should be confused, exaggerated, and inaccurate is not surprising.

Although four heavy bombers were lost, the 8th Bomber Command once again proved that it could contend with the German fighters and hold their own. And, while the accuracy of the Lille bombing was not exemplary (some bombs fell miles from the aiming point) and there were too many unexploded duds, severe damage was reported in the target area. It did not erase the general successes of the previous missions. The 8th Bomber Command had also impressed the skeptical British, who, as Eaker wrote to Arnold, "acknowledge willingly and cheerfully the great accuracy of our bombing, the surprising hardihood of our bombardment aircraft and the skill and tenacity of our crews."

As for the "surprising hardihood of our bombardment aircraft," the Boeing Company during this period received an unsolicited endorsement of their product from pilot Lieutenant Clark M. Garber, Jr., who wrote enthusiastically after an experience he had with a B-17. The incident not only points up the strength built into the B-17 but also an important though little appreciated hazard of formation flying.

"We had left our base that day with a maximum load of bombs, gasoline, and ammunition, bound for the continent," Lieutenant Garber wrote. "A big cloud loomed ahead of us and we flew into it, and all the rest of the world vanished. Our squadron was flying instrument formation from then on . . .

"After about fifteen minutes of this, a shadow suddenly loomed big ahead of us. It was another B-17, the leader of our formation, and he was turning into us from ahead and to the side. It was just one of those things that is apt to happen when the soup is thick as it was that day.

"At the speed we were traveling, we were due for a smashup. I yanked the nose of our ship up and to the right, trying to climb and turn at the same time. We were loaded too heavily for that, and we went into a stall. We hung there for an instant, our nose pointing into the sky with the ship's tremendous load pulling at it. Then the Fortress went over on one wing—and fell onto its back. From there it screamed into a vertical dive.

"What we had done was a maneuver not unusual for small planes, but one that four-engine bombers were never designed to stand. Something else a heavy bomber was never built to do is vertical dive. And now we were doing that.

"It was a pretty sickening sensation, heading down there. All this time I didn't know where we were or where the ground was, because we were in the clouds. Our indicated air speed was better than 350 miles per hour, which means

The Lockheed P-38 Lightning, the first American-built fighter plane to escort the B-17s on a mission. They were to play an important role in the North African Theater to which they were transferred after a few missions out of England. The P-38s wingspan was 52 feet; fuselage: 37 feet, 10 inches. Powered by two Allison liquid-cooled engines its top speed was around 400 mph; range: 1500 miles and ceiling 40,000 feet.

at that altitude we were actually traveling somewhere between 400 and 450 mph. I could hear those heavy bombs rattling around in the bomb compartment like ten pins.

"According to the slide rules, there was no chance of our pulling out of the dive. The strain would tear the wings off a loaded ship the size of ours. But there wasn't any choice—we were goners if we didn't try it. So I held my breath and started to pull out.

"There were tearing noises. The bombs had ripped loose and they were crashing out through the bottom of the ship. Then—the bomber came up level—and the wings were still with us.

99

"During the ship's tumbling, both the bombardier and navigator had their heads driven through the glass windows. Two of the gunners were thrown half out of the ship, where somehow they managed to hang on by their fingers. Other crew members pulled the gunners back inside.

"We brought the ship down to a safe landing, then, and we were a pretty happy bunch of boys . . . Our ship is back in shape and in service again now, just as good as ever. Meanwhile, we've changed her name from *Hellzapoppin* to the very appropriate one of *Borrowed Time* . . . She's a great ship . . ."

Assured by such endorsements, Eaker was able to turn his attention to the problem that his superiors regarded as the primary one. It was almost like a sequel to the Great War.

Although the 8th Bomber Command was the first American fighting force to bring the war to the Germans, it was not the only one to suffer casualties. The so-called wolfpacks of submarines took their toll along the Atlantic life-line over which the needed supplies were transported to England and to Russia. In time also, the U-boats appeared in American coastal waters to sink transports within sight of American shores.

For a while, the convoy system introduced during the First World War, afforded the best means of protection. But by early 1942 the Germans had almost 250 submarines at their disposal, about a hundred of which were active, so that the pack system was devised to harass convoys. When a submarine commander sighted a convoy he radioed all the other submarines in the vicinity to close in for attack. As the number increased, the Germans were able to string the packs along the entire Atlantic shipping route. Thus the convoy would be under attack practically the entire way across the Atlantic which tired the crews and lowered efficiency and rendered the ships more vulnerable.

All through 1942 the sinkings rose, went up sharply in October and reached a peak in November of 117 ships. Not only was the loss of life terrible, but also valuable supplies and equipment (as well as the ships) were sent to the bottom. If this were permitted to go on—and it was proving a difficult problem for the naval forces and the coastal sub-chasing aircraft—it would have a serious deleterious effect upon the future of "Torch," the invasion of North Africa scheduled for November.

After seizing France the Germans set up U-boat bases along the Bay of Biscay. These shelters to which the submarines could come for servicing, repair, and other work were regarded as impervious to heavy bombardment by the Germans. Although constructed inland, they could be entered directly from the Bay of Biscay through concrete entrances which led underground. The side walls were eight feet thick and the roofs were eleven foot thick reinforced concrete. Once inside this pen, the submarine could be readied for its next foray, free of disruption.

Because of the limited number of bombers available to the 8th Bomber Command (some of its units were already tied-up in the preparations for the North African invasion), it was decided that instead of attempting to strike at the submarine construction yards inside Germany, the turn-around ports in the Bay of Biscay would be the targets in the 8th's first official phase of its wartime program —the war on the sub-pens. That it was to prove as costly as it was inconclusive (the Germans were correct in their boast about the bombproof pens) soon became evident.

Two B-17s collide over England while forming up for a mission. The tail section of one may be seen just below the smoke cloud in the center; the other tail section is slightly above and to the right. Fog was an ever present danger to B-17 crews.

The sub-pen phase opened on October 21, 1942, with an attack by ninety bombers on the base at Keroman, a small fishing port about a mile and a half from Lorient. The Lorient mission was only the third that the 8th had been able to carry out during October, a month of miserable weather conditions which had caused the canceling of eleven missions.

When the formations—four groups had been sent out—arrived over Lorient it was found that at the specified bombing altitude of 22,000 feet heavy overcast made sighting on the target impossible. Three of the groups thereupon abandoned the mission and turned for home. But the veteran 97th Group elected to complete the mission, if possible. Its tiny force of fifteen B-17s moved down to 17,500 feet, under the overcast, and dropped thirty one-ton bombs on the target area.

Although flak was negligible, fighter opposition was ferocious and in the battle near the target area, the 97th lost three B-17s to the FW-190s, the yellow-nosed

Abbeville Kids of Göring's special squadron. The attack impressed both the Germans and Frenchmen with the accuracy of the bombardment, but little major damage was actually done. Two subs, not in pens, were damaged and a workshop or two was demolished. But the heavy bombs did not penetrate through the roofs of any of the shelters—when they were hit at all.

Of the five submarine sites in the Bay of Biscay—Brest, Lorient, La Pallice, Bordeaux, and Saint-Nazaire—the latter was nicknamed "Flak City" by the bomber crews. When it was initially attacked on November 9 it was from a low level in the hope that greater accuracy might bring greater results. The B-17s approached at altitudes ranging from 7500 feet to 10,000; the B-24s remained up around 20,000. The result was that the B-17s became targets for intense and accurate antiaircraft fire. Three B-17s went down and over twenty were damaged of the thirty-one attacking. It was the last attempt to attack any sub-shelter from so low an altitude, but Saint-Nazaire's reputation as "Flak City" did not diminish.

The cumulative effect of repeated attacks was found more effective than low-level attacks and such major bases as those at Lorient and Saint-Nazaire were visited by the heavies with as much regularity as weather and logistics permitted. If the sub sites were neglected for even a short while, however, activity quickly picked up and they were back in operation as if they had never been bombed.

One of the heaviest strikes upon Saint-Nazaire was made on January 3, 1943 —it was the first since November 23. A new bombing technique was introduced on this mission which was to have an important effect upon future operations. Instead of each plane dropping bombs individually, all bombardiers released when they saw the bombs leave the bomb bay of the lead plane. This technique resulted in greater accuracy (for the most skilled bombardier and pilot were in the lead aircraft) and a massive concentration of strikes in the target area.

However, on this particular mission, the bomb run was made into a high gale which practically cut the flying speed of the B-17 in half. As they faced into the wind, the planes seemed to hover in place over the target. They were almost stationary targets for the antiaircraft gunners below. Also, instead of attempting to follow the formations as was the usual practice, the flak gunners introduced their own innovation. They predicted the area through which the B-17s would have to pass on the bomb run and filled that area with flak bursts. Three Fortresses were shot down over Saint-Nazaire on that mission and dozens returned in various stages of damage.

Fighters, too, were murderously fearless in their attacks. Ever since the November 23 mission to Saint-Nazaire it was noted that the German fighters had developed a new attack approach. They no longer attacked from the stern, but from the "twelve o'clock high" spot directly head-on. This innovation has been credited to Oberleutnant Egon Mayer, who had noted that the fire power from both B-17s and B-24s was weak in the nose area. There were blind spots that neither the nose guns nor even the top-turret gunner could cover from the front.

Diving head-on into a formation of B-17s was not a tactic for an inexperienced pilot. The formations could bring tremendous fire power to bear despite the blind spots, but a head-on attack was a fleeting thing because of the tremendous closing speed of the two aircraft. An error of judgment could mean a wasted pass by the fighter or a mid-air collision.

Among the seven B-17s that did not return from "Flak City" on January 3, one carried Arizona Harris into the Bay of Biscay. He was not the only American airman to die that day, but he was the only one to choose, with a show of stubborn valor, the time and place.

Harris was top-turret gunner and crew chief of the B-17 piloted by Charles Cramner. Another pilot, William Casey and his crew aboard the *Banshee,* witnessed the exploit of Arizona Harris.

"His name was really Arizona," Casey later told newspapermen, "and he was one of the best top-turret gunners you ever did see. He usually fired in short, quick bursts, to keep his guns from overheating and he didn't miss—not often. He already had two FW-190s to his credit, and he had an Air Medal, too, that he was going to show to his father and his two brothers and his married sister when he got home [Tempe, Arizona]."

Over Saint-Nazaire a direct hit by flak blew off the underside of the B-17's nose "so that the bombardier and navigator simply disappeared and nobody knew what became of them," and two engines went dead, with No. 3 smoking badly. Because of this Cramner was forced to leave the comparative safety of the rest of the formation, though Casey, disobeying standing orders, tried to remain close-by to give the crippled Fortress some support. The formation had dropped down to about ten feet above the water to discourage fighter attacks from below; with his two bad engines, Cramner needed all the altitude he could hang onto to get his B-17 home. He managed to stay up at 1500 feet.

Casey watched with horror when "all of a sudden, about forty miles northwest of Brest, six Focke-Wulf 190s and a Messerschmitt 109 came hurtling out of nowhere. They spotted the limping Fortress, and one after another they made a pass at it from behind."

After the first sweep by the fighters, two parachutes were seen to billow out behind the B-17; these were probably waist gunners. The chutes barely opened before they hit and the men sank into the icy Bay. Another two flared out and remained in the air long enough for some of the fighters to circle them a few times. "Whether or not they machine-gunned the fliers is something that can't be proved, so why think about it?" Casey said.

"But when the Fortress settled into the sea—and Charlie Cramner, who stayed with his ship as a captain should, set her down as gracefully and gently as if he had four engines and a six thousand foot runway under him—then the Germans did strafe her, and you could see the steel-gray sea boiling under the rain of bullets.

"But there was something else you could see, and that was the guns in the upper turret still blazing even as she settled. She settled fast; she lasted only about half a minute. But the top turret was still spitting as the waves closed over it . . ."

By this time there was no way for Harris to escape from the ditched B-17. He had not even gone into the radio compartment, according to regular ditching procedure which was done to protect the surviving crew members from too much bouncing around and injury from loose parts. Instead Arizona Harris had chosen to stay at his post all through the battle—no one actually will ever know why—

to continue fighting the German fighters even at the cost of his life. Even as the freezing waters closed over the turret so that only the gun muzzles pointed out at the sky, Harris continued to fire the guns.

Besides the aggressive German fighters, as exemplified in the story of Arizona Harris, the sub-pen phase of the 8th Bomber Command encountered two early obstacles. There was the weather, which had deteriorated through the late autumn on into the winter. Not only did it contribute to the cancellation of mission after mission, with resultant effects upon the morale of crews, but those missions that were actually carried out were not very successful because of poor visibility and nerve-wracking flying conditions; in addition there was a high percentage of colds which made high-altitude flights with oxygen masks miserable.

Even more of an impact was made on the 8th when its men and machines were diverted into the North African invasion, "Torch." Its two most experienced heavy bomber groups, the 97th and 301st, as well as two P-38 fighter Groups and two Spitfire Groups, were committed to "Torch," as the nucleus of the newly formed 12th Air Force.

With the loss of men and planes, without replacements or service parts, all of which were poured into the top priority "Torch" operation, the 8th Air Force was seriously reduced in fighting strength. Those men and machines remaining in England were overworked, consequently, for whatever missions were scheduled and, weather permitting, were carried out fell with unrelenting regularity to the same men and planes. Even spare parts were hard to come by and ground crews learned to improvise or scrounge parts from the "hangar queens," B-17s beyond repair from battle damage. The once proud 8th Air Force was reduced to a kind of poverty. It was General Arnold's belief that the diversion to "Torch" had set the bomber offensive back four months. And General Spaatz, who could see the situation firsthand, actually considered suspending operations of the 8th

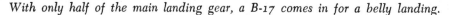

With only half of the main landing gear, a B-17 comes in for a belly landing.

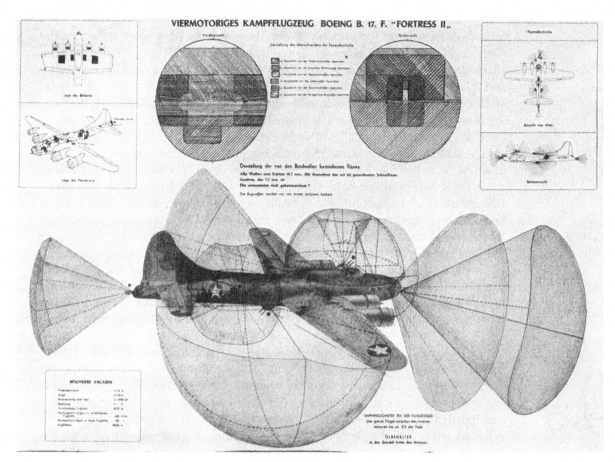

A German poster designed to instruct Luftwaffe pilots how to attack the B-17F, a Viermotoriges Kampfflugzeug ("four engine fighter airplane"). The shaded conic and hesmispheric areas indicate cones of fire from the gun positions. Smaller diagrams in the upper left corner indicate (top) gas and oil tanks and (bottom) position of armor. Cross-hatched circles show overlap of cones of fire from front and rear of plane. Nazi pilots were instructed that the most vulnerable area was the entire wing between the inboard engines (notation in bottom right of poster).

Air Force until it could be built up to strength. Instead, they continued to operate when they could with what they had.

General Dwight D. Eisenhower was placed in over-all command of the North African invasion and since D-Day was to occur early in November he chose to direct the operation from Gibraltar rather than England. Six B-17s of the 97th Group's 340th Squadron were selected to transport General Eisenhower and his staff to Gibraltar on November 5. The flight leader, also the commander of the squadron, was Major Paul W. Tibbets, Jr., (who would later command the B-29 *Enola Gay* that dropped the atom bomb on Hiroshima) in whose B-17 Eisenhower would fly. His deputy, Major General Mark W. Clark, was to fly in the next Fortress; other top officials were more or less evenly distributed among the six B-17s so that no single plane carried too many of equal importance.

The Fortresses, with their mystified crews, lined up on the Hurn Airdrome, south of London, awaiting the arrival of their distinguished passengers. The planes were stripped down and carried no bombs and the crews were briefed for a dash from Hurn to Gibraltar around Portugal. As the planes waited in the misty, cold morning Eisenhower arrived and boarded Tibbets' *Red Gremlin;* Clark climbed into *Boomerang* and into the Fortress of John C. Summers, pilot, and Thomas F. Lohr, co-pilot, came Major General James H. Doolittle, Medal of Honor hero of the Tokyo raid and commander of the 12th Air Force. Following him were Brigadier General Lyman L. Lemnitzer, Colonel Thomas J. Davis (both on Eisenhower's staff), and eight British generals.

"The large number of passengers with baggage was the reason we had to strip down as far as possible for the long trip," Lohr recalls. "The only guns on the ship were the fixed emplacements, the top turret, the ball turret, and tail guns." Information had leaked out that Eisenhower's absence from his usual London headquarters was because he had been called to Washington for a conference. It was hoped this ruse might throw off any attempt by the Germans to intercept the heavily loaded, undergunned B-17s.

About 8:15 in the morning the "Cyclones" roared to life as the six planes prepared to take off. They pulled out along the taxi strip until Tibbets swung his Fortress across the strip, parallel to the path of the oncoming planes which in turn swung to the side, preparatory to an engine check before actually taking off.

But Summers and Lohr found themselves in trouble; for some reason their hydraulic system was not functioning and they continued on toward the other B-17s. Frantically Summers and Lohr pumped the practically useless brakes (as visions of burning Fortresses appeared before their eyes if they collided), manipulated the tail wheel and the engines to maneuver the great plane from its collision path. All this was accomplished, although their wingtip practically grazed the plane in front of them and their tail surfaces seemed about to sweep into the other plane also. By gunning all four engines, Summers and Lohr were able to pull their plane away from the other one. Exhausted, they cut the engines. The five B-17s continued with the flight while Doolittle's party had to wait until the following day when the hydraulic system was put back into shape. They would make the flight to Gibraltar alone.

By dawn—November 6, 1942—they were on their way. They were making the turn toward Gibraltar off Cape Finisterre, Spain, when they sighted four black specks in the distance above them. Up till then the flight had been uneventful and amiable.

"Early in the trip," Lohr relates, "General Doolittle [came] forward to talk to us. He told us he had never flown a B-17. I remember him as being very friendly. You have to remember it was our responsibility to see that there was nothing wrong with the hydraulic system and we weren't too sure about the repercussions."

A flight of Junkers Ju-88, four in all, had taken off that morning from a field in France on a reconnaissance flight over the Atlantic. There seemed to be quite a lot of activity which they intended to investigate. They were ready to return to their base, and low on fuel, when they spotted a lone plane in the distance. Their leader, a Lieutenant Molder, decided to investigate. They were searching for shipping and transports, but an unexplained aircraft was interesting.

The men in the B-17 had also seen the four planes, some hoping that it was their fighter escort. With practically no guns they would be no match for enemy

Thomas F. Lohr, co-pilot of the B-17 which took General Doolittle to Gibraltar, and later a prisoner of war in Germany after parachuting into the Sahara.

fighters. And, considering the heavy brass aboard, it seemed a logical conclusion. But because as little notice as possible was hoped to be stirred up by the initiation of "Torch," no arrangement was made for fighter escort. Besides, they were still well out of fighter escort range. The four specks had to be German planes.

The Ju-88s dived on the B-17, breaking up into elements of two which for a time merely flew alongside the bomber. Without waist guns the men in the B-17 were unable to fire at the German fighters. This may have puzzled the pilots for they made no attempt to attack. All other guns were manned as the adversaries studied each other. Finally the twin-engine German fighters pulled ahead of the B-17, turned and raced in to attack.

Summers threw the plane into an evasive maneuver by cutting the throttles to slow up and by applying a fast rudder. This confused the attackers and though they fired they missed the B-17 completely. With engines at full throttle now, Summers tried to outrun the Ju-88s. The fighters circled around and prepared for another pass.

As they closed a 20-mm cannon shell exploded inside the cockpit of the B-17, shattering the windshield and the instrument panel, filling the cockpit with smoke and wounding co-pilot Lohr. Number 3 engine had also been hit and the propeller began windmilling. Summers had his hands full keeping the plane in flight just above the surface of the water. He was not able to feather No. 3 engine because of this and the wild propeller threatened to pull out the engine.

Fortunately the low fuel supply of the Ju-88s saved the B-17 from further attacks. Lohr, with a bad arm wound, remained in his seat until the crisis was past. Once the engine was feathered and the four German planes left them, Lohr felt he could leave the cockpit.

". . . I went down to the navigator's compartment to get my arm bandaged. I brought the medical kit down with me and asked one of the brigadiers to fix it up for me. I don't recall his name but I remember jawing him out because he wouldn't apply the sulpha package in the kit. Later when I was in the hospital at Gibraltar he came to visit me. There was a big hullaballoo, everyone popping to, picking up and being military. It was the general coming to see me. Evidently he wanted to apologize for not applying the sulpha powder. He said he read on the package that you weren't supposed to use it except on the advice of a physician.

"I then went back to the co-pilot's seat and called Doolittle (to serve as Summers' co-pilot). Actually, of course, any pilot can fly and land a B-17 without a co-pilot, so it wasn't as serious as it seemed. It would have been important, of course, if there had been another attack and the pilot had been hurt. I remember passing Doolittle in the bomb bay and him giving me a fatherly pat on the shoulder.

"The greatest service Lemnitzer performed was to get out the flask when I came back with the shot-up arm. (To carry any kind of liquor on a military plane is strictly *verboten!*) I remember arriving in Gibraltar a few hours later with a pleasant glow."

Two days later "Torch" opened when the Allies struck at Algiers and Oran in the Mediterranean and Casablanca on the Atlantic. Montgomery's British 8th Army was pushing toward the "Torch" landing areas from the east at El Alamein, where he had broken through Rommel's line. The objective was a meeting of the converging Allied forces in Tunisia.

The heavy bombers did not take part in the "Torch" assault but they would see action once suitable air bases were secured in Africa. "The American carrier-borne Navy aviation at Casablanca, and the British Fleet Arm at Oran," Doolittle reported to Arnold, "did the larger part of the air fighting. By the time the airports were secured, they had destroyed, either in the air or on the ground, the majority of the French aviation." It had been hoped that the French would permit the Allies to land without opposition, but that had not proved to be the case. Thus the British had to engage with their former allies and the Americans fought against a people with whom they were not at war.

As soon as possible an airdrome for the heavies was constructed at Biskra, an oasis and winter resort near Oran. In the African campaign the function of the B-17s was directed more toward air-ground cooperation rather than strict strategic bombardment. Because the key to the African battle lay in supply, the B-17s of the 97th and 301st Groups were dispatched to bomb the shipping in the harbors of Tunisia, particularly Bizerte, and Nazi airfields. It was also possible to range to the north of Africa into the Mediterranean to strike at Axis installations on the island of Sardinia, Sicily, and to the Italian mainland itself.

The bombings not only denied Rommel's forces desperately needed supplies and reinforcements, but also began the softening up for Churchill's hoped-for attack at the "soft underbelly of Europe."

One of the Fortresses sent to Africa, *Hell's Kitchen* was a veteran of the 97th Group's 414th Squadron and had begun its war career in the second mission of the group when the airdrome at Abbeville was bombed during the Dieppe catastrophe.

On February 26, 1943, several B-17s of the 97th Group, *Hell's Kitchen* among

One of the most reproduced photographs of the air war of World War II. The B-17 is "All American" of the 414th Squadron, 97th Bomb Group. Just before this photo was taken it had been attacked by an Me-109 whose pilot was probably killed. Out of control the Messerschmitt sliced into the aft section of the B-17, practically cutting the fuselage in half and taking away the left elevator. Having completed a mission over Tunisia the pilot, Kenneth R. Bragg, had an hour and a half of flying to do before he could attempt to land the ship at Biskra.

them, were sent out to bomb Italian cruisers near Sicily; the secondary target was Sardinia from which Axis planes were active.

For belly-turret gunner Sergeant Allie Moszyk it was the twenty-third mission of his rather brief career—he had only been in the Army Air Corps for a month over a year. The mission had not begun too well for him for, because of the shortage of ground crews, the plane's crew members had to gas-up and bomb-up their own plane. It was while he was assisting with the fueling that Moszyk fell off the wing. Though not seriously injured, he could easily have stayed home on that particular mission. But there was a serious shortage of men and he chose to go on the raid. Because of the lack of hands, ground officers actually served on KP and Moszyk received a jolt one day when he was served powdered egg by a KP with the rank of lieutenant colonel. Air crews were regarded as the elite and were spared the duties that fell to the ground men.

Hell's Kitchen's regular pilot was ill on the day of Moszyk's twenty-third mission so co-pilot Norbert Kirk took over the left-hand seat. A devout Catholic, Moszyk carried an improvised rosary he had fashioned from a shoelace, having lost the one he brought overseas with him. They were about 15,000 feet over Sicily when they were attacked by a flock of Me-109s and FW-190s. The latter especially buzzed around the Fortress with ferocious tenacity, jumping in on either side and from the tail. Curled up in the ball position Moszyk could not get a good bead upon the FW-190 which had got on their tail firing 20-mm cannon shells at them.

What Moszyk did not know was that Philip Trapani, in the tail gun position, was having trouble with his twin fifties which had frozen. He had just reached

109

for the lever to charge his guns when a 20-mm shell exploded in the tail, severely injuring him in the arms and legs.

Almost at the same instant Moszyk, seeing the FW on their tail firing shouted into the intercom, "Pull up the tail, sir!" and received a direct hit (apparently aimed at the tail gun) in his turret. In a flash the FW-190 dived below and out of the way. There was a great explosion inside the turret, smoke and bits of shrapnel filled the ball and Moszyk felt his arm go numb and his face was covered with blood. His radio was dead so he climbed out of the ball turret to attend to his wounds. Surprised that he could still walk around, Moszyk decided to investigate the tail-gun position to see how Trapani was making out. He found the tail gunner bleeding profusely and without an oxygen mask. Placing his mask upon the wounded Trapani, he hurriedly tried to tie a tourniquet around his arm. He then found a walk-around oxygen bottle for himself and went forward to inform Kirk that he would need some help to attend to Trapani.

Kirk had his hands full, for he had already feathered No. 3 engine, and No. 1 was afire. He and the bombardier "Gabby" Gardner returned to the tail-gunner, noting on the way that Robert Jones, the radio operator, was also wounded but continued to send messages.

Trapani was conscious by then and it was found that when he had reached out to charge his guns the 20-mm shell had exploded against the arm (later it was learned that the bone was badly shattered and the arm had to be amputated). Moszyk and Gardner gave the wounded man first aid and were shocked to find that they had to open five first-aid kits before they could find one that contained morphine. However, Trapani refused the morphine because he was

Typical Air Force luxury in North Africa, 1942.

Oran.

Distinguished guests visit the 414th Squadron. Crews are briefed as Winston Churchill and party look on. To the Prime Minister's right are Anthony Eden and General George C. Marshall.

afraid if he had an injection he would never wake up again. They managed to stop some of the bleeding in both arm and leg.

They then turned to Moszyk, himself with arm and leg wounds, and his face badly cut up from the splinters that had ricocheted in the ball turret. Luckily the structure of the turret had deflected the full impact of the cannon shell and his injuries were not serious. Because of the wounded men aboard Kirk wanted to land at an emergency field at Bône, but they continued on to Biskra instead. Before they landed he asked Moszyk to get back into the ball turret to see if any of the tires had been shot up. One had been so that when they came into their field on three engines, the fire in No. 1 had gone out, they had only one tire.

Kirk brought *Hell's Kitchen* in gingerly and balanced it on the single good tire, then when the flat touched down the plane swung around bending a couple of propellers. Their plane was met by anxious members of their squadron, including Richard Murfitt, the regular pilot. He was shocked when he saw the plane and the bloodied Trapani and Moszyk.

"Kirk," he demanded, "what have you done with my crew?"

Both the wounded men were hospitalized; within two weeks Moszyk was out, but Trapani's arm required amputation and he remained in the hospital for a month before being evacuated to the United States. (After the war, and following several additional surgical treatments, he died from the wounds he received over Sicily.) Moszyk received the Distinguished Flying Cross for his role in attending to the severely wounded Trapani and for giving up his own oxygen mask. He was later returned to the U.S. to serve as a gunnery instructor.

111

The Eighth Air Force B-17s over Bremen.

10. Winter of Our Discontent

Before he left for Casablanca early in January 1943, Winston Churchill sent a brief, complaining memo to his Secretary of State for Air in which he made a point of noting that "the Americans have not yet succeeded in dropping a single bomb on Germany."

Spaatz, Eaker, and thousands of 8th Air Force men were fully aware of this fact. The Prime Minister, however, assumed that there were greater numbers of men and planes available than actually existed. When he said that there were twenty thousand men and "five hundred machines all laid out in East Anglia," the fact was that 8th Bomber Command barely had a hundred planes and crews to continue with the submarine pen offensive. The crews, planes, and supplies, as has been said, were shunted into "Torch."

The RAF, on its part, had been penetrating into the heart of Germany on area bombing missions at night for two years. While this method lacked precision it enabled the British to drop heavy bomb loads on the enemy. It was the American belief that the RAF's night area bombing was not economical nor as truly effective as the more precise daylight bombardment. The American strategy aimed at specific factories, marshaling yards and other targets which, if hit, would cripple the German economy. The British method of saturation bombing placed bombs in the general location of a military target, damaging both the target area as well as the areas around it. The American method killed fewer civilians, of course.

The British were skeptical of daylight bombing during the winter of 1942–43 because the 8th Air Force had not actually proved its case. The green crews had managed to place their bombs on targets with remarkable precision, but to no great effect. The weather handicap scrubbed many missions and fighter opposition appeared to be growing stronger, antiaircraft more accurate; losses, the British argued, would mount prohibitively. Night bombing was the only sure method of carrying the war into Germany.

As General Spaatz recalls, "There was plenty of pressure on me to do something, but I didn't want to lose crews needlessly by sending them out before they were as ready as they could possibly be. So I held back, despite the pressure."

It was at the Casablanca conference (January 14–23, 1943) that Churchill proposed to call an end to the daylight bombardment by the Americans and hoped to persuade Roosevelt that the 8th Air Force should join the RAF in nighttime area bombings. Spaatz, who was Eisenhower's Commander-in-Chief of Allied Air Forces, called General Eaker, commanding the 8th Air Force, to come to Casablanca to put forward the case for strategic bombardment by day to the Prime Minister.

To Eaker, the double approach to the bombardment of Germany was complementary rather than competitive. But the controversy between the Allies, however friendly, was not contributing to the combined effort. When he arrived at Casablanca, Eaker was disturbed to learn that the Prime Minister had already placed his point of view before the President, and it had been decided to discontinue daylight bombing.

"That doesn't make any sense at all," Eaker told General Arnold, who gave him the news. "Our planes aren't equipped for that [night bombing] and our crews aren't trained for night bombing." During the period of transition, while the Americans were being retrained, the Germans would be given a chance to recover from what little damage had already been done and could meet them even stronger than before.

Arnold arranged for Eaker to see Churchill on the following day. The Prime Minister opened their discussion with the explanation that his views in no manner implied a lack of confidence in Eaker or his crews. It was just that the early missions of the 8th Air Force had proved costly—"your losses are sometimes 10 percent on a mission"—and too few. In addition, Churchill pointed out, the Americans had been operational for five months and had not dropped one bomb on German territory.

Eaker explained that the poor operational record could be attributed to the draining away of their strength by "Torch," and inexperience. Both of these would soon not bother them. He also gathered his reasons for continuing with daylight bombardment. If targets could be hit with precision, there could be more damage done with smaller forces. Specific, critical, targets—such as factories—could be hit by day; night bombing might saturate the area but miss the target itself. Day bombing imposed a strain upon the *Luftwaffe* for, despite the American losses, the German Air Force was also being decimated. He feared too that the time lost on training crews would have its effect upon the war's outcome

*General Henry H. Arnold,
General of the Air Force.*

and that American crews would probably suffer more training casualties than they would operational casualties.

The Prime Minister was particularly impressed with a passage in Eaker's notes which read: "If the RAF bombs by night, and we bomb by day, bombing around the clock, the German defenses will get no rest." Churchill used the phrase, "bombing around the clock," when he spoke before Parliament after returning from Casablanca.

Although not completely convinced by Eaker's arguments, Churchill conceded that he should have the opportunity to prove his case. When next he saw Roosevelt, Churchill informed him that he withdrew his objections to the daylight bombing program—at least until it had been given a fair trial.

It was thus at Casablanca that, besides the decisions to invade Sicily, to launch a cross-Channel invasion in 1944, to fight Germany until the Allies beat them into an "unconditional surrender" (the phrase was Roosevelt's), the Allies would also plan for a Combined Bomber Offensive which would deploy the air power of the British and Americans in an all-out effort in the "destruction and dislocation of the German military, industrial, and economic system and the undermining of the morale of the German people to the point where their capacity for armed resistance is fatally weakened." At the same time a system of target priorities was established. First on the list was the German submarine construction yards; second, the aircraft industry; third, transportation; fourth, oil fields and plants and, finally, other industrial targets. It would not be until the following June that this CBO plan would be put into effect and not without some alterations in target priority. But however tentative this plan might be, for the Germans it would mean a terror and devastation that had been known up to that time, only to their

114

victims. The democracies, "soft, spoiled and ineffectual," would teach the super-men how to war.

All during the initial phases of the North African campaign the depleted 8th Bomber Command continued with its attacks on the Bay of Biscay sub-pens whenever possible. Within three days after the end of the Casablanca conference, Flying Fortresses appeared for the first time over Germany. Fifty-three B-17s attacked Wilhelmshaven; the target: the U-boat construction yards on the North Sea, about three hundred miles from East Anglia. Weather was, as usual, far from ideal, but while the formations were given attention by antiaircraft guns over the Frisian Islands and Germany, only slight damage resulted. Even more surprising was the lack of fighter opposition despite the fact that the attackers were not protected by Allied fighters. Three planes, however, were knocked down, two were shot down by fighters and one, a B-24, when it collided with a FW-190. The unexpected daylight raid had apparently caught the *Luftwaffe*

Wilhelmshaven from the air. The B-17s approach in typical formations as the Germans release smoke to obscure the targets. Wilhelmshaven was the first German target attacked by the 8th Air Force after several missions against points in occupied countries.

offguard; in addition, all the best fighter units were stationed in occupied France or along the Eastern front.

On the next mission to Wilhelmshaven, members of "The Writing 69th," war correspondents, were permitted to fly with the 8th Air Force in order to observe an air attack firsthand. While arrangements were being made for the correspondents to hitch rides aboard the planes, a public relations officer approached the writers, explaining that he had a problem.

"I know you like to fly in the Fortresses," he told them, "but we have an outfit of men flying the B-24s, too. The men in the Libs generally go out on the same missions with the B-17s but it's always the Flying Fortresses we read about. Maybe some of you would like to go with the B-24s, eh?"

"Not me," said Walter Cronkite and five other journalists. They preferred the B-17s for no better reason than they did look better in the headlines. Not, however the man from the New York *Times*, Robert B. Post. The *Times*, he suggested, was not interested in headlines. He intimated that the great newspaper was above such things and said he would fly with the Liberators that day (February 26, 1943). So while Cronkite and the other war correspondents climbed into the B-17s, Post was driven off to the Liberator base. By a tragic coincidence, he was the only correspondent who did not return from Wilhelmshaven. The B-24 in which Post was a passenger was one of the seven planes that were lost.

In March the marshaling yards at Hamm, in the Ruhr Valley—"Happy Valley" to bomber crews—the heart of Germany's industrial might, was the chosen target. Four groups had assembled over England but by the time they had approached the Dutch coast, the weather had turned against them. One group returned to its base, two others bombed the last-resort target at Rotterdam and only one, the 91st Group with fourteen B-17s, continued to Hamm.

The skies were clear over the target and the bombing was quite accurate but an attack by fifty German fighters accounted for four of the 91st's B-17s. The Hamm mission was proof that daylight bombing could be accurate and it also proved the need for fighter escort.

The next attack on the German homeland occurred on March 18, when the Bremer Vulkan shipbuilding yards at Vegesack were attacked. These yards were fourth in importance to the construction of submarines. It was one of the 8th's historic missions.

A B-17 tail gunner, Sergeant Casimer P. Piatek, kept a diary of his missions, the fifth of which was the one to Vegesack. His impressions of that mission were written on his return from that raid. "On March 18 we were briefed for Vegesack," he wrote, "it was our [the 303rd Bombardment Group's] first target in Germany and we were plenty excited about it. After our first raid we picked up a new left waist gunner whose name was Francis J. Ryan from New Jersey. Everything went along fine and we bombed the target with good results. The flak over Vegesack was really rough.

"After we left the target we were attacked by about fifteen or twenty FW-190s and ME-109Fs. I kept firing at fighters for about fifteen minutes and then all of a sudden a 20-mm shell burst in back of me in the tail, knocking out our oxygen on the left side of the ship. I called all the fellows over Interphone to switch over to the other side which they did in no time 'flat.' The very next thing I knew I was hung to the top of the tail position and we were in a very steep dive. We dove from 23,000 feet to about 12,000 feet.

116

Crew of the Miss Bea Haven, *many of whom participated in the historic bombing of Vegesack which proved that strategic bombardment was more than a phrase. Standing in the rear are Lieutenant T. Rotham, Lieutenant D. Stettler, Lieutenant W. Roseberry, and Lieutenant G. McClung. In front are Sergeant C. Piatek, Sergeant R. Coykendall, Sergeant F. Ryan, Sergeant Roberts, Sergeant J. Traban, and Sergeant Vogel.*

"After we were in level flight again I found out my guns were jammed so I started crawling to the waist position. I got to the tail wheel and we went into another dive, I could see Traban and Ryan [the waist gunners] stuck to the top of the ship. After we leveled out again we were about 200 feet above the water.

"I took one look at Ryan and his face was one mass of Blood. I thought he was a goner sure as 'Hell.' Then I went to the Radio Room and saw Gentry lying on the floor with damn near half his side blown out. Then I looked at Phillips and he had three 7.9 slugs in his right leg between his ankle and knee.

"I then looked out the Radio Hatch and saw about six foot of our horizontal stabilizer missing. The cowling from our No. 2 engine was shot off and knocked the stabilizer off. The Pilot couldn't feather No. 2 engine and it kept windmilling all the way home. It vibrated so bad we thought the ship would fall apart.

"The navigator came to the Radio Room and told us we should prepare to ditch the ship in the North Sea. He then noticed Gentry on the floor and told the Pilot we couldn't ditch because Gentry was hurt so bad, so the Pilot said we would stick it out.

"The Pilot then told me to keep an eye on our stabilizer and to let him know just when it was weakening. I don't see where that would have done any good, because if it would have come off we would have gone down 'Nose First.' The Navigator then spotted the coast of England, and we began looking for a place to land so we could get Gentry, Phillips and Ryan to a Hospital. The Navigator spotted a Fighter Field, so Coykendall cranked down the landing wheels, and I was told to crank the flaps down.

"We hit the soft grass with a perfect landing in spite of a flat tire, one Engine completely out and two others throwing oil all over the place.

"We all got out of the ship and put Gentry, Phillips and Ryan into the ambulance and started to inspect the ship. We found six direct hits by 20-mm, two in the nose of the ship, one by the Navigator's window, one under the Pilot's feet, one in No. 2 Engine, one in the Radio Room which got Gentry, one in the vertical stabilizer, and one behind me which got the oxygen system. We had about 150 to 200 holes in the ship all total. We stayed at the English fighter field that night and the best part of it was 'Jerry' came over that night and bombed the town where Gentry, Phillips and Ryan were in the Hospital. They also dropped a few near the field where we were.

"When we got back to our own Base we found the fellows just about ready to distribute our clothing among themselves as they had given us up for lost. The Operations Officer wouldn't let us fly the next few missions. He said we needed a rest, 'Which I admit We Did.' Captain McClung was awarded the Distinguished Flying Cross for this raid which he rightly deserved. Also on this Vegesack raid a Bombardier from our Squadron was awarded the Congressional Medal of Honor . . . He is one Boy from our Squadron that the Eighth Air Force will never forget."

This "one Boy," Lieutenant Jack W. Mathis of San Angelo, Texas, and his accomplishment that day prompted the following message from the British Prime Minister:

> All my compliments to you and your officers
> and men on your brilliant exploit, the effective-
> ness of which the photographs already reveal.

General Eaker was gratified to receive this gracious message, along with another from Sir Charles Portal, Chief of Britain's Air Staff, recognizing the effectiveness of the 8th's bomber effort. He was, after the Vegesack mission, to say "The men and the machines have proven themselves. Vegesack was a successful conclusion to long months of experimentation in daytime, high-level precision bombing. After Vegesack comes a new chapter."

Lieutenant Jack Mathis was commended for "conspicuous gallantry and intrepidity above and beyond the call of duty" for his contribution to the writing of the new chapter that began with Vegesack. He was lead bombardier of the 359th Bombardment Squadron (303rd Group) in the B-17 named *The Duchess*. As lead bombardier, Mathis would do the aiming for the entire squadron with the aid of AFCE (Automatic Flight Control Equipment): on the bomb run he would literally control *The Duchess* through a system whereby the Norden bombsight was connected with the auto-pilot. During this run, while the bombardier guided the plane with unusual accuracy, there was no evasive action—and would not be until the bombardier signaled "Bombs away!" Only then would the pilot again assume control of the plane.

Just as *The Duchess* approached the target it ran into a heavy flak barrage. Mathis was crouched over the bombsight carefully aligning the sights on the target. They were now on the run.

118

"Bomb bay doors open," he announced. The pilot removed his hands from the control column. The flak was close and heavy and the squadron was taking hits. The plane carrying Sergeant Piatek was one of them. About ten yards away and slightly below *The Duchess* a black puff of flak blossomed with a red center. A jagged piece of metal tore through the bombardier-navigator compartment, breaking one of the windows on the right side of the nose.

Mathis was thrown back against the navigator and both were tossed against the bulkhead of their compartment. Leaving the slightly dazed navigator, Mathis crawled back to his bombsight; his seat had been blown out of position, but the sight was still on its platform apparently untouched. He knelt over the sight, checked his settings and released the bombs—the rest of the squadron then followed suit—and said, "Bombs . . ."

The navigator, timing the fall of the bombs, glanced over at Mathis and saw the bombardier reaching for the bomb door retracting lever. Thinking that something had gone wrong with Mathis' intercom, he completed the bombardier's call, ". . . away!"

The pilot could now begin evasive action to throw off the aim of the antiaircraft gunners. Then the navigator saw that Mathis had collapsed over his sight. He was dead; the small piece of flak had shattered his arm and torn out a large wound in the abdomen. Jack Mathis was mortally wounded when he crawled back to his sight to drop the bombs on Vegesack. They landed directly on target, as did most of those released by the other planes in the formation.

Jack Mathis was one of the first of the 8th Air Force B-17 crew members to be awarded the Congressional Medal of Honor, the nation's highest military decora-

Lieutenant Jack Mathis, lead bombardier, 359th Squadron, 303rd Bombardment Group, whose performance during the Vegesack mission won him the Congressional Medal of Honor.

Strike photo: Vegesack, March 18, 1943.

tion. His story has a sequel. His brother Mark, who had served with the medium bombers, had himself transferred into his dead brother's squadron and even flew in *The Duchess* using the same bombsight. Mark Mathis bore a personal hatred for the Germans and hoped to avenge his brother by completing his missions for him (Jack Mathis was killed on his fourteenth mission). Mark Mathis was listed as "missing in action" on his fourth mission, to Kiel's shipyards.

While the U-boat campaign, regarded as the primary menace to the Allies, continued, other targets were not overlooked. A foretaste of what was to come occurred on April 17, 1943, when the largest attacking force to that time was dispatched to Bremen's Focke-Wulf plant. Of the 115 Fortresses sent, 107 bombed the target—and sixteen never returned. It was the heaviest loss to date. Even before the formations were within radar range a German observation plane attached itself to the edge of the First Bombardment Wing's B-17s and alerted the fighters of the approach.

All the way to and from Bremen the B-17s were subjected to what was described as "the most vicious and concentrated fighter attacks yet encountered." The attacks were especially severe on lead ships on the bomb run, when evasive action was impossible. Stragglers were also picked off by savage attacks by *Luftwaffe* fighters. The price paid for the effective bombing, sixteen B-17s, plus forty-six damaged, was high. But production in the Focke-Wulf plant was seriously disrupted and eventually the facilities were moved deeper into Germany, to Marienburg.

120

One of the Fortresses which returned from the costly mission to Bremen was the *Memphis Belle*, one of the most publicized aircraft of the war which, despite flak and fighter attacks, managed to bring its crew home without one major injury. Although the crew accumulated fifty-one decorations, the only Purple Heart was awarded to tail-gunner John P. Quinlan for what he described as "a pin scratch on the leg."

The *Memphis Belle* was also the first B-17 to complete its (or rather the crew's) quota of twenty-five missions. The April 17 attack was the twenty-first; four missions later the *Memphis Belle*, carrying its crew returned to the United States on a morale-building tour selling U. S. War Bonds. The *Memphis Belle's* penultimate mission to Wilhelmshaven was filmed in color and widely shown during the war also. Pilot Robert K. Morgan later piloted the first B-29 to bomb Tokyo.

Among the other "firsts" of the 8th Air Force of this period was the bestowing of the Medal of Honor upon the first hero to receive it while still living. Sergeant Maynard Smith hardly lived up to the conventional expectations of the Air Force

Target: Bremen as viewed from a B-17. Bombs have already fallen into the Focke-Wulf components plant.

The Memphis Belle, *first 8th Air Force plane whose intact crew completed its full quota of combat missions in June, 1943.*

hero. He lacked the generally clean-cut quality of the typical airman—he was short, scrawny, and not given over to "wild blue yonderisms." And, after he received the Medal of Honor from the hands of no less a personage than Secretary of War Henry L. Stimson, he became even more so.

"Snuffy" Smith, as he was inevitably called, was on his first combat mission as luck would have it to the sub-pens at "Flak City," Saint-Nazaire. The plane had dropped its bomb-load and had received only a single flak puncture in the left wing. Visibility was poor and much of the flying was done over water. Suddenly land appeared and the planes prepared for their descent. Almost instantly the group was caught in a heavy flak concentration. Owing to an error in navigation the group had begun to put down over the occupied French coast, mistaking it for England. Two ships off the wing of the B-17 carrying Smith went down and then German fighters attacked.

The pilot pushed the Fortress down to the water, hoping to keep the fighters away. But the fighters continued their attack.

The intercom was shot out and the top turret gunner came into the cockpit to announce that the ship was afire. The co-pilot, Robert McCallum, "looked back through the bomb bay and all I could see was bright red flames, like looking into a furnace." Fire extinguishers did very little good and the panic-stricken waist gunners and radio operator had already parachuted into the Channel. The tail gunner was seriously wounded by a 20-mm shell and both navigator and bombardier were wounded seriously enough not to be able to help.

122

Crew of the Memphis Belle. *Harold P. Loch, Cecil H. Scott, Robert J. Hanson, James A. Varinis, Robert K. Morgan (the pilot), Charles B. Leighton, John P. Quinlan, Casimer A. Nastal, Vincent R. Evans, and Clarence E. Winchell.*

Smith had to hand-crank himself up out of the belly turret to find out what had happened. He found the wounded tail-gunner and applied first aid. He saw that the shell had set the radio compartment aflame and immediately jettisoned the explosive oxygen bottles and ammunition and began fighting the fire with anything he had at hand, clothing, boots, anything (as his legend grew in the 8th Air Force, it was even suggested that he had used urine).

From time to time Smith would leave off fire-fighting to man the waist guns to fight off attacking FW-190s. In spite of these several distractions, Smith managed to drive off the German fighters and also put out the fire in Number 649's radio room by smothering it with his hands. He had saved the ship and all the men remaining aboard. The plane came in without controls or a tail-wheel but without further incident.

General Eaker remembers that when the time came for the presentation of "Snuffy" Smith's Medal of Honor, the tough little sergeant was easily located. He was serving a hitch on KP for some misdemeanor or other. Nothing serious, of course, but meriting some form of punishment. No one dared to break a Medal of Honor recipient.

Following the ceremonies, Smith took to inscribing his letters, British style, *"Sgt. Maynard H. Smith, C.M.H."* After four additional missions he was relieved of combat duty and faded into the vast anonymity of the Air Force for the rest of the war.

A more typical Medal of Honor mission was that of Flight Officer John C.

Lieutenant General Jacob L. Devers, ETO Theater Commander, and Major General Ira C. Eaker, CO, 8th Air Force on hand to see the Memphis Belle *off for the United States.*

Morgan of the 407th Squadron, 92nd Bombardment Group. Morgan, an adventurous New Yorker, had been serving with the Royal Canadian Air Force (thus the Flight Officer rating) before he transferred to the 8th after the U.S. came into the war. On July 26, 1943, Morgan was co-pilot on Lieutenant Robert Campbell's Fortress, *Ruthie II*. The target was the Continental Gummiwerke A. G., a rubber plant in Hannover.

"We were on our way into the enemy coast," the navigator of *Ruthie II*, Keith J. Koske, related at the mission's debriefing, "when we were attacked by a group of FW-190s. On their first pass I felt sure they had got us for there was a terrific explosion overhead and the ship rocked badly. A second later the top turret gunner, Sergeant Tyre C. Weaver, fell through the hatch and slumped to the floor at the rear of my nose compartment. When I got to him I saw his left arm had been blown off at the shoulder and he was a mass of blood. I first tried to inject some morphine but the needle was bent and I could not get it in. As things turned out it was best I didn't give him any.

"My first thought was to try and stop his loss of blood. I tried to apply a tourniquet, but it was impossible as the arm was off too close to the shoulder. I knew he had to have the right kind of medical treatment as soon as possible and we had almost four hours flying time ahead of us, so there was no alternative.

"I opened the escape hatch, adjusted his chute for him. After I adjusted his chute and placed the ripcord ring firmly in his right hand, he must have become

124

excited and pulled the cord, opening the pilot chute in the up-draft. I managed to gather it together and tuck it under his right arm, got him in a crouched position with legs through hatch, making certain again that his good arm was holding the chute folds together, and toppled him out into space. I learned somewhat later from our ball turret gunner, James L. Ford, that the chute opened OK. We were at 24,000 feet about twenty-five miles due west of Hannover and our only hope was that he was found and given medical attention immediately." (Weaver was picked up almost as soon as he hit the ground and given immediate medical attention by the Germans; in December his squadron mates learned that he was well and a prisoner of war in Stalag Luft IV.)

"The bombardier, Asa J. Irwin," Koske related, "had been busy with the nose guns and when I got back up in the nose he was getting ready to toggle his bombs. The target area was one mass of smoke and we added our contribution.

"After we dropped our bombs we were kept busy with the nose guns. However, all our attacks were from the tail and we could do very little good. I had tried to use my interphone several times, but could get no answer. The last I remember hearing over it was shortly after the first attack when someone was complaining about not getting any oxygen. Except for what I thought to be some violent evasive action we seemed to be flying OK.

"It was two hours later when we were fifteen minutes out from the enemy coast that I decided to go up to check with the pilot and have a look around."

Colonel James S. Sutton, commanding officer of the 92nd Group, described what had occurred in the cockpit two hours before: "Just as the pilot took over the controls (Morgan piloted during take-off and up to the combat area), the first group of enemy aircraft attacked. The first pass knocked out the oxygen system to the waist, tail and radio positions. A moment later, a frontal attack from out of the sun at two o'clock put a 20-mm and a .303-caliber shell through the windshield on the co-pilot's side, totally shattering it. One of them hit the pilot in the head, splitting open his skull. The pilot fell forward over the wheel, wrapping his arms around it, causing the aircraft to nose down sharply.

"F/O Morgan at once grasped the controls from his side and attempted to pull

The end of the Memphis Belle's *twenty-fifth mission.*

Secretary of War Henry L. Stimson bestows the Medal of Honor upon Sergeant Maynard H. Smith for his actions on his first combat mission to Saint-Nazaire.

the plane back in formation. This was accomplished only by sheer brute strength against the struggling of the semi-conscious pilot, who was a six foot, 185 pound, heavily muscled man. At this time it was determined that the interphone had been shot out as well as the aft oxygen system, and F/O Morgan could not call for help."

The waist, tail, and radio gunners had succumbed to anoxia and were no longer able to fire their guns. Morgan assumed they had parachuted from the gyrating aircraft. Campbell was still alive though completely unconscious of what he was doing and held onto the control column instinctively. The B-17 moved crazily through the formation as Morgan attempted to counteract the dying pilot's struggles. His visibility was limited because of the shattered windshield on his side of the cockpit, although he could see above and to the side. Realizing that if they left the formation the German fighters would shoot them to pieces, Morgan decided to continue flying.

This meant that he had to pilot the plane with one hand and hold off the dying pilot with the other—which he did, all the way to the target, where *Ruthie II* dropped its bombs.

When Koske entered the cockpit he was shocked to see that "Morgan was flying the plane with one hand and holding the half-dead pilot with the other, and he had been doing it for over two hours!

"Morgan told me we had to get Campbell out of his seat as the plane couldn't be landed from the co-pilot's seat as the glass on that side was shattered so badly you could barely see out."

It took the two men thirty minutes to remove Campbell from the pilot's seat.

126

Lieutenant John C. Morgan, Medal of Honor winner for his mission, as co-pilot, to Hannover. Unable to call for help because the intercom system had been blown out, Morgan flew his B-17 all the way to the target and back, despite the fact that he had to fight against the dying pilot's grip on the control column.

Finally they did and Koske took him into the bombardier's compartment where Irwin held Campbell to keep him from slipping out of the open hatch.

When Morgan brought the plane over the English coast all fuel gauges were in the red for the gas tanks had also been hit and much fuel was lost. Despite the heavy traffic over the first field he saw, Morgan moved into the pattern and brought the plane down. They found that damage to their radio made it impossible to communicate with the field's control tower. The revived tail gunner, John Foley, cranked the wheels and flaps down by hand and John Morgan landed the plane. Campbell died an hour and a half after they reached England.

Morgan himself always believed that it was Koske who had had to make the tough decision which "took guts and brains"—and which saved the life of Tyre Weaver. The mission had been a harrowing one and unique in its details though, as was said, characteristic of the Air Force valor. John C. Morgan would experience yet another air adventure which would end his career as a B-17 pilot over Berlin the following year when he would be blown out of his plane with his parachute in his arms, and finish his World War II career in a German prison camp.

The Hannover strike was but one which took place during the week of July 24-31, 1943, which came to be called "Little Blitz Week," when the 8th Air Force attacked sixteen major industrial targets in the greatest sustained air offensive to date. On July 24 the 8th Air Force bombed targets in Norway for the first time. At Trondheim harbor installations were hit and at Heroya the still uncompleted Nordisk Lettmetal works, important to Germany's supply of aluminum, magnesium and nitrate. The next day the B-17s struck at the U-boat yards at

Hamburg; on the twenty-sixth they struck again in the combined bomber operation with the RAF, which bombed at night. Hannover was a target that same day. "Little Blitz Week" closed with missions to the Focke-Wulf factories at Oschersleben, Warnemunde, and Kassel.

On June 10 the Combined Bomber Offensive Plan, which had been decided upon at Casablanca, came into effect and the 8th Air Force's strategic bombardment passed into its second major phase: concentration upon the German Air Force by bombardment of factories, installations and, as would be inevitable, aerial combat. Other strategic targets, marshaling yards, factories, etc., would not be ignored, but the main weight would be placed upon eliminating the *Luftwaffe* as a factor in the German war machine. It would be necessary to the planned cross-Channel invasion of France, of course, and also to the further application of the mission of the growing 8th Air Force.

During May five new B-17 groups—the 94th, 95th, 96th, 351st, and 379th—became operational; the 92nd, which had been functioning as a training unit was also placed back into operational status. The 100th Bombardment Group (H), which would become notorious as "The Bloody 100th," was ready for combat missions in June. By the end of the year there would be a total of twenty-two heavy bombardment groups stationed in the British Isles. Almost simultaneously, the newly activated 15th Air Force, in the Mediterranean Theater, began to grow by taking its heavy bombardment units, including the veteran 97th and 301st groups from the 12th Air Force. The build-up for the all-out onslaught on Germany was on.

The bombardment groups were organized in September into three divisions: the First and Third Bombardment Divisions (H) were comprised of B-17 and

Not all the danger was encountered in the air. The 95th Group had barely become operational when on May 27, 1943—just fifteen days after the Group had debarked from the Queen Elizabeth—*it suffered a ground accident. While crews were loading up for a mission an explosion occurred on the base killing nineteen men and seriously injuring twenty.*

Explosion at Alconbury, base of the new 95th Bombardment Group. Four B-17s were completely destroyed and eleven others were put out of action for weeks until repairs could be made.

the Second Bombardment Division (H) of B-24 aircraft. Each division, in turn, was further broken down into four Combat Wings of three groups each, so that when the 8th reached full operational strength, each Division consisted of twelve groups. The First Bombardment Division was placed in command of Major General Robert B. Williams, the Second in command of Brigadier General James P. Hodges, and the Third was in command of Major General Curtis E. LeMay. Major General Frederick L. Anderson, Jr., assumed command of the 8th Bomber Command under Major General Ira C. Eaker at the head of the 8th Air Force. General Spaatz was Commander-in-Chief of all the American Air Forces in the European Theater.

Although the 8th Air Force lost some of its promised units to the organizing 15th Air Force, it was able to plan impressive missions on the basis of the newly operational groups. In the summer of 1943 three of the B-24 groups were reassigned to Lieutenant General Lewis H. Brereton's 9th Air Force in Egypt for the second American strike at the Ploesti oil fields in Rumania. (The first occurred on June 2, 1942, when thirteen B-24s led by Colonel Harry Halverson bombed Ploesti. All bombed the target but only four planes returned.)

The second Ploesti mission, flown at low level, was a disaster in which the Air Force lost fifty-four B-24s of the 163 that succeeded in reaching the target area. It was one of the costliest, and still most controversial bombardments of the war. The loss in terms of men and aircraft was excessive for the results obtained. But the Ploesti strike was only the first in a series that were to follow.

On the first anniversary of the 8th Bomber Command's first raid on German occupied territory (the Rouen-Sotteville marshaling yards), just sixteen days after Ploesti, a bold mission was formulated for the 8th Air Force heavies. The plan was to deliver a double-pronged blow on August 17 at the German Air Force directly by attacking the Messerschmitt fighter factory at Regensburg in

129

A German B-17 photographed at Orly Airport, Paris. This is a Flying Fortress captured intact by the Germans and placed into the hands of the ZS-1, Zerstorer Schule I ("Destroyer School I"), and used to train German fighter pilots how to attack the B-17. Fortresses without swastikas or other German markings were also used to join formations and radio information to attacking German fighters.

South Bavaria and indirectly by hitting, almost simultaneously, the ball-bearing plants at Schweinfurt.

"It was a bold strategic concept," General Eaker has said in retrospect, "one of the most significant and remarkable air battles of the Second World War . . .

"Regensburg-Schweinfurt was the bloodiest and most savagely fought air battle up to that time. The flight crews demonstrated a determination and courage seldom equalled and never surpassed in warfare. It demonstrated that enemy fighters could exact a heavy toll on unescorted bomber formations, but could not stop them. Our bombers could and did press through to their assigned targets. It set a pattern and a precedent for all bombing missions which were to follow. It created consternation at the highest levels in the Third Reich.

"Speer, the German charged with over-all responsibility for weapons production, reported to Hitler after this raid that if such assaults could not be stopped by the *Luftwaffe*, weapons making was doomed, and the war was lost.

"This battle resulted in the recall of many squadrons of German fighters from the Eastern front at a critical time there, in a vain effort to meet the bomber onslaught. Even the heavy and tragic losses in this mission, nearly 20 percent of the attacking force, taught a valuable lesson. It demonstrated clearly the need for long ranged fighter escort, stimulated production and hastened delivery of these types to the 8th Air Force in England.

"Finally, it was one of the great air battles of the pre-invasion effort to reduce the *Luftwaffe* to impotence, so that a seaborne land invasion of Europe could be made without prohibitive casualties. Schweinfurt-Regensburg was a dramatic symbol of the strategic air operations which destroyed Germany's *Luftwaffe*, and made it impossible for that force to be of any consequence against

130

Allied landings in France on June 6, 1944. The gallant sacrifices of the 8th Air Force Bomber crews therefore saved thousands of lives of Allied sailors and soldiers crossing the beaches on D-Day."

The Regensburg-Schweinfurt mission was historic, too, because it marked the deepest penetration into Germany to that time (Regensburg was over five hundred miles from East Anglia and Schweinfurt nearly four hundred); it employed the largest force dispatched—376 Flying Fortresses, of which 315 dropped bombs on their respective targets. It was the first shuttle mission of the war, for the forces attacking Regensburg, the 3rd Air Division, did not return to England but continued on southward to bases in Africa. This was as much due to necessity as to imaginative planning, for because of Regensburg's distance from the English bases, the B-17s would hardly have enough fuel to return after engaging in evasive maneuvers under attack. Continuing on instead of turning around and heading back, as was customary, served also to confuse the *Luftwaffe*.

But, despite this and all other factors, the August 17 mission resulted in the loss of sixty B-17s, twenty-four on the Regensburg strike and thirty-six on the Schweinfurt.

While some of this heavy toll might be attributed to the ferocity of the attacking *Luftwaffe*, using every device and tactic it could muster—from 20-mm cannons to rockets and even dropping bombs down upon the attacking B-17s —part of the heavy loss must be attributed to the slight slip-up in the original plan caused by weather.

As originally projected the Regensburg force was scheduled to take off first and ten minutes after it had crossed the enemy coast, the Schweinfurt force was supposed to take off. The bulk of supporting fighters were assigned to the 3rd Air Division (Regensburg) because it was felt that the heaviest German attacks would occur on that leg of the mission. Diversionary forces were also sent out over the occupied countries, concentrating especially on airdromes, to engage the *Luftwaffe*.

"On August 16, 1943, after a month of dreary waiting for suitable weather in the target area," General Eaker recalls, "the forecast indicated the attack could go on the following day, and orders were issued to launch the assault on the morrow. Unfortunately, the English bases were fog shrouded on the morning of the 17th. The 3rd Air Division got off, due entirely to the fact that LeMay's groups had been practicing instrument take-offs for some time. LeMay displayed then the qualities of leadership which would result in his selection as Chief of Staff of the Air Force 18 years later.

"The 1st Division got off later [three and a half hours later], as weather lifted slightly, but was too far behind to benefit from the cover provided by the 3rd Air Division. German fighters had time to land, refuel and rearm after engaging LeMay's Regensburg force, and strike the 1st Air Division all the way to their targets at Schweinfurt and all the way home."

This same weather prevented a few of the American fighters, P-47 Thunderbolts equipped with long-range gas tanks, and Spitfires, from fulfilling their missions. Also the diversionary missions of the mediums were canceled. For the 3rd Air Division this meant a constant battle across Germany to Regensburg, one of the most intense of the war, and for the 1st Air Division it meant a battle going and coming. The Germans called in fighter squadrons from Holland, Belgium, Germany, Austria, France, and Italy to attack the bombers.

131

Regensburg's Messerschmitt Me-109 factory is attacked by the 8th Air Force's 3rd Air Division. The river coursing through the photograph is the Danube. After attacking Regensburg the B-17s continued on to Africa in the first 8th Air Force Shuttle Mission.

Conditions in the air were incredible. Flak was light but fighter attacks were intense. "I can't remember looking out," one crew member reported, "without seeing a bunch of them falling out of the sky like big dirty drops of rain." The crews which returned claimed 288 German fighters shot down, which was probably exaggerated but was still an indication of the ferocity of the attack.

The air was literally filled with burning debris, parachutes, bodies, and parts of the bodies of airmen. To some, it appeared that they would all go down before they ever reached the target. "After we had been under constant attack for a solid hour," reported Lieutenant Colonel Beirne Lay, Jr., flying as a special observer with the 100th Bomb Group to Regensburg, "it appeared that our group was faced with annihilation." As the last group in the formation, the one hundredth was subject to more violent attacks for it was this position in the formation that the German fighters found to be most vulnerable.

"Seven of us had been shot down," Colonel Lay continued, "the sky was still mottled with rising fighters, and it was only 1120 hours, with target time still thirty-five minutes away. I doubt if a man in the group visualized the possibility of our getting much further without one hundred percent loss."

Despite the almost constant attack, the 3rd Air Division achieved excellent results in bombing the Messerschmitt factory at Regensburg. Every important building was hit and a good number of completed Me-109s were destroyed on the ground. At Schweinfurt the results were not so good, but severe damage was done on the two main bearing plants, production was interfered with and the

Reconnaissance photo taken after the bombing of Regensburg. The factory area is heavily pock-marked by bomb craters.

Germans began to consider the reorganization of their industries. This disruption would have a considerable effect upon the war beyond that of actual bomb damage.

In the face of the heavy losses, plus the great amount of damage to those planes which returned, the 8th Air Force concentrated for a time upon sending smaller numbers of bombers out over the occupied countries within range of fighter cover.

During August and September the new B-17Gs began to arrive in England; equipped with the new "chin" turret the Fortresses were now more capable of meeting the head-on attacks of German fighters. Also during this period the detached units flying B-24s, which had been sent to Africa for the Ploesti mission, were returned and the average daily strength of heavy bombers went up to 373. While this was still small, by September 6, the 8th was able to muster a force of more than four hundred bombers for another attack on the aircraft industry, particularly the VKF ball-bearing works at Stuttgart.

This mission, which General Arnold was to call "a complete failure" after the war, was regarded optimistically at the time. In truth, it was almost a repetition of the Regensburg-Schweinfurt mission without the results. Once again the weather interfered and of the 338 planes dispatched none succeeded in seeing the target because of the overcast. They were then attacked by more than a hundred fighters; forty-six B-17s, catching a glimpse of Stuttgart through a momentary break in the clouds, dropped down to salvo their bombs into the

B-17s of the 1st Bombardment Division (Triangle on the right wing tip) during the mission—"a complete failure," according to General H. H. Arnold—to Stuttgart. Dense cloud cover over the target made precision bombing impossible; forty-five Fortresses did not return from this mission.

center of the city. The rest of the attacking force, which added up to 262 of the original 338, attacked various targets of opportunity. A total of forty-five B-17s was lost during the air battle and to accurate flak.

Because it had made no less than three bomb runs before it dropped its loads, some planes of the 1st Bomb Division consumed so much gas that they were unable to make it back all the way across the English Channel. Air-Sea Rescue pulled 118 American airmen out of the waters of the channel after the Stuttgart mission.

The bad weather during this period underscored the need for special radar equipment then being developed. So-called Pathfinders using the British evolved H2S, a radar device which scanned the ground under the clouds and which could be read by a trained operator like a map, were developed. The American variant of this device was designated H2X, or by its operators in the bombers, "Mickey."

"Mickey" was used for the first time on the important shipping port at Emden. Although not technically a strategic target according to the definition of the Combined Bomber Offensive plan, the location of Emden on a seacoast would make it simpler to identify by the inexperienced though trained users of the device. Although not a complete success, the first use of radar in blind-bombing proved that it could be effective and somewhat safer from fighter opposition than visual bombing.

The second week in October, running from the eighth to the fourteenth, was to bring far-reaching effects upon the future of the strategic bombardment program of the 8th Air Force.

On the eighth of October 357 heavies bombed targets in the Bremen-Vegesack

134

Marienburg: before.   *Marienburg: during.*

Marienburg: after.

area with a loss of 30. This mission was significant for it was the first in which another radio device called "Carpet" was used to jam German radar. On the ninth a force of 378 bombers were dispatched to bomb a number of targets in Poland and East Prussia. The latter force, consisting of a hundred B-17s (of which 96 succeeded in bombing the target) attacked the Focke-Wulf assembly plant at Marienburg, its most distant target yet.

A B-17 of the 94th Bombardment Group leaves Marienburg after bombing the Focke-Wulf assembly plant in what General Eaker called "a classic example of precision bombing." This photo shows how the bombs were dropped on target and not on the little settlements nearby which were militarily of no consequence.

On Sunday October 10, 1943, Hermann Göring was to arrive at Marienburg to dedicate the recently completed runway. The occasion was permanently postponed when the B-17s had appeared over the plant just before noon on the day before almost completely destroying the factory and the new runway in what General Eaker called "the classic example of precision bombing." In the adjacent Marienburg prison camp, Corporal James McLoughlin of the British Expeditionary Force, watched and cheered as the high concentration of bombs fell into the factory area. The camp was not touched.

McLoughlin observed the effects of the bombing firsthand when he and other prisoners were set to work clearing up the wreckage and pulling out dead Germans.

"It was every bit as bloody good fun as opening Christmas parcels," he said later after he had arrived back in England as a repatriated prisoner. The Prime Minister, using less colorful language, asked General Arnold to "convey to General Eaker and his Command, the thanks of the British War Cabinet for the magnificent achievements of the Eighth Air Force in the Battle of Germany in recent days, culminating in the remarkable success of last week."

On the very next day the 8th took off to hit the important rail junction at Münster. The German fighters came up in force and appeared to use a new tactic, concentrating on a single group during the battle. Thirty Fortresses were knocked down, but it was a single group, the 100th, which suffered the effects of the new *Luftwaffe* technique. Of the thirteen planes sent out by the 100th Group only one, *Rosie's Riveters* piloted by Lieutenant Robert Rosenthal, returned to England.

"It appears to have been a catastrophe . . ." read one teletype report back in England. To the men at Thorpe Abbots, where the "Bloody" 100th was stationed, it was not appearance but a fact. The equivalent of an entire squadron had been wiped out. Not all the men were dead, of course, for many had bailed out and would serve time in German prison camps, but the empty places in quonset huts and in the mess halls affected morale.

The final tragic climax of that winter came on October 14, 1943, when Mission 115, a return to Schweinfurt, cost the 8th Air Force another sixty B-17s

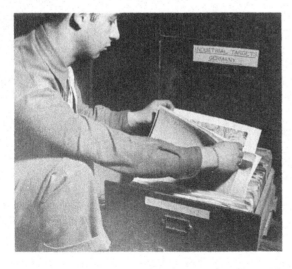

The beginning of Mission 115, getting out the target folder containing maps, photos and all of other information pertaining to Schweinfurt.

Despite heavy fighter operation, and at the tremendous cost of sixty B-17s, the 8th Air Force fought its way to Schweinfurt to bomb without fighter escort. It was one of the most intense air battles of the Second World War.

One of Schweinfurt's ball-bearing plants after being bombed by the 8th Air Force's heavy bombers. As was usual, reconstruction work was begun immediately after and the plant was soon back in operation.

Members of the 305th Bombardment Group receive a gift from the infantry—a Nazi flag taken down at Schweinfurt after being taken by the 42nd ("Rainbow") Division. This was in recognition of the 305th's heavy losses on Mission 115.

138

. . . and some six hundred crew members "missing in action." The loss was especially tragic because the attack on Schweinfurt was to have no decisive effect upon the output of ball-bearings, so essential to various war industries. Weather again was a factor in Mission 115, for though the two B-17 forces, the 1st and 3rd Divisions, were able to assemble over England with the aid of radio equipment, the 2nd Division of B-24 units was unable to make formation because of poor weather conditions. Of the attacking forces, the 1st Division experienced the heaviest losses—a total of forty-five Fortresses—with the 305th Group, once commanded by LeMay, leading the list. Of the sixteen planes dispatched by the 305th, thirteen were shot down before reaching Schweinfurt. The 306th Group lost ten planes, the second greatest number of losses suffered by a single group. Curiously, the so-called "Bloody 100th" Group lost no planes on the Schweinfurt mission.

When the 42nd (Rainbow) Infantry Division, under the command of Major General Henry J. Collins, captured Schweinfurt they took a Nazi flag measuring 8 by 15 feet flying over the city. In recognition of the 8th Air Force's role in making it possible for them to take German cities with low casualties the flag was sent back to England to be presented to the 305th Group. It was the first time such a trophy was presented to the Air Force by the Army Ground Forces. The inscription read: *To the Eighth Air Force. The Rainbow has revenged your losses at Schweinfurt!*

11. Impious War

In view of the succession of heavy losses suffered by the 8th Air Force during the winter of 1943 it became obvious that without fighter escort deep penetration into the heart of Germany would have to be seriously curtailed, if, not abandoned altogether.

The months devoted to the destruction of the *Luftwaffe* were, it seemed, wasted, for despite the heavy—and costly—attacks upon the German aircraft industry, the number of German fighters rising to meet the bomber formations increased rather than the opposite. While the RAF concentrated upon "Happy Valley" (the Ruhr), the 8th Air Force attempted to deal more directly with the problem of the *Luftwaffe*. Area bombings of industrial areas were believed to be undermining German civilian morale (which was not actually the case). There was a growing doubt, however, as to the effectiveness of the American daylight campaign. Concern was expressed over the resurgent *Luftwaffe* and

140

its possible effect upon "Overlord," the cross-Channel invasion which the Combined Chiefs of Staff hoped could take place on May 1, 1944.

General Arnold was critical of the inability of the 8th Air Force to send out larger missions into Germany, regularly and more often. He felt that too many bombers were kept on the ground, some of them because of inefficient maintenance, and not enough were dispatched on combat missions. Neither Arnold, nor anyone else at the time, was fully aware of the amazing recuperative powers of the German aircraft industry and of the effectiveness of its decentralization. Nor were they fully aware of the fact that, despite the exaggerated claims, especially by bomber crews, the missions were taking a serious toll. Nazi pilots of top quality were being worn out or killed and the *Luftwaffe* was being directly affected although it was not immediately noted. Despite the increase in fighter production, there was not a simultaneous increase in the number of first-line pilots to fly the planes.

Nor was Arnold fully aware of the weather problem. Not only might it be poor over England making take-offs and assembly hazardous, but even if it were fine over the bases, it might be bad over the target areas. True, Eaker had been steadily building up an impressive stockpile of B-17s, and to a lesser extent, B-24s, but the crews to man them were not available. There was an especially acute shortage of combat crews in October–November 1943, partly because replacements had not been arriving fast enough and partly because of the high cost of operations exemplified by Regensburg-Schweinfurt, Stuttgart, Münster, and Schweinfurt.

Even those B-17s that returned from those missions were damaged and required various levels of maintenance. This was complicated by a shortage of tools, spare parts, and trained personnel.

The fact is that the 8th Air Force was expected to accomplish its full commitment to "Pointblank" (the code name for the Combined Bomber Offensive in preparation for D-Day) with only a fraction of the required crews and planes.

It was a time of soul searching and a time for seeking possible solutions. Among them must be the building up of forces in Britain which, if commensurate with the mission of the 8th, Eaker promised, would help solve the problem. Another solution was put forward: bombing Germany from Mediterranean bases as they became available to the Allies already moving up the Italian boot. It would, in part, solve the problem of weather and would confuse German defenses expecting attacks only from the direction of England. It would also place some of the dispersed industries within reach of the heavy bombers. It was this thinking which led to the organization of the 15th Air Force in November 1943. Actually it resulted from the reorganization of Doolittle's 12th Air Force into the 15th Air Force, with Doolittle in command, and the 9th Air Force, with Brereton in command. The 15th would then introduce a second strategic air force into the European Theater of Operations. (The 9th later moved to England to serve as a Tactical air force of the Allied Expeditionary Air Force which was especially activated to take part in the invasion of Europe.)

In time the effort of the air forces based in Italy grew so much in importance that General Eaker was sent there to command the Mediterranean Allied Air Forces (the 12th, 15th as well as other units including RAF). Doolittle was transferred to Europe to head the 8th Air Force; his place with the 15th Air Force was assumed by Major General Nathan F. Twining. By mid-January

Maintenance crew working on a Fortress; Number 3 engine is being readied for a change. In the foreground crew chief Olin K. Leathers checks flight report with A. Szymanoske, instrument inspector.

1944, Eaker had left "Pinetree," where he had spent almost two years, reluctantly saying that he found it "heartbreaking to leave just before the climax."

The climax came quickly. The two years, which had been at times as heartbreaking as was his leaving to Eaker, was a period of learning, of experiment. Some lessons had cost a good deal, but the crews had learned well and they had proved their mettle. Their B-17 was the best combat aircraft ever built. If their beginnings had been tentative, perhaps a little wasteful (such as the sub-pen campaign), they had learned something about target selection and accuracy.

The miracle was that the Air Force had taken thousands of civilians and transformed them into pilots, one of the most exacting occupations known to man. Men who had never flown before were somehow taught to be fliers who were given the most advanced aircraft up to that time and then took them out to take part in extremely complex operations. This in itself was no simple job. The Air Force, particularly, pioneered new teaching methods which resulted in remarkably capable airmen. This applied also to the ground crews, also mainly ex-civilians who were given the job of keeping the most complicated machines in existence in combat condition.

These civilians, part-time warriors, led by the professionals without whom they would have been lost, went about their daily work as if hazard and heroics were common commodities. They had never flown before—and, after the war ended, many never flew again. But while they were airborne, they performed epical deeds.

142

Members of the 305th Bombardment Group ground crew experience one of the hazards of their work. This plane, which returned fully loaded with bombs from an aborted mission because of bad weather, caught fire while a new carburetor in Number 4 engine was being tested. When the fire became uncontrollable the plane was taxied away from other planes. It then exploded. There were no injuries.

The climax that Eaker knew was coming was made possible by the tremendous piling up of aircraft in Britain and the arrival of crews—plus the arrival of the North American P-51, the Mustang, as an escort aircraft. The Thunderbolt and Lightning had already arrived and, once they had been given "longer legs" (that is, increased range through the use of drop tanks carrying additional fuel), proved to be effective, potent fighters. But it was the Mustang which was able to range the farthest. It was then possible for fighters to escort bomber formations all the way to Berlin and back.

The latter weeks of 1943, the 8th Air Force restricted its missions to the range of the fighters; there were no deep penetrations into Germany. The 15th Air Force began its operations on November 2, dropping bombs upon the Messerschmitt factory at Wiener-Neustadt in Austria—and then it too was socked-in by weather.

Allied pessimism toward the strategic bombardment program would have been a good deal less had they known of the true conditions inside Germany and of the problems confronting Göring's *Luftwaffe*. The *Reichsmarschall* and his Fuehrer had a serious falling out after a devastating RAF raid on Cologne the night of May 30, 1942. Hitler went so far as to accuse the German fliers of cowardice and threatened them with courts-martial, executions, and other reprisals. He even blamed the Russian debacle upon the *Luftwaffe*.

A year after the Cologne attack, propaganda minister Paul Goebbels secretly confided to his diary that "The day raids by American bombers are creating extraordinary difficulties . . . If this continues we shall have to face serious con-

143

Typical young pilots who have just completed primary training at the Hancock College of Aeronautics, Santa Maria, California; their next step will be basic training. Hancock was one of many private training schools taken over by the Army Air Forces to train pilots. From Squadron A, Class 44-C (1943) are C. J. Graham, R. B. Frost, H. E. Brooks, Instructor W. C. Keller, M. G. Gregory and W. G. Becker.

The P-51 Mustangs arrive in ETO. The long-range fighter, by December 1943, made escort to and from distant targets inside Germany possible. These fighters are watching over B-17s headed for Merseburg, a well-guarded oil target.

144

A second strategic air force, the 15th Air Force, comes into action from Italy. This formation is dropping bombs upon an aircraft factory at Wiener-Neustadt, near Vienna, where Messerschmitt Me-109s were manufactured.

sequences which in the long run will prove unbearable . . ." Among the possible unbearable consequences this twisted little man discussed with his leader was the choice of whom they should surrender to—the British-Americans or the Russians.

The Anglo-Americans, unaware of the critical condition in Germany, which had all but disintegrated into one vast unconfined insane asylum, considered their own position and hesitated about continuing with the Combined Bomber Offensive. Practically the only inkling they had of the effects of the B-17 missions upon the Germans was from an order intercepted by the RAF radio in which Göring demanded that the *Luftwaffe* "must destroy the Fortresses, regardless of everything else." Pilots who did not carry out this dictum were subject to court-martial. In its way, this too was a tribute to the effectiveness of the B-17 and the 8th Air Force.

It was not actually until the beginning of 1944 that the 8th Air Force was

145

truly at a point in terms of experience, men, and planes and even in a definition of its mission, where it could begin to do the job it was created to do. Sixteen and a half months had not been wasted but the price had been high and to no discernible effect. The sub-pen campaign had been carried out against General Eaker's protests and he had been proved correct. Except for minor disruption, the costly attacks on the Bay of Biscay installations had had no real effect upon the course of the war. The German submarines were more efficiently dealt with by Allied naval forces and Coastal Command.

Precision bombardment upon marshaling yards, too, proved frustrating. Once bombardiers had achieved pinpoint accuracy and could hit the targets with amazing exactness, it was found that with an efficient German labor force, plus the forced labor of captives, the rail yards were back in operation within a few days.

The concentrated campaign against the *Luftwaffe,* the assembly plants, the ball-bearing factories, the rubber factories, had proved—at least so it seemed— equally frustrating. But finally the decision was made to continue with the Combined Bomber Offensive as had been formulated at Casablanca. Lieutenant General Carl Spaatz was placed in command of the newly formed U. S. Strategic Air Forces in Europe "to plan and direct heavy bombers based in England and Italy, and coordinate their efforts with the night operations of the RAF," in the words of General Arnold in his report to the Secretary of War. "Our air power in Europe had been built slowly because of the needs of other fronts, aircraft losses, and the sheer physical size and complexity of the bases required. At last," Arnold concluded, "we were ready for the job ahead."

Following the second Schweinfurt mission, through the last weeks of 1943 and into January, the 8th Air Force generally stayed close to home, choosing targets within fighter escort range. Because of the weather there was a good deal of radar bombings through the overcast. On January 11, 1944, the first major mission of the U. S. Strategic Air Forces was carried out from England when large formations (over six hundred heavy bombers) struck again at targets of the German aircraft industry. Of this large number of bombers dispatched only 238 B-17s actually succeeded in attacking after entire divisions were called back because the good weather did not hold. And because the formations approached Berlin within ninety miles, the German fighters attacked with more than usual fury. The cost to the 8th Air Force that day was sixty B-17s. While high, it was not as critical to future operations as had been the devastating Schweinfurt mission. The crews and planes continued to arrive in England. Also, the Mustangs had accompanied the bombers to the target area and back.

Continued bad weather again forced a break in the campaign against the aircraft industry begun in the summer. Then, on Sunday, February 24, 1944, the weather cleared over vitally important targets within Germany. The time had come to unleash the tiger.

"Nearly a thousand AAF bombers escorted by fighters attacked fighter-plane factories at Brunswick, Oschersleben, Bernberg, and Leipzig in our heaviest assault of the war up to that time," General Arnold reported. "A large part of the force was directed at the Messerschmitt 109 assembly factory and aircraft component plants at Leipzig. Defenses there had been alerted by an RAF area attack the night before, and the Nazis rose in force. One gunner reported, 'The Luftwaffe had all their planes up but their trainers.' Another said, 'We caught

146

Protecting its own, a Focke-Wulf FW-190 attacks a burning B-17 which has just bombed the Focke-Wulf factory at Oschersleben. This was the first important mission of the newly formed U. S. Strategic Air Forces (USSTAF) on January 11, 1944.

flak, rockets, and trailing attacks. Twenty-millimeter shells came zinging past with our names and rank on them, everything but our serial numbers.' Enemy fighters attacked some bomber formations for three hours, making head-on attacks in groups of ten or more.

"Bombing results were good.

"Production was stopped at the Leipzig and Bernberg factories, which together had been making 30 percent of all single- and twin-engined fighters. Output at Brunswick fighter assembly plants had been interrupted by previous attacks, and Sunday's bombardment put them out of business 4 more months.

"The RAF bombed that night.

"On Monday, Lieutenant General Doolittle's Eighth Air Force heavies were over in force again [but could not bomb the major targets at Brunswick because the weather had closed in; the bombardiers were forced to switch over to radar bombing instead of visual and, though they hit the city, did not hit the aircraft factories]. Tuesday they were joined by bombers of the Fifteenth Air Force based in Italy, the first coordinated attack of the U. S. Strategic Air Forces in Europe. [Wednesday was a "stand-down," no missions were flown because of the weather. Tuesday's mission was marred also by weather conditions over English bases resulting in collisions while the groups assembled for the trip to Germany. General LeMay ordered the 3rd Division, scheduled to bomb Schweinfurt, to cancel.] On Thursday," General Arnold continued, "the Eighth and the Fifteenth struck another coordinated blow at German aircraft production. On Friday, for the fifth time in the week, we struck at aircraft factories. More than 2000 planes from the Eighth and Fifteenth Air Forces set out for Regensburg, Augsburg, Furth and Stuttgart. The operation set a record for size; it climaxed five days of assault against one of Germany's most vital and well-protected industries . . .

"Those five days changed the history of the air war.

A mid-air collision. This is the top plane which sliced into the B-17 lead plane of a formation. Debris still trails behind.

"From this time on, the Luftwaffe, converted into a defensive air force, was no longer an effective defensive air force. It was still potent, but it could no longer challenge our aircraft anywhere and everywhere we flew over German-held territory. From that day the Luftwaffe rose to battle only when it believed it had local superiority or when high-priority targets were under attack.

"Instead of fighter-plane production being quadrupled as planned, the German output for March 1944 was less than in August 1942, and the April figure was lower than March. By frantic dispersal of plants and desperate repairs, the Luftwaffe maintained considerable capacity, but it never recovered from those five days in February.

"We paid a price for the air," Arnold admitted in summarizing those operations which came to be called The Big Week. "We lost 244 heavy bombers [carrying 2440 men] and thirty-three fighter planes during [those] five days."

Although General Arnold's report tended toward optimism, viewing as he did these operations from a distance, he did not exaggerate results. He was also writing for a select audience and hoped to make a favorable impression. Not every day, as has been parenthetically indicated within brackets, of "The Big Week" was successful. But, despite his enthusiasm, Arnold erred only slightly in evaluating this week of operations when he stated that it "changed the history of the air war." He might have, except that he would have been severely criticized by ground warriors, eliminated the word "air." One of the ultimate effects of "The Big Week" was evident when "Overlord" was launched on D-Day, June 6, 1944, and General Eisenhower could assure his troops that "If you see fighter

Cut in half, this Flying Fortress, the lead ship of a bombing formation, falls to earth. Trapped inside by the forces of a spin, the men were unable to parachute to safety.

aircraft over you, they will be ours." With the *Luftwaffe* all but erased from the skies, it was possible to make the Normandy landings at a remarkably low cost. Some advance payment for "D-Day" was made during the sorties of "The Big Week."

On the opening day, February 20, twenty-one heavy bombers were lost of the approximately one thousand in the striking forces. One of the Fortresses that did return from that day's strike on Leipzig (one of the twelve targets) was piloted by William R. Lawley, Jr., of Denison, Texas. As his B-17 approached the bomb release line, Lawley could be thankful that flak was light and inaccurate—even the fighters seemed to remain at a respectful distance.

But Lawley's troubles began at the moment of "bombs away," for bombardier Harry G. Mason informed him that for some reason their bombs had not dropped when he released the switch. At practically the same instant a dozen or more German fighters careened in for the attack. The Fortress recoiled under the weight of heavy cannon fire.

A 20-mm cannon shell burst inside the cockpit, killing the co-pilot instantly and wounding Lawley. He then heard Mason report that an engine was aflame. The weight of the co-pilot's body against the control column threw the plane into a dive. And because of the blood that had covered the instruments and windshield, Lawley could neither see out of the plane nor read his instruments for a time.

While Mason fought to get rid of the bomb load, which made control of the crippled plane even more difficult, Lawley, though more seriously wounded than

Hit by flak over Wiener-Neustadt, B-17 crew members bail out of their stricken plane. An open parachute may be seen behind the plane. Another airman may be seen just behind the right wing. Railroad yards cut through the center of the picture.

he was aware, fought with his waning strength to get the Fortress under control. He ordered the crew to bail out only to learn that, including himself, eight were wounded—two so seriously that they were unable to jump. He would have to remain with the ship. He punched the extinguisher button and the flaming engine stopped burning and Lawley found he could relax a little, but just then another engine caught fire as another swarm of fighters piled in on the crippled Fortress.

While the wounded gunners continued fighting the Germans, Lawley managed to get the second fire under control and Mason succeeded in salvoing their bombs. The bombardier came into the cockpit and saw that Lawley was on the verge of collapse because of his wounds and the exertion of flying the plane. That he had remained conscious as long as he did was a miracle, but he slipped into painful oblivion when he saw Mason there to help. Mason had had pilot training before he was transferred into bombardier training and was able to keep their B-17 pointed toward England.

As quickly as he spotted a fighter base, Mason managed to bring Lawley back to consciousness. The pilot, making a great effort, kept himself conscious by sheer will power as he took over the controls. As they approached an engine ran out of gas and another burst into flame; and they could not lower the gear. Lawley brought the Fortress in for a wheels-up landing. Sparks flashed as the belly of the Fortress scraped the concrete and careened onto the grass; the propellers were

150

The B-17 of William Lawley after he brought it in for a landing following a mission to Leipzig on February 20, 1944—the first day of "The Big Week." Lawley received the Congressional Medal of Honor for this mission.

Lieutenant William R. Lawley.

rather neatly bent back and the plane skidded to a stop. Fires were quickly extinguished and ambulances rushed the wounded to the hospital. For his part in the Leipzig mission Lawley was awarded the Medal of Honor and Mason and radio operator T. A. Dempsey were decorated with Silver Stars. Dempsey administered to the wounded crew members and manned the guns of the most seriously hurt men.

Not so fortunate, though he too was given the Medal of Honor, was Sergeant Archibald Mathies. On that same opening day of "The Big Week" Mathies was aboard a B-17 in which the co-pilot was killed and the pilot was unconscious. Mathies managed to get the Fortress under control (though unlike Mason in Lawley's plane, he had no flight training) and headed back for England. Mathies died trying to land the plane with the help of the pilot. Lieutenant Walter E. Truemper, navigator in another B-17, faced a similar situation on the same day. The co-pilot was dead and the pilot unconscious so Truemper flew the badly damaged Fortress back to England. Once there, however, he ordered the crew to bail out; he then attempted to land the plane so that the injured pilot could be given medical attention, but died in the crash-landing.

The weather brought a merciful close to "The Big Week," for crews were exhausted and the cost continued to mount, beginning with twenty-one on February 20 and rising to sixty-four (the 8th AF losing thirty-one and the 15th AF

151

Sergeant Archibald Mathies, who died while attempting to land a B-17 with a dead co-pilot and an unconscious pilot.

Lieutenant Walter E. Truemper, 8th Air Force navigator and Medal of Honor recipient during "The Big Week."

losing thirty-three) on February 25. Despite this, there was an excitement about the next major target—Berlin.

The RAF had been hitting Berlin with its area, saturation bombings since the night of August 25–26, 1940, but it was not until March 1944 that the American Fortresses appeared over the German capital. Berlin was not selected merely because it was Germany's capital—although that was, as the fury mounted, reason enough—it was the site also of several important industries. Also, because Berlin was Berlin, the Americans hoped that attacks upon the sacred city would bring out the fighters to be destroyed by American gunners in the bombers and by the potent little "peashooters," the Mustangs which escorted the B-17s and B-24s to Berlin and back.

The first attempt occurred on March 3, 1944, but was canceled because of poor weather conditions which worsened as the formations flew over the North Sea toward Germany. On the next attempt some units took off into a snowstorm and some never even got off the ground. One wing, the 13th, managed to get as far as the German capital. A recall had gone out from Division HQ, but while some of the planes turned back, others went on because, they later insisted, they had not heard the recall order. Thus it was that twenty-nine planes of the 95th and 100th Bombardment Groups were the first 8th Air Force aircraft to drop bombs on Berlin—"Big B," as it came to be known. Losses were light and the bombing was not very effective because of the cloud cover over Berlin, but all this was forgotten in the excitement of the first American strike on the Nazi capital.

Two days later more than six hundred heavy bombers, escorted by Mustangs and Thunderbolts, returned to Berlin. The weather had improved and some visual bombing was possible. But there was yet another difference: on March 6 the *Luftwaffe* was out in force and accounted for eleven of the fighter escorts and sixty-nine B-17s.

Coming in for a belly landing.

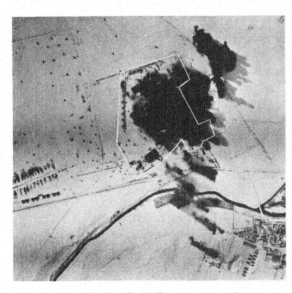

The Big Week: bombs fall on an aircraft assembly plant making Ju-88s, at Bernburg, Germany. A good concentration of hits billow up in smoke in the target area. Finished planes may be clearly seen against the snow.

The 8th Air Force drops bombs on Berlin. The first attack was made on March 4, 1944 and continued practically until the war's end. Berlin was a military as well as political target.

153

Flying as co-pilot in the lead ship on that March 6 Berlin strike was Lieutenant John C. Morgan, holder of the Medal of Honor for taking his B-17 to Hannover and back despite the fact that his pilot had been fatally injured and would not release his death-hold on the control column. Pilot of the plane was Major F. A. Rabo; flying in the plane was Brigadier General Russell, Air Executive of the mission.

Russell had been standing in the traditional spot for the Air Executive, between and behind the pilot and co-pilot. As the formation approached Berlin, Russell changed places with Morgan. They were at 21,000 feet and except for flak the day was described as "fairly quiet" by Morgan. The plane was on its bomb run when a heavy concentration of flak burst all around it.

Both engines on the right wing burst into flame and another fire started in the navigator's compartment. Rabo coolly remained on course until the bombs were dropped on target, for the success of the mission depended upon the accuracy of their drop. All other planes were to drop when they saw the bombs leave the bomb bay of the lead ship. After the bombardier sang out, "Bombs away!" Rabo pulled away from the rest of the formation. They were losing altitude and had dropped about 1500 feet when the Fortress exploded.

"I had been holding my chute in my hand from the time I had left my seat," Morgan recalls, "so the explosion . . . found me flying through space, with my chute still in my arms—unhooked. Everything had occurred so rapidly that the natural fear one has of approaching death hadn't been felt. The one thought which absorbed my mind was to get my parachute pack attached to my harness, which after what seemed hours, I did."

Morgan was only about a thousand feet from the ground before he managed to get his chute on and pulled the ripcord. He worried a little about the possibility of the chute not working at all, but it opened and he floated for a short while and then hit the ground hard enough to be bruised. The Germans greeted him "with the customary display of arms and belligerence. They weren't too friendly, but I didn't receive expected mistreatment." Goebbels' "Kill Orders" were in force and fliers could expect little kind treatment from civilians even if they were not lynched or pitchforked to death. The *Luftwaffe* deliberately interfered with the carrying out of the "Kill Orders" by racing to the scene of an emergency landing, or chute landing, to rescue the American or British fliers from the "good" German civilians or the SS.

Such desperate savagery revealed the internal German deterioration. At the same time the air battle decimated the *Luftwaffe* to a point where it was no longer regarded as a serious threat. It could not be ignored, for, when it was able to, the German Air Force struck back. But as far as the strategic bombardment program was concerned, the attack on the aircraft industry phase was over.

Number-one priority was then shifted to oil. On May 12, 1944, concentrated attacks were begun on the known oil-production centers and the synthetic oil-production plants. Without a *Luftwaffe* to protect them the oil centers were more vulnerable than they had been before. Flak was still a serious deterrent, but the B-17s and B-24s of the 8th Air Force and the 15th Air Force began to drop heavy bomb loads on the facilities at Brüx, Merseburg, Zeitz, Bohlen, and the infamous Ploesti.

Germany's oil industry was centered in eighty-one targets—twenty-three synthetic oil plants and fifty-eight oil refineries. A reduction of the German oil supply would not only affect the distressed *Luftwaffe*, but would also seriously curtail

154

15th Air Force B-17s encounter a typical flak concentration over Vienna after attacking the Schwechat Oil Refinery. Oil targets were among the best guarded by antiaircraft guns.

A Messerschmitt Me-410 banks after making a pass at a Fortress. The "Square H" on the wing identifies the B-17 as one from the 388th Bombardment Group. The photograph was taken by Victor A. LaBruno over Brüx, during the oil campaign.

A ground rocket just misses a B-17 over Germany.

the activities of the army and navy. Road transport too would suffer so that the entire German war machine would break down.

By June 1944 the oil campaign had reached a climax when more than 1500 Flying Fortresses and Liberators of the two strategic air forces fanned out over Germany to smash a dozen refineries and synthetic plants at Hamburg, Magdeburg, Ostermoor, and Politz. The Germans instituted elaborate defense measures to frustrate the oil offensive. The *Luftwaffe* conserved its fighters until it was certain the oil targets would be attacked—then it would take to the air in force. Some 12,000 antiaircraft guns were moved into areas ringing the oil targets— in some places the antiaircraft concentrations were double that around Berlin itself. Heavy smoke-screen devices were set up to confuse bombardiers. Great labor battalions with huge quantities of equipment and repair materials were stationed near the oil centers so that repair and reconstruction might be under way even before the attacking bombers returned to their bases in England and Italy.

The supply of German fuel and lubricants dropped catastrophically. The German High Command, as was reported in *Impact*, the Air Force secret wartime magazine, "faced with skyrocketing consumption to combat a large-scale Russian offensive in the East and the Normandy invasion in the West, found their oil production cut almost in half in only two months of attacks. Their reserves, which had looked so generous a few months earlier, were already shrinking dangerously. But this was nothing. By August (1944), production was down to 37 per cent. Three weeks later, Ploesti, which had been nine-tenths destroyed by the 15th Air Force, was captured by the Russians. This freed the bombers of the 15th, who redoubled their efforts against Vienna and Silesia . . . Production for September shrank to 23 per cent. The enemy, now desperate, was being relentlessly squeezed between the jaws of mounting demand and dwindling supply. There was no fat to draw on. The home front had been living on starvation rations for some time. The *Luftwaffe*, already weakened by the aircraft campaign, was literally dying of thirst. Its training program was shaved to minuscule proportions, all gas being saved for combat operations, and even that became rarer and rarer as the weeks went by."

Destruction of the synthetic oil centers had additional impact upon the German war machine. The production of two important chemicals, nitrogen and methanol, both essential to the manufacture of explosives, were closely tied into the synthetic oil centers. Ninety per cent of these two chemicals was produced in the synthetic oil plants destroyed by strategic air attacks. This not only created crucial shortages in the supply but also contributed to lessening the effectiveness of ammunition, particularly artillery shells, because the salt used in these shells was increased to make up for the lack of nitrogen. A postwar study by the United States Strategic Bombing Survey would conclude that the oil offensive phase of the air war would prove to be the most conclusive of all. Had it been begun earlier (although the wisdom of such a move must be questioned; until the *Luftwaffe* was checkmated all attacks inside Germany were painfully costly), the war in Europe might have ended sooner. Had the strategic bombardment offensive been pursued fully in all its phases, General Spaatz maintained during and after the war, Germany could have been beaten without the necessity of invasion.

"D-Day should have been a field day for a strong *Luftwaffe*," General Arnold wrote. "Thousands of ships and boats and landing craft crowded the Channel. A dominant German air fleet could have created incalculable havoc. The Germans were aware of their opportunity. Their success in the initial phases of the war was largely conditioned on the employment of air power. While the *Luftwaffe* was now depleted, it had, for months, husbanded its strength in the hope of giving violent opposition to our air attacks on vital targets.

"On D-Day the Allied Forces, sea, ground, service—all struck at the most vital target of all, the overland route to Berlin. Yet the *Luftwaffe* failed to appear.

"The AAF and the RAF had made it impossible."

In preparing for the launching of "Overlord," the heavy bombers joined in heavy attacks upon tactical targets such as enemy airfields, railroad yards, transportation targets, communications, gun installations, and bridges. In these operations, the heavies were joined by the medium bombers and the fighters of the 9th Air Force under command of Major General Hoyt S. Vandenberg.

On "D-Day" itself B-17s and Liberators joined with Allied naval forces to pound

B-17s bomb a German airfield near Saint-Dizier, France, on June 4, 1944, in preparation for "D-Day."

The Mission Board of the 8th Air Force B-17s on June 6, 1944.

Elements of the invasion fleet seen from a B-17 over the English coast on "D-Day."

the Normandy beach defenses before the troops made the landings. Medium bombers and fighters ranged over a radius of a hundred miles from the beachhead zones to strike at communications centers, airfields, troop concentrations, railways and truck convoys, disrupting enemy efforts to bring in reinforcements. Few pilots saw an enemy plane.

Aside from giving some ground support to the troops, such as the display of "carpet bombing" at Saint-Lô, or in stopping the German last gasp, the Ardennes breakthrough popularly known as "The Bulge," and diversion to "Crossbow" targets, the heavy bombers concentrated on strategic targets.

The technique of "carpet bombing," which had not proved very effective at Cassino, was tried again nonetheless when the timetable of the Allied advance across France was interrupted. In order to clear a path before General Courtney H. Hodges' First Army, a concentration of bombs was dropped into an area just in front of American troops only 250 yards wide and 7000 yards long. Despite

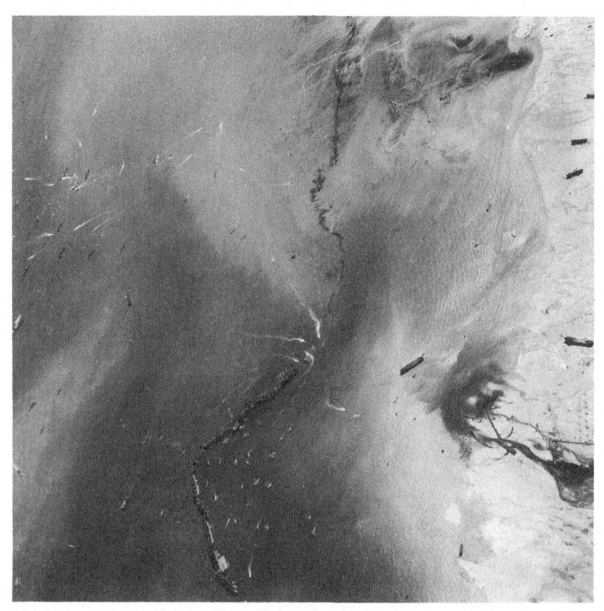

Normandy beachhead: the irregular line of ships was formed by deliberately sinking them to form a breakwater which protected shipping facilities at the beachhead.

The Normandy beach after the battle had moved inland; a Republic P-47 Thunderbolt lies on the battle-scarred beach.

159

Ships come into Normandy, troops dot the shore and vehicles move inland.

A V-1 "buzz bomb" photographed over the English countryside—and an example of what it did when it landed in a populated area. The V-1 and the more vicious V-2 were the final terror weapons used by the Germans when their cause was hopeless. No useful purpose was served by the V-weapons whose sole reason for being was to strike blindly at the enemy.

the care and precision used in the carpet bombing, some bombs fell short—into American troop concentrations, killing more than a hundred Americans including Lieutenant General Lesley J. McNair. It was a tragic error, but the troops were able to get through.

"Crossbow" targets were those connected with German V-weapons, the V-1 "buzz-bomb," and the V-2 rocket. Both weapons were unmanned and were aimed in the general direction of the targets, possibly the most senseless weapons of the war. Control of these secret weapons was of course out of the question and they plunged to earth anywhere—and in the case of the V-2, without any warning. To state that these struck at military targets would be ridiculous.

The Allies were aware of the existence of German "secret weapons" but were not certain what form they would take. One week after the Normandy invasion the first V-1 landed in the middle of London. In September the first V-2, a twelve-ton rocket, exploded in the London area; sixteen seconds later a second struck. The rocket caused about twice as many casualties as the V-1 and Churchill demanded countermeasures be taken.

The ski sites of the V-1s and launching sites of the V-2s were bombed (although to no great effect as it was learned later) and Peenemünde, the German experimental station on the Isle of Usedom in the Baltic Sea, was attacked heavily.

The so-called Vengeance weapons, although originally called *Versuchmuster* ("experimental"), proved a problem until their sites were captured by ground troops. The race across France had begun. By August American troops were in Paris and, if the war would not end by December—and there was no better reminder of that than the Battle of the Bulge—the Germans were on the run.

The King and Queen visit the underground headquarters of the 8th Air Force at Wycombe Abbey. General Todd leads, the Queen follows while the King listens to General Doolittle; General Orvil Anderson is behind Doolittle with General William Kepner of VIII Fighter Command.

The build-up: new B-17Gs ready for delivery to combat units of the 8th Air Force. This gives some idea of the overwhelming numbers that were to go into action against the Germans in the final months of the war over Europe.

By autumn of 1944 transportation targets were given number-one priority in the strategic campaign; this was to be the final phase of the strategic program. It was at once tactical and strategic: the Fortresses and Liberators struck at marshaling yards and the fighters swooped down to strafe trains. It was estimated that the Germans lost about two hundred cars a day, every day. Railyards congested with wreckage and troops were denied much needed supplies and transportation. By February 1945 Germany was all but defeated before the fury of the air war and the advancing land armies of the Americans, British, and Russians. It was at this time that one of the most controversial bombings of the war occurred, the joint attack upon the city of Dresden (February 14, 1945) by the RAF and 8th Air Force.

It was during this final phase of the air war that a curious and possibly unique incident occurred. On November 23, 1944, spotters of a British antiaircraft unit near Cortonburg, Belgium, were astonished to see a B-17, its landing gear down, approaching their gun positions. As the gunners put in a call to their Operations Room at nearby Erps-Querps, the Fortress came in fast for a rather rough landing on a plowed field near the gun position.

It bounced to within thirty yards of the gun crew and came to a sudden stop when one wingtip dipped and dug into the ground. The propeller buckled and the engine stopped but the other three remained in operation.

John V. Crisp arrived upon the scene about twenty minutes after he had been notified of the plane's approach. The three propellers continued revolving, but no one had emerged from the B-17.

Crisp finally discovered the front entrance underneath the fuselage and was able to get inside the plane. He found no one aboard, "although evidence of fairly recent occupation was everywhere."

He managed also after some experimentation to turn off the four engines and then proceed to inspect what came to be called "The Phantom Fortress."

"I next looked at the navigator's table," Crisp has written. "The aircraft log was open and the last words, written some time before, were 'Bad flak.'

"We now made a thorough search and our most remarkable find in the fuselage was about a dozen parachutes neatly wrapped and ready for clipping on. This made the whereabouts of the crew even more mysterious. The Sperry bomb-sight remained in the Perspex nose, quite undamaged, with its cover neatly folded beside it. Back on the navigator's desk was the code book giving the colours and letters of the day for identification purposes. Various fur-lined flying jackets lay in the fuselage together with a few bars of chocolate, partly consumed in some cases."

George J. Hansen, then serving with Advanced Headquarters, 8th Air Force Service Command in Brussels, sent a crew out to investigate the mysterious aircraft. On checking the plane's serial number, he learned that it had come from the 91st Bombardment Group and that the crew was already safe in England.

The build-up: only a fraction of the B-17s which stockpiled in Britain for the strategic air war.

The build-up in the air. B-17s of the 381st Bombardment Group head for German targets above the clouds.

As far as the eye can see, great formations of Flying Fortresses bringing war to the war makers in Germany.

What had happened was that the plane, on a mission to Merseburg oil targets, developed trouble just before reaching the target area. The plane was not able to climb with the rest of its group and, in addition, was plagued with a malfunction of the bomb racks. Then a direct hit knocked out No. 3 engine and another filled the center of the plane with a tremendous flash. "We had been hit in the bomb bay," pilot Harold R. DeBolt reported later, "and I'll be darned if I know why the bombs didn't explode."

With one propeller windmilling and the weather closing in, DeBolt headed for England and then changed his mind, for the plane was obviously not going to make it back to East Anglia. He then pointed the B-17 toward Brussels and ordered all loose equipment jettisoned to lighten the load. It was then that two

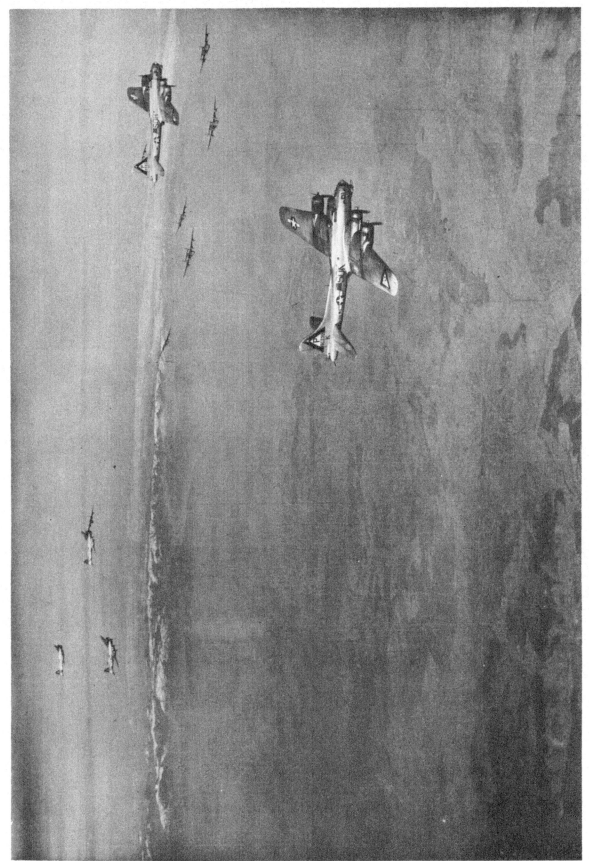

B-17s of the First Division are joined by B-24s of the 2nd Division over Germany.

A B-17 comes to grief near the Rhine; the Fortress was shot down while on a photo mission. Geometric lines are trenches. Members of the crew may be seen just above the plane.

The end: Bad Abling Airdrome, Germany after the surrender of Germany.

166

engines quit. Setting the B-17 on automatic pilot, DeBolt ordered the crew to bail out, leaving the plane last.

All landed safely—and so did their stricken B-17. What had undoubtedly happened was that after the crew jumped, with justification as far as they could discern, the trouble in the engines cleared up and the beautifully designed, stable, B-17 flew itself. Its malfunctioning engines, however, would not keep it up and it simply came down as described by John V. Crisp. To his uneducated eye the plane appeared to be undamaged and what he thought were the crew's parachutes were probably extra chute packs.

Throughout the war there were other reports of B-17s which continued to fly though pilotless, but the Phantom Fortress was the only one that succeeded in landing itself more or less intact.

But this was but an incident in the mounting air offensive in the European war's final phases. Through the winter of 1944–45 the heavy bomber attacks continued with ferocity. The RAF hammered Germany at night and was followed by day with double pronged assaults by the 8th Air Force in England and the 15th in Italy; Germany lay almost completely vulnerable in the bomber streams that came from what must have seemed all directions at all hours.

The Third Reich was pulverized into an inferno of wreckage, demoralization, and chaos. Denied lubrication, the source of which was struck with near immunity during that last winter of the war, the German war machine shrieked to a halt, a crippled shambles, unable to move. By April 1945 the Strategic Air Forces had exhausted their targets. Plans were already under way to divert the weight of its terrible destructive power to the Pacific. The lessons so painfully learned, perhaps, could be applied in order to save Allied lives—and ultimately, even the lives of the enemy.

BALLAD OF THE BLOODY CENTURY

*Don't get the notion that your job
is going to be glorious or glamorous.
You've got dirty work to do, and you
might as well face the facts. You're
going to be baby-killers and
women-killers . . .*

COL. DARR H. ALKIRE
CO, 100th Bombardment Group (H)

12. The Bloody 100th

In the summer of 1944 First Lieutenant Stanley Russell of Sudbury, Massachusetts, on pass in London, quite naturally found his way to an American club where he could find some refreshment and, perhaps, a little adventure not readily available in East Anglia. The handsome young navigator, with very little effort, found himself dancing with an attractive WAC officer. Names were exchanged and as they danced other typical information was shared: home towns, marital status, current assignment, etc.

The very desirable young woman was obviously connected with one of the Air Force headquarters in the vicinity of London. She finally asked Russell where he was stationed. He hesitated for it was a violation of security to reveal such information, even to a fellow Air Force member. At the base they received talks on the subject and posters bloomed everywhere declaiming "A slip of the lip," etc. But it would certainly do no harm to reveal the name of the railroad station at which one might leave the train. It was a curious place name (England was full of them) and was grist for many a pun mill.

"Diss," Russell informed the girl, "is the station stop."

Her face clouded and she stopped dancing and stepped away from the startled Russell.

"I'm not going to dance with you," she told him. "I don't want to have any-

171

Lieutenant Stanley Russell

Stanley Russell's office window.

thing to do with you. Not after what you men did." She turned abruptly and left Russell standing in the middle of the dance floor, without a partner and with no idea of what he, or anyone else had done.

Major Robert Rosenthal joined a gathering of 8th Air Force airmen one day and the talk, as usual, was shop. Techniques of evasive action in a Flying Fortress, turning into fighter attacks, how to ditch without breaking the fuselage in half and other such technical subject matter of their strange temporary trade were discussed as if it were indeed normal (which for the moment it was). Accredited missions were compared (the 8th Air Force retired a man after twenty-five missions) and it turned out that Rosenthal had reached forty.

This excited comment, but this was nothing compared to the reaction when Rosenthal informed the other airmen that he was from the 100th Bombardment Group.

"Nobody lives long enough in the 100th," he was told, "to get in forty deals."

Sergeant Joseph Bonem, tail gunner with the 306th Bombardment Group, teamed up with another Air Force sergeant, whom he had never seen before, to explore the delights of Piccadilly. Before long the two youngsters, each barely twenty, shared confidences. Bonem, a taciturn Midwesterner, was rather disconcerted by his companion's sad story. He told Bonem that he was certainly marked for death.

"I'm not going to make it," he said almost sobbing. "They just put me in the 100th Group. I haven't got a chance."

Except for the legend that grew up around it, the 100th Bombardment Group (H) was no different from any other that served in the air war against Germany. It was as typical an American unit as any other, it had its hot pilots, heroes, misfits, "characters," its madmen and its cool operators in the same proportions as all other groups. It was predominantly a civilian fighting outfit with all its related good points and bad.

The 100th Bombardment Group (H) was created on January 28, 1942, when Special Order ⚹300 was cut into a stencil by a clerk at Gowen Field near Boise, Idaho. Shortly after, air and ground men began to gather rather haphazardly at the Walla Walla Air Base, Washington. Although no Group Commander had yet been assigned, Captain Karl Standish, group adjutant, more or less filled the bill. Captain John C. Egan was named Operations Officer, but there were no operations—nor were there any B-17s with which to train.

Early in November the squadrons were established; the 349th was commanded by Captain William W. Veal, the 350th by Captain Gale W. Cleven, the 351st by Captain John B. Kidd, and the 418th by Captain Robert E. Flesher. Almost simultaneously four B-17Fs were delivered, one to each squadron and with air crews under command of Lieutenant Oran B. Petrich (349th), Lieutenant Norman H. Scott (350th), Lieutenant Roland T. Knight (351st), and Lieutenant Everett E. Blakely (418th).

Practice flights could then be scheduled and crew training began at once; likewise the ground crews began to familiarize themselves with the complex B-17. Most had come from technical schools and were still weak in practical work on an operational aircraft.

173

On November 14 Colonel Darr H. Alkire arrived to command the group. The next day he called an assembly of the group in the base theater to make a typical speech of introduction and to define future plans. "Pappy" Alkire, as he came to be called, endeared himself immediately to the ground crews by emphasizing the importance of their contribution to the group's future (this became known as the "Keep 'Em Flying" theme). Alkire proceeded to deflate the airmen, who tended to look upon themselves as something special, and to strut around in characteristic "fly-boy" fashion.

"Don't get the notion that your job is going to be glorious or glamorous," Alkire told them. "You've got dirty work to do, and you might as well face the facts. You're going to be baby-killers and women-killers . . ."

As the group completed different phases of its training it moved to different bases. By the end of November the 100th was stationed (the number of crews having reached thirty-six) at Wendover Field, Utah. In January 1943 it was at Sioux City Army Base, an improvement over the primitive Wendover, for a third phase in training stressing formation flying and navigation. By mid-January overseas packing had been begun when unexpectedly the Air Force decided that the 100th should be broken up instead of sent to combat as a unit. Only Alkire's determination to hold the 100th together and his ability to argue prevented the dispersal.

Although the 100th was not disbanded, it certainly was scattered. In February, with the ground echelons sent to Kearney Army Air Field, Nebraska, the air crews were sent to a half dozen bases where they were ostensibly supposed to instruct. Instead they rusted. With practically nothing to do, some idle airmen casually took time off, went AWOL, one even managed to squeeze in a wedding and honeymoon on, as it might be put, "GI time."

"We were all conceited," Harry H. Crosby now recalls, "and quite impossible. We were undertrained and not as good as we thought we were."

This was proved in a comedic performance by the group which cost Alkire his job. At the end of March a series of "showdown" inspections were initiated as part of the processing for overseas shipment. The aircrews began to straggle back and by mid-April the 100th Group had a full complement of thirty-seven B-17 crews.

A practice mission was scheduled for April 20, a simulated bomb run, from Kearney to Hamilton Field, California—a distance of almost 1300 miles. Twenty-one planes were to participate in the mission in this high-altitude test. The elements were to rendezvous over Salt Lake City before proceeding on to California.

No one took into consideration the fact that most of the crews had been practically inactive for almost three months. Their own conceit would not permit them to realize it themselves.

The result was a fiasco. Planes of the 100th Group were scattered over the American west, although five managed to make it to Hamilton Field, among them the plane commanded by Captain John B. Kidd—described by Crosby as "the only air leader who knew anything." Three B-17s landed in Las Vegas, one of them carrying an embarrassed Colonel Alkire.

But worse: one B-17 of the 100th put down at Smyrna, Tennessee. In truth, this could not be attributed so much to poor navigation (as it would seem) as much as to the characteristic lackadaisical attitude of the pilot, whose wife just happened to be in Smyrna. This was, indeed, devotion which preceded the call of duty.

In time, all but three planes arrived at Hamilton, but the damage was done. Alkire was relieved of his command (the charge: "incompetence") and Operations Officer Egan was reduced to a squadron command.

The 100th Group was stepped back a phase and returned to Wendover for further training and inspections under the command of Colonel Howard M. Turner, an assistant to General Arnold. After some shaking up and intensive additional training the air echelons began moving overseas toward the end of May. By the middle of June 1943 the 100th Bombardment Group (H) was placed on the operational list. They continued to fly practice missions to familiarize themselves with the English terrain and with their station ⚹139 at Thorpe Abbotts, near Diss, County of Norfolk. On June 22 B-17s of the group participated in a diversionary sweep over the North Sea, while the main 8th Air Force formations made the first large-scale attack in the Ruhr Valley on the synthetic rubber plant at Hüls.

The first member of the 100th to experience a combat flight was Major John ("Bucky") Egan who had preceded the rest of the unit as one of the advance party. Egan was to become one of the group's most colorful members; he was dashing, dour, and given over to speaking in a dialect that could only be described as Runyanesque (of which samples will be offered below). A full month before the 100th went out on its uncredited diversion flight, Egan flew on a combat mission to gain experience. When he did not return that evening Major Miner F. Shaw, the 100th's S-2 (Intelligence), in an excess of zeal, reported Egan "missing in action." It turned out however that the plane in which Egan had flown ran into a bit of trouble over Germany and was forced to land at another base.

At 6:00 in the morning of June 25, 1943, the 100th Bombardment Group took off on its first official mission. The weather was typically English; clouds were thick and visibility was poor. One B-17 could not find the formation during assembly and returned to base; another, piloted by Samuel Barr, developed propeller trouble and, too, was forced to return. The remaining seventeen 100th Group Fortresses were led by Major Gale Cleven in the high squadron (Captain Mark Carnell pilot) and by Major Robert Flesher in the low squadron in the B-17 flown by Lieutenant John Swartout.

The 100th's planes then joined the other groups comprising the 13th Combat Wing—the 95th and 390th—which in turn joined the other elements of the Third Division. In all 275 Fortresses assembled (although only 167 succeeded in reaching the targets for the day) to bomb convoys near Bremen and targets of opportunity in Germany.

The group was barely ten minutes out from the English coast when a B-17 materialized out of the clouds and tagged onto the formation. The sides of the fuselage bore the letters VGY and the serial numbers on the tail were 42-3726, but it was not one of the planes which belonged in the 100th's Wing. The unidentified Fortress trailed along with the group until they were over France, then it turned away and attached itself to other formations; over Germany it rejoined the 100th.

There was no communication exchanged between the mystery B-17 and the other planes in the formation; when they were over Germany and flak began

One of the Luftwaffe's B-17s. Those which were used to track bomber formations carried no German markings, but were left as they fell into German hands. Later in the war no strays were permitted to join B-17 formations and were even fired upon by Fortress gunners if they attempted to do so.

Colonel Neil B. Harding, commanding officer of the 100th Group during its most difficult period, greeting an old friend, Lieutenant Colonel John M. Bennett, Jr., who has been credited by many ex-100th Group members with saving the unit—and their lives.

Over the fjords of Norway on the Trondheim mission; the planes are from the 95th Bombardment Group, like the 100th Group a part of the 13th Combat Wing.

176

to burst around them the intruder turned away into the clouds. Although they did not know definitely, members of the group were certain that the plane was a captured Fortress which the Germans used to track the formation, alerting by radio the fighter bases and flak concentrations along the way.

Then suddenly from below they saw their first German fighter, an Me-109. It darted up, fired a burst, rolled over and was gone. More Me-109s appeared attacking in train; they were joined by Focke-Wulf 190s and the Ju-88s. The intercoms rattled with warnings and shouting of the clock positions from which the fighters attacked. The battle was intense and of the eighteen B-17s lost by the 8th Air Force that day, three were from the 100th Group: the crews of Alonzo Adams, Paul Schmalenbach, and Oran Petrich (the latter was the pilot of one of the first air crews of the group).

Five hours later, when they returned to Thorpe Abbotts, the once-cocky 100th Group members were veterans—and they were minus thirty men. They had been friends known over a period of time whose presence had been taken for granted and now they were gone. The illusionary, the irrational, reality of war had suddenly come home, especially to those who temporarily free watched horror-stricken as the three B-17s seemed to dissolve into the overcast. It could have been them.

The following week, on July 1, 1943, Colonel Neil Harding, a graduate of West Point and a famed football coach for Army, was assigned to the 100th Group as its commander replacing Colonel Harold Q. Huglin. Harding, whose nickname was "Chick," was a seasoned flier and no stranger to the Flying Fortress. He took part in the early South American Good Will tours of the 2nd Bombardment Group, and in fact, flew the fifth B-17 to leave the Boeing factory in 1937. On July 20, the RAF officially turned over the base to Colonel Harding; it would be the home of the 100th Bombardment Group (H) for the next three years.

In July, after Harding took command, the 100th took part in one of the historic missions of the 8th Air Force, the long twelve-hour flight to German U-boat installations in the harbor at Trondheim, Norway. The round trip was a 1900-mile flight; the larger force attacked the Nordisk Lettmetal (magnesium, aluminum, nitrate) plant then nearing completion and the smaller force dropped bombs on Trondheim. The target was found to be obscured by clouds so that part of the mission was abandoned as it was against the policy of the 8th Air Force to attack indiscriminately over occupied countries; thus eighty-four planes returned to England without dropping their bombs. Heroya was bombed by 167 planes and Trondheim by forty-one, among them the B-17s of the 100th Group. Of the entire force of planes attacking only one, from another group, was lost. Hit by flak over Heroya, the pilot managed to land in Sweden.

For the 100th, except for two planes lost over France early in the month, July was wonderfully free of incident until the twenty-fifth, when another B-17 went down over Warnemunde. The crews were acquiring experience and self-assurance.

Among these self-confident men was navigator Harry H. Crosby, then a First Lieutenant of Des Moines, Iowa. For his part in the Trondheim mission he received the Distinguished Flying Cross. Despite a brilliant mathematical turn of mind, the sensitive, even mercurial, Crosby was a romantic. He was, in fact, responsible for one of the strangest decisions ever made during the Second World War. On August 12, 1943, the 100th was dispatched to the Ruhr to bomb various military targets in that flak-laden industrial heartland.

"We were sent to bomb as our primary target an industrial section of some city in the Ruhr, I think, Gelsenkirchen," Crosby now remembers. "As we flew eastward with the entire Ruhr Valley on our left we could see that the Ruhr would be completely obscured and in those days before blind bombing (i.e. with the use of radar equipment), we had to have visual reference to the ground or we could not find our target.

"Instead of turning north to cross over the Ruhr, our formation turned right looking for a target we could see. In those days we were given a primary target, a secondary target, a tertiary target and a series of targets called targets of opportunity. As I remember some built-up installation in Bochum or Recklinghausen was our second and third targets, but they too were obscured by cloud cover. Therefore, our bombardier James R. Douglass began a run on Bonn, which was listed as a target of opportunity.

"It just happened that the night before, after I had been given a pre-briefing, I had returned to my quarters and was playing some records on what in England was called a gramophone . . . I had the complete *Third Symphony* (*Eroica*) and the complete *Fifth Symphony*. As I played the records I rather idly read the inscription on the inside cover of the album. I noticed without paying much attention that Beethoven had been born in and had gone to school in Bonn.

"On the next day, 25,000 feet in the air, when we started our run on Bonn, I looked down and saw a series of buildings which I presumed to be the University of Bonn. Instantly there flashed through my mind the thought, 'That must be where Beethoven went to school!'

"I grabbed Douglass by the shoulder and said we would not go to Bonn. Over the intercom someone asked me why not and, after giving the pilot a new heading, I explained that this was where Beethoven went to school.

"In those tense moments for some reason nobody objected and we made a run on a marshaling yard in Cologne which was listed as a target of opportunity. We were the lead ship in the whole Eighth Air Force that day and therefore the entire formation followed us . . ."

Five days later on August 14, 1943, the 100th flew to Regensburg on the first shuttle mission of the war. It was their contribution to the day's double attack on the Me-109 plant at Regensburg and the ball-bearing works at Schweinfurt. The lead ship was piloted by Captain Everett E. Blakely, with the team of Crosby and Douglass as navigator and bombardier, respectively. Major John B. Kidd flew with them to lead the 100th's planes. The 100th was in low position, tail-end charlie—the least desirable spot in any formation for it was a favorite attack point for German fighters.

Although fighter support by Thunderbolts was scheduled for the day, the men in the 100th Group, last in the fifteen-mile-long formation were not to see any. But they were to see plenty of Me-109s and FW-190s which attacked ferociously. Major Gale Cleven's squadron, in low position, was hardest hit, three B-17s went down almost at the time of the first attack, cutting his strength in half.

The hapless men in the 100th, desperately fighting back, watched the planes

Harry H. Crosby

in their group, burning and falling. Of the twenty-two 100th planes dispatched, nine were lost on the Regensburg mission, more than a third of all lost (twenty-four) that day on the strike.

It was the plane of Captain R. Knox that initiated the infamous legend of the "Bloody 100th." According to an Air Force observer flying with the 100th that day what occurred was this: Knox found himself in serious trouble after one of the fighter attacks. For a time his plane lagged with one engine out and, practically a stationary target, he became the focus of sustained fighter attacks. A second engine went out.

The wheels of the B-17, according to the observer, were lowered. This was the signal to the *Luftwaffe* that the plane had surrendered and, according to the Code of the Air, once this was done attacks upon the bomber would cease. To guide Knox toward a German airdrome a few fighters pulled alongside, forming a little cluster. Then for some reason, possibly because the engine trouble had cleared up, the gunners aboard the B-17 blasted the escorting German planes out of the sky. The wheels went up and the plane made a dash for home.

The 100th encounters flak over the target.

Within fifty seconds the maddened fighters tore the plane to pieces and it too went down.

After this flagrant violation of the Code of the Air, so the legend went, the 100th Bombardment Group was marked for extinction by the *Luftwaffe*. The Me-109s and FW-190s would ignore all other planes in the bomber formation, concentrating upon the 100th; it had become a personal grudge; the *Luftwaffe* against the Bloody 100th.

So it certainly seemed as the 100th Group and the other planes of the 8th Air Force fought on to bomb Regensburg with "impressive accuracy" according to official opinion. What remained of the 100th—thirteen of the original twenty—dropped when they saw Douglass in the lead plane drop his load of 250-pound incendiaries. Flak boomed and crackled around them and the bomb bays were quickly closed and they headed over the Alps for North Africa.

All was not well there when they arrived, those who were fortunate to make it. No real arrangements were made to house the air crews nor to service the planes. "Strangely enough," Crosby recalls, "my worst memories are not of the incessant beating that the 100th took; instead I remember an incident that happened while we were in North Africa. The mission was so fouled up with poor coordination between the 8th and 12th Air Forces that when we got to North Africa (at Berteaux and Telegerma), the only detachments that were there were a finance corps and some postal clerks. As a result, someone pumped 2780 gallons of kerosene into our B-17 wing tanks thinking it was high-test gasoline. We had to pump a hand apparatus for about fifty-six straight hours before we finally got the kerosene out of our tanks."

Such incidents convinced Colonel LeMay that the time had not yet come to establish a regular run of shuttle-missions between England and North African

Remnants of the 100th Group in North Africa after the Regensburg mission.

Lieutenant Owen D. Roane's plane on the Regensburg to Africa shuttle mission, the first such mission by the 8th Air Force. Roane was all of twenty years old at the time he was in command of Laden Maiden.

bases. Heavy bombers required facilities and ground crews to keep them operational. The fast moving war in North Africa made it impossible to establish permanent bases to explore the idea of the shuttle bombings.

Before they returned, the men of the 100th managed to get in some characteristic sightseeing and made some curious friends. One such new-found friend was responsible for a crisis when the 100th returned to Thorpe Abbotts. The tattered remnants of the once-large formation was settling down onto the field when the radio in the tower crackled. It was the worried voice of Lieutenant Owen D. Roane—"Cowboy" to practically everyone in the group, and one of the best pilots.

"Stand by," Cowboy radioed. "Stand by, I'm coming in with a frozen ass!"

Roane's B-17 the *Laden Maiden*, was met by ambulances when it touched down and came to a stop on the hardstand. Worried medics rushed to the plane where they met the frozen ass, "Mohammed," a quite cold (though he was wrapped in blankets) tiny African donkey.

There were additional crises, for Roane's wasn't the only plane to return with the little beasts aboard. When this news leaked out to be published in *Stars and Stripes*—London papers copying—it was found that the United States Army Air Forces had violated the "Importation of Dogs and Cats Order (1928)." This greatly upset H. M. Ministry of Agriculture and Fisheries which, with stout heart and printed order, went into action. The Office of the Ministry of Agriculture and Fisheries immediately applied for the location of those stations at which the African donkeys had stolen into the kingdom.

The Air Force, looking out for its own, refused to release the asked for locations, giving as a reason the fact that the addresses of said stations were "restricted." Tempers flared and it seemed an international incident almost erupted. It was reported by Sergeants Bud Hutton and Andy Rooney that "Gunners talked of getting their caliber .50s out of armament shops and defying the redcoats."

The incident eventually quieted, partly because requests from the Ministry were lost in the labyrinthine channels. The African donkey, like the American airmen, however, succumbed to the vagaries of English weather and in time the international incident was settled by the grim reaper.

The five missions after the one to Regensburg would not have added any details to the legend of the Bloody 100th; all were carried out without any losses. Four planes went down when the airfield at Beaumont le Roger was attacked on September 3. On the sixth, three planes were lost; on the fifteenth, one plane went down over Paris; the next day one more 100th B-17 was lost over Bordeaux. These were tragic personal losses, but not spectacular.

On the other hand, the airmanship displayed by young Lieutenant Sumner Reeder on the September 6 mission was spectacular. He was piloting the *Squawkin' Hawk II* on a raid on Stuttgart when four fighters attacked while the plane was on the bomb run. The nose of the Fortress blew open with the impact of 20-mm shells. Reeder's co-pilot, H. E. Edburn, was killed, the bombardier, P. Delao, and the navigator, R. Engel, were both seriously wounded. And the shell which had killed the co-pilot had also wounded Reeder himself. The oxygen system was practically out and one wing tank was punctured. The fighters turned, poised, and dived in for another attack.

Reeder dived his crippled Fortress into the comparative safety of the formation below him. The fighters followed. Though undoubtedly weakened by his

After the return from North Africa. The crew of Laden Maiden, *gather round "Mohammed," the celebrated "frozen ass." In the back row are R. Stroble, J. Jarvie, A. Hauge, P. Healey, C. Comb, R. Stuart. In front are C. Campbell, A. Stipe, D. Schmucker and O. Roane.*

Owen D. "Cowboy" Roane of Valley View, Texas.

Lieutenant Colonel Sam L. Barr, CO of the 349th Squadron and Major Sumner Reeder, who also commanded the same squadron for a time. After he returned to the U.S. on completing his tour of duty, Reeder was killed in a routine flight over the Gulf of Mexico.

wounds, Reeder flew with amazing skill and made it possible for the gunners to drive off the fighters. When this danger seemed past he decided to seek a lower level as the oxygen supply seemed dangerously low.

Almost as soon as they left the formation the fighters swarmed around the plane again. Reeder put the B-17 into a dive, aiming for some clouds for possible shelter from the fighters. In the clouds he had to dodge from one to another while the fighters attempted to get in more shots. This game of hide-and-seek went on for an hour; the fighters left eventually possibly because they were low on fuel.

Somehow, without the aid of navigation, Reeder found the English Channel. The dying co-pilot was removed from the cockpit and Reeder was joined by the wounded Engle who assisted him as much as he could.

Reeder set the *Squawkin' Hawk II* down on an RAF fighter base without brakes without so much as shaking up the wounded aboard. Reeder was awarded the Distinguished Service Cross for his remarkable performance on this mission. Although the plane barely remained airborne, he never once suggested that they bail out because of the seriousness of the injuries of Delao and Engel (who would not have survived a parachute drop). During the two hour battle Reeder not only piloted with consummate skill, but he also bolstered up the crew with occasional wisecracks over the intercom and snatches of songs.

Late in September the 100th lost the *Damdifino II* in an extraordinary manner. A mission had been scrubbed so it was decided it would be a good idea to send the Third Division out on a practice mission using Pathfinder (radar blind bombing) equipment. Lieutenant J. Gossage and his crew, finding their regular plane still loaded with bombs, switched to the *Damdifino II* for the practice run. All this plane's guns were stored in the nose.

As they approached the selected practice Target Area, Gossage was astonished to see the guns in the lead ship (he was in Number 2 position) firing at what should have been a friendly escort of P-47s. About a dozen German fighters flashed down upon the formation. Aboard the *Damdifino II* someone managed to get a nose gun in position, but the attackers darted by firing their cannons.

Chunks of the plane's fuselage flew off into the slipstream and one 20-mm shell tore through the right wing behind the No. 3 engine setting the oil tank ablaze. Not until they attempted to tighten up to the lead plane, piloted by Sammy Barr, were they aware of the engine fire. Barr frantically waved them away pointing to their right wing.

Gossage prepared to ditch the plane in the Channel, but then realized that the longer they remained aloft the better the chance of blowing up. He gave the order to bail out. Though they were losing altitude fast and the wing was blazing furiously, the bomb-bay doors were opened and nine men jumped. By the time his turn came, Gossage could see he was too low to jump so he stayed with the ship, setting it down in the water hoping that the spray would extinguish the fire. The ship would sink, of course, but at least he would not be blown to bits.

The fire had burned the control surfaces on the wing and flying was difficult; the B-17 came in nose first, buckling the front of the plane. Gossage, though wedged inside for a few moments, crawled out and waited for Air-Sea Rescue to pick him up. The men who had bailed out floated around for about an hour before the British ships arrived to retrieve them. Both co-pilot and navigator were dead when they were picked up; three others were missing. It had been a costly practice mission.

It was on October 8, 1943, that the 100th made the Bremen mission. "The prelude to this mission was normal," wrote Lieutenant Harry Crosby in his report to Colonel Harding. "There had been a couple of days of pre-briefing in which the pilot, navigator and bombardier made secret trips to air division headquarters. The general idea was that we, and many hundreds of other planes of heavy bombardment, were out to 'Hamburg' Bremen.

A ditched B-17. The dinghy holds some of the crew while they await the arrival of
the British Air-Sea Rescue ships.

Captain Everett E. Blakely, first
pilot of Just A Snappin' on the
mission to Bremen.

"The unusual thing on this trip was that we were to lead the Third Combat Wing. This meant additional strain and responsibility on the part of our crew but it was a load to which we were more or less accustomed after having been in this position a few times previously. Major John B. Kidd, who had done such a creditable job leading the 100th Group on the important Regensburg Raid, was the command pilot sharing the piloting duties with Captain E. E. Blakely, now squadron commander of the 418th Squadron. Our co-pilot, Lieutenant Charles A. Via, rode in the position of tail gunner serving the vital function of formation control officer. Staff Sergeant Lyle E. Nord acted as radio gunner and assistant to Technical Sergeant Edmond C. Forkner.

"Briefing, take-off and assembly of the group were as usual except that the group formed in the record time of eighteen minutes. The group climbed to 9000 feet and passed over Buncher Eight [a navigational aid, a reference point for navigators], at Framlingham, about forty seconds behind the briefed time of 1246. However, the 100th Group, in the lead position, was joined by the 390th and the 95th without difficulty. The Thirteenth Combat Wing passed over Spalding in excellent defensive formation at the exact time as briefed, 1312. By essing slightly, our combat wing fell into position as the Third Combat Wing as scheduled. At 1329 the Fourth Air Division, in unquestionably the best formation flown during my experience, passed over the English Coast nine miles north of Splasher Beacon Number Four.

"The course flown was nearly as briefed but a few minutes were lost due to slight discrepancies in turns and metro data. The journey over water was made unnecessarily hazardous due to the fact that planes which aborted instead of clearing the formation persisted in attempting to fly through our combat wing formation. On one occasion an entire six ship squadron in good formation flew between the 100th and 390th Groups. Six minutes later a flight in equally good formation threaded itself through our formation. Two minutes later a single ship with what appeared to be a 'T' marking on the tail, repeated the process.

"At 1441½ our combat wing started the turn onto land near the island of Borkonny. At this time we had twenty-one ships in our group formation and our other two groups were in total or nearly complete strength. We crossed the coast at 1456 on course. Although a slight haze and a two-tenths undercast of low stratus were present, it was possible to determine our exact position by pilotage [visually]. Reception on GEE Navigational Equipment [radio] failed upon crossing the coast due partially to jamming and lack of strength on transmission of the A marker. We approached Groningen on course and turned toward the Initial Point two miles to the left of course in an effort to clear the combat wing ahead of us.

"On the approach to the I.P. it was observed that Emden, apparently remembering the two previous trips [September 27, October 2] of the Eighth Air Force to that area, had sent up a dense smoke screen. Also it was noted by several members of the crew that FW-190s, instead of devoting all their efforts on the Fortresses, in a few cases turned on our escort, long range P-47s, and engaged them in combat. The escort apparently was ahead of us defending the lead combat wing of the air division.

"The I.P. was reached at 1521 . . .

"Earlier in this narrative I have classed this mission as 'usual.' From this point on that classification no longer holds true.

186

Third Division B-17s over Bremen on October 8, 1943. The Germans attempt to obscure the railroad yards with smokescreen. These planes are from the 388th Group, 45th Combat Wing which frequently joined the 100th Group on missions.

"By now much of the ground haze had cleared away. My calculations had been proving accurate in my dead reckoning. But all these opportunities to check my navigation were unnecessary. Everyone on the crew knew that the intense black cloud ahead of us marked the vicinity of our target, the town of Bremen. I have been exposed to flak before and haven't been particularly perturbed by its presence. I remember that in all of those instances each little burst of 'Flieger-abwehr-kanonen' was a distinct mean-looking little black ball. But now, over Bremen, each little ball had lost its individuality and the whole thing was blended into a huge angry cloud.

"Too late I realized that our combat wing had been briefed to fly at an

187

altitude too similar to that of the previous wing, for we sailed right into the midst of that cloud. I could just visualize the gunners on the ground checking back on their computations and sending up volleys using the same data . . . At any rate, two minutes before we hit the target our plane was hit by the first burst of flak. Our ball turret operator, Staff Sergeant William F. McClelland, announced in a calm voice that his turret had been struck, but not pierced, by a flak burst. From that time his turret operated in a jerky fashion.

"Thirty seconds before the bombs were dropped a burst of flak hit our nose compartment shattering the window to the right of the bombardier's head. One fragment struck the bombardier Lieutenant James R. Douglass, in the left side. It tore through his clothing and ripped the cloth of his flak suit but did not touch his skin. Despite this distraction, and I am certain that Lieutenant Douglass thought he had been injured by the expression on his face, he continued the manipulation of his bomb sight and bombs were away at 1525. Even accepting the fact that we had been hit by flak, annoyed by fighters, and had been searching for a target obscured by the typical smoke screen, our own and PRU [Photographic Reconnaissance Unit] photographs show that his bombs were dropped accurately and destructively.

"A mere matter of seconds later our Number Four engine was destroyed by flak, the control wires were shattered and the left elevator was ripped to shreds, plunging our plane into a sort of spinning dive, completely out of control . . .

"We were plunging down in a helpless, careening dive. Flames were blazing from our Number Four Engine. Our control surfaces were all cut and torn. (I might add, parenthetically, that the 95th Group reported later that we were seen to fall into a flat spin, on fire, and that three parachutes were observed to open from our plane.)

"The normal reaction on the part of our pilots should have been to think of their own personal safety, or in cases of extreme nobility of character perhaps they would have been thinking about the other members of the crew. But they did not, even in this crisis, forget for one minute that they were the leaders of a great formation. Their first thought was of the crews behind them. In unison, as we fell into our dive, the words came over the interphone to our tail gunner, 'Signal the deputy leader to take over.'

"I can't help but think that as they fought for their lives they might have been excused for being too busy to think of their command, but such was not the case.

"By this signaling the remainder of the formation was notified immediately that we had been hit and were aborting. This act would have prevented any planes being pulled even a few feet out of position into danger from the enemy aircraft buzzing about. (It was the misfortune of the 100th Bomb Group that the deputy leader was destroyed at this time and so many of the flight leaders likewise, that the group was left to do its best by tacking onto the 390th Group.)

"Back in the radio compartment our young radio operator knew what was going on. He knew he was in imminent danger of his life. But he also had a duty to do. Consequently he still remained at his position and radioed in to Wing Headquarters that 'The target was bombed at 1525.'

"For 3000 feet Captain Blakely and Major Kidd fought to get that plane under control. It was only because of the superior construction of our bomber, and its perfect maintenance, plus the combination of two skilled pilots, that we

Just A Snappin', *the Fortress in which Blakely, Kidd, and Crosby went to Bremen and back. The plane never flew again.*

ever even recovered from that dive . . . If I were an expert on stress and strain analysis, or a mechanic, or even a pilot, I would dwell at length on the manner in which the plane was restored to normal flying attitude. As it is, the procedure defies my description. But I am certain it was a very great accomplishment."

Pilot Everett Blakely's description was a simple comment, "You can lose altitude awfully fast when one engine goes sour and your controls are chewed to ribbons. We dropped for 3000 feet before Major Kidd and I could regain control . . . Most of the crew not strapped to their seats were thrown to the floor, shaken severely—but at last the ground was once more back where it ought to be, instead of standing up on one ear. Once more we were in level flight and, at least temporarily, safe."

Crosby's narrative report continued: "At 19,000 feet we were . . . able to look out the windows (and) were temporarily assured to note that the ground was now in the right place. A hurried consultation was held over interphone to determine a plan for fighting our way back to England.

"The following facts had to be considered: We had lost all communication back of the top turret, so it was impossible to determine the extent of injury and damage. Our control wires were fraying as far back as the top turret operator could see. At least two of the crew had reported being hit immediately after we left the target. One engine was in such bad condition that bits and finally all of the cowling were blasted off. We were losing altitude so rapidly probably because of the condition of the elevator that any but the shortest way back was beyond contemplation . . . So we headed across the face of Germany for home.

"From this point till we crossed the coast at 1635 this narrative is necessarily lacking in details. I wish that I could have been in on the interphone communications which passed between the members in the rear of our ship. For one thing, I could have known the exact times at which we were subjected to tail attacks, and known the exact circumstances under which our gunners destroyed twelve for sure and scored a possible and another enemy aircraft as the Luftwaffe continued its usual policy of singling out a lone aircraft and concentrating all attacks upon it.

"As it was, my lack of information and the fact that I was so busy getting us back in the direction for home, didn't click with the information of our intelligence service and their *RADAR* control so we received credit for only the destruction of seven planes. But every member of the crew is positive of twelve.

189

"We've always known we have a good crew. Away back in 1942 when the 100th Bomb Group was first formed, the first crew which served as the nucleus of the group was Lieutenant Blakely's crew. It had been formed from selected material from three first phase schools. This condition caused the crew to suffer from the stigma of being called the 'model crew.' They held several engineering records such as flight for endurance and maximum performance which lasted for seventeen hours which drew them commendations from a general in the Second Air Force. I personally am a recent addition to the crew, necessitated when their regular navigator was made group navigator. But with all of this, aside from being regular guys, and devoted to duty, and good at it, our gunners waited till that day to not only prove themselves but also to illustrate just how vitally important it is that all crew members must be tops at their jobs when *that* time comes.

"As we ploughed across Germany with Captain Blakely and Major Kidd carefully nursing the loss of each precious foot of altitude and flying at 120 miles an hour, we were subjected to the threat of innumerable attacks from enemy fighters. I will say that there were other straggling Fortresses who received a lot harsher treatment than we did that day. And I will venture a reason for this fact.

"Ahead of us a lone B-17 was limping along. A flight of three Messerschmitts were harassing it, darting in and out but not attacking it. Finally all three swooped in and fired for a long time at the bomber. The bomber didn't go down but neither did any of the fighters. And those three small planes kept attacking that plane receiving no damage to themselves till finally the B-17 caught on fire. It was with a helpless feeling that we saw our last ally turn over, spin slightly and then burst into a huge ball of flame.

"Now the victorious Germans turned to us. And now comes the reason that we were able to return. From that point on, there wasn't one single attack upon us that at least one enemy fighter wasn't destroyed. I believe that Technical Sergeant Monroe B. Thornton got the first one.

"On this attack which came slightly from the right, Sergeant Thornton started firing when the fighter was about 800 yards away. At about 300 yards the effect of his firing began to show and the propeller fell off. Lieutenant Douglass and I both saw the pilot jump. Thornton got a couple of others too. One of them was an Me-110. It came at us high and from the right side. Another plane was flying with it in a stacked, slightly echeloned, position. Thorny says that it was firing at us before he was able to get his sights on either of them. The right engine of the fighter caught on fire and pieces flew off the left engine or wing. Our left waist gunner saw two occupants bail out and both chutes open. His [Thornton's] third came very near to the Holland border.

"Lieutenant Douglass got one. It was a JU-88 that flipped around a long time before it came in on us. It came into about 300 yards and ended up in a vertical bank with its belly toward us. I saw almost the whole tail assembly shatter off before it fell into a spin. Smoke was pouring from its rear as it went down.

"Three minutes later another JU-88 came at us from ten o'clock. I was positive that my shots were hitting the plane at its exposed belly but the plane did not go down. It made no more attacks.

"Back in the tail, waist and radio compartments, our gunners were paying a heavier price for their planes. About the time that we went over the target Lieutenant Via had reported that he was hit. We didn't know whether he meant his compartment or himself. That hit was a serious flesh wound in his right leg. But this didn't stop his shooting. As nearly as we can tell from his and the waist gunner's reports he destroyed his first for that day soon after Thornton hit his number one.

"Two Me-210s came in together after hovering for some time at 1000 yards. Lieutenant Via picked out the second one and the left waist gunner and the radio gunner say it disintegrated in midair. His second claim was the partner of one that our top turret gunner destroyed. Thornton saw it blow up nearly five hundred yards out.

"Credit must be given to Lieutenant Via's shooting but when another fact is considered, his performance can be called truly heroic. In between his first and second planes, Lieutenant Via had had a projectile pass from the fat of his hip through his pelvis, severing his sciatic nerve, opening several blood vessels and passing on out his hip. Yet, even with this horrible injury, Lieutenant Via stuck to his position and didn't come out till we had crossed the enemy coast.

"I hope that mentioning them in any certain order won't detract from the heroism of any of the gunners. Staff Sergeant Lyle E. Nord was pretty busy scratching flak fragments out of his face, head, neck and clothing, but he still managed to bring down a fighter from a difficult position. Two Me-210s came in stacked up from about 600 yards out. Nord took one of them and our left waist gunner the other. The plane side-slipped to the right, then blew up. Pieces of the fighter splattered against our plane.

"I've saved the waist gunners till now. They each got two, but the price was infinitely great. Staff Sergeant Edward S. Yevich has a double compound fracture in his forearm and a deep gash in his leg. Staff Sergeant Lester W. Saunders fought a gallant fight against death but succumbed in a hospital bed one week after our return.

"Yevich had been seared across the back by flak fragments at the target so he had a grudge against the first fighter who approached from the left side. He got it going away and two members of the crew saw it explode in midair.

"Saunders, at the other waist window, had already knocked his first fighter down too. (It was an Me-210.) Almost immediately after Yevich's first went down, a 20-millimeter shell tore through the left waist window into the pit of Sergeant Saunders' stomach and hurled him back against the other side of the plane. I believe it was the same shell which hit Yevich's gun and ricocheted into his arm. Yet in this gravely wounded condition, both of these gunners actually retained their positions and each one of them knocked out another fighter.

"After his first remark, we hadn't heard much from Staff Sergeant William F. McClelland. It wasn't till shortly before our crash landing that I learned why. He had destroyed two aircraft with his damaged turret before he himself was hit. The first flak that hit him tore deep into his scalp. But he kept at his position. Later another burst, or perhaps an exploding 20-millimeter scraped his face and made shreds of his oxygen mask, headset and clothing. Some place along the line he received an injection of flak in his leg. When the last volley rendered his turret useless—the door was blown clear off—he climbed out into the radio compartment. As we crossed the Dutch coast another burst of flak hit the flak suit on which he was lying and threw him into a bloody heap.

"All this time the pilots had been pretty busy piloting and I was occupied with navigating. The terrain was distinctive so it wasn't hard staying on the course we had selected. I did try to use the GEE box and I am positive I would have had a fix at 8000 feet over the German-Holland border, but some sort of projectile came through the floor and shattered the cathode tube. The radio, along with most of the electrical equipment, was long since non-functional.

"We crossed Germany and Holland on a line thirty miles north of Lingein, Ommen, and Zwolle. We evaded all known flak areas and large towns. I remember a feeling of futility I experienced when explosions burst in and around our compartment. I was so certain that I was safe from flak area, yet here it was all around us. I yelled out over the interphone for someone to tell me where the flak was coming from. The bombardier told me that those explosions were 20-millimeter shells. I didn't feel any better . . .

"I remember another instance when the bombardier turned around and looked at me. Two holes appeared on each side of the compartment and cotton batting sifted down as a bullet went between us. I don't remember his looking back at me again.

"Finally at 1620 we hit the Zuider Zee. We realized our predicament was still acute but just the same that water looked good to all of us. To avoid known fighter fields we turned to a course of 340 degrees to cross over the West Frisian Islands. I was uncomfortably aware that a few weeks ago a big formation on a practice mission was attacked by enemy fighters at precisely that point.

"I hadn't even considered the coastal batteries. At our usual altitude they didn't bother us at all. But at 7000 feet, flying at 120 miles per hour even pop-guns would have been a menace.

"They threw everything at us. Whole acres of some sort of light guns flashed up at our ship. Tracers from machine guns laced all around us. In credit to their gunnery we can say that we were hit plenty. Our number three engine, revolving feebly at least, now was non-existent. The whole situation was a series of cracking noises much like the closing of a book as volley after volley hit their target. Captain Blakely and Major Kidd were risking everything in some last evasive action. One of them would see flak on one side and jerk the plane on one heading. The other would spot some on his side and back we would go. Their efforts were effective, though, because we got through their last defense.

"We had survived everything that the Germans could send up at us but there was still one thing to consider—gravity. Crossing the coast had cost plenty and we were now at 3990 feet and sinking rapidly. Major Kidd asked for a heading to the closest part of England and I gave it to him.

"My ETA (Estimated Time of Arrival) ran out and then some. As I checked back over my figures I glanced at my airspeed indicator and thought it looked suspiciously immobile. I rapped on it with my fist and the needle dropped to zero. It was then that I learned from a consultation with the pilot that we were making only 120 miles an hour instead of 150 as I had believed. I hurriedly redid my calculations and gave a correction in our heading. But I knew we were a long way from home.

"Ditching seemed the next answer. Lt. Douglass went back to make the

192

preparations. Two minutes later he was back with the news that we couldn't ditch, that our crew members were in too bad a condition to endure the movements ditching would cause. Moreover, our dinghy compartment was in shreds and at least one of them was in ribbons. That was the first that we in the front had learned of the severity of the situation back in the rear of the plane.

"Our next out was to lighten the load of the plane. We threw everything away. Our guns went first and the ammunition with them. I threw away my flying equipment, my GEE box, my radio, anything with even an ounce of weight. Now comes an amazing fact: Although our airspeed still remained at 115–120 miles per hour, a very small number of miles above the stalling speed of our plane, Captain Blakely not only managed to keep the plane level but actually gained three hundred feet of altitude.

"England seemed so far away. The ship was listing in such an attitude that our floating aperiodic compasses stuck on the side. I figured the sun should hit the plexiglass front of the plane and called the pilot to correct him every time he went someplace else.

"We hit England at 52°47′ N.; 01°37′ E. By now our gas problem was serious. The very first airport sighted, at Ludham, seemed large enough and occupied, so we prepared for a crash landing.

"Most of us ganged up in the radio compartment. Sergeant Saunders walked unaided to the radio compartment and smiled at us as we bustled about. I

Return from Bremen: Old 393 after crash-landing on an unoccupied RAF base.

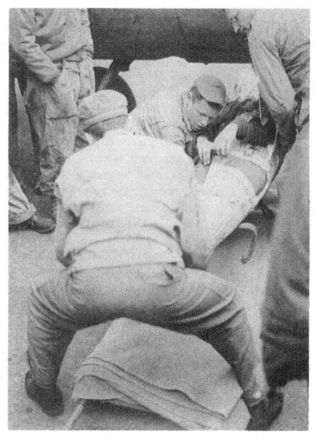

Removing the wounded from "Old 393."

193

Walking away from headquarters of the 100th Bomb Group: Robert Rosenthal, Saul Levitt, ex-radio operator of the 100th turned writer for Yank *and Harry H. Crosby.*

didn't dream how seriously he was injured because he kept cheering us up with his motions [thumbs up and thumb and forefinger circled]. When he noticed in his dazed condition that excitement was about, he thought we were again being attacked so he tried to crawl to his turret to help ward off the fighters he thought were present. It was almost impossible to stop him.

"I do not intend to omit the conduct of Technical Sergeant Edmund G. Forkner. He has always seemed young and perhaps excitable but he was all there on this trip. He had completely stopped the flow of blood from all wounds, he had disinfected all injuries. He had calmed his patients with morphine. He had them all covered with blankets to lessen the shock of the approaching landing and the mental shock of their pain. He had encouraged them all during the crossing. Moreover, even though his key had been shot away he still managed to send out distress signals by pounding his finger on his throat mike! [Actually, Forkner sent messages by touching two exposed wires of the smashed radio.]

"Thornton cradled Lieutenant Via with his body in the waist, since the latter's condition prevented his being moved. The rest of us cushioned ourselves as best we could for a landing we knew was going to be rough." Only ten gallons of fuel remained and the tail wheel would not go down.

Pilot Blakely tells the story of the landing: "The ship touched the ground. Instantly the cables operating the brakes snapped. The elevator was useless. The plane wouldn't taxi, wouldn't steer. With the terrific momentum you get even at 100 mph we plowed down that vacant airport toward a huge tree. And no power on earth could stop us.

"The tree crashed us between No. 2 engine and the pilot's compartment. That was lucky because another three inches to the right and it would have

194

crushed the pilot and copilot. We had slowed down to maybe fifty mph by then. The force behind our smash swung the ship savagely around to the left in a half circle.

"The nose compartment was completely destroyed. The plane was a wreck, scrap metal only. The salvage crew counted 700 holes from the rear to the cabin alone! They counted up to 800 and then got tired of counting."

"But we were on the ground," Crosby continued in his narrative to Colonel Harding. "Even the triumph of this was negated when we learned we had picked an unused field. The planes we had seen on the perimeters were dummies. And medical aid was still two hours away.

"We did everything we could. Aid was summoned immediately. The rockets we had fired had been seen from Coltishall so it wasn't long before some RAF medical officers arrived. We are extremely grateful to Flight Lieutenant Nolan of the Coltishall RAF Base for his medical care. Two ambulances arrived and our four wounded men, all busily engaged in cheering each other up were loaded into them and soon were under expert medical care at the Norwich and Norfolk General Hospital."

In writing of this mission to his wife, Crosby—although leaving out certain details—closed the letter with a characteristic gesture.

"But now we are on the ground," he wrote to his young wife. "Via has a very bad injury in his hip which will take months to cure. Staff Sergeant Lester Saunders has a cannon hole clear through his stomach which goes out his back. Staff Sergeant Edward Yevich has a compound fracture of his left arm and numerous small injuries. Staff Sergeant Mac McClelland is suffering from shock and a bad wound. Be sure to write them all [Crosby was not aware of Saunder's fatal wound yet] at our same address. Mention how grateful we are for their gunnery . . . And, Jean, there are just two reasons that I am here today. One of them is because of Blake's superb piloting and the other because of the skill of our gunners . . . They came through when they were really needed . . . Also I wish you would send Charlie Via a book of crossword puzzles."

The Bremen mission was over. Of the thirty 8th Air Force losses of that day, seven had been 100th Group planes. Among them was that of Bucky Cleven, one of the 100th's Iron Men, whom no one believed would ever go down. It had been rough, but there was nothing about it that would justify the 100th's reputation as the "Bloody 100th"; in fact, practically two months had transpired since the so-called Knox Incident on the Regensburg strike.

And then came Münster.

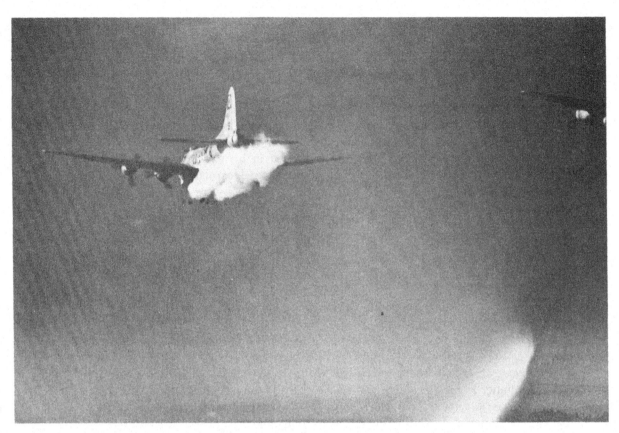

The 100th Bombardment Group (H) on target. This photograph was taken at the instant that the lead plane released the smoke markers over the target.

13. "Rosie's Riveters"

Robert Rosenthal, graduate of Brooklyn Law School, had not yet begun to practice law although he was working in a law firm, when he enlisted in the U. S. Army. The date of his enlistment was December 8, 1941—he was twenty-five years old. He had never piloted an airplane before in his life and had never thought about it. But according to the curious workings of the Army classification system, he was informed that he had all the qualifications of a good pilot, particularly of a heavy bomber.

By the first of January 1942, Rosenthal had reported in to Maxwell Field, Alabama, for preflight training which lasted for nine weeks. He then graduated to primary training and was actually flying by the end of the first week. When the course was finished he had logged sixty-five hours in the air, and many more hours in classrooms on all the phases of flying, aerobatics, map reading, and an introduction to instrument flying in the Link Trainer. He had "staged" from preflight to primary training. The next step was basic flying school where it was finally determined whether or not the cadet will go on to advanced training. In the case of Robert Rosenthal, the heavy bomber classification proved correct and he went into advanced training flying twin-engined planes.

196

Harry Crosby, Robert Rosenthal, and Woodrow McGill parking their vehicles near the Officers' Club. "Rosie" had learned to operate a bicycle by this time.

On completion of this training, he went on to Hendricks Field, near Sebring, Florida, for Pilot Transition Training on the B-17. Here Rosenthal would be carefully observed to see if he had those qualifications necessary to be an "airplane commander." He not only had to prove his flying ability but also his familiarity with all of the Pilot's Information File. This was a vast collection of technical information, Do's and Don'ts, and other materials which would have to impress the candidate of the responsibilities of command: he would be accountable for nine lives besides his own and an aircraft which cost well over a quarter of a million dollars.

Rosenthal had not trained with the 100th, but happened to be in England by August 1943 and was sent to the Group's 418th Squadron as one of the replacements following the heavy losses on the Regensburg mission. Major J. C. Egan was then commanding officer of the 418th and, after watching Rosenthal handle a B-17, commented, "I think this boy Rosenthal is quite a flier."

But he was not very good at maneuvering a spindly British bicycle. As "airplane commander," Rosenthal was issued along with a good deal of other matériel, a bicycle for getting around the wide vistas of Thorpe Abbotts. He found himself heavily burdened by all this issue but somehow managed to get himself upon the cycle. He carried a load of gear in one arm, had draped his life preserver around his neck, and set off in the general direction of his quarters.

Rosenthal managed to do pretty well, for he got some distance away from the supply hut and was pedaling his uncertain way along a little dirt road. A shift in the load contributed to a series of unusual course changes which came to a sudden, damp conclusion as Rosenthal, newly issued supplies and bicycle plunged down an embankment into one of those charming little ditches that run along the picturesque rural English roads.

Lying in the water (which was not deep), Lieutenant Rosenthal felt there was only one thing to do in this emergency as he lay there, face up in the

197

ditch: he inflated his Mae West. This was probably the only time during all of the Second World War that a member of the 8th Air Force was thus saved from British waters.

Rosenthal's first combat mission was the harrowing one to Bremen on which "Bucky" Cleven was shot down and from which Blakely returned with a badly shot up B-17. The next day the 8th Air Force went to Marienburg, on the longest mission flown up to that time, to place the bombs with remarkable precision on the Focke-Wulf assembly plant. The 8th lost twenty-eight planes that day, none of them from the 100th Group.

Robert Rosenthal's third combat mission, one per day for three days running, was to Münster. It was this ill-fated mission that made the reputation of the "Bloody 100th."

To avenge the loss of his friend Gale Cleven over Bremen, Major John—also nicknamed "Bucky"—Egan insisted that he lead the mission. When told that "Bucky" Cleven had gone down, Egan's reply was characteristic: "I'm browned off more than somewhat and will bring a load not of what Farmer Gray hauled away and dump it all over those Germans!

"The mission had not been set up for me to kill the hated Hun," Egan admitted, "but as a last resort to stop rail transportation in the Ruhr Valley. Practically all of the rail workers in the valley were being billeted in Münster. It was decided that a pursuit and fighter-bomber attack could not effectively stop up Ruhr Valley. A good big bomber raid could really mess up the very efficient German rail system by messing up its personnel."

Rosenthal had no personal grudge to make the Münster mission something special. Bremen had been very bad, Marienburg had been exhausting—but he had one thought in mind and that was to do what he could to end the war. At twenty-five he was a little older than many of the other pilots, more mature, less given over to high jinks (such as riding bicycles around inside the Officers' Club), and more quietly reflective. Unlike many who had become involved in the war, Rosenthal knew why the United States was in it. His family was safe back in Brooklyn but, as he tried to explain to a fellow officer, "We have the opportunity and ability to stand up for the things in which we believe; we can help those people—captive in Germany and in occupied countries—who can't speak and act for themselves. A human being must look out for other human beings or else there's no civilization. We are morally obligated to fight."

Thirteen planes from the 100th Group took off for Münster; only one, *Rosie's Riveters*, returned.

Those who awaited the return of the B-17s from Münster were shocked to see one lone Fortress, battered, full of holes and with only two engines. As *Rosie's Riveters* sputtered down to a perfect landing an appalling realization quickly spread through the base—the 100th Group had practically been wiped out.

And, except for *Rosie's Riveters*, not one of the 100th planes had succeeded even in reaching the target. They were attacked just as the formations were approaching the IP, just about the time when the P-47s had to turn around. Without fighter escort the Fortresses were now open to attack.

One combat report, as it came in over the Third Division teletype read: "The most vilent [sic] and concentrated attack yet made on this division by

198

L. F. Darling, M. V. Bocuzzi, J. F. Mack, C. C. Hall, W. J. DeBlasio, R. H. Robinson, R. C. Bailey, R. Rosenthal, C. J. Milburn, W. T. Lewis.

Major John "Bucky" Egan, 418th Squadron and Major Gale "Bucky" W. Cleven, 350th Squadron. Two of the 100th's most colorful figures, both men were shot down, the former on the Münster mission and the latter over Bremen. They then spent much of the war as guests of the German government.

199

E/A [Enemy Aircraft] was encountered. E/A engaged totaled between 200–250 planes, mostly Fw 190s, Me 109s, Ju 88s, Me 210 and Me 110s . . . The fighters appeared to stay out of range. Me 110 firing at formation with long-range guns slung under each wing and lob[b]ing explosive cannonshells from 200–1500 yards. Ju 88s attacked from 800–1000 yards firing rockets from under each wing (two distinct puffs were seen from each ship) . . . A new feature was the appearance of enemy bombers flying parallel to our formation at 1500 yards firing rocket guns. Heavy AA fire was intense, accurat[e] and damaging . . . it was continuous through the target area . . ."

Among the first to go was the Fortress in which "Bucky" Egan led the 100th. "Just as we approached the IP, I called out to the group that our high cover was leaving, watched them go, looked straight ahead and said: 'Jesus Christ! Pursuits at twelve o'clock. Looks like they're on us!'

"This whole thing was disastrous more than somewhat . . . As for our ship, it was obvious that we'd had it. [The pilot, J. D.] Brady and I pulled off our oxygen masks to say simultaneously . . . Number Two has quit . . . There goes One . . . and there goes Three. Number Four proceeded to run away. Dave Solomon came up from the nose looking quite messy to tell us that we have to leave the formation because Hambone Hamilton had numerous holes in him and wanted to go home. I assured him that we had left the formation."

One by one the men in the distressed plane jumped. As he floated down Egan became the target of three FW-190s firing at him, helpless in his parachute. "They came in, and do you know what?—they started shooting at Mrs. Egan's little boy Johnnie, who told himself that this was a situation he couldn't talk himself out of. My chute was now full of holes, and so was Mrs. Egan's little boy.

"They came back for another pass at me, and I took a very dim view of the whole thing. They finally left, probably thinking that I am very dead, not knowing that I'm Irish."

Though wounded by the fighter attacks, Egan managed to land without further injury and escaped capture for a while. He was eventually to catch up not only with "Bucky" Cleven in a German prison camp, but also had a no doubt touching reunion with the first commander of the 100th Group, the deposed Colonel Alkire. There is no doubting the fact that having the two "Buckies" on their hands complicated the war for the hapless Germans. Cleven, in fact, eventually escaped and returned to Thorpe Abbotts.

Over Münster Rosenthal completed his bomb run; his two engines were already out, both waist gunners were wounded, one seriously. The interphones were out and the oxygen system was shot up; a rocket had gone through the right wing, ripping a large ragged hole in the skin. The flak was heavy as the plane dropped its bombs.

"After the drop," Rosenthal related, "the fighters began queueing up; they seemed to be coming in hordes. I had the plane all over the sky: chandelles, lazy Esses, every manner of violent evasive action. The fighters eventually became discouraged and left and, losing altitude, I headed home."

The lone plane returned to the base, firing the flares which signaled wounded aboard and Rosenthal brought it down as gently as possible. As the shaken men tumbled out of *Rosie's Riveters,* one gunner shouted, "I'm through flying

200

in these things. That's enough!" Rosenthal rode away in the ambulance accompanying his wounded gunners to the hospital. It came to him then that it would be a deadly war; the two earlier missions had been relatively simple.

In his diary, tail gunner William J. DeBlasio summarized the depleted emotions of the crew: "By the grace of God we were the only ship to come back. Our pilot brought us home safely."

The word spread through Station 136, to the other bases and through the heavy bomber units of the 8th Air Force. The *Luftwaffe* had got the 100th Group. The facts grew, as they did in those times, into rumors and the Legend of the Bloody 100th burgeoned. The gap in time from the supposed "Knox Incident" and the disaster over Münster was completely disregarded.

There was no doubt about one tragic fact: the equivalent of an entire squadron had been erased from the group's roll. The *Luftwaffe* that day had introduced a new technique—and it was having the desired effect—of concentrating upon a single group in its attacks. If they were fortunate enough in knocking down enough planes the effect upon morale would be devastating. The absence of 120 men would be noted; one-quarter of the 100th Group's airmen were gone. No doubt about it, as far as the rumor factory was concerned, the *Luftwaffe* was out to get the 100th.

One other factor no one seems to have noted at the time, or since, was that on October 14, the date of the dread "Black Thursday" Schweinfurt mission, the 100th did not lose a single plane. Coming only four days after Münster, it was impossible, of course, to put up a large force, but the 100th scraped up eight planes and crews which were led to Schweinfurt by "Cowboy" Roane. If the *Luftwaffe* harbored a personal grudge against the men of the 100th, it certainly suspended it on the one day when logic would dictate it should have been much in force.

But the folk tale had begun its diffusion, accumulating details as it spread throughout England. One of its most important centers was Stalag Luft I, the German prison camp for airmen near Barth, Germany. It seems to have reached every possible corner where two airmen happened to meet. Only the *Luftwaffe* seems to have been unaware of their personal war against the 100th Group.

The legendary "Rosie" had achieved his own folk quality. When he appeared at 3rd Division Headquarters to report upon the Münster raid, his brief description of what he and his crew had done elicited what amounted to effusive and high praise from General LeMay: "Good job."

On the day of the Regensburg-Schweinfurt mission there arrived in England a man who was to affect the fortunes of the 100th Bomb Group a good deal, Major John M. Bennett, Jr. A Texan—non-Texans, Bennett believed, were "almost foreigners in the 8th Air Force"—with a long tradition of military service behind him. In later years, Marvin Bowman who was the S-2 for the 100th, recalled Bennett as "about the coolest and meticulous operator you ever heard of."

He was an old friend of Neil Harding and proceeded to look him up as soon as he had settled at 3rd Division Headquarters. Harding, having only recently lost two top squadron commanders, Cleven and Egan, needed a replacement so, as Bennett put it, "I inherited the 349th."

Bennett was the complete officer—a gentleman, scholarly, but thoroughly un-

Strike photo: Schweinfurt, October 14, 1943. On this mission the "Bloody 100th" lost no planes although sixty 8th Air Force planes were shot down.

deceived by the facts of war. His decisions were hard, objective, and final. On his first combat mission Bennett went to "Happy Valley," the Ruhr, with the 100th. In his letters home Bennett was to reveal some of the emotions he rarely permitted others to know.

"After the intelligence officer [Marvin Bowman] finished, the operations officer, Lieutenant Colonel Jack Kidd, gave us the time for take-off and instructions for group, wing and division assemblies. He also went over our route into the target and out again, explaining where we would meet our fighter escort for invasion and withdrawal. Next the weather officer gave us complete

202

data on clouds, direction of winds at various altitudes and temperatures. This was followed by the communications officer who gave us the various frequencies and channels to be used on the radio: group frequency, wing frequency, division channel, fighter to bomber channels for air-sea rescue, and many others. You really need a blonde switch-board operator in a Fortress . . ."

The trip into "Happy Valley" was not uneventful and pilot Ollen Turner was obliged to bring *Skipper* home without No. 2 engine which had been knocked out over the Ruhr.

"Let's get the hell out of here," Turner shouted after their bombs had dropped and turned the plane for England. They watched eight parachutes blossom out of one of their Fortresses, one of its engines burning fiercely. By diving, the pilot extinguished the fire and returned without his crew. Four later returned to England.

"We are now out of the Ruhr," Bennett wrote to his father. "I have flown through 'the valley of the shadow of death.' The 23rd Psalm notwithstanding, I feared plenty of evil. Maybe I should go to church more often."

On November 16, 1943, Bennett was in command of a large force sent by the 8th Air Force to bomb an electrolysis plant in Rjukan, Norway, which the Germans were using to manufacture high explosives.

"Because of the short days in late November and the long distance of the mission," Bennett wrote, "we had to take off before daylight and climb through low hanging clouds at 400 feet and assemble on top. This is always a bit nerve-wracking as each plane carried six 1000 pound high explosive bombs and full over-load of gasoline (2800 gallons). This means that the airplane has a gross weight of approximately 65,000 pounds, which is well above its originally designed maximum of 52,000 pounds. Even in broad daylight with perfect weather I would be nervous with this load.

"The success of our take-off and climb through the overcast was due to no skill of my own, but to Lieutenant Owen D. (Cowboy) Roane from Valley View, Texas."

After assembling the group, Bennett led them to 14,000 feet and out over the North Sea for Norway. As had been hoped, the trip across the North Sea was uneventful and no German fighters were encountered. The mission was so planned that the American bombers would arrive over the Norwegian factory during lunch hour (between 11:30 and noon). It was hoped thus to keep the number of Norwegian casualties down to a minimum. But because of the smoothness with which the operation had proceeded, the 100th Group arrived over the target eighteen minutes early.

Bennett ordered the formation to swing out over the North Sea, where he led them in a large circle for about fifteen minutes. This concern for the lives of noncombatant neutrals, even if they were actually working for the Nazi war effort, was typical of all 8th Air Force missions over occupied territories. But it also gave the Germans plenty of time in which to alert whatever fighters were in the area and to prepare their antiaircraft guns.

As the 100th approached the coast the flak began to come up; coming in at 14,000 feet (actually 11,000, for the altitude of the target was 3000 feet), made accurate flak sighting fairly easy. Bennett saw the plane of Pete Biddick pull out of the formation with a smoking engine (recalling then how he had "volunteered" Biddick for the job, promising him it would be a "milk run"—an easy mission). A ship from another group, burning, plunged into the North Sea. Bennett counted ten parachutes. He was relieved to see German patrol boats headed in the direction of the descending chutes.

As they came in on the bomb run, the 100th ran into the prop wash of the 95th Group which had preceded them over the target but had not bombed because of cloud cover. Bombardier Robert Peel, however, saw the aiming point and the 100th dropped its bombs squarely on the target. The navigation of Joseph Paine had been flawless also.

"We had a successful strike," Roane recalls, "but caught the devil back at critique [3rd Air Division] for bombing out of turn and one and one-half minutes early. We passed over in order but two previous groups failed to drop due to clouds. John Bennett went to bat for us, as we had no rank aboard."

Biddick, in the one 100th Group plane which had been hit on the mission, succeeded in making it back to Scotland. His only recorded comment was, "Milk run!—those dirty . . ."

Winter had set in over England and over Europe so that missions were fewer and the men had time to consider their miseries. One of them was the scarcity of coal. Of course, the Nissen huts were so constructed that comfort in them was laughable. Also the curious little stoves in them had undoubtedly been designed for some other purpose than basting by-standers, but no one had succeeded in finding out what that was.

However, they did throw heat for a time and it felt good so long as you could scrounge the necessary fuel. The method devised by both officers and men was technically known as "midnight requisitioning." One crew had developed a pretty good method. Since, of necessity, the ball turret gunner was the smallest member of any crew he was assigned a special function in the operation. A group of them would slip out into the night to the fenced enclosure where the supply of coal was kept, taking barracks bags with them.

After making certain that they were unobserved by guards or other unauthorized personnel, they would bodily heave the turret gunner, barracks bag in hand, over the fence. On one of these occasions, a turret gunner was stealthily chucking coal into the bag when a light flashed on him. It was the officer of the day.

"Sergeant," the OD demanded, "what are you doing there?"

From the top of the coal pile came the meek, completely honest, reply, "Stealing coal, sir."

Through these cold, bitter winter months the 100th went out regularly on missions, several to the fateful Bremen, even Münster was visited again. There were either no losses or very low losses over the period from the Rjukan mission (October 16, 1943) to the strike upon a German airfield near Chartres (March 2, 1944). A total of thirty-seven sorties was credited to the 100th and the highest losses occurred over Frankfurt on February 3, 1944, when three planes failed to return. In this entire period of approximately five months, the 100th Group lost a total of thirteen planes.

During this period it was evident that Colonel Harding was quite ill but refused hospitalization, telling Bennett that he had "no time to be sick." When the 100th suffered its greatest losses, or if it was believed a mission was to be a tough one, Harding made it a point to fly with the Group on that mission. His indomitable courage and selflessness almost cost him his life. When he was

204

A white Christmas.

finally forced to permit himself to be sent to the hospital, where surgery was required, Harding was near death. Quick medical treatment saved his life and eventually he was evacuated to the States and sent to Walter Reed Hospital in Washington.

Before he left, Harding had appointed Bennett to the post of Air Executive of the 100th Group. As Marvin Bowman was later to reveal, Bennett "was responsible for rejuvenating the group after it had fallen into innocuous desuetude . . . Our bombing record and casualty record were, I believe, the worst in the 8th Air Force when Bennett was sent down from Thetford (3rd Division Headquarters) to find what was wrong. He flew a few missions, talked to the right people (among them a guy named Bowman) and the result a few weeks later was a wholesale shakeup. Things changed rapidly after that, and it wasn't till much later that we realized that Bennett was the guy responsible . . . The boys may not have liked him too well, but how they respected him! Of course, we who knew him better came to like him very much."

Although he was initially a Squadron Commander, Bennett was to prove to have much more power than a mere squadron CO. Resolutely and with what must have been regarded as a ruthless objectivity, Bennett went to work on the 100th during his service as temporary commander. The losses at Regensburg, Bremen, and Münster had affected morale. And it wasn't helped when one Squadron Commander greeted new crews with the words, "I don't want to know your names; you're going to be shot down soon so why should I know

Frank Valesh, described by writer John R. Nilsson as "the 100th's most prodigal pilot," used up no less than seven B-17s, most of them, such as this one, in the line of duty. There was one in which he had taken up two Red Cross girls and sheared the wings off during a landing (no one was hurt). Valesh's planes were all named Hang the Expense; *this one which had been hit by flak on a mission was named* Hang the Expense III.

your names!" This same CO was known to go through the boxes of crews missing in action before they were sent to next kin, pilfering out anything he regarded as valuable.

"There was bad morale through losses," Bennett now recalls, "and two bad apples" in command of a couple of squadrons. They went very quickly and were replaced with good men. Bennett began to instill a respect for and, if need be, a fear of discipline. "He wasn't running any 'wild blue yonder' outfit," Harry Crosby has said. Some of "our leadership at the time was very much in the romantic, old flyboy P-39 frame of mind, and they were very poor at teaching any kind of discipline, let alone air formation. It was considered very dashing to break off formation and come home alone in the clouds on the slightest pretext . . . As a result, when fourteen bomb groups were in the air, the 100th always flew the very worst formations and we were in the logical position to be hit. On a number of occasions, I flew in the lead plane of another group, and would look back at my own group and be shocked to see it spread all over the sky."

Bennett changed all that. One of the near sufferers was the romantic Crosby himself. As part of his program of stiffening up the discipline, Bennett expected real snap-to reactions to his summons. It almost seemed to be a form of harassment.

His crisp voice would echo through the group's Tannoy (public address system), "Captain Crosby, will run—not walk—to my office!" It chanced that once when this announcement crackled in Crosby's barracks, he was taking a shower. When he did not appear in what Bennett considered a reasonable amount of time, the p.a. system crackled again, "Captain Crosby is AWOL and will be treated accordingly."

Seconds later a slightly damp and somewhat angry Crosby dashed into Group headquarters. With cold eyes Bennett summoned him into his office and closed the door. Though practically soundproof the glass enclosed office was open to everyone's view. Crosby was still angry by Bennett's treatment and told him so. Bennett, his eyes still cold and his arm movements obviously those of an angry, scolding man (as far as those who could see knew), began to question Crosby about his home town, about other personal matters—but all the while pointing an angry finger under Crosby's nose, or otherwise seeming to display anger—in a soothing voice. He was actually measuring Crosby (one of the group's finest navigators) and getting acquainted. Crosby calmed down and the men talked for a while and, as he left, Crosby would have appeared to have been in a chastened mood. For the benefit of the silent observers, Bennett put his arm about Crosby's shoulders and said, "Don't worry, everything will be all right, my boy."

This was the hard-headed John M. Bennett, Jr.

He immediately took to Robert Rosenthal and soon put him at the head of the 350th Squadron after the CO, Major M. J. Fitzgerald, was shot down.

"Because he was smart and had all the courage and determination in the world," Bennett wrote of Rosenthal, "he went up fast. He was a natural leader of men . . ." Bowman found Rosenthal "one of the great figures of the Air Force; a shy, modest, and patriotic gentleman of truly amazing courage and achievement." When Rosenthal's military career ended he had been awarded sixteen decorations, among them the Distinguished Service Cross for "extraordinary heroism in connection with military operations against the enemy"; the Silver Star (with cluster) for "gallantry in action"; the Distinguished Flying Cross (with cluster) for "heroism or extraordinary achievement during aerial flight"; and so on including the Air Medal (with seven clusters), the Purple Heart (with cluster) and British and French decorations.

The 100th Group, on its part, was awarded a Presidential Citation for its attacks on Berlin on March 4, 1944. Along with one of their Combat Wing teams, the 95th Bomb Group, the 100th was to achieve the distinction of being the first American airmen to bomb the German capital.

"Overcoming unusually hazardous weather conditions," the citation read, "which forced all but one other unit of the 8th Air Force to bomb targets of opportunity or abandon the mission, the 100th Bombardment Group (H) resolutely continued on to the German capital in the first American operation over Berlin, 4 March 1944. The mission was successfully completed despite solid layers of clouds and dense, persistent, vapor trails which lasted throughout the perilous flight. Accurate antiaircraft fire was encountered in the target area, and the bomber formations were continually harassed by sharp attacks from twenty to twenty-five enemy aircraft from the initial point to the rally point."

It was an impressive event, historically, but not from a purely military aspect. The planes had been called back but, according to those who succeeded in bombing, this recall was not heard by them. It was probably a matter of their zeal and the proximity of Berlin—they had come this far and it seemed wrong to go back. So they found little holes in the cloud cover and bombed. In all probably thirty planes made an ineffectual strike. The 95th lost four B-17s on this mission and the 100th one.

Two days later, March 6, 1944, the 8th Air Force was out in force (660 heavies attacking) over Berlin. Rosenthal, who had gone on the March 4 strike, was not flying that day with the 100th which, after a long period of good luck was once again to emerge from an air battle—called by one fighter pilot who was there "the most intense air battle of the war"—as the "Bloody 100th." Over Berlin on March 6, 1944, the 100th Group suffered its greatest loss of the entire war—fifteen B-17s. The 8th Air Force lost a total of sixty-nine bombers and eleven fighters.

Morale at Thorpe Abbotts went down.

Lieutenant Colonel John Bennett, who had been appointed Air Executive just the day before by Colonel Harding, found himself in a predicament. On Sunday, March 5, Harding informed Bennett of his decision and on March 6, Harding was rushed to the hospital with a serious gallstone condition. That day the 100th left fifteen aircraft one half of the attacking force and 150 men in Germany. Bennett was now acting Group Commander of the 100th and to his dismay found that the very next mission was to be to Berlin.

Bad weather canceled any possible missions for the seventh, but on Wednesday, March 8 the 100th was scheduled to make the deadly trip again.

"I was dumfounded," Bennett recalls, "and don't remember what I said, if anything. I slipped into another room where I could call Wing Hq. I explained to them that the morale of our men was terribly low after Monday's losses, and that I was afraid that possibly everyone would abort."

Major Bowman, now the S-2, could only shake his head doubtfully. The operations officer was less reticent than either Bennett or Bowman. Cursing the high command for what they were doing he angrily said, "What are those fools trying to do, kill all of us?"

Bennett was given permission to lead the Wing and the 100th was able to muster up enough crews to put up fifteen planes. Bennett would lead and, as deputy leader in the high squadron, was Captain Rosenthal (flying his twenty-fifth mission—the last of his tour of duty).

208

A Fortress from the 447th Bomb Group goes down, No. 3 engine afire, over Berlin on March 6, 1944. The white square on the tail indicates that the plane is from the 3rd Division to which the 100th Group also belonged. Fifteen 100th Group planes were lost on this day's mission.

Bennett did not sleep the night of March 7. He wondered what the reaction would be the next morning at briefing.

"When we have an easy target and a short mission," he wrote to his father, "everybody cheers at briefing when the curtain is pulled back. When morale is good, and we have a deep penetration into Germany, there is a good-natured groan. On the morning of March 8, 1944, when the curtain was opened there was not a sound."

Bowman, "Major B" to the airmen who were fond of the peppery former World War I pilot, showed them pictures of the Erkner ball-bearing plant which was the target for the day. He could not bring himself to engage in the usual wisecracking comments as he generally did.

Operations explained the procedure. The 45th Wing was to lead the 8th Air Force, followed by the 13th Wing which was to be led by the 100th Group.

As they proceeded on their mission Bennett found himself checking with the formation control officer, who was always stationed in the tail gunner's position of the lead plane, to see how many planes of the 100th were following. They were then joined by the other groups of the 13th Combat Wing, the 95th and 390th. Ahead of them Bennett could see the 45th Combat Wing (96th, 388th, 42nd Groups); above were the P-47 escorts.

"How many do you see now?" he asked Lieutenant Charles Stapleton in the tail.

209

"All fourteen, sir."

Bennett later said that he "was strongly moved. These fine young men were following me in spite of what had happened on their last trip to Berlin. There were a few abortions out of the high group, but none out of the 100th."

Over Dümmer Lake, where the 100th had suffered so badly two days before, the P-47s turned back; the P-51s were supposed to join the bombers at this point. But for some reason the "little friends" did not appear.

Then Bennett saw fighters to the right and high above them flying parallel to the formations. Then, with breath-taking suddenness, the fighters whipped around and plunged into the bomber formations.

The *Luftwaffe!*

The Fortresses began shuddering with the rattle of the .50-calibers training on the attackers. The fighters came in in waves of as many as fifteen abreast, concentrating on the 45th Wing in the lead. Nine B-17s went down from the 45th Wing, including the lead plane and the deputy leader; the fighters then plunged through Bennett's 13th Combat Wing. Four planes from the 95th Group and the 390th Group broke out of the formation and fell. In Rosenthal's squadron the plane flown by Lieutenant N. Chapman began to smoke and dropped from the formation. Chapman brought the ship under control and joined Bennett's formation to continue on to Berlin.

Bennett estimated that about 150 Me-109s and FW-190s attacked them as they approached the turning point about fifty miles south of Berlin. In the confusion resulting from the loss of their lead planes, the elements of the 45th Wing missed the turn and continued on a wrong course. Realizing this Bennett assumed command of the attack on Berlin and led his Wing to the target on what was the first visual bombing by the 8th Air Force on Berlin (the previous attacks had been either through intermittent clouds or complete cover). The 45th Wing planes, having seen Bennett make the turn, swung around also to follow the 100th to the target. About then the "little friends," P-51s, appeared to drive off the German fighters.

After "Bombs away," Lieutenant Chapman was forced to leave the formation and when Bennett last saw him he had the plane under control. "I hope he crash-landed safely," Bennett thought. "The fifteen ships of the 100th Bomb Group had delivered the goods. The trip home was uneventful."

Not completely. When they came in over Thorpe Abbotts it appeared that the men in *Rosie's Riveters* had gone mad. Even the otherwise careful, wise, undemonstrative "Rosie" himself went wild. The giant aircraft swooped down out of the sky, the tips of the four propellers barely missing the ground and roared at the tower. All the while, from the plane itself, came a stream of flares of all colors, like some aerial Fourth of July display. Even stranger was the fact that from the tower itself, the center of military discipline and businesslike demeanor, came an answering barrage of multicolored flares and shouting led by the squadron commander, Major Blakely, himself.

This curious behavior began when they had passed the enemy coast and "Rosie" took up the intercom and said, "Interphone discipline is now a sack of something." The B-17 echoed with wild shouting, ribald song, good-natured curses and general roughhouse. There was also a demand from the crew, practically in unison.

"Give us a beautiful buzz job, 'Rosie'!"

210

Lieutenant Colonel John M. Bennett. The medal is the Silver Star awarded to Bennett for leading the March 8 Berlin attack after the lead wing had been disrupted by fighter attacks.

Rosie's Riveters had completed its twenty-five missions, its twenty-five invasions of enemy territory and had come safely home—and were ready to "stand a tip-toe" when the day was named. They had gone to Bremen and to Münster, and they had been to Regensburg and had just now returned from "Big B." The quiet, calming, skilled "Rosie" had brought them home again.

Now he regaled them with such flying as anyone had rarely seen. When they pulled into the hardstand they were met in style. Each man rode to the post-mission interrogation in his own private jeep, except radio operator Michael Bocuzzi, who had no less than an MP's motorcycle as means of transportation. It was said that even the hard eyes of veteran crew chief J. E. Woodard filled with tears.

There were celebrations that night and a shock for all, for "Rosie" had no intentions of leaving the 100th Group, or to stop flying. He would take a week off, go to Scotland perhaps, and then come back for another tour.

It was a difficult decision to explain. Everyone looked forward to that last mission, though many feared they would not live to fly it. It was the hope and dread of every air crew, that count. The percentages were against them, if you believed in numbers (fifteen missions was the average lifespan of a bomber crew); and if you really believed in numbers you never flew a mission Number 13, but 12A. The irony of being shot down on your last mission was enough to send a man to the flak house.

Rosenthal did not expect anyone to understand his feelings, which were complex, nor did he expect anyone to adopt his attitude. Nor, most of all, did he enjoy trying to put it into words. "I had simply set my own standards for myself and didn't feel any arbitrary tour of duty set by the Air Force would apply," he would say, his already healthy glow growing redder. He secretly felt that it all sounded "stuffy." "I had to do what I could for as long as I was able."

He had no idea that what he was doing would make him the true legend of the 100th Group. That "moral compulsion" of wanting to see the war through to the end and his incredible ability to handle a B-17 were to make him one of the 8th Air Force's folk heroes. But unlike the folk hero's, Rosenthal's exploits were not exaggerated and their telling never originated from him.

At debriefings interrogation officers were exasperated by his laconic replies and the mere reporting of facts. "The flak was meager," he would say. "We landed with our flaps out."

"Were you hit?"

"A little."

"We never get anything out of you."

It was on his second tour that Rosenthal experienced one of his classic adventures. He was commanding officer of the 350th Squadron and, in May 1944, flew as command pilot on one of the missions to Berlin that month. Technically, therefore, Rosenthal was not the pilot of the plane. They had completed their mission and were returning to England. They had encountered a little flak over the Ruhr and had heard it rattle against the plane but there was no evident damage.

They were flying along peacefully when, inexplicably, the oil pressure in No. 1 engine dropped. Something was wrong. Rosenthal, in the co-pilot's seat, reached over to punch the feather button. Instead of feathering the engine ran away.

The B-17 shuddered and vibrated violently as the propeller whined and shook, threatening to tear off the left wing. Little tongues of flame licked from under the cowling. The pilot was at a loss as to what he should do. They could bail out and spend the rest of the war in a German prison—and they would have to do that before the wing snapped, trapping all of them inside the spinning aircraft.

The pilot turned the plane over to Rosenthal.

Obviously something had to be done about the wild propeller. Rosenthal pushed forward on the control column, pulled back on the throttles, and then lifted the nose. He dipped and snapped the great plane, hoping to toss the uncontrollable propeller away from the plane.

Suddenly it went, like a wild, lethal, three-bladed buzzsaw away from No. 1 engine and toward the plane. Striking the propeller of the adjacent engine, it sliced away half of each of the three blades and, thus deflected, careened backward to strike the tail shearing off about half of the rudder and fin.

At least their wing would not snap off. Rosenthal feathered No. 2 engine and carefully tested the controls. With only two engines—and both on the same side—they lost airspeed and altitude. Without the rudder there was no lateral control except that which could be accomplished with the ailerons.

The fire went out, they were more or less airborne but they were also over

Germany, barely able to keep up flying speed and unable to maneuver. They were what the *Luftwaffe* loved, a lone B-17 in trouble. They wistfully watched as the rest of the formation continued on to England. Standing orders were to leave planes that could not keep up with the formation, for that would only put all ships in jeopardy.

They still had over three hundred miles to go when Rosenthal saw specks in the sky. Fighters. The ten men in the sluggish Fortress waited as the gunners pointed their fifties at the approaching fighter. A single plane came toward them, approaching with evident care, waiting to see what would happen. His silhouette grew larger in the gunner's sights.

It was a Thunderbolt, a "little friend"!

In the P-47 was Captain Charles N. Keppler, leading a flight of three additional fighters—although they were not observed by the men in the B-17. But with this powerful ally, Rosenthal knew that they could depend upon Keppler's protection and ordered all the possible jettisonable equipment thrown out of the plane, including guns. Thus relieved of the weight, the airspeed of the Fortress rose above the hundred and five mile an hour stagger through the air. Rosenthal was able to maintain flying speed with the two remaining engines; one stall and they would have been finished.

With the Thunderbolts darting around them, Rosenthal headed for home. The two straining engines were burning gas voraciously and when he tried to transfer fuel from the dead side of the wing, found that the transfer engine was burning and the fuel line was leaking. They had fifty gallons in No. 4 and seventy gallons in No. 3—and a long way to go.

As a precaution Rosenthal asked the radio operator to contact Air-Sea only to learn that the liaison set had been put out of order by the vibration of the plane. They then contacted Keppler, who told them he had already contacted Air-Sea Rescue.

"Thank you," Rosenthal told him.

They seemed to crawl through the sky. When they came over the North Sea, the P-47 pilot said, "Rescue launch below you now." There was some lessening of the tension in the bomber; at least if they had to ditch some of them had a good chance to make it.

The English coast showed up as a dim line in the distance. They were down to 3000 feet over the Channel and their fuel practically nil. Desperately they all looked for the first possible place to land.

Then an engine coughed, sputtered, and went dead. The prop was feathered and the Fortress struggled to keep flying on one engine. They saw a field coming up. Rosenthal dived the plane toward the field to gain a little more speed, carefully putting the plane into a landing attitude.

The strip appeared under them; there were more sputters from his right. About twenty feet above the runway their last engine conked out. Gently the wheels touched the runway and "Rosie" had brought them home again.

While waiting for someone to come and get them, for they had landed in an emergency field which was a long distance from transportation, Rosenthal and the crew got out of the plane. They could see that their trouble had been caused by a single tiny piece of flak which had gone into the oil sump of No. 1 engine. They had been able to fly for quite some time until the oil had drained out. Then the engine fused and the prop went wild.

The B-17 brought home by Robert Rosenthal with two engines out (note sheared off prop blades on No. 2 engine, sliced off when prop from No. 1 engine was snapped loose by Rosenthal's maneuvering). The tail also was cut away by the propeller. Part of the way was made with only one engine. As Rosenthal brought the plane onto the runway the last engine died out also.

"Well," as Rosenthal frequently said, "if you get home it's a milk run." They removed their flying gear and sunned themselves while they awaited transportation.

Eventually men gathered around the plane and before long, an officer drove up in a jeep, screeched to a halt and demanded to know, "Who the hell put that plane there?"

"No one put it there, sir," one of the crowd offered, pointing to the men basking in the sun (and no doubt unconsciously embracing the earth), "these men *flew* it here."

The captain studied the plane for a moment and before he jumped back into his jeep said, "We're bound to win the war!"

On D-Day, a little less than a month later, the 100th Group flew no less than seventy-eight sorties. "Mayor B" briefed them for their part in this great historic event. He read a secret message from Generals LeMay and Doolittle: "The Eighth Air Force is currently charged with a most solemn obligation in support of the most vital operation ever undertaken by our armed forces."

Lieutenant Colonel Thomas S. Jeffrey, Jr., the new commanding officer of the 100th Group, led the first mission of the day. By this time Lieutenant Colonel Bennett had been assigned to Wing Headquarters and would go eventually to 3rd Division Headquarters to serve on the staff of General LeMay.

Jeffrey was an outstanding leader and proved to be in the Bennett tradition. A strict disciplinarian he maintained the 100th Group in top form.

Although the second mission of the 100th on D-Day failed to drop its bombs, the third led by Captain Robert Rosenthal, bombed a bridge to help seal off

Sam Barr, Robert Rosenthal, Thomas Jeffrey, Sumner Reeder, and John Kidd. Reeder and Kidd were leaving the 100th Group for other assignments.

the invasion area. It was a stirring sight to Rosenthal. "There was a feeling of excitement about the mission—there were thousands of ships below us. Suddenly the whole thing had a new meaning—you became a part of something." On D-Day Rosenthal was able to see what it was that he had been working toward for so many months.

But, as John Bennett was to observe, "a man's luck just doesn't last indefinitely." On the mission to Nuremberg in September 1944 Rosenthal's luck caught up with him. Flak again had struck his ship and there was no possibility of stretching it over the Channel. All that he could do was try to stay up for as long as possible and possibly crash land within allied lines. The crew elected to remain with "Rosie" rather than to bail out over Germany.

When it was obvious that they were losing altitude fast, Rosenthal spotted a field in which to set the plane down. It was a rough landing and the uncontrollable Fortress plowed across the field with a roar, digging up the earth, shedding pieces of airplane and finally crashing into a tree.

When he was pulled out of the cockpit with a broken arm and nose, Rosenthal was happy to see that his luck had held. The Free French, to whom he had dropped supplies only a few weeks before, rescued Rosenthal and the other two injured crew members from the plane and took them to a nearby U. S. Army hospital. Two days later he was flown back to England and sent to the hospital in Oxford. He had a steady stream of visitors, many of whom brought him "gallons of ice cream and candy."

Major Eugene Rovegno, the group's engineering officer, was a favorite with the young pilots and, when the opportunity came to join in an unusual shuttle mission which took the 100th, led by Colonel Jeffrey, from England to bomb the oil refinery at Ruhland he eagerly hitched a ride. The formations proceeded from there to Russia where they remained a while, loaded up again and set course for Foggia, bombing an oil refinery in Poland on the way, and were guests of the 15th Air Force in Italy for a while. From Foggia they struck at a marshaling yard in Rumania, returned to Italy and finally headed back for England, dropping bombs on a marshaling yard in France, en route. In all two weeks were spent away from Thorpe Abbotts.

215

Robert Rosenthal after a crash-landing in France.

Poltava: after the American bomber formations landed in Russia on an extended shuttle mission, German planes paid a visit during the night. This photo was taken during the attack showing flares and antiaircraft fire.

The shuttle mission to Poltava, which began on June 21, 1944, was to prove doubly historic. It was the 8th's first mission to Russia, a fact which prompted such otherwise grounded "paddlefeet" (a term for them used by airmen) as Bowman and Rovegno eager to participate. The ground had already been prepared for the mission, which enabled the 8th to bomb deep inside Germany and then continue on to Russia instead of returning to England, by General Eaker, who had lead the first such mission from Italy.

The target, at Ruhland, was just south of Berlin and the bombing by 114 Fortresses, with an escort of seventy Mustangs, went off as planned and the formation pushed on to the fields in Russia, located at Mirgorod, Piryatin, and Poltava. The 100th was to land at the latter base, along with planes from other groups. They were not aware of a trailing German He-177 which observed their landings and then flipped away into the clouds.

That night they experienced their second touch of history. Poltava suddenly lit up under a great shower of flares and then erupted with the bursting of more than a hundred tons of bombs. The Germans, without the loss of a single aircraft, succeeded in destroying forty-three B-17s and damaging twenty-six; fourteen P-51s were demolished and others damaged. More seriously, twenty-five Russians were killed and one American. General Spaatz later admitted that the

Poltava: the morning after. American bombers of the 3rd Air Division, 452nd Bomb Group, lay strewn over the airfield. In this attack on the Russian field on June 21, 1944, forty-three B-17s and fourteen P-51s were destroyed.

217

raid on Poltava was the "best attack the *Luftwaffe* ever made on the AAF."
An attempt was made to repeat the success on the following night upon the other
bases but not with the same success. When the time came to leave Russia for the
next leg of the shuttle, of the original force the 8th was able to get seventy-one
Fortresses and fifty-five Mustangs off the ground on June 26. Inexplicably, considering its reputation, none of the Bloody 100th's planes were destroyed in the
surprise attack.

Carried as passengers on the flight were Rovegno and Bowman. It was on the
trip from Russia to Italy that they encountered fairly heavy flak. Major Harry
Crosby kept a remarkable diary of this historic trip and reported that the plane
of Captain "Bucky" Mason (there seems to have been no shortage of "Buckies"
in the 100th) was badly hit and trailed along behind the formation. There was no
fighter opposition and the flak had stopped so Mason called the lead ship asking
for Rovegno.

"Hey you old coot," he said, "you better get your hammer and nails ready.
This duck I'm riding is about to fall apart."

"But Major Rovegno already had his own troubles," Crosby wrote. "Over the
target [his plane] had been struck by flak. His predicament makes one of the
classic stories of the war. The piece of flak that hit him just bruised his knees,
then dropped at his feet. Major Rovegno, the last four numbers of whose serial
number are 6788, bent down to pick it up. On it were the numbers 6787! He
yelled over the interphone, "Hey, let's get the hell out of here! The next one has
my number on it!"

While that part of the 100th continued on its trail-blazing shuttle mission with
the other planes of the 8th Air Force, other members of the 100th took part

*Major Eugene Rovegno, Engineering officer
of the 100th.*

in an unusual mission: Flying at a dangerously low altitude to drop supplies to the French Maquis who were fighting the Germans.

Robert Rosenthal took part in that mission. After he had been released from the hospital he was assigned to wing headquarters where, as Bennett was to write, "he was very unhappy because he wasn't allowed to fly. When his arm was finally healed, he raised so much hell around wing headquarters that General [Harold Q.] Huglin allowed him to return to the Century Bombers."

It was as Major Rosenthal that he returned to his original squadron, the 418th, which he had joined as a lieutenant just over a year before. When the 100th was selected to lead the entire 3rd Division it was Rosenthal who was chosen to lead it to Berlin.

The date was February 3, 1945. The Russians were within thirty-five miles of the German capital and the targets were the marshaling yards within the city in order to prevent supplies and reinforcements from being shipped to the Eastern front.

Colonel Bennett had seconded the choice of Rosenthal to lead the mission (it was unusual for a squadron commander to lead a Division; this was generally done by a Wing Commander or a Group Commander). The decision was approved by General Earle E. Partridge, 3rd Division commander who had replaced General LeMay who, in turn, had left for the Pacific Theater.

February 3 proved to be "a beautiful morning and the silver bombers were glistening in the early morning sunlight," Bennett noted as he piloted his fighter plane, in company with his friend Hunter Harris, to observe the B-17s forming up for the mission. "As many times as I had seen this sight, I was still thrilled at it. The magnitude of the mighty 8th Air Force was an inspiring sight." (That

Return from Italy: Colonel Jeffrey, Colonel Bennett, and Major Marvin Bowman on the 100th's completion of the shuttle mission from England to Russia to Italy and return to England.

Low level mission: dropping supplies to the Maquis *in France. The French Resistance fighters were in need of guns and ammunition so selected groups of the 3rd Division were chosen to do the job, among the 100th and the 94th, whose planes are seen here.*

day nearly a thousand B-17s went to Berlin.) "Hunter and I circled over the lead group and violated radio silence with such phrases as, 'Atta boy, Rosy,' or 'Give 'em hell, Rosy.' Major Rosenthal, an excellent air leader, obeyed all standing instructions and remained silent."

The great air armada approached the German capital practically unchallenged by the *Luftwaffe*. As Air Commander Rosenthal on his fifty-second mission would coordinate the mission and make the final decision as to whether or not they would bomb. All the other operational responsibilities were also his. They were coming in high over Berlin (possibly at 27,000 feet) when the flak, accurate and thick, began to come up.

Rosenthal was already on the bomb run when a direct flak hit put an engine on fire. The others in the formation watched with surprised horror. The blazing plane continued on the run. The fire spread and it appeared that the bomb bay too was burning. But the lead ship completed the run and then they heard Rosenthal's voice. "Take over, Dave," he said to Major D. K. Lyster, deputy lead.

The French present the Croix de Guerre avec Palm *to members of the 100th who took part in the drop to the* Maquis. *Lieutenant Colonel Bennett is the recipient here.*

As the men watched, aircraft 379 pulled away from the formation burning fiercely. Anxiously they began counting the chutes while, for some reason, the crippled plane remained in level flight. It was obvious now who was at the controls. The count reached eight when aircraft 379 flashed brightly for an instant, stood still then disintegrated, leaving nothing behind but floating bits of red hot metal, four orange balls of fire—the gas tanks—and dirty black smoke.

"Christ," an awed voice said over an intercom, "Rosie went down."

The flak had proved to be murderously accurate over Berlin that day—"a beautiful day," as Rosenthal would later recall it. He was of course referring only to the clear weather. The plane shuddered under the impact of the flak and the air filled with the noises of ripping metal. No. 1 engine spouted flame, a great white sheet spilling into the airstream behind the wing; the fabric-covered aileron shriveled, exposing the graceful metallic structure. The plane bounced again under another hit. The pilot, Captain John Ernst, continued with the run, his eyes darting toward Rosenthal, who mentally weighed the possibility of their continuing against the other possibility of a mid-air explosion before they made it.

They kept going and bombardier Lieutenant E. Lockhart zeroed in on the Erkner factory and the bombs fell from the blazing Fortress; the rest of the group dropped on the leader. Then Rosenthal pushed the alarm bell signaling "Abandon ship," and ordered Ernst to supervise the bail-out. He then informed Lyster that they were leaving the formation. Another hit set the bomb bay on fire and the middle of the B-17 was an uncontrollable mass of flame. In making his exit

221

". . . the burning plane continued on the run . . ."

Ernst had dropped through the still open bomb bay. He caught his leg on a jagged edge, cutting it so badly that it had to be amputated.

The B-17 had now descended to about a thousand feet. Rosenthal, certain that all who were able had leaped from the plane, put it on autopilot and, adjusting his chute harness, left the flight deck. The nearest exit was the forward emergency door just below and in front of the pilot's compartment. Rosenthal squeezed down toward the door, and as he did saw that a man still remained in the ship. He would never know that man's identity, for he had been decapitated.

There was no time now for anything but to plunge through the exit in the bottom of the plane. Rosenthal hardly had time to pull his ripcord (he waited as long as he could, but the ground was now dangerously close) before the ship exploded. The force of the detonation struck him and tossed him around in the air.

Because he had headed the plane toward the Russian lines, by then on the outskirts of Berlin, Rosenthal hoped that those who had been able to get out of the plane would land among the Russians. As it turned out, only three, including himself, were picked up by the Russians. Others were captured by the Germans, one of whom was lynched by civilians.

When he landed, which was hard, Rosenthal fractured his arm—that is, the arm just barely mended, was broken again. He was forced to hold his .45 pistol in his left hand while awaiting the next development. He saw a group of soldiers approaching and wasn't certain whether they would prove to be Russian or German (only the German civilians might prove to be less welcome than the latter).

With his right arm dangling helplessly, "I just poised there waiting. They came at me very quickly, but I noticed, in my haze, that they were driving a jeep."

They were Russians—he had managed to land on the right bank of the Oder River.

But the Russians were not certain who the tall man, holding a gun, was. Rosenthal was wearing a green RAF flying suit and looked quite German. One of the soldiers lunged at him with his bayonet. Rosenthal dodged as well as he could in his condition, shouting, "Americansky! Americansky!"

But the Russian had lunged again, despite the fact that Rosenthal had made no attempt to shoot him. Rosenthal, in desperation tried another tack, "Americansky! Stalin! Roosevelt! Jeep!," he shouted at the Russians.

"I must have sounded too happy to be a German, for the man who had been lunging at me put down his gun and embraced me."

He was taken before a Russian general and sent to a former German hospital which had been taken over by the Russians and where his arm was set. There was no way to send Rosenthal back to Thorpe Abbotts through the lines, so it was decided that he would be evacuated to the east.

After four days in the hospital Rosenthal and others were sent off toward Poland. For almost a week he was billeted in a farmhouse near a Russian airfield. Rosenthal hardly represented the Air Force at its sartorial best. Besides the sling, which did not remain sterile for long, he wore his flying boots (he had no shoes), his green flying jacket and a Russian soldier's hat. The Russian fliers threw some rather blinding vodka parties, as was their wont, and if his arm pained him, Rosenthal never noticed it. Not even when he rolled off his improvised bed, which was nothing but a couple of planks placed on saw horses.

As he moved farther into Poland, however, his accommodations improved. He was put up by a Polish family, a mother and son, the latter a former Polish Army officer. The family was cultured and before the war had hit them, quite wealthy.

But because of the American guests they found their food supply even more inadequate than normally. The son came to Rosenthal, the ranking officer in the little group, and explained that they were running out of food. Perhaps if Rosenthal explained to the Russian commander, their food allotment might be increased. The American agreed and, dressed in his nondescript outfit, accompanied the Pole to the Russian headquarters.

Once there, they demanded to see the general, explaining that Rosenthal was an American officer of almost equal rank and therefore worthy of more than passing consideration. Finally they were admitted.

But they also encountered some serious language problems. Rosenthal spoke only English. The Pole could speak English and some German. Therefore, when they finally confronted the Russian general who sat impassively behind a large desk studying them with a cold suspicious eye, they were joined by yet another man. He was a German prisoner of war who could speak German and Russian. The chain was complete, with but one weak link (the German): Rosenthal would tell the Pole what he wanted the general to know, the Pole would tell the German and then both could only hope that the German would tell the Russian what had been said.

There seemed to be some difficulty from the start. The Russian general seemed to be totally unimpressed with an officer in the Air Force of an allied army. He might very well have been totally unaware of it.

There was one further inconvenience. Each time the German addressed the

Russian general, he would click his heels and bow so excessively that he managed always to bump into or to shove Rosenthal.

Rosenthal began patiently enough. He was Major Robert Rosenthal of the American Air Force and was billeted with a Polish family whose food he and the other Americans were devouring. Since the Russians had placed them in the homes of the Poles, and they were all allies, perhaps the Russians could restock the food supply of the Polish family.

It was not, apparently, getting through—and the German continued with his heel-clicking and bumping into Rosenthal.

Finally the gentle Rosenthal reached his limit. "The next time he bowed I kicked him in the fanny and he went flying right over the general's desk.

"The Russian stood up, guffawed and said, 'Americansky!' We got the food, too."

Two days later Rosenthal was in Moscow.

"In Moscow," John Bennett reported, "the Russians kept Rosy loaded with vodka. He says he remained just barely conscious for thirty days [actually Rosenthal was in Moscow less than a week, but the story isn't too exaggerated]. He was entertained by Averell Harriman, the U. S. Ambassador and many others [including the press]. At the opera he was given a box [and at the ballet he sat close enough to the Japanese ambassador to have created an international incident, but didn't]. He must have been a quaint figure when fully charged with vodka and wearing his winter flying boots, green flying pants, and RAF fur coat, dirty arm bandage and a Russian cap with a red star."

His social round completed, Rosenthal was anxious to return to England. He took the train to Kiev, which was a shattered remnant of a city. From Poltava, at which the 100th had landed on its shuttle mission, he flew to Teheran (where Roosevelt, Churchill, and Stalin had agreed on the date of the invasion of Europe), to Cairo, to Greece, to Naples, and finally back to England.

Thus ended Major Robert Rosenthal's fifty-second mission.

While Rosenthal enjoyed his circuitous excursion—the closest he ever came to a furlough during the entire stay in England—the 100th Group continued rounding out its fighting history.

After that fateful February 3 mission, there were fourteen more flown in the remaining days of the month, all of them without a single loss. March, too, began with hopeful promise when, on the second, the group went to Ruhland and Dresden to bomb factories and returned to England intact. But the next day over Brunswick the 100th suffered its first loss to a German jet fighter. Until March 1945, the jet attacks upon the bomber streams had been sporadic and uncoordinated. Then the increase in numbers and a development of tactics proved them to be terribly formidable.

As the 100th Group approached Brunswick they were attacked by waves of Messerschmitt 262s. The sleek-bodied Me, its two engine pods slung under the wings, flashed through the formation from the rear. In its sudden trajectory, it left a burning Fortress, piloted by Jack W. Thrasher, behind. For a few moments Thrasher struggled to hold the plane in the formation and, disintegrating, it fell through the clouds.

The jets came out in force again when the 100th Group returned—for the last time—to Berlin on March 18, 1945. Four Fortresses with the Square D on the tail fell under the fleet assault of the Me-262s. Worst hit was the B-17 piloted by Edward "Duke" Gwin of Whittier, California. The great bomber was shorn in

Lieutenant General Carl A. Spaatz, commander of the U. S. Strategic Air Forces, congratulates Captain Sumner Reeder to whom he has just presented the Distinguished Service Cross, second only to the Medal of Honor of all American decorations.

Generals Doolittle and LeMay at the 100th's 200 Mission party. To LeMay's left are Lieutenant Colonel George W. Dauncey and Major Sam Barr of the 100th Group.

half by the guns of the Messerschmitt and almost instantly whipped into a tight gyrating fall. Some of the crew got out: Don Reigel, the co-pilot, Herbert Hamann (who helped pull Reigel out of the twisting fuselage half), José Griego, the tail gunner, who was isolated in the severed tail, and Norman Heilbuth. Gwin, however, last seen fastening his parachute straps, was trapped in the cockpit and "rode her in." The phrase was his own, from a parody Gwin had composed based on "Casey Jones."

Meanwhile, the rumors were that the Germans were all but beaten. The jets, however, were a serious threat even if they were not as skillfully manned nor as aggressive as the German fighters once had been. Besides, the flak was as vicious as ever. By the end of March the 8th Air Force was to lose thirty bombers to the jets alone.

Major Horace Varian, 100th Ground Executive, Lieutenant Colonel John M. Bennett and men of the 100th who received the Purple Heart. Bennett shakes hands with Major Albert M. Elton who replaced "Bucky" Cleven, after he was shot down, as commander of the 350th Squadron.

"Bucky" Cleven (center) returns to the 100th Group after almost two years in German prison camps. Cleven escaped in April 1945.

During those latter March days, specifically from the twenty-first through the twenty-fourth, the 8th Air Force and Bomber Command concentrated on isolating the Ruhr and in smashing German defenses in preparation for the crossing of the Rhine River. Among the prime targets were German airfields (with special attention to the jet bases), marshaling yards and storage areas.

The 100th's participation in these assaults cost two bombers, which brought the March loss total to seven B-17s. April, the group's last official operational month, took an equal number of planes and crews.

Purely "strategic" targets were becoming scarce as the ground forces raced

Major William H. Utley, then serving as Ground Executive for the 100th, bids goodbye to Major Glenn Miller, the famed danceband leader who led the Air Force Band. Shortly after this photo was taken, Miller disappeared over the English Channel on a flight to France.

toward Germany. To restrain last-ditch stands or resurgences by the Germans the bombers returned again to targets that had been somewhat neglected.

Among them were the sub-pens at Kiel, over which the 100th suffered its first casualties in the month of April. Four days later, on April 7, the 8th Air Force encountered one of its most severe jet attacks, losing seven bombers—among them two 100th Group B-17s. The 100th's last battle with the *Luftwaffe* occurred on April 10, 1945; lost were the planes flown by Lawrence L. Bazin of Girard, Kansas, and Delbert D. Reeve of Tipton, Iowa. Eleven days later—April 20, 1945—twenty-nine aircraft of the 100th Group took off from Thorpe Abbotts to bomb Oranienburg's marshaling yards. On completing the mission, twenty-nine planes returned to Thorpe Abbotts. Mission Number 306 had been the 100th Bomb Group's last combat flight. The flow of blood had ended.

Mercy missions, however, kept the 8th Air Force occupied. One of them was flown on May 1 and carried out in cooperation with the Germans. To bring relief to civilians in occupied Holland, the Fortresses were loaded with food canisters. A truce was declared and the B-17s came in low over Amsterdam; the "target" was the oval race track near the city over which hundreds of small chutes blossomed. The B-17s returned to England and the war ended a week after.

Robert Rosenthal, having recovered from his injuries of the Berlin raid (and undoubtedly from Moscow's vodka), flew his last mission after VE-Day. As quickly as possible the 8th Air Force began evacuating American prisoners from German camps. In addition, when the concentration camps were uncovered, it was decided to free as many of those prisoners by air as was possible. For some it meant the difference between life or death.

It was that enterprising dreamer, Harry Crosby, who arranged for Rosenthal's last mission. He burst in upon the latter and soon had Rosenthal quite excited over an unusual mercy mission, flying PWs out of Germany. As he waxed enthusiastic, Rosenthal found himself carried along by the Crosby magic, picking up his gear and hurrying out to the tarmac and the waiting B-17s. All the while he assumed Crosby was to come along as navigator. It was not quite so.

As Rosenthal prepared for the flight, Crosby came up with a large carton

227

In one of the last encounters with the Luftwaffe on April 7, 1945, Sergeant W. Dudecz in a 100th B-17 shot down an Me-109. The fighter, probably carrying a dead pilot, continued on into the Fortress with the result as seen in this picture. The parallel slashes were made by the Me-109's propeller. This plane continued on to bomb the oil storage tanks at Buchen and returned to Thorpe Abbotts. The tail gunner was not aware of the collision until the plane had landed.

and poured the contents over his head. It was DDT (a special precaution which not only protected Rosenthal but also the susceptible prisoners). The cloud of powder barely settled before Rosenthal sat again at the controls of the Fortress and, waving goodbye to the grinning Crosby, pointed the nose toward Germany.

The liberated prisoners were French and filled the plane to full capacity. "They were seated all over the floor; some even stood in the bomb bay," Rosenthal recollects. It pleased Rosenthal that he was not carrying bombs. Because his passengers were French he had decided to take them a hundred miles out of their way to enable them to see the Eiffel Tower while the Fortress, dipping gently, circled Paris.

As many of the liberated prisoners as could at a time crowded the waist-gun positions to see the city from the air. They cheered and shouted despite the airsickness of many who were violently ill.

"It was a very rewarding mission," Rosenthal said. It ended his own personal crusade on just the right humanistic note. And the Legend of the "Bloody 100th" was closed.

FESTUNG EUROPA

*. . . if a single enemy bomber reaches the
Reich, my name is not Hermann Göring—
you can call me Meier!*

14. The 15th at Foggia

The 15th Air Force was never destined to achieve the celebrity of its companion strategic arm, the 8th Air Force. Possibly this was because it was formed relatively late in the war, after most of the headlines had been written and the novelty of the air war had worn off a little with the folks back home. Also, because it was based in Italy it was, like practically all units, ground and air, relegated to a kind of second-class participation in what in the public mind was a minor theater of war. If the western front seemed more dramatic, the Italian front—the entire Mediterranean Theater of Operations, in fact—was no less critical to the eventual defeat of the Axis. Some of the World War I romanticism, of course, was responsible. France as the traditional battleground for great armies was simply more familiarly interesting and men died in Italy wondering if anyone realized what went on there.

Although the 15th Air Force was regarded as a "new" air force, it was in truth one of the oldest, for its strategic element was comprised of such veteran units as the 97th Bomb Group (once of the 8th) and the 301st Bomb Group (also a veteran of the 8th), both of which, it will be recalled, had been detached from the 8th to become part of Doolittle's 12th Air Force for the North African campaign. During this operation the 12th's heavy bombers served in the dual function of tactical-strategic aircraft, supporting land forces and also bombing the harbors and shipping in and around North Africa and Italy.

231

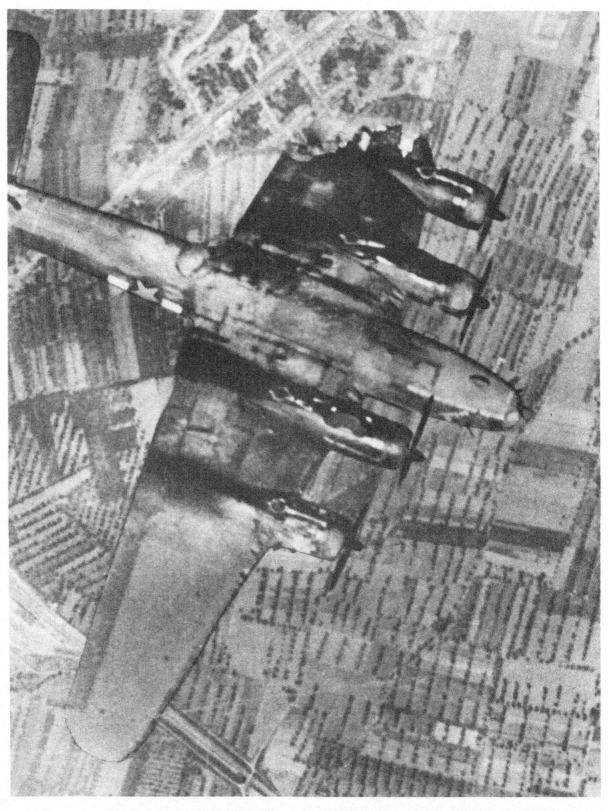

Hit by flak over Naples, this 97th Group B-17 falls to earth half its right wing off. The pilot somehow succeeded in straightening it out momentarily; only five parachutes were seen to open.

While such employment of heavy bombers was not ideal it demonstrated a valuable lesson in the use of tactical air power and allied joint command. The 12th united with the RAF's Desert Air Force, and with Lieutenant General Lewis H. Brereton's 9th Air Force, a tactical unit, to push Rommel's Afrika Korps out of Africa. When the Allies converged on Tunisia these air forces were combined as the Northwest African Air Forces under command of General Spaatz.

When Eisenhower directed his attention toward Sicily, it was this combined air force which demonstrated one of the most effective employments of air power up to that time. The island of Pantelleria lay in the path of the route to Sicily. The German and Italian planes based on Pantelleria would certainly interfere with any attempts to gain Sicily. Heavy air attacks were laid on Pantelleria in May of 1943 and after twenty-five days of overwhelming bombardment, Allied troops were able to invade without a single loss of life. Strategic bombardment had taken an objective without the use of either sea or land forces. When Pantelleria surrendered all aircraft that still remained on the island were destroyed and the Italian Air Force had practically ceased to exist. The way was open for the conquest of Sicily and southern Italy, which would be the first foothold upon Hitler's *Festung Europa*.

The 15th Air Force, therefore, was created on November 1, 1943, from heavy and medium bomber units of the "old" 12th Air Force and Brereton's 9th Air Force (which was then transferred to England to become the Tactical Air Force of the Normandy invasion). Doolittle was placed in command of the 15th which was formed to work in coordination with the still undermanned and underequipped 8th in England as the heavy bomber component of the Southern Front.

Although it was hoped that the 15th, stationed under blue Mediterranean skies, would be able to operate when the 8th was socked in by English weather, it was soon learned that the 15th would encounter the same problem. In addition there was the climb over the Alps whenever the 15th was to reach its targets. Although the Alps were not technically a serious obstacle for the B-17, which could easily fly over them, it was, in the words of Stanley J. Kavan who flew over them, "perilous territory to cross when losing altitude."

If you were forced to return from a target with one or two engines out, you couldn't go over or around the Alps. There was no ditching possible as in the English Channel, for example. There was also the problem of flying through clouds over the Alps which not only carried the threat of icing but also interfered with visibility. "That was always an unpleasant experience," Kavan recalls. "The normal tactic was to spread out to one-hundred-foot intervals and hold straight and level at a set speed. Sometimes it only took a minute to get through, but there was always the chance of collision or vertigo."

Collision might result from the normal turbulence of formation flight, from tricky air currents among the Alps; vertigo might occur when the pilot lost contact with reality. If, for some reason, his instinct convinced him that his instruments were wrong, he might dive the B-17 into the Alps all the while thinking he was in level flight. Kavan witnessed the results of such occurrences after the formation emerged from a cloud (or it sometimes occurred when they were flying over water) and where there had once been twelve Fortresses there were now only eleven, or ten. And all without any word from the missing planes.

Like the 8th, the 15th Air Force was committed to the over-all strategic program entailing the neutralization of the *Luftwaffe* both in aerial combat and by destroying the factories on the ground. At times it would be ordered away from strictly strategic operations to support the Italian land campaigns such as the landings at Anzio and the bombardment of Cassino.

When the bombing of Monte Cassino occurred on February 15, 1944, the 15th Air Force was but one unit in the great Mediterranean Allied Air Forces commanded by Lieutenant General Ira C. Eaker. Doolittle had been sent to England to command the 8th; he was replaced by Lieutenant General Nathan F. Twining at the head of the 15th Air Force. Eaker served as head of the MAAF, the strategic components of which consisted of the 15th and the RAF's No. 205 Group. This complex of powerful air striking forces was further under command of General Spaatz whose United States Strategic Air Forces coordinated its operations.

General Eaker did not approve of the bombing of Cassino with its ancient abbey, contending that it would serve no useful military purpose. That the Germans were using it as an outpost is still controversial, but both General Eaker and General Jacob Devers observed a radio antenna on the abbey's roof when they flew over it, prior to the bombing, in a Piper Cub. Aside from its historic and religious significance, the abbey, reduced to rubble by bombardment, and the town of Cassino would only impede the advance of the infantry. However the pressures from ground commanders were urgent enough and Eaker acquiesced. On February 15 the abbey was attacked by waves of heavy and medium bombers (after the area had been showered with leaflets urging the Italians inside to leave). Five hundred tons of bombs reduced the abbey to a pile of stone. A month later the town of Cassino, which lay at the foot of Monte Cassino, was likewise pulverized. Although the bombing, as such, was effective, Eaker was proved correct in his objections to using heavy bombers for the effort.

Although the Germans continue to insist that they did not use the abbey as a military observation post, it would seem unlikely that two such responsible officers as Eaker and Devers would have invented a radio antenna in order to be able to do a job they did not particularly want to do. The German positions in and around Cassino did block the Allied advance up the Italian peninsula. However it appears years after the event, at the time it was a military necessity General Sir Henry M. Wilson could not overlook.

The 15th Air Force was more effectively employed in its proper function as a strategic air force. Once it moved into the bases around Foggia in Italy, the 15th was able to reach objectives in southern France, Germany, Poland, Czechoslovakia, and the Balkans, some of which were difficult to reach from England. Beginning with an attack upon the Messerschmitt plant at Wiener-Neustadt on November 2, 1943, the 15th Air Force gradually, with occasional diversions to the Italian land campaigns, increased its strategic offensive. Aircraft factories were hit during the February 1944 "Big Week" in conjunction with the 8th's operations; ball-bearings were the objective in attacks upon Turin, Italy, and the dread Schweinfurt. Marshaling yards were struck all over Europe, as was shipping—and it must have seemed to the Germans that no corner of the Reich was safe from the heavy bombers.

One aspect of the 15th's operations which contributed greatly to the winning of the war was its reduction of Ploesti in July–August 1944. During this period

234

The bombardment of the abbey on Monte Cassino.

235

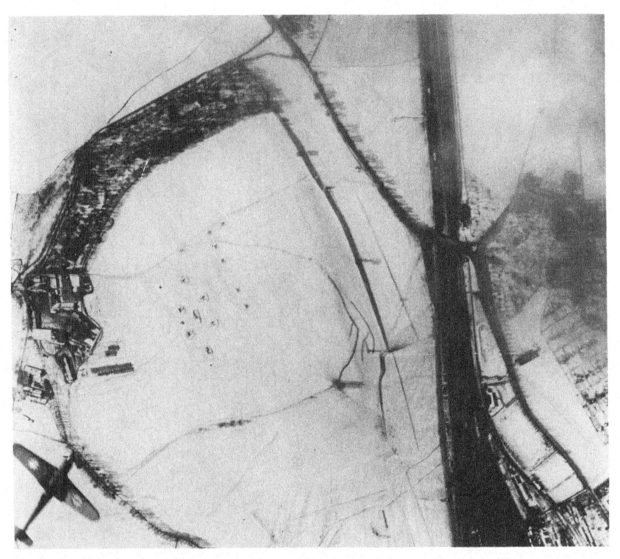

A German fighter (lower left) flies under a B-17, from which this photograph was taken during a strike by 15th Air Force planes during the "Big Week" of February 1944. The target is an aircraft factory at Regensburg.

the 15th carried out a series of heavy attacks on this prime oil target. These bombings practically destroyed all of the cracking facilities at Ploesti which meant that crude oil would have to be shipped to refineries in the Hamburg area, Austria, Hungary, or Czechoslovakia. Synthetic production was also severely attacked. This represented nearly half of Germany's liquid fuel and almost all of its aviation gas output.

The synthetic fuel centers were concentrated in eight great plants and about a dozen smaller ones—all good targets. The synthetic plants could not be dispersed and relocated like the aircraft factories. The machinery was complex and the processes were continuous, requiring heat, pressure, and chemicals. The plants were vulnerable because of their huge stores of hydrogen and manufactured fuel which were highly inflammable.

Exploding in mid-air after being hit over the target at Nis, Yugoslavia this B-17 from the 483rd Bomb Group goes down taking its crew with it. Tracks of the marshaling yards may be seen beneath the still intact wing. It was near Nis also that 15th Air Force P-38s strafed, by mistake, a Russian column killing a general, two other officers and six enlisted men, besides setting vehicles afire. Russians then forbade Americans to fly over their zones without clearance.

One of the biggest strikes on oil was carried out by the 15th when it dropped 800 tons of bombs on five refineries in the Vienna area and 375 tons on Bratislava, across the Danube, in Czechoslovakia on June 16, 1944. At the same time, the 8th Air Force took a little time off from supporting the Normandy invasion to bomb the Misburg refinery near Hannover.

Vienna, pilot Stanley Kavan recalls, was an unpopular city because it was surrounded (as Ploesti had been) with a heavy ring of flak guns. So were, in fact, all fuel targets such as Blechhammer, Brux, Ruhland, and Regensburg. Transportation targets, the final phase of the strategic offensive, were also tough, especially those in the Vienna area (which was sensitive, too, because of the oil), Hungary, and Yugoslavia.

The 15th Air Force was the first to fly a shuttle mission to Russia. On June 2, 1944, a formation of B-17s led by General Eaker took off from Foggia, bombed a marshaling yard at Debrecen, Hungary, and proceeded on to land at Poltava.

237

Stanley J. Kavan, B-17 pilot, 463rd Bomb Group.

The shuttle missions were given the, as it eventuated, appropriate code name "Frantic." Although designed to assist the Russians in their offensive against the Germans, it was difficult to clear targets with them and to arrange for bases on which the American planes could land.

Frustrating and seemingly endless negotiations were required before Eaker could get the green light from the Russians to make the missions. Leading a formation of 130 Fortresses, with an escort of seventy Mustangs, Eaker was able, finally, to launch the assault. Although neither German fighters nor flak were encountered over the target, one B-17 exploded in the air—the only loss on the trip to Russia.

Eaker recalls a pleasant and warm welcome from the Russians at Poltava and Mirgorad, where the B-17s were based. "The local people were very friendly, particularly at first," he said. "They were kindly and cordial and the young girls especially, who worked on the base, were friendly toward our crews.

"About the third day some people from Moscow arrived and things changed. The girls objected, for some of them beat the newcomers on the head with clubs. But we were told to keep our crews inside the compound; no American magazines were permitted to be given to Russians."

While he was there Eaker was able to convince the Russians of the benefits to

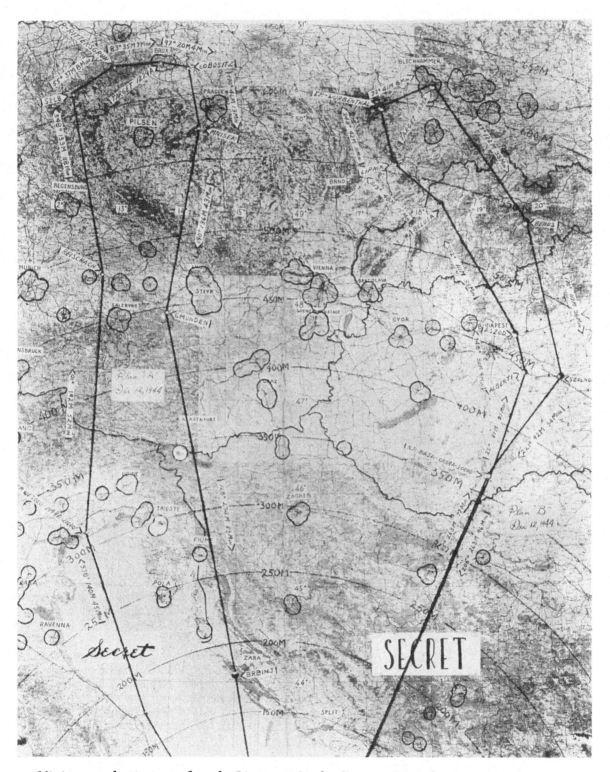

Mission map showing route flown by Lieutenant Stanley Kavan on December 12, 1944, to Blechhammer. Mileages and compass headings are indicated on each leg of the trip. Cloud-like figures are known flak concentrations. Another force of 15th Air Force planes went to Brux. Routes to and from targets were planned in order to avoid the flak centers.

239

Returning from the first shuttle mission to Russia, June, 1944. On the return trip the 15th bombed the Focsani Air Base in Rumania.

When a "Little Friend" needs a "Big Friend." After escorting the 2nd Bomb Group to an oil target at Blechhammer this P-38 found itself in difficulty after a flak hit knocked out one engine. For protection the Lightning moved into the comforting zones of fire of the B-17s.

Having completed its bomb run over the Farencvaros Railroad Yards near Budapest, Hungary, this Fortress received a direct hit. Although five parachutes left the plane, there was no possibility of any others. The flak tore away the entire front of the plane carrying off pilot, co-pilot, bombardier, navigator, and undoubtedly hitting the top-turret gunner. The plane remained poised like this only for a moment before falling.

Flak did this to the B-17 piloted by Guy M. Miller and Thomas M. Rybovich over the Debreczen railroad yards in Hungary. Although no one was injured, it was quite a feat to bring the plane back to Foggia. The tail wheel collapsed during the landing, causing the bend in the fuselage.

On the way to bomb the oil refineries at Blechhammer, these 15th Air Force B-17s are seen in a typical setting: over the Alps, flying through the turbulent contrails of the preceding groups.

Working with the B-17s were the B-24 units. The Liberator, bombs spilling from its belly, was struck by flak over Blechhammer during the bomb run. The plane was from the 465th Bomb Group, the pilot: Lieutenant Colonel Jack Lokker.

241

them as well as the Allies if they could carry out shuttle bombings. Without the necessity of making the return trip it would be possible to make deeper penetrations into Germany. The Russians seemed to agree and appeared to be co-operative. This opened the way for the series of shuttle missions in which both the 15th and 8th Air Forces took part. But by September the Russians lost interest and refused permission to Allied planes to land on Russian bases. This attitude took its most tragic turn when the Russians refused to help the Poles in Warsaw who had risen against the Germans. Denounced by the Russians as "reckless adventurers who had risen too soon and without Soviet incitement," the Poles were left to fight without aid although the Russians were nearby. Relief missions by the RAF and the U. S. Air Forces were flown but not until September 8, 1944, was permission reluctantly granted for another "Frantic" operation. Supplies were dropped into Warsaw but only a fraction fell into Polish hands and, because of the Russian delay, time had run out for the beleaguered Warsaw.

The B-17s returned from their missions to Foggia in the same condition as the battered Fortresses in England, although flak was more of a problem than the fighters, the *Luftwaffe* being all but done after "The Big Week." It was during this period that one of the most astonishing incidents involving a B-17 occurred.

Sergeant James Raley of Henderson, Kentucky, was a B-17 tail gunner in the 15th Air Force. During "The Big Week," just as they were approaching the target, Raley heard over the intercom that they were at 19,000 feet. A moment later he was thrown violently around inside his gun position, and he heard a loud ripping noise. Peering through his window Raley could see another Fortress burning and nosing toward the ground. Apparently in the close formation there had been a collision.

Trapped inside the gun position, Raley could feel his plane spinning down also. The plane described crazy convolutions through the air as it tossed around the sky on its way to earth. Raley knew he was falling from 19,000 feet and had no chance of getting out of the plane. He was sure he would die.

The erratic plunge stopped, although it must have seemed a lifetime to Raley, and he heard the sounds of sliding impact. This was it. Raley closed his eyes.

When he opened them he was amazed to see pine trees around him. They had made it! Then almost in panic, he began to fight his way out of the damaged plane, afraid of fire. Grabbing some candy and his shoes, he pushed his way through the bulkhead to get into the forward part of the plane.

There was no forward part of the plane. Raley had dropped 19,000 feet in the B-17's tail section. The collision had just cut the fuselage at the point where the part in which Raley was stationed formed an inefficient glider. By pure accident the distribution of weight in conjunction with the empennage formed a crude motorless aircraft. Part of the way Raley had glided and part of the way he was tossed end over end, but at the time of impact he was in a glide and thus did not hit with the force which could have killed him. The trees in which the tail section landed did the rest.

Very shaken by this unusual experience (another was reported as happening in the tail of a B-24), Raley removed his flight boots, laced up his GI shoes and then walked for weeks through the Italian mountains until he was able to rejoin his outfit. The other nine men in the B-17 were never heard of again.

242

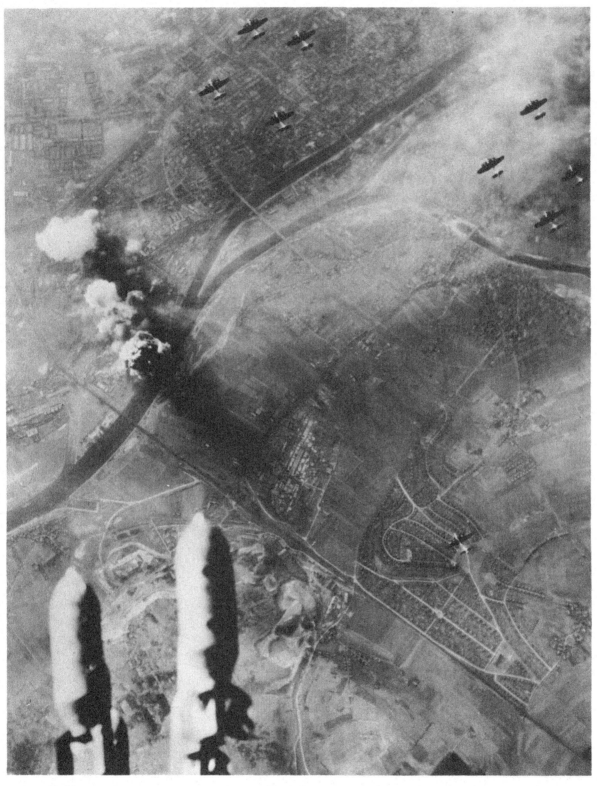

The Fortresses strike the oil storage facilities at Regensburg (December 18, 1944).
Storage tanks, distillation plants and rolling stock received direct hits.

The 15th Air Force, like the 8th, took part in the invasion of France—the invasion of Southern France on August 15, 1944. When the German jets became a serious problem the 15th, along with the 8th was dispatched to bomb the factories and airdromes. But even more telling in the counter-jet campaign was the lack of fuel.

The strategic air forces were rapidly running out of targets. Ground forces encircled or over-ran the once invincible *Wehrmacht*. The 15th's first assault on Berlin occurred on March 24, 1945. Like the 8th the 15th was dispatched on more satisfying missions such as the dropping of food to starving populations cut off from supplies by the war and evacuating prisoners of war.

Mission accomplished.

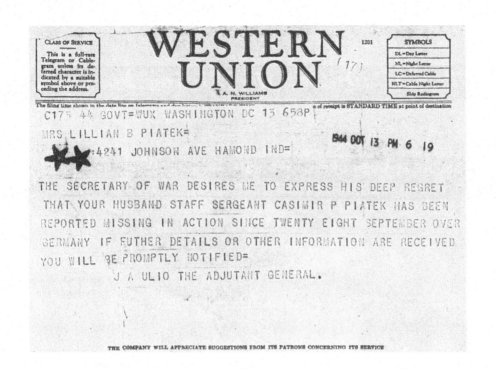

15. POW

The B-17 had begun its bomb run—the target was a marshaling yard near Saarbrücken—when one engine stopped. They had come this far so the pilot chose to feather the prop and continue on the run. But the strain on the remaining three engines was too much for the heavily loaded plane. A cylinder head blew and an engine began burning—and instants later the Fortress vanished in a flash and a billow of black smoke. Nothing remained of the wings which simply shriveled and floated down through the oily cloud in small bits of metal. The fuselage separated into its three components. The pilot and co-pilot were killed instantly but in the three sections several simultaneous events took place.

The bombardier, Daniel Gilmore of Luling, Texas, seeing the plane seriously ablaze, was just reaching for his parachute when the B-17's explosion blew him through the nose. As he fell unconscious for perhaps 10,000 feet he gripped the chute pack tightly. When he recovered from the shock of the explosion he found himself falling through space with his chute in his hands instead of on his back. As he fell he struggled to snap the hooks which, somehow, he managed to do. The chute billowed up over him and he fell three miles from the German lines inside France.

The navigator merely followed Gilmore through the nose of the plane. One of the waist gunners was blown through the side of the ship and never recalled opening his chute. The top turret gunner was just leaving via the escape hatch when the explosion occurred and was blown from the plane also.

Arthur E. Weiss of Chicago, the radio operator, was thrown to the floor by the explosion. When he came to his senses he had only to roll himself to the

How To Bail Out of the Flying Fortress

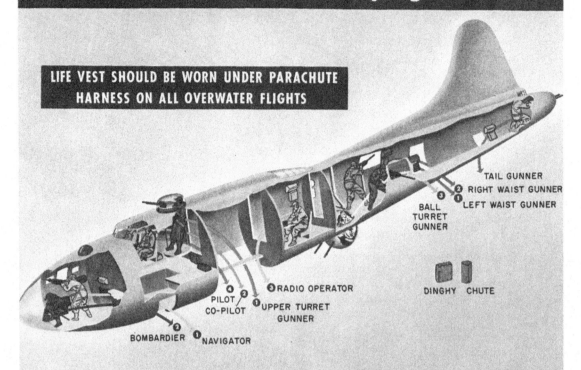

LIFE VEST SHOULD BE WORN UNDER PARACHUTE
HARNESS ON ALL OVERWATER FLIGHTS

TAIL GUNNER
RIGHT WAIST GUNNER
LEFT WAIST GUNNER

BALL
TURRET
GUNNER

DINGHY   CHUTE

RADIO OPERATOR
PILOT
CO-PILOT   UPPER TURRET
GUNNER

BOMBARDIER   NAVIGATOR

Procedure When Wearing Conventional Seat or Back-Type Parachute

When an emergency develops in the air and it becomes necessary to bail out of your airplane, there is no time for confusion or second-guessing. The procedure must be automatic. The instructions below, and the diagram, show through what hatches and in what order crew members should make their exit. Ground drills based on this procedure will help you obtain the efficiency and speed necessary to abandon your airplane successfully and safely. Wherever possible, jump from the after end of the hatch. Where several crew members bail out of the same exit, each should inspect the others to make sure that all are wearing a full complement of equipment securely fastened.

PILOT—Exits fourth out forward end of bomb bay. (Alternate exit, out front entrance door.) Is last to leave plane.

CO-PILOT—Exits second through forward end of bomb bay.

BOMBARDIER—Exits second through front entrance door.

NAVIGATOR—Exits first out of front entrance door.

UPPER TURRET GUNNER—Exits first out forward end of bomb bay.

RADIO OPERATOR—Exits third through after end of bomb bay.

RIGHT WAIST GUNNER—Exits second through main entrance door.

LEFT WAIST GUNNER—Exits first out main entrance door.

BALL TURRET GUNNER—Exits third out of main entrance door.

TAIL GUNNER—Exits through small emergency door in tail.

Procedure When Wearing Quick Attachable Chute Harness...

When the order is given over the inter-com to "Abandon Airplane," each crew member will remove the individual seat-type dinghy and breast-type parachute from their respective positions near his station, snap them onto his QAC harness, and exit through the hatch specified. The following instructions, used with the diagram, show the positions of the dinghies and the parachutes, the correct exit hatch, and the order of bailing out. Where several crew members bail out of the same hatch, each should check the others to make sure that all are wearing a full complement of equipment, securely fastened. Wherever possible, jump from the after end of the hatch. Remember, a life vest should be worn under the QAC harness on all over-water flights. The lanyard on the dinghy should be snapped onto the D-ring on the life vest.

Periodic ground drills will familiarize your crew members with the operations of the QAC harness and the order of bail-out.

PILOT—Parachute mounted on floor, directly behind pilot's seat in pilot's cabin. Dinghy worn in seat position. Pilot is fourth to exit through forward end of bomb bay. (Alternate exit, out front entrance door.) Last to leave plane.

CO-PILOT—Parachute mounted on floor directly behind co-pilot's seat in pilot's compartment. Dinghy worn in seat position. Exits second through forward end of bomb bay. (Alternate exit, through front entrance door.)

BOMBARDIER—Parachute mounted in navigator's compartment on starboard wall directly opposite navigator about half-way up on wall. Dinghy mounted in navigator's compartment near floor on starboard side, half the distance forward from bulkhead. Exits second through front entrance door.

NAVIGATOR—Parachute mounted on bulkhead armor plating directly above door, on inner side of navigator's compartment. Dinghy mounted alongside and to rear of bombardier's dinghy. Exits first through front entrance door.

UPPER TURRET GUNNER—Parachute mounted on floor just forward of bomb bay bulkhead on port side. Dinghy mounted on forward wall of bomb bay bulkhead in turret compartment, directly below entrance to bomb bay. Exits first through forward end of bomb bay.

RADIO OPERATOR—Parachute mounted on starboard wall just forward of rear bulkhead of radio compartment, three-fourths way up side of wall. Dinghy mounted directly beneath radio operator's parachute. Exits third through after end of bomb bay.

RIGHT WAIST GUNNER—Parachute mounted on starboard wall just forward of rear door and even with top of door. Dinghy mounted directly beneath parachute. Exits second through main entrance door.

LEFT WAIST GUNNER—Parachute mounted on wall immediately aft and on same level as left waist window on port side. Dinghy mounted directly beneath left waist gunner's parachute. Exits first through main entrance door.

BALL TURRET GUNNER—Parachute mounted on aft starboard side of rear bulkhead of radio compartment, about even with top of door. Dinghy mounted directly beneath ball turret gunner's parachute. Exits third through main entrance.

TAIL GUNNER—Parachute mounted on starboard wall immediately aft and slightly above rear gunner's escape hatch. Dinghy mounted directly beneath parachute. Exits through small emergency door in tail.

"How to bail out of a Flying Fortress."

246

shattered edge of the fuselage, push, and was falling. His chute opened and he was safe.

The ball-turret gunner was in his position when the explosion came and had to get out of the turret before he could even get his chute on. He found it less than a foot away from the jagged edge at which the fuselage had snapped. As this remnant of the B-17 fell to earth Samuel M. Longtine of Marquette, Michigan, climbed out of the turret, put on his chute and jumped.

In the tail gun position Michael J. Kuzel of Ironwood, Michigan, found himself spinning end over end in the detached section. Centrifugal forces pinned him inside during the gyrations but he could move from time to time whenever the tail section smoothed out the path of its fall. But there was a serious problem: Kuzel's chute had opened while he was still inside the tail section. He gathered up the wildly fluttering silk in his arms and jumped clear, hoping that it would not catch on the jagged edges of the tail section. He made it also.

What happened to a Fortress crew that had to bail out over enemy territory? Those who were neither captured nor killed (by incensed civilians) sometimes managed to make it back to England over various routes. Most were captured and spent the rest of the war in a German prison camp as *Kriegsgefangenen*, prisoners of war—or as they themselves preferred, "Kriegies." Then began a life of almost unremitting boredom punctuated by escape attempts and other events of interest.

Joseph Wackerly was an aerial gunner-radio operator with the 305th Bomb Group. His story is typical of the "Kriegie." He and his crew mates were new to the 305th where, after a run of missions, they were taken off combat temporarily for training as a PFF crew. This crew operated lead planes, Pathfinders, equipped with radar for bombing through clouds.

As new members of the 305th, a group which had been once commanded by General LeMay, Wackerly and the others were invited to a squadron party for a typical hearty welcome.

"We were awakened about 3 A.M. and told that we were to fly Deputy PFF Lead for the 92nd (our old group) which was leading the 8th Air Force on a strike against Berlin," Wackerly continues. "We left our ball turret gunner in the barracks because his place was taken up by the PFF equipment operated by a lieutenant, who was a new addition to our crew."

The date was March 22, 1944. "The Mickey operator's position was directly across from me in the radio room and as I left my seat to see that the bombs were all out of the racks (after the bombs had been dropped), a piece of flak came through the floor and he looked at me and I looked at him and it wasn't necessary to say a word.

"It just seemed to me that the flak was drawn to us by the PFF equipment because I don't think they missed us many times. We were hit directly over the target so that would mean that the fighters would be off in the wings waiting for the flak to let up and then they would come back in. There weren't too many missions when we had trouble from the fighters, it was mostly always the accurate flak. This was the way it was with most of the fellows that I talked to in Germany.

". . . after dropping our bombs we were forced to drop out of formation because of hits on two of our engines. Lieutenant Burnett, our pilot, ordered the bail-out when it became apparent that because of the loss of gasoline and the

Prisoner's Identification Card.   Prisoner of War mug shot.

inability to feather the props on the two useless engines we would be unable to reach the North Sea.

"As far as going down in a chute is concerned, it was just something that had to be done. I guess I was always afraid that the pin would not come out but I can remember the good feeling when with just one soft pull the pin just popped out so nice and easy. We were less than a thousand feet up when we were ordered to jump so it didn't take long to reach the ground.

"We were picked up shortly after near the town of Oldenberg and were told that the pilot was dead. I think that most of the fellows will tell you that the German civilians were a greater threat to our ever reaching prison camp than the soldiers. I can understand their bitterness, but it sure is an unhealthy feeling when you hear them inciting a crowd. One of their pet calls was 'Hang the bastards!', in perfect English, too.

"We were taken to the interrogation center in Frankfurt; here we were split up—the remaining officers to one camp, three to the enlisted camp in Latvia and Sergeant Billy Lewis and myself to Stalag Luft I, Barth, Germany. Because this was an Officers' camp and we were enlisted men, we were given the manual work around the camp."

Already a guest of the Third Reich in Stalag Luft I were Lieutenants Lewis Pinkussohn and Thomas T. Keasbey, the former a navigator-bombardier from the 44th Group (a B-24 unit; Pinkussohn still feels that if he had been in a B-17 that day in February 1944 he would not have had to jump over Germany). Keasbey was a B-17 pilot with the 95th Group, one of the Wing companion groups of the 100th, who went down over Berlin during the great air battle on March 6, 1944.

After leaving the Interrogation Center the men were issued a Red Cross parcel containing cigarettes, shaving equipment, underwear, and other invaluables and given baths—although not in that order. Wackerly's contingent had spent five days in boxcars traveling across Germany before they arrived at Barth. Food was scanty and on the primitive side.

An American officer was in charge of the prisoners and an attempt was made to maintain some form of military discipline and a routine which might

248

make their enforced stay more bearable. The prisoners were assigned to barracks (called blocks) and rooms or bunks in the blocks.

They were issued nine bed slats on which the lumpy mattress was placed. There were generally two roll calls per day and the bed slats were counted regularly for the wood could be put to several uses by ingenious prisoners intent upon escape.

Since the Germans were having trouble getting food, the prisoner of war did not fare too well nutritionally. To the regular issue of German food was added the contents of the Red Cross parcels that arrived intermittently or from home. For better eating, the men generally pooled their food supplies which were turned over to those best qualified to prepare food.

Among the first acts of all prisoners was to communicate with their families. The War Department, as a matter of course, sent the next-of-kin the rather chilling telegram with the words "missing in action" in it. This could mean anything, but was sent to the families of those known to be missing in order to prepare them for whatever was to come. Long gaps in correspondence always worried the next of kin and the telegram was, if a little frightening, at least some word.

This was followed shortly after with a letter which attempted to reassure the relatives of the missing. "I know that added distress is caused by failure to receive more information or details," wrote Major General James A. Ulio, the Adjutant General, in a letter that was always personally signed. "Therefore, I wish to assure you that at any time additional information is received it will be transmitted to you without delay, and, if in the meantime no additional information is received, I will again communicate with you at the expiration of three months.

"The term 'missing in action,'" Ulio explained, "is used only to indicate that the whereabouts or status of an individual is not immediately known. It is not intended to convey the impression that the case is closed. I wish to emphasize that every effort is exerted continuously to clear up the status of our personnel. Under war conditions this is a difficult task as one must readily realize. Experience has shown that many persons reported missing in action are subsequently reported as prisoners of war, but as this information is furnished by countries with which we are at war, the War Department is helpless to expedite such reports. However, in order to relieve financial worry, Congress has enacted legislation which continues in force the pay, allowances, and allotments to dependents of personnel carried in a missing status."

The International Red Cross at Geneva, Switzerland, served as the clearing house for clearing up "the status of personnel." Also the Germans issued a postcard with which the prisoner could communicate with his family as soon as he had arrived at a permanent camp.

As soon as it was known that a man was a prisoner of war in Germany, the office of the Provost Marshal immediately informed the next of kin how they might communicate with the prisoner and how they might send parcels (one parcel and two tobacco labels were issued every sixty days). "Care should be taken," they were warned, "when preparing next of kin parcels to avoid using stickers or other material which bear patriotic slogans either within or on the outside of the parcels."

One of the prized issues was given the prisoners by the War Prisoners' Aid of the YMCA, "A Wartime Log." Into this chunky volume with the rough tan cover

Kriegsgefangenenpost

Postkarte

Mit Luftpost
Par Avion

Taxe perçue   P₁.

Gebührenfrei

Absender:
Vor- und Zuname:

Empfangsort:

Straße:

Gefangenennummer:

Lager-Bezeichnung: Luft 1
via Stalag Luft 3

Land:
Landesteil (Provinz usw.

Deutschland (Allemagne)

Stalag Luft I, Barth, Germany—panoramic vista showing some of the barracks and the town hall in the distance. Crack in original glass negative accounts for scratch on film.

Postcard supplied by the Germans to prisoners for notifying next of kin of their whereabouts and state of health. All prisoners' incoming mail was censored at Stalag Luft III near Sagan, Germany.

the men in German prison camps noted their thoughts, dreams, hopes, and remembrances of times past. Poetry would seem to have been a favored occupation, ranging from the humorous to the solemn—and all of it quite unpolished though heartfelt and sincere.

A Combat Airman's Prayer

Please, dear God, let me soar
O'er green and yellow fields once more,
Where there'll be no dirty clouds of black,
Bringing forth that anguished cry of "Flak!"
Where sight of speck out in the blue
Will not mean "Watch it—fighter at two!"
Where no screaming demon from out of the sun
Makes every man jump, and with flaming gun
Endeavor to pay another life
To the devil who started this world wide strife;
If you don't think this too much of a boon,
Well, please dear God, please make it soon.

—ANON—

The prisoners also made drawings in their logs—cartoons, portraits of fellow prisoners, maps on which they followed the course of the war. Someone always managed to have a radio which was tuned into BBC and then the news was disseminated via the camp newspaper *POW.* The men drew the floor plans of their homes, made lists of their menus in camp and the ones they would devour when they returned to their homes.

BREAKFAST:
Fresh peaches (with cream)
Corn flakes (with thick cream)
Toast (lots of butter and jam)
Coffee and milk

250

Guests of the Third Reich, Stalag Luft I, a special prison for fliers. The Luftwaffe, as a rule, treated their fellow airmen better than other prisoners of war were handled in other camps. The men are gathered in a vegetable garden. B-17 pilot T. F. Keasbey is second guest from right.

LUNCH:

    Scrambled eggs (with sliced tomatoes & bacon)
    Milk
    Fresh fruit

DINNER:

    Martini (pecan and almond nuts)
    Shrimp cocktail
    Soup: chicken noodle
    Entre: roast beef
    Vegetables: peas, potatoes (mashed)
    Salad: hearts of lettuce (Russian dressing)
    Dessert: Brandied peaches
        Coffee and brandy

This was drawn up with loving attention to detail as may be gleaned from the parenthetic afterthoughts. However on the very next page of the log from which the menu was taken is the following bulletin:

Office of the Group Commander
Group I, U.S.A.A.F. North Compound
Oflag Luft I. Barth, Germany

                              Feb. 3, 1945

1. Menu: Breakfast-Oatmeal. Bring your own Klim [powdered milk] cans as bowls will not be available if water is not on. Dinner: will be announced later.

2. Official: Commencing today, if we have not received word that water is on by the time of this bulletin, we will begin construction of a well to alleviate the present water shortage. Anyone having experience in the construction

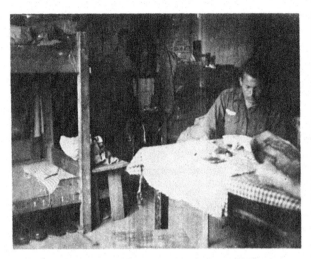

Interior shot of a barracks, Stalag Luft I made with a camera using glass negatives. Lieutenant Lewis Pinkussohn reads at the table.

Still life, Stalag Luft I, by Thomas T. Keasbey. The KLIM cans were used as cooking utensils, name tags, made into stove pipes, soap dishes, reflectors, picture frames and dozens of other objects.

of water wells, please report to Bl. 9, Rm. 5 immediately after morning roll call for the purpose of supervising a detail in the construction of a well. 3. Official: Due to the present water shortage, it is highly imperative that every man do his utmost to purify water before consumption and take special precautions with regards to water shortage. All water absolutely must be boiled before consumption, as well as for washing purposes. In no case will snow be used for washing faces, etc. as chilblains will result. The latrines must be flushed each time after use. This may be accomplished by keeping the large wooden tub filled at all times. The squadron commanders are directly responsible to see that these regulations are enforced without exception.

Four days later there was yet another warning: ". . . bits of glass have been found in German bread. Bread should be sliced thin and in the light, and the slices examined before consumption."

As the Allies (in the case of Stalag Luft I it was the Russians) approached, the regulations became more stringent. By late February the Red Cross food parcels were not coming through (they did arrive toward the end of March) and the coal supply was short.

On March 18, 1945, the bulletin board carried a tragic note: "*This Headquarters regrets to announce the death of Lt. E. F. Wayman, who was killed by the Germans when he forgetfully attempted to attend church during an Air Raid.*"

To keep themselves occupied, besides plotting escapes, the men organized games, clubs, study groups, discussion groups, libraries, even built models of their favorite aircraft. They also formed orchestras, glee clubs, and produced musicals, as for example *Hit the Bottle,* a musical comedy in three acts with songs by N. Bliss and J. H. Lashly and book by Nelson Gidding. *Hit the Bottle* opened on July 3, 1944, at "The Little Theater off Times Square—Way Off—" at Barth, Germany. Two of the songs were entitled "My Dreams Never Let Me Down"

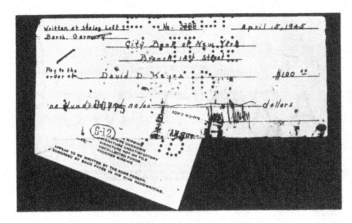

This check drawn upon the National City Bank of New York and written on a plain sheet of paper (following a game of chance) at Stalag Luft I, was cashed in the United States after the payee was released from the camp.

An escape map prepared by Thomas Keasbey against the day when he was hoping he could make a break.

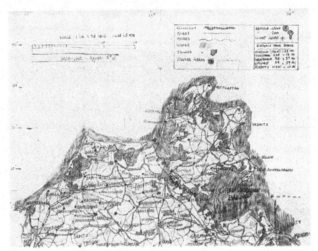

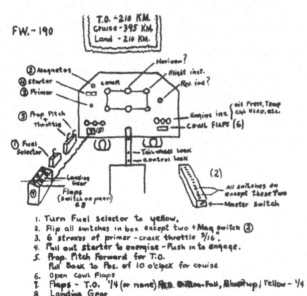

Cockpit diagram of the Focke-Wulf 190 indicating all the necessary details a pilot would need to know to fly the unfamiliar plane out of Germany.

BARTH

HARD TIMES

Vol 1   No. 1   LAST 1   SATURDAY MAY 5th 1945   PRICE 1 D- BAR.

Editor: F L E. R. INKPEN   Assoc: 1st Lt N. GIDDINGS   Publisher: 1st Lt D. MacDONALD   Printing: F LT J. D. WHITE

RUSSKY COME!

As seen by LOWELL BENNET, I. N. S. War Correspondent.

RELIEVED!

Colonel Zemke intended to write this appreciation of the relief of Stalag Luft I, but unfortunately necessary duties have made this impossible. He has, in his own words, "taken a powder" to make final arrangements with the relieving Soviet forces.

It is therefore my privilege to introduce this Memorial Edition of the BARTH HARD TIMES.

During the successes, reverses and stagnant periods encountered during this struggle, our newspaper has faithfully recorded the German war communiques and expanded upon them in capable editorials.

With the redemption of a continent, our exile is ended. Our barb-bound community will soon be a memory. So, on behalf of Colonel Hubert Zemke and myself, to all our fellow-kriegies: G O O D
L U C K !

G. C. C. T. Weir.

WHAT D'YE KNOW- JOE!!

BRAITHWAITE FINDS UNCLE JOE

Contacts Russian Infantryman at Crossroads
Five miles South of Stalag One.

Major Braithwaite and Sgt Korson, our Stalag scouts, raced out to a cross-roads 5 miles south of Barth with the order, "find Uncle Joe". This was 8 p. m., May 1.

They searched southward, defying a rumored Russian curfew which was about as brief and emphatic as their own order: "EVERYONE stay put; anyone seen moving will be shot on sight."

Meanwhile, Wing Commander Blackburn's telephone crew were ringing numbers in Stralsund, hoping a Russian would answer the phone and we could break the big news of our presence. "Try the mayor," they asked the girl (who was still working Barth's phone exchange). "Not a chance," said she. "Barth's mayor poisoned himself and Stralsund's mayor has sprouted wings."

Scouts Braithwaite and Korson pushed on 3 miles. The scenery: thousands of people everywhere, sitting down, waiting.

The last issue of the Barth Hard Times—*also the first.*

254

(There's a lovely brunette/That I haven't seen yet . . .) and "A Woman's a Woman." The boys, though not eating too well, were still healthy in spirit.

Toward the end of April 1945 the situation inside Germany had deteriorated badly. Keasbey, inside Stalag Luft I with Pinkussohn, Wackerly, and "Red" Morgan watched and noted it down in his diary.

APRIL 30, 1945—Jerry military personnel leaving camp with families. Going out on bikes, carts, carriages, horses, trucks, cars and on foot. Some drunk— No harm shown to Kriegies. All day long installations at Flak School were blown up—plus supply dumps, radar, etc. About a thousand men picked up parcels at Flak School (Red Cross). Civilians left behind made a few outbursts in trying to obtain parcels. Many civilians had R.C. parcels in their possession. 2330: no guards in any tower of the camp . . .

MAY 1, 1945—0645. Chow in the sack. M.P.'s (our own) in all towers. White flag flying where swastika used to fly. Each man given 3 R.C. parcels to last him 10 days at most . . . Russian patrol at gate at 2230. *Hitler dead!!*

MAY 2—*Some* were able to get to Flak School to loot. Brought back chairs, tables, beds, shoes, boots, hats, sabers, daggers, guns, medals, etc. (everything imaginable). Many men take off to see Germany and the sights. Don't remember having been told not to go, but they said we should stick around for the planes which are to arrive soon. *Ha!!* Went into Barth and saw Russians taking over a town. Very wild, but very little damage done. More done by civilians in town and U.S. officers and EM (enlisted men). Some men were able to get wine and other fairly drinkable liquor! Red flag on Barth steeple.

MAY 4, 1945—Impatient to get home—Still eating like mad.

MAY 5, 1945—First Yanks (from Evac. Hospital) came in Main Gate at 1600 . . . Men went mad with joy at seeing them. Rode in on a jeep. American, Russian and British Flags flying!!

MAY 7-9—Still waiting!

MAY 12—B-17s start evacuating Barth.

MAY 13—Left in B-17 for France. We landed near Laon, France around 1430. Taken by trucks to camp outside Rheims.

On May 24, 1945, Keasbey in a stateroom in the SS *Monticello* left Southampton for the United States. His diary ends here with the word *"Sheets!!"*

Little Friends.

16. "Little Friends" and the Dying *Luftwaffe*

Although it was true that the B-17 could withstand a good deal of punishment from fighter attack and antiaircraft fire, it could not absorb all possible .50-caliber fire, cannon fire, rocket fire and remain airborne. It was not therefore a "Flying Fortress" in the sense that it could take a direct hit in a critical spot or take sustained fighter attacks.

The B-17 could probably take more than any other bomber of the war, as has been seen. But until long-range fighters were introduced which could serve as escort to and from the target, the men in the B-17s and B-24s suffered terribly. They never turned back, but the price was—as was proved at Schweinfurt and Ploesti—exorbitant.

In their fashion, the strategic bombers contributed toward the solution of the *Luftwaffe* problem during the counter-air campaign by bombing the factories, assembly plants and the airdromes and in aerial combat, even if claims were exaggerated. The oil campaign, too, was to have its effect upon the German Air Force. But until these long-range programs took effect the *Luftwaffe* was a formidable, courageous, and deadly adversary.

All deep penetrations of Germany by the B-17s were rendered hazardous because the fighter escorts had to turn back practically at the German border, somewhere between Emden and Cologne. Then the German fighters would pounce on the formations and take their heavy toll. They lost some of their own but never in the numbers claimed by bomber crews. Most of the early missions of the 8th Air Force were made with scant protection from the *Luftwaffe* and the price was paid on the Schweinfurt–Regensburg mission and the return to Schweinfurt in October, 1943.

It was just the day after that mission that the improved Lockheed P-38 Lightning was ready for action. A high-flying twin-engine fighter, the P-38 eventually could achieve an effective escort radius of 1500 miles and was ·the first American fighter which could match the performance of the Messerschmitt Me-109.

Because it was a heavy aircraft, the P-38 was not as maneuverable as its adversaries, but it was fast, tough and, because of its two-engine layout, could lose one of them and still return home. It was also heavily armed, some models carrying a 20-mm cannon and four .50-caliber machine guns in the nose. As it was supplanted by the P-47 and P-51 as a fighter, although serving in that capacity also until the end of the war, the P-38 was put to several different uses, such as bombardment and photography.

The Republic P-47 Thunderbolt, also known as "The Jug" to its pilots, was a tricky plane to develop but once it had been perfected proved to be one of the most effective of all American fighters. The Thunderbolt's armament, consisted of from six to eight .50-caliber machine guns. It was also, by far, the heaviest fighter plane, its gross weight in the later models reaching 21,000 pounds (the Douglas C-47 Cargo plane weighed 26,000).

The Thunderbolt was an extremely rugged aircraft capable of taking a good

Fighter pilots were generally younger than bomber pilots and displayed a more aggressive and adventurous temperament. Closing the canopy of his P-38 is nineteen-year-old Royal D. Frey of the 20th Fighter Group at Kings Cliffe, England. Frey was "hacked" (shot down) over Brunswick on February 10, 1944, on an escort mission. He was sent to "that rest haven on the Baltic," Stalag Luft I—a prisoner of war camp under the supervision of the Luftwaffe.

A Republic P-47, Thunderbolt, one of the most rugged fighters ever built. This "Jug" flys off the starboard wing of a B-17 of the 91st Bomb Group.

A North American P-51 Mustang releasing rockets from under its wings. The P-51 may have been the best fighter craft of the Second World War.

The Lockheed P-38 Lightning, the first American designed fighter plane capable of competing with the British Spitfire as a serious threat to the German Me-109 and FW-190.

258

The Messerschmitt Me-109, the Luftwaffe's first-line fighter when the Second World War began. Subsequent models appeared throughout the war, this one being one of the later Bf-109Gs.

deal of battle damage. By late 1943, equipped with drop tanks, the P-47 was able to accompany the B-17s and B-24s to Berlin and back.

The most effective escort of all was the North American P-51 Mustang, originally designed for the RAF as a replacement for the P-40. Ignored at first by the Army Air Forces, the P-51 was hailed by the British as "the best American fighter that has so far reached this country." They even compared it favorably to the Spitfire, which though a fine and potent fighter aircraft was unable to achieve the range necessary for the Battle of Germany.

Not too late, though tardy, did the Americans recognize the potency of the beautifully designed little Mustang. Though it too was designed for limited-range fighter defense to meet the needs of the British, the P-51 was modified for American use into a long-range fighter. The first units using the American version arrived in England in November 1943 and flew the first escort mission in December. By March of the following year the Mustang was challenging the *Luftwaffe* over Berlin. Powered by a single Rolls-Royce–Packard engine, the P-51 was armed with from four to six .50-caliber machine guns.

By January 1944 the Americans had two, possibly three, extremely effective "Little Friends," to protect the big bombers on their strategic attacks.

The best of the German fighters, which were on standing orders to concentrate their attacks upon the bombers (ignoring the fighters, if possible), were the Messerschmitt Me-109 and the Focke-Wulf FW-190. The former was one of the oldest of all German fighters while the latter was introduced after the war had begun. These aircraft, plus such twin-engined fighters as the Messerschmitt 110 (which was no match for the single engine fighters) bore the brunt of the aerial battles that were designed to take place over Germany. The Focke-Wulf

259

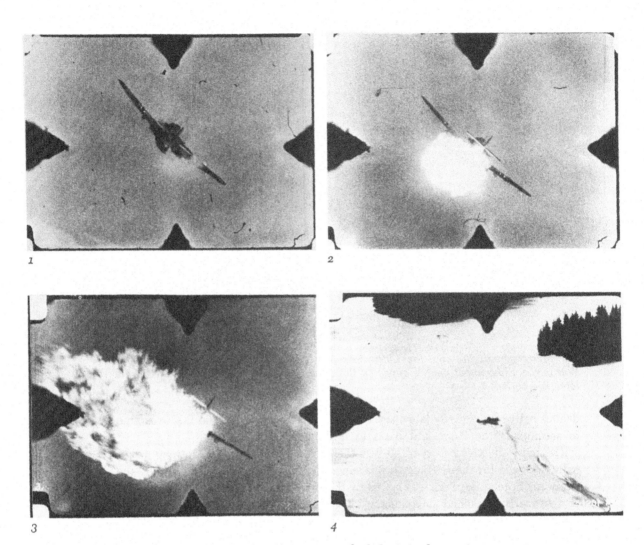

A gun-camera sequence in which Lieutenant Lee G. Mendenhal of Anahuac, Texas, shoots down an Me-109.

was especially a serious contender in this contest, but it was to be handicapped, as was the entire *Luftwaffe*, by the German High Command.

At first the High Command, Göring, Hitler, et al., did not believe that the American day bombers had a chance against the *Luftwaffe*, which was dispersed in the form of a peripheral defense in France and along the Eastern Front. At first there was no central means of defense for the Reich because no one believed it would be necessary. But when the B-17s first appeared over German territory this long-held belief was rendered meaningless. The next one adopted was that the Allies would not be able to develop fighters capable of escorting the bombers deep into Germany—the subsequent losses would discourage such assaults. And despite the fact that more and more American fighters were encountered over German cities, even Göring refused to accept that as a sign of things to come.

Secure in the false hope that the diffused *Luftwaffe* could stop the bombers from reaching the Reich, Adolf Galland's suggestion that a system such as had proved effective in the Battle of Britain be adopted to stop the B-17s was turned

A newly completed Focke-Wulf 190 rolls out of the plant at Oschersleben, Germany. One of the best fighters of the war, the Focke-Wulf 190 was regarded by German pilots as superior to the Me-109. Oschersleben was bombed severely by the B-17s.

down cold. The German High Command was, with an unusual hold on unreality, hoping that the bombers could be stopped and the German people would never realize the seriousness of the German military situation in 1943. While the British night raids at this time were numerically greater than those of the American day raids, and placed a terrible strain upon the civilian population, the few close to Hitler who actually recognized the possible consequences, admitted that the precision attacks would eventually prove the most costly to the war industries.

Under the rain of the combined blows of the British at night and the Americans by day, production of fighters of the Me-109, for example, dropped from 725 in July to 357 in December. And then came "The Big Week" in February 1944, specifically aimed at the German Air Force.

The curious paradox is that despite heavy losses by the *Luftwaffe* and the concentrated strikes on the aircraft industry, the German aircraft production actually rose to new peaks in 1944. There were several reasons for this. The most important probably was because of the efficiency and intelligence of Albert Speer, the German Minister of Armaments, who removed the jurisdiction over fighter production from the Air Ministry and took charge. Also through dispersal of the factories it was difficult to strike conclusively at the aircraft industry, as it was at oil. Also, damage to factories as revealed in strike photos was overrated. Likewise, so was the number of German fighters shot down by bomber crews. If the numbers submitted by crews were to be taken at face value, there should have been practically no *Luftwaffe* by 1944.

In a sense, there wasn't. The Normandy invasion was accomplished practically unopposed by German planes. The Allies did not know that only the 3rd Air Fleet equipped with from eighty to a hundred German fighters was within striking distance of the beaches. Even so, heavy fighter concentrations in overwhelming numbers stood ready to eliminate all *Luftwaffe* attempts on D-Day.

But there was an even more serious problem: from June 1944 on it was all

261

Captain Alvin Juchheim, Grenada, Mississippi, accounts for a FW-190 from which the pilot ejects himself.

but impossible to get enough aviation fuel. Speer was forced to admit that by September 1944, of the minimum of 160,000 tons required he was only able to supply 30,000.

Internal feuding in the desperate German High Command was to have its effects also. As early as August 1940 a cancellation order came from Hitler which abandoned all research and testing on aircraft that could not be put into production within a year. While this was not followed to the letter, the decision was to have far-reaching effects upon the German experiments with jet aircraft which might easily have turned the tide against the American day bombers had they been produced in time and in sufficient numbers. In the spring of 1943 the Messerschmitt Me-262, the first warplane to be powered with a turbojet engine, was ready to be manufactured, after a long period of testing, in large

262

The Messerschmitt Me-262, the first military jet fighter.

Another view.

numbers. Even the conservative Göring was impressed with the fighter. Luckily, for the Allies at least, Hitler would not give priority to the fighter for mass production. And when it was finally approved for quantity production it was on the understanding that the Me-262 would be used as a bomber—this because Hitler was obsessed with the idea of retaliation more than with protecting the hapless civilians within the Reich.

Consequently the few jet bombers that were produced (a total of 1433) were misused and the few that saw combat—less than a hundred—proved what a potent weapon the jet fighter might have been. Only thirty B-17s were knocked down by the Me-262s, but the jet's great speed of almost 600 mph made it difficult to overtake. It could flash through a bomber formation doing its damage with four 30-mm cannons and be out of sight a moment later.

Another German innovation was the introduction of a rocket fighter, the Messerschmitt Me-163 *Komet*, the first rocket powered fighter ever used. The egg-shaped craft was actually still in the experimental stage when it was turned over to operational groups late in 1944. It was a difficult plane to fly, had a tendency to explode on landing and, because it dropped its two-wheel dolly after taking off, caused serious pilot injuries when it landed.

The *Komet*, like the Me-262, was fast (also like the jet fighter it had a speed around 600 mph) although its range and endurance were very limited. It could remain in flight for about ten minutes. This meant that in order to be effective against the bomber formations, fighter units would have to be based almost in the path of the bombers; this was difficult to ascertain in 1944–45, for almost all of Germany had become the province of the B-17s.

Even fewer *Komets* than Me-262s became operational, but those that did proved quite effective against the bomber formations. One rocket pilot shot down three B-17s in succession by darting through the groups. The *Komet* could only shoot up above the B-17s and then swoop down firing its two 30-mm cannon before having to land for more fuel.

But the *Komet*, too, had come too late partially because of the conservatism of the German High Command, which did not want to develop such radical aircraft and because the original designer Alexander M. Lippisch and Wilhelm Messerschmitt did not get along. In addition Messerschmitt did not encourage the design because it had not originated with him. Thus did human failings affect larger projects.

The *Luftwaffe* expired as a victim both of the Allied fighter superiority and of German High Command incompetence. It had proved itself the master of inferior air forces but in time, when quality as well as quantity turned in the Allies' favor, the German Air Force was done. They had been betrayed by their Fuehrer and by their ineffectual leader Göring. Too late did the *Luftwaffe*, as did the *Wehrmacht*, discover that they had surrendered their traditions to a mad little ex-corporal of World War I. Strategies and tactics meant nothing to Hitler who, letting his imagination and instincts guide him, had brought them a series of early victories. These served only to blind the professionals to the facts. When the first B-17s appeared over Wilhelmshaven on January 27, 1943, the handwriting appeared on the walls of *Festung Europa*; and the professionals knew it.

A year later with large escorts of "Little Friends" the big bombers ranged practically unchallenged over all of Germany, deracinating the roots of Na-

An Me-262 is on the tail of an American Mustang as the gun camera of the plane behind the jet—a Mustang also—opens fire. This fight took place during a heavy bomber mission on oil targets.

A Messerschmitt Me-262 flies through the gun-camera of an American P-51 fighter.

265

The rocket fighter, Messerschmitt Me-163B, Komet. These strange planes took off from the wheeled dolly arched up through the bomber formations and landed almost immediately after. They were deadly to bombers and to the Komet pilot alike, being heavily armed and very volatile.

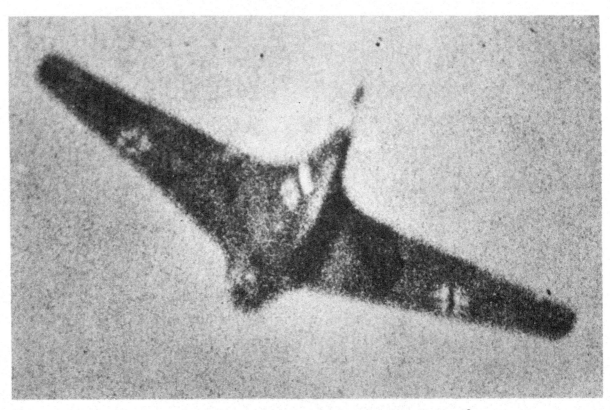

A rare photo: the pilot of a P-47 has a Komet in his gun sights for a fraction of a second. He shot it down.

266

One of the German last ditch weapons. The Ju-88 (on the bottom) was filled with high explosives and controlled by the FW-190 on top. When the target area was reached, the Ju-88 was released from the "piggy-back" arrangement and guided to the target by radio from the FW-190. This tandem set-up was captured by the Americans.

tional Socialism while, tragically, destroying the homes of its chief victims—the German people—and killing or maiming them. War was defined for them in the simplest terms—as it had not been in the First World War. It was a terrible lesson, not easily forgotten.

The "single" enemy plane that Göring boasted would never appear over sacred German soil, not only materialized but was multiplied literally into the thousands, the big bombers shepherded by weaving, aggressive, "Little Friends."

When the *Luftwaffe* could not rise to challenge them, the fighters dropped down to "the deck" when it was safe to leave the bombers. The Jugs and Mustangs wreaked havoc—only this cliché succinctly expresses it—on the ground. Unopposed they swooped down to strafe the roads, broke up troop concentrations, flamed supply dumps, disrupted rail travel, shattered any and all vehicles they could find and pummeled airdromes, destroying German aircraft *in situ*.

To the once majestic *Luftwaffe*, this was the ultimate nightmare for, as has been reported by survivors, the pilots watched with tears of frustration in their eyes. Without fuel they could not even leave the ground.

On April 16, 1945, General Spaatz sent personal messages to Generals Doolittle and Twining which, in part, read: "The advances of our ground forces have brought to a close the strategic air war waged by the United States Strategic Air Forces and the Royal Air Force Bomber Command.

"It has been won with a decisiveness becoming increasingly evident as our armies overrun Germany . . .

"All units of the U. S. Strategic Air Forces are commended for their part in winning the Strategic Air War and are enjoined to continue with undiminished effort and precision the final tactical phase of air action to secure the ultimate objective—the complete defeat of Germany."

That came within a month. On May 7, Germany surrendered unconditionally to the Allies. A week before Hitler, founder of the glorious Third Reich, which he had boasted would last for a thousand years, killed himself in Berlin. His body, and that of Eva Braun, his wife for one day, were soaked in gasoline and burned, like rubbish or old leaves, in the garden of the Chancellery. The smoke of their fire writhed up to mingle with the pall of a burning Berlin.

The Fuehrer had taken 30,000,000 souls with him before his dream sputtered out in a ghastly whimper.

SUPERFORTRESS

My God!

A member of the crew of
the *Enola Gay* on August 6, 1945.

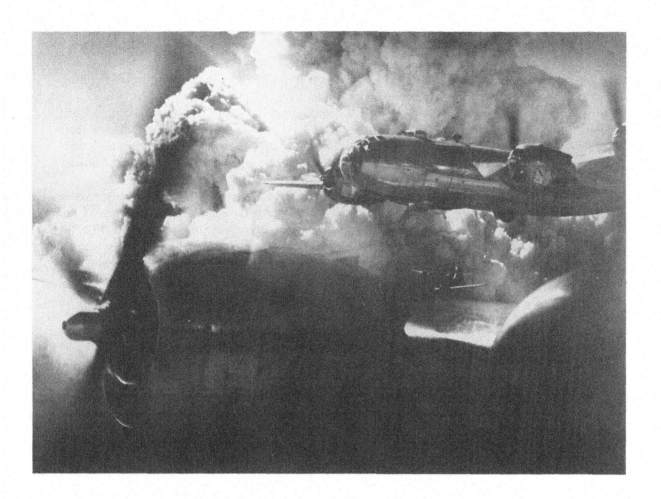

17. Sunset

The ill-fated Japanese attack on Midway cost them heavily in ships, planes, and men and, by extension, would cost them the war. If the action in the central Pacific was a dismal failure, ending all threats to Hawaii and the West Coast, the northern flank of Yamamoto's force did succeed in landing on the islands of Kiska, Attu, and Agattu in the Aleutians. Even this small victory was a bitter one, for the major objective was the American base at Dutch Harbor and American resistance made landings there impossible. But the Japanese did hold islands dangerously close to the American mainland.

The Aleutian Islands campaign, which officially ran from June 3, 1942, through August 24, 1943, was one of the most difficult and least known of all. The 11th Air Force operating from bases in Alaska (Fort Mears, Cold Bay) and Umnak Island (Fort Glenn), had to contend with weather conditions that could only be described as atrocious. Despite winds which could buckle metal runway matting, fog and general murky weather, the 11th Air Force, by bombing with B-17s and B-24s, strafing with its P-40s, contained the Japanese invaders. In October 1942 the Japanese began to abandon Attu and Agattu and reinforce their hold on Kiska. This installation was so heavily bombed and so regularly under American attack that holding it seemed senseless. Ground troops invaded Attu to route out the invaders in May 1943, and after three weeks of heavy fighting wiped out the Japanese garrison there.

When American and Canadian forces turned to Kiska, the main Japanese base, on August 15, 1943, they found it abandoned. Late in July the Japanese had boarded their ships and slipped away in the fog. The threat to the North American mainland was over—and the threat to the Japanese mainland via the Kurile Islands, north of Japan, began.

In the Southwest Pacific MacArthur moved inexorably up the bloody-runged ladder toward the Philippines, along the northern coast of New Guinea. At the same time, in the Central Pacific, under the command of Admiral Chester W. Nimitz, American forces moved upward from Guadalcanal in the Solomon Islands. From these hard-won bases, taken by the Marines in savage battles, the 13th Air Force was able to reach out and bomb the Japanese holdings at Rabaul in coordinated attacks with Kenney's 5th Air Force. The 7th Air Force, originally stationed at Hawaii, began moving toward Japan in its "one damned island after another" operations. As MacArthur's forces moved toward the Philippines in a series of brilliantly conceived moves, Nimitz's forces converged upon the Marianas Islands: Guam, Saipan, and Tinian.

The reason, which was hardly obvious to armchair strategists nor yet to the Japanese, was that bases were required for a new battleplane, the so-called Superfortress. American, British, and Australian sea and land power were devoted to securing these bases for this new aircraft which no one had seen, although had heard rumors about.

Boeing's Superfortress shared a common ancestor with the B-17—"Old Grandfather," the XB-15 of 1937.

Initial studies for a "super bomber" were begun in 1938 when Boeing proposed a design of an improved B-17 with a pressurized cabin to increase crew efficiency and comfort during long high altitude missions. By eliminating the need for oxygen masks this could be achieved. Encouraged by the Air Force, Boeing proceeded with the study.

The next year, the Air Force recognizing that the European war would be a serious threat to American security, began to consider the possibilities of a bomber design which was faster, could fly higher and carry a heavier bomb load than the B-17 and B-24. Bids were requested from aircraft manufacturers on such an aircraft. Of the four responses, two companies later withdrew. Convair produced a few B-32s which were used in the Pacific. But it was Boeing's B-29 which was to decide the issue there.

Because of the heightening emergency, the Air Force began placing orders for the plane before it was actually fully tested. There were serious problems and heartbreaks associated with the development of the B-29.

The request for bids was dispatched on January 29, 1940; large scale production was authorized on May 17, 1941, and the first flight, with test pilot Edmund Allen at the controls, occurred on September 21, 1942. Even as the planes were being built, testing continued to eliminate all the usual "bugs" of a new aircraft —a testing which generally would have taken twice the time as was granted the B-29. One of the bugs was a tendency for the engines to catch fire in flight and it was this that would echo the tragedy of the 299. Just as Leslie Tower was killed in testing the B-17 prototype so also was another irreplaceable pilot-engineer Edmund Allen to die while testing the B-29.

272

The B-29 Superfortress, successor to the B-17. Among the aerodynamic refinements introduced into this aircraft were flush-type rivets, butt joined external "skin," completely retractable landing gear, pressurized cabin and remotely controlled gun turrets. The B-29 carried thirteen .50-caliber machine guns.

Edmund "Eddie" Allen, the famed test pilot who died in a B-29 crash during the testing of the new aircraft.

On February 18, 1943, an urgent radio message was flashed to the tower at Boeing Field. "Eddie" Allen was coming in with the second completed B-29 with a blazing wing. As sirens wailed on the field, those who were there knew that the plane was down. To the north of the field a black column of smoke rose into the dreary sky.

Tragically the plane had crashed into an office building before it could reach Boeing field and besides Allen and all the Boeing employees aboard the B-29, nineteen office workers perished in the crash.

This crisis in the B-29 program might have had an unfortunate effect upon the outcome of the war in the Pacific except for the faith in the aircraft which Arnold and Air Force personnel more closely associated with the development of the B-29 had. Specifically they were Major General Kenneth B. Wolfe and Brigadier General LaVerne G. Saunders and their staff. The problem was mechanical and not in the design of the aircraft. In time, of course, it was solved and the B-29 was ready for delivery to the fighting zones.

It is not generally known that the Superfortress was to have gone to the European Theater, but by December 1943 the B-17 build-up had progressed so well that it was possible—at last—to begin the accumulation of planes, supplies, and men in the Pacific.

The B-29 was a third again as large as the B-17; its wing spanned 141 feet 3 inches and its long cylindrical fuselage stretched to 99 feet. Its resemblance to the B-17 was slight, much like that of a younger though bigger brother. The sweeping tail fin was the most obvious and the horizontal tail surfaces were practically identical except in the construction. The greatest difference was in the long, narrow wing which carried the plane, its bomb load and the four Wright Cyclone engines, each with eighteen cylinders in double rows capable of more than a 2000 horsepower pull.

To maintain a smooth airflow the gun positions were remotely controlled, engines were faired into the wings and the tricycle landing gear retracted into the fuselage (in the nose) and the wings. Even flush rivets were used to keep air resistance to a minimum. The B-29 could carry a bomb load up to 10,000 pounds up to 4000 miles.

To meet its commitment to the B-29 program Boeing expanded its facilities at Wichita and, as with the B-17, other manufacturers, Bell and Martin also produced B-29s.

The first use of the B-29s in the Pacific war was mounted from bases in India and China. On April 24, 1944, the first B-29 landed in China where bases had been built with the help of Chinese laborers (more than 700,000) virtually by hand, without the aid of modern equipment. By mid-April, in this crude manner, the Air Force engineers had prepared five fields in India and four in China.

On June 5, 1944, the first B-29 mission took off from an Indian base to bomb Bangkok, Thailand. Ten days later, the newly formed 20th Air Force bombed Yawata, in Japan proper—the first air attack since the Doolittle raid in April 1942. The Japanese homeland was now within striking distance of Allied air power.

But the long flights were wearing on both men and aircraft and not very conclusive. Weather at bombing altitudes was found to be a serious deterrent to bombing accuracy and its requisite visual bombing, although radar proved quite effective. The long missions from Indian and Chinese bases made lighter bomb loads necessary to permit the heavier fuel loadings for the flights. Damage to targets was not very gratifying.

It was not until Nimitz's forces moved into the Marianas in June 1944 and were able to take Guam, Saipan, and Tinian that the B-29 would be able to begin its Pacific mission. Almost before the fighting had stopped engineer aviation battalions moved in to construct airfields. Five great bases were built, two on Guam and Tinian and one on Saipan. The first B-29 of what was to be the 21st Bomber Command landed on Saipan on October 12, 1944. The strategic bombardment of Japan was about to begin.

A flight of B-29s returning from a 3000-mile flight to Japan headed for North Field (top of photo) Guam in the Marianas. Until these islands were taken by the Marines, the B-29s were forced to operate from inadequate or too distant bases in India and China.

Flak over Nagoya, Japan.

Hit on a bomb run over a Japanese target, this B-29 plunges to earth ablaze and trailing fragments of burning wing. Eleven men made up the crew of a B-29, one more than that of the B-17.

A Japanese fighter plane goes down over its homeland after an encounter with a B-29 formation.

Target: Tokyo, specifically the Musashino engine plant.

A Yokohaman in the ruins of his city.

Dropping incendiaries over Japanese targets. Although Japanese cities were highly susceptible to fire attacks the weather over Japan made accuracy difficult until General LeMay made the decision to bomb from lower altitudes than was usual for the B-29—or even the B-17.

The Marianas were about 1500 miles from Japan which meant a round-trip flight of about 3000 miles, which was well within the range of the B-29, but was a treacherous wide expanse of water for a plane in distress. When the small volcanic island of Iwo Jima was secured by the U. S. Marines in February–March 1945, the last comfortable land link fell into place. Only about eight miles long, Iwo Jima was located about midway between the Marianas and Japan and would become the haven for B-29s in distress and the base for the P-51 escorts.

The first strike from the Marianas against Tokyo took place on November 24, 1944, when a force of 111 Superforts led by Brigadier General Emmett O'Donnell in the *Dauntless Dotty*, piloted by Robert K. Morgan who had commanded the *Memphis Belle*, struck at the Musashino engine factory, just north of the Japanese capital. Only twenty-four of the attacking planes succeeded in bombing the target so that, although historic, the mission was no strategic success. The "bugs" were still being worked out of both plane and men. The tactics which were proving so effective in Europe obviously did not apply in the Pacific. The high winds at bombing altitudes interfered with bombing accuracy so that even a large force of B-29s did not seem to bring effective results.

Major General Curtis LeMay, once commander of the 3rd Division in Europe, had been transferred to India to assume command of B-29 operations there. On January 20, 1945, he was placed in charge of the 21st Bomber Com-

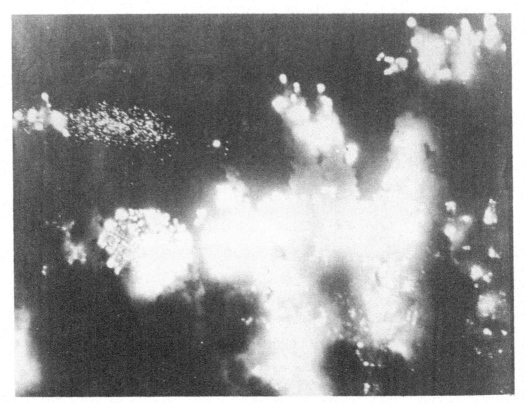

The effects of a night incendiary raid upon the industrial center at Shizuoka (aircraft engines) shortly after the 20th Air Force B-29s dropped its bombs.

Shizuoka by day, devastated and hopeless. The war is over here.

When the island of Iwo Jima was taken it was possible for "Little Friends" to escort the B-29s to Japan, taking off from Iwo to meet the Superforts flying from the Marianas. Fighter attacks upon the Japanese homeland were carried out by sending out formations of Mustangs which followed the B-29s, equipped with navigational equipment for the long flight.

mand, with headquarters on Guam. After observing the poor results of the early bombing missions, LeMay made one of the most radical command decisions—and one of the most conclusive—of the war.

On the morning of March 9, 1945, air crews were shocked to learn that henceforth they would abandon the high-altitude mission for which the B-29 was designed and bomb Japanese targets from the unprecedented altitudes of 5000 to 8000 feet. These attacks would be carried out at night with incendiary bombs and almost all armament would be removed from the planes in order to increase the bomb load. This was a dramatic switch in tactics and the crews were naturally apprehensive as to the results, especially as it would affect them.

That night about three hundred B-29s took off to bomb Tokyo at low altitudes and left over fifteen miles of the city's heart burned out. Also left behind were fourteen B-29s, but despite this, LeMay's plan had worked. The precision neces-

279

P-51s as seen from the left-waist window of a B-29. The object in the center of the picture is the gun-sight of the type which controlled the gun turrets in the B-29.

Fujiyama, Japan, as seen from the nose of a B-29.

280

The Enola Gay *lands at Guam.*

sary for a systematic destruction of Japan's war economy was possible at the lower altitudes. This devastating technique was then applied to Japan's industrial centers with particular attention being given to Tokyo, Nagoya, Yokohama, and Kobe; by the war's end. a total of sixty-nine Japanese cities were burned out. Although Japan's ability to wage war was collapsing in a burning ruin, the Japanese warlords refused to acknowledge it.

The necessity for invading the Japanese homeland seemed inevitable. Toward this end, MacArthur had kept his promise and, with the aid of the Third Fleet, had returned to the Philippines in October 1944. The fighting was as furious as any during the Pacific war and, at Leyte, the Japanese introduced its desperately wasteful *Kamikaze* suicide attacks. Suffering most heavily from these onslaughts were the ships of the naval forces. Although these attacks were to have no effect upon the course of the war they did present serious problems to the Navy. The *Kamikazes* were shot from the sky by antiaircraft fire, by carrier-based fighters and B-29s bombed the bases from which they were dispatched. In time the attacks lessened, not only because of the Allied defenses but because the Japanese were withholding the bulk of their aircraft for the last-ditch defense of the home islands.

The strategic island of Okinawa, just 362 miles from the southernmost Jap-

Hiroshima, August 6, 1945.

anese island, Kyushu was the final island steppingstone. Again the fighting was bitter and casualties were high on both sides: 109,600 Japanese were killed and 12,500 Americans dead or missing. But by June 1945 after three months of the bloodiest fighting of the war, the Allies were poised in a deadly circle, ready to spring upon the Japanese homeland.

D-Day for this invasion was set for some time in November. Based on the home islands of Japan were an army of 2,000,000 soldiers and an air armada of 8000 planes of all types. If the fighting at Iwo Jima, Guadalcanal, Tarawa, and Okinawa had been fanatically expensive, the battle that was to come, however handicapped the Japanese were by the fire raids, promised to be worse.

Hiroshima, after the bomb had fallen.

Nagasaki, August 9, 1945, the final blow in the war which had begun at Pearl Harbor.

"It was to combat invasion that we hoarded all our aircraft," stated General Kawabe, commander of the Japanese Army Air Force, "refused all challenge to fight the Third Fleet, the city-destroying Superfortresses and the hard-hitting FEAF [Far Eastern Air Forces, commanded by Gen. Kenney and consisting of the 5th and 13th Air Forces] which was blasting targets on Kyushu . . . But while we waited, the air war was carried to such extremes of destruction . . . that the Emperor decided to capitulate on the basis of the Potsdam Declaration."

Had this capitulation not occurred the toll in lives, Japanese as well as Allied, might have been astronomical. The estimates went into the millions. But the invasion that Japan awaited was not to come.

On Monday morning, August 6, 1945, a single bomb was dropped from the *Enola Gay*, piloted by Colonel Paul W. Tibbets, Jr., once of the 97th Bomb Group which had initiated the American heavy bomber attacks from England and who flew General Eisenhower to Gibraltar to open the African campaign. It was as if history had come full circle.

284

Hiroshima was a city of 343,000 people and an industrial center chosen as the site for the dropping of the first atomic bomb. In a single burning flash more than half of Hiroshima vanished and more than 70,000 people with it. It was a stunning blow which impressed the crew members of the *Enola Gay* more than the Japanese High Command who chose to ignore a surrender ultimatum.

Three days later an even more powerful bomb was dropped on the port city Nagasaki from *Bock's Car*, a B-29 flown by Major Charles W. Sweeney. Although the bomb on this mission was more potent than the Hiroshima "Little Boy" bomb, the loss of life was fortunately less. Over 35,000 people died as a result of the dropping of "Fat Man" on Nagasaki, August 9, 1945.

These two terrible blows, which were to cost the Japanese civilians unimaginable personal tragedy and large numbers of casualties, ended the Pacific war. Although it is scant consolation to the scarred survivors of Hiroshima and Nagasaki, their sacrifice undoubtedly saved two million lives. The unprecedented desolation and casualty toll of the two bombs afforded the Japanese High Command the excuse to save face and on August 14, 1945, surrendered unconditionally. The formal surrender took place aboard the battleship *Missouri* on Sunday, September 2. The Rising Sun had set.

The advocates of strategic bombardment and the heavy bomber were vindicated by the victory over Japan. No invasion had been necessary after the A-bombs had been dropped. But even before these two events, the Japanese industries were burned out enough to have caused the Japanese to consider an end to the fruitless fight they were by then waging. Had their High Command responded to this, the bombs would never have fallen upon Hiroshima and Nagasaki.

But they did. No one, not even the men who backed the development of the B-17 and its ultimate development, the B-29, and those who preached the doctrine of strategic bombardment, wished that such steps would be necessary. But they were.

After six years of the worst man-made agony in history, peace had come again. It was almost as unreal as the war had been. Only time would reveal whether or not the lessons it had taught would be lost upon man, particularly those of strategic bombardment. If so, then man would also be lost as quite suddenly the hardy, beloved, and destructive B-17 was transformed into not much more than a toy.

It had served, unlike any other heavy bomber, through all of the Second World War. It had become a legend in its time, a tribute to the men who had conceived, designed, and built it—and a monument to the remarkable young men, most of them boys, who flew it. These men, and this plane, accomplished one of the most frightening missions ever demanded of men and aircraft. Together they helped to end history's last "Glorious War."

The legacy of Dresden: the end of the Third Reich.

EPILOGUE: THE LEGACY OF DRESDEN

When Göring boasted before the onset of the Second World War that his *Luftwaffe* would make it impossible for an enemy aircraft to fly over the Reich (he referred specifically to the industrial Ruhr), there were few among his admirers who would have attempted to contradict the pink, beaming, arrogant, and cherubic German *Reichsmarschall.*

Less than a month later his *Luftwaffe* demonstrated what it could do in coordination with the German troops and Panzer divisions. The Germans introduced the concept of lightning warfare—the blitzkrieg—to the world. With ruthless and characteristic disregard for anything but its own ends, the apparently indomitable German war machine raced across Poland, crushing everything in its path.

The *Luftwaffe* was employed mainly as a tactical adjunct to the ground forces, its screaming Stukas terrorizing the refugees choking the roads in an attempt to flee the battle zones. But there were actually no clearly defined battle

286

zones in the style of good old-fashioned war; as the Stukas strafed the columns, clearing a path for the advancing Wehrmacht, they left behind them a terror of confusion and death. The Germans had also introduced the concept of modern total war in which all, soldiers and civilians, were grist for the mills of Mars.

The Polish Air Force, weak and equipped with obsolete aircraft, was no match for the Messerschmitts which were faster and more heavily armed than anything the Poles could muster. In about two days of war the Polish Air Force no longer existed, wiped out on the ground.

Within twenty-seven days after crossing the Polish border in an undeclared war (after, of course, providing for an "incident"), the Germans were in possession of Warsaw. With the Russians moving in from the east and the Germans from the west, the Poles had no chance.

Göring's *Luftwaffe* had proved itself, particularly in its devastating ground support with the frightful Stukas (these were equipped with noise-making devices which added to the terror), and in contending with inferior and outnumbered Polish and French aircraft. Obviously the preening Göring knew whereof he boasted. That his 1500 or so long-range bombers were primarily intended for tactical support of land army operations or, because of a deficiency in armament, might prove easy victims to heavily armed fighters seemed unimportant in the heady run of victories.

The only opponent, actually, confronting Germany was Britain. Both adversaries approached the employment of strategic bombardment warily and tentatively, confining their attacks mostly to strictly military targets or the dropping of leaflets upon enemy cities.

And then occurred the first bombing of a city of little military importance. During the afternoon of May 10, 1940, three bombers appeared over the German city of Freiburg, attacked and left behind fifty-seven dead, thirteen of them children.

"This kind of aerial terrorism is the product of sick minds of the plutocratic world-destroyers," Dr. Goebbels would say three years later. "A long chain of human suffering in all German cities blitzed by the Allies has borne witness against them and their cruel and cowardly leaders—from the murder of German children in Freiburg on May 10, 1940, right up to the present day."

Herr Goebbels did not reveal of course that he knew then, and in 1940, that the planes that bombed Freiburg were Heinkel 111s which had been dispatched to bomb a fighter airfield in France, got lost in the clouds, and bombed one of their own cities. Nor did Goebbels refer to the bombing of Rotterdam, which occurred four days after the bombing of Freiburg, a systematic, methodical, and one would be tempted to say Germanically thorough, destruction of a portion of an open city.

"Rotterdam," General Henri Winkelman, the Dutch commander announced, "bombed this afternoon, suffered the fate of total war . . . We have ceased to struggle."

The German bombers, ironically, dropped their bombs on the center of Rotterdam at the same time that surrender negotiations were under way. Although propaganda at the time exaggerated the casualties (30,000), the sixty or so attacking He-111s literally saturated the city with bombs killing about 980 and rendering 78,000 homeless. Although the attack could not be termed strategic, for it had been brought to bear as ground support, the distinction to the people of

German Heinkel He-111s which took part in the daylight bombing during the Battle of Britain and which, by mistake, bombed the German city of Freiburg. German propaganda accused the French and British for bombing the unprotected city although aware of the true facts. Designed in 1935 as a bomber, the plane was originally used as an airliner to disguise its actual function. British Hurricanes and Spitfires were more than a match for it.

Rotterdam was unimportant. The British initiated, thereafter, the strategic assault upon the Ruhr on May 15-16.

Even more importantly, the Germans emphasized the concept of total war: people against people, not army against army. The tragedy is that, like the Freiburg bombing, the wiping out of Rotterdam was probably an error. The attacking planes continued on to Rotterdam although they had been called back when it became known that surrender negotiations had begun.

It has been said that war is an art; it is not. War is a succession of more or less controlled calamity—and even what control exists (which is never revealed on large-scale maps with their impressive lines and arrows) is frightfully dependent upon whim, chance, luck, and any number of unpredictable variables.

Germany had launched the Second World War and it had won impressive victories by using quite new methods of warfare. When its juggernaut leaped over the supposedly impregnable Maginot line, Germany proved, even more than the military realized, that the concept of a static "front line" was truly passé. So was the innocent civilian, many of whom lay strewn along the roads of Poland, in the center of Rotterdam and—ironically—Freiburg.

The gloves were off. On the night of August 24-25, 1940, bombs fell on the city of London for the first time since the First World War. On the night of August 25-26 the RAF dropped bombs upon Berlin. Thus was begun the reprisal

288

The RAF's "Stirling," the first British heavy bomber to bring the air war to the German people. Although its wing span was four feet shorter than that of the B-17, its high undercarriage makes it appear to be a much larger plane. The "Stirling's" limited altitude range curtailed its use later in the war and was eventually supplanted by the Lancaster and the Halifax.

raids, a deadly stick-on-the-shoulder retaliatory game in which each power took turns in attacking the cities of the other.

The RAF carried the war into the Ruhr Valley and the Germans, recalling the boast of Göring began to ask bitterly, "Where is Hermann Meier?" The air raid sirens, which wailed with unrelenting regularity, were called "Meier's Hunting Horns." Total war was turned upon its practitioners.

Since the war the Germans, somewhat encouraged and backed by some British writers, have adopted a curious pose in reference to the subject of the strategic air war. In a curiously dishonest book, *The Bombing of Germany* (Holt, Rinehart and Winston, 1963), the German writer Hans Rumpf marshals a battery of cold, precise statistics which are used to suggest that the real victim of the Second World War was Germany. The most chilling aspect of the book however is its tacit acceptance of war itself, just so long as it is "civilized" and, no doubt, fought on German terms. Although the American Air Forces are blackened here and there in the book, it is the RAF which is painted as the most cruel villain. Because, early in the war, the RAF learned that it was unable (like the Germans during the Battle of Britain and the London Blitz) to take the terrible losses which were inevitable during day bombing raids and had concentrated on nighttime bombing, the concept of "area" bombing was adopted.

This meant that when a military target was to be hit at night, the only possible means of actually hitting it (and frequently it was missed altogether)

Five hundred pound incendiaries shower down upon Kiel's U-Boat installations. One canister has broken open and scatters the individual stacks. Incendiary bombs though not as explosive as the HE (High Explosive) caused more damage by starting uncontrollable fires.

German fire-fighters survey the damage done to a Focke-Wulf plant at Kassel after B-17s had attacked it.

was by saturating the area in which the target lay. The result was that dwellings around the target area were also struck, civilians killed and wounded and their homes destroyed. This was regarded as perfectly proper for London, Birmingham, Portsmouth, and Coventry but unlawful and cruel when applied to Essen, Kassel, Stuttgart, Berlin, and Hamburg. In short, the concept of half a war.

In *The Bombing of Germany*, Herr Rumpf employs such phrases as a "lawful act of war," the "ideals of humanitarianism in war" and the "acknowledged laws of humanity in war," as if such exist and as if these were practiced by the Germans and not by the Allies. War, then, is acceptable if played according to rules.

Rules imply legality, but strategic bombardment was not a legal form of war. True, the bulk of the American bombs fell upon military targets but as the war reached the climax before the bloody *finale*, even the Americans helped the British destroy the lovely little German cities.

The facts assembled by Herr Rumpf are carefully chosen, just as other facts (especially those pertaining to German atrocities) are ignored.

Without a doubt the Germans suffered and terribly, the innocent along with the guilty. But in the glorious days of the Third Reich who did not belong to the Master Race and who did not worship at the altar of Hitler and who did not condone the acts of war, as long as things were going well?

Even the "good" German generals who were, after all, exponents of the fine classic approach to war, did not attempt to depose Hitler because he had committed crimes against all human reason but because he was giving the German military caste a bad name. As a war leader, the mad little World War I corporal was to prove himself the Allies' "own dearest enemy."

The German cities and their inhabitants paid for all this. So long as the war remained in Poland, France, Holland, and Britain it was a nice war. But when "Meier's Hunting Horns" began to blow and their cities were destroyed, their homes burned, their children killed, it was not a very glorious war after all.

That terrible personal tragedies on an enormous scale resulted from strategic bombardment cannot be denied, but it does seem that the popular position since the war is an attempt, as followed the First World War, to misplace the guilt. Had Hitler and his cheering, triumphant Germans never invaded Poland in 1939 then it is very likely that Dresden would not have been all but obliterated in 1945.

Impressive numbers are appalling, but so is each individual tragedy. Piling on of detail after detail of how terribly many innocent German women and children were killed is also awesome, but death by freezing in a supposed medical study is no less terrible than being fused with the street paving by fire.

Strategic bombardment has been called a failure because it did not always eradicate the military installations or factories it was supposed to bomb. Nor did it break civilian morale as many believed it would. These so-called "terror raids" were not the main objective of the RAF area bombings but merely a hoped for side effect. The Battle of Britain had amply proved that the human spirit is capable of withstanding impossible punishment; there was no reason to believe that the Berliner was less brave than the Londoner.

Of all German cities, Berlin was struck most often and most heavily—no less than 363 attacks—during which 45,517 tons of bombs were dropped. Berlin was, as has been said, both a military as well as political target, the heart of Hitler's Germany. It was a costly target to hit and the Allies suffered great losses over

Aftermath

B-17s of the 91st Bomb Group over Berlin. Smoke trails indicate release point.

Berlin: elevated railroad station in Nollendorf-Platz.

Berlin, with its ring of flak guns and fighters. After the *Luftwaffe*—which is rapidly becoming the scapegoat responsible for Germany's losing the war—was neutralized, it could not defend the German capital as well as it would have liked. But when the fighters rose to attack the bomber formations they fought gallantly and desperately. The "Big B" was never a popular target for the bomber crews. But when the war came to a close, it had been reduced to rubble as had many other historic cities.

If examples of medieval architecture, such as that at Dresden, were destroyed, so were the exponents of primordial political ethics and social concepts. Tragically, the innocent suffered and the innocent did not number among them merely the classic examples of women, children, and the aged. The great masses of soldiers were equally innocent. The Germans had permitted themselves to be deluded and led by madmen into committing massive brutalities that still jars the imagination and belief. One day they found themselves in a burning asylum. Hitler had built a fortress around Europe and, in the phrase of Franklin D. Roosevelt, "forgot to put a roof on it."

Great architectural treasures were devastated (as they also had been in London and Coventry) and examples of art, too, were destroyed in the frightful fire storms. But one wonders how much of that art had been looted from conquered countries.

In total war there really are no innocent civilians, for the means are produced by them. Civilians supply the weapons, the ammunition and even the beautifully efficient German ovens. Thus a good German businessman appealed to the SS in Belgrade for business, saying in reference to "equipment . . . for the burning of bodies" that he was "submitting plans for our perfected cremation ovens which operate with coal and which have hitherto given full satisfaction." The firm, C. H. Kori, went so far as to "guarantee the effectiveness of the cremation ovens as well as their durability, the use of the best materials and our faultless workmanship."

Nothing was too good for the 5,000,000 enemies of the German Reich.

Although knowledge of the death camps was denied by Germans after the war, such an open bid for business would tend to obviate that. Undoubtedly large numbers of Germans were unaware of extermination camps, but they were unaware of a lot of aspects of the Thousand Year Reich. All they knew was that the weak, ineffectual British and Americans were flying over with their Lancasters and Flying Fortresses and teaching them how to war.

They would look up, and then around them asking, "Where's Hermann Meier?" Where was the *Luftwaffe*? Where was the fuel, the oil and the steel? The now damned strategic bombardment program had wiped them out. While it was not a complete success, it was not a failure and without question contributed to the fall of Germany. This was accomplished at great cost to the young men—none of them brutal killers, nor, for that matter were their leaders—who flew in the heavy bombers.

Young American lives (and British too) were lost in great air battles. It was a fearful kind of barter, the hope being that each life might be traded for a moment or an hour nearer the war's end. There was no means of knowing, at the time, whether or not this would prove true. We now know that the casualty toll for the 8th and 15th Air Forces up to May 8, 1945, was 24,288 killed, 18,804 wounded, 31,436 taken prisoner, and 18,699 missing. A great number of the missing have never been heard from and may be presumed dead. The loss rate of bomber crews, if analyzed statistically, was second only to the infantry.

Had the price paid achieved the hoped for results? A year after the war's end Senator Elbert D. Thomas of Utah published an article in a popular magazine in which he stated that "One of the outstanding hoaxes of military history was the myth of 'precision bombing.' There was no such thing." He then proceeded to prove his point with an amazing compendium of misinformation and a surprising ignorance of the mission of the air forces.

Those who had suffered the weight of this mission, professional airmen and

293

In this unusual sequence a B-17 from the 94th Bomb Group is the victim of a formation accident. The Fortress was under the plane above when the bombs were released upon Berlin. One bomb cut off the horizontal stabilizer of the B-17 sending it down toward Berlin. No parachutes were seen to open.

294

A P-47 Thunderbolt of the 12th Air Force flies over Hitler's one-time retreat at Berchtes-gaden. The Fuehrer had made a promise as he came into power. "Give me four years and I promise you," he declared, "you won't recognize your towns!" It was one of the few promises he was able to keep.

others who should have known, had other views. *Generaleutnant* Adolf Galland, who had commanded the fighter forces for a time, said, "In my opinion, it was the Allied bombing of our oil industries that had the greatest effect on German war potential . . . [Also] disorganization of German communications in the West by strategic bombing caused withdrawal to the German frontiers. In the last two months of the war, the crippling of the German transport system brought about the final collapse."

Alfred Krupp, head of the German armament empire, stated that "Allied air attacks left only 40 per cent of the Krupp works able to operate . . . These plants of mine, and German industry as a whole, were more hampered by lack of speedy and adequate transportation facilities since the beginning of 1943 than by anything else."

General Feldmarschall Hugo Sperrle said, "Allied bombing was the dominant factor in the success of the [Normandy] invasion. I believe the initial landing could have been made without assistance from the air forces, but the break-through that followed would have been impossible without the massive scale of bombing, particularly of German communications far in the rear. Allied air power was the chief factor in Germany's defeat."

The broken and deposed Hermann Göring had this to say: "Allied precision bombing had a greater effect on the defeat of Germany than area bombing, because destroyed cities can be evacuated but destroyed industry was difficult to replace.

"Allied selection of targets was good, particularly in regard to oil. As soon as we started to repair an oil installation, you always bombed it again before we could produce one ton.

"We didn't concentrate on the four-engine Focke-Wulf planes as heavy bombers because we were developing the He-177 and the Me-264, which was designed to go to America and return . . ."

Thus the defeated proclaimed immediately after the fall of the Third Reich. Since then, however, out of the ashes have risen such apologists as Hans Rumpf who reveal a decided lack of remorse and little more than passing recognition of the fact that Hitler, backed by Germans grown arrogant and rapacious by easy victories, had plunged the world into total war.

All that seems to remain of historical fact is that the Germans suffered heavily at the hands of the Allies and, ultimately, through betrayals, or because of Hitler (just like "the last time" of the Kaiser's war) lost. Few of these apologists specu-late on what kind of a world it might have been had the Germans won—or to what military extremes they might have gone had they been able.

Much is made of Germany's inability to strike back at the Allies in kind—that is, with heavy retaliatory strategic bombing. This was not Nazi humanitarian-ism but rather simple ineffectuality. The German Air Force had not been de-signed for strategic bombardment and when Hitler awakened to its possibilities, it was too late: the RAF and the U. S. Air Force had canceled it out for him. However, had Germany been able to launch its "New York Bomber" (the Me-264, wistfully mentioned by Göring), armed with an atomic bomb (on which the Germans were working) there can be no doubting that New York would have suffered heavily during the Second World War.

As it was, the V-1s and V-2s were pointed in the general direction of England with no real knowledge of where they would actually come to earth. England itself—and her people, the old, women, and children—was the target; military definitions no longer held.

The basic error in the thinking of so many who now decry the "work" of the strategic bombardment forces is that, as stated by military analyst Liddel Hart, it was "the most uncivilized method of warfare the world has known since the Mongol devastations."

What, indeed, is civilized about any aspect of war? It is not the means, but war itself which is the major tragic illusion. Still, there are those who are willing to accept it so long as it can be played according to the rules of the nineteenth century.

This is their theme, just as it is the theme of the tract by Rumpf, one of whose chapters is entitled "At Least There Was No Gas War." There was—at Dachau, at Buchenwald, at Mauthausen and Auschwitz.

SUPPLEMENT

General Anderson (center) and Colonel Potts at the moment of decision.

MISSION: A PHOTOGRAPHIC ESSAY

In the pages that follow an attempt is made to show pictorially the meaning and complexity of a B-17 operation from onset to completion. It should be noted that no attempt is made to recreate any specific mission (therefore those who make a career of identifying every 8th Air Force tail marking and each individual B-17 should not be dismayed by the juxtaposition of anomalous aircraft or groups). The photographs were chosen primarily for their photographic quality or because of their rarity.

The decision to mount a major air attack was not lightly taken, nor was it a simple one. In the early months of the 8th Air Force's operations from England, the decision was made by Generals Spaatz and Eaker. Toward the latter months it fell to General Orvil A. Anderson, deputy commander for operations, and to Colonel Ramsey Potts, director of bombing. Many factors weighed on the mind of a man before he made this decision: how many planes were operational, what was crew status, the weather conditions over the bases and targets, etc. Once, however, the decision was made a terrible chain of events ensued. Whatever happened after that, unless the mission was canceled, someone had to die.

Potts and Anderson begin by working out details, routes, flak concentrations, etc.

The groundcrew works through the night.

Intelligence prepares maps and other pertinent material.

300

The Fortress is "operational."

Bombing up.

Briefing.

Jeep ride out to the hardstand.

Sweating it out.

Turning over the props, before starting engines.

Line-up.

Airborne and assembling over England.

The tail-gunner's view.

Passing over the Channel.

Contrails: joining up with the "Little Friends."

The marker rocket signals the drop area.

Bomb-bay doors open.

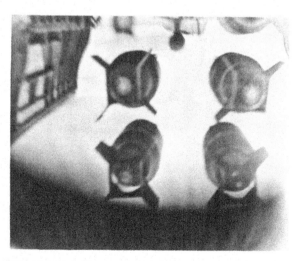

Bombs away!

Target: synthetic fuel and chemicals, Ludwigshaven, Germany.

Thunderbolts move in to meet the Luftwaffe.

Feathered prop on No. 4 engine.

Tail-gunner in action; a small flicker of flame begins on the right wing behind No. 4 engine.

The last fall.

Direct hit by flak.

Waiting at the station.

305

Two flares indicate wounded aboard.

Coming in.

The "meat-wagon" chases the B-17.

Battle damage.

Journey's end.

The wounded.

The wounded.

Mission's end.

Their tour is over.

Interrogation.

Intelligence Officer briefs Generals Spaatz, Doolittle, and Turner on the results of the mission.

307

THE FLYING FORTRESSES: A TABULATION

Note: This chart represents a capsule history of the B-17s from the prototype Model 299 through the B-17G; such variants as the B-17H, the Navy PB-1 and others, including postwar B-17s used as Drones by the Air Force for missile target practice and as test beds are not included. These were not actually new designs but modifications of the Gs. All performance figures were taken from official Boeing files; while these do not coincide with other published figures, it would seem that these represent the most authentic. Where the figure is not known, as in the case of some of the performances, it is omitted (indicated by a dash). It might be pointed out that maximum range varied directly with the bomb load as well as with the weight of fuel. Likewise, fuel capacity varied from model to model: the 299 carried a maximum of 1700 gallons and the B-17G, equipped with bomb-bay tanks, carried 3600 gallons. Likewise the weight of the airplane both empty and with full pay load varied widely; so did the bomb load and armament. By the war's climax, the B-17 could carry up to 20,000 pounds of bombs, depending on the distance to be flown—the longer the distance to target, the lighter the bomb load.

A word about the USAAF serial numbers: all Air Force planes were, and are, identified by a model designation and a serial number. The model designation was stenciled on the left side of the fuselage, under which the serial number also appeared. These were generally placed below the navigator's window. The serial number was stenciled on the fin portion of the tail. The first two numbers indicate the year the plane was built. Therefore aircraft number 36-153 was built in 1936, and so on through 44-85841, which was built in 1944—the last B-17G. When these numbers were painted onto the tails, the "3" and "4" of the year prefix was dropped, as was the hyphen, so that B-17 numbered 230319, was built in 1942 and carried the Air Force serial number 30319.

When vast numbers of B-17s were being manufactured, not only by Boeing but also by Douglas and Vega, a system of Block numbers was introduced to assist in keeping the various models straight for purposes of maintenance and servicing (interchangeability of parts, etc.), so that the model designation was further complicated by such attachments as is evident in B-17G-90VE, or B-17F-35DL. The first would have appeared on a Vega built B-17G of Block number 90 and the second plane was a Douglas built B-17F of Block number 35.

There were one hundred B-17Gs built in Vega's Block 90 (Serial numbers 44-8901—44-9900). All aircraft in this block were identical and modifications upon them were to be the same upon arrival at modification centers. In short, the Block system was a means of keeping track of the large numbers of Fortresses, more or less the same. Because the serial number is sufficient to identify the model, block numbers are not included in the tabulation.

Hamilton Standard constant speed three bladed propellers were used on all B-17s; beginning with the "G" the broad-bladed "paddle" propellers were installed which increased the ceiling of the aircraft. These too were manufactured by Hamilton.

A total of 12,731 Flying Fortresses were produced in the period 1935–45. Of this total, Boeing built 6981; Douglas Aircraft: 3000 and Vega (Lockheed): 2700. Approximately 4750 B-17s were lost on combat missions.

USSAF Model Designation	Boeing Model number	Wing Span	Fuselage Length	Power Plant	Weight Empty (lbs.)	Gross Weight (lbs.)
None	299	103' 9⅜"	68' 9"	Pratt & Whitney R-1690 750 HP	21,657	32,432
Y1B-17	299B	103' 9⅜"	68' 9"	Wright R-1820–39 850 HP	24,465	34,880
Y1B-17A	299F	103' 9⅜"	68' 9"	Wright R-1820–51 1000 HP	31,160	44,000
B-17B	299M	103' 9⅜"	67' 10.2"	Wright R-1820–51 1000 HP	27,652	37,997
B-17C	299H	103' 9⅜"	67' 10.6"	Wright R-1820–65 1000 HP	29,021	39,065
B-17D	299H	103' 9.3"	67' 10.6"	Wright R-1820 1000 HP	30,963	39,319
B-17E	299O	103' 9.38"	73' 9.73"	Wright R-1820–91 1000 HP	33,279	40,260
B-17F	299O	103' 9.38"	74' 8.9"	Wright R-1820–65 1000 HP	35,728	40,260
B-17G	299O Chin turret	103' 9.38"	74' 8.9"	Wright R-1820–97 1000 HP	36,134	38,200

Top Speed	Cruising Speed	Range (Maximum)	Service Ceiling	Armament	USAAF Serial Numbers	Number Built
236	140 @ 70%	3,010	24,620	Five .50 or Five .30	—	1
239	175 @ max.	2,430	27,800	Five .50 or Five .30	36-149 — 36-161	13
271	183	—	38,000	Five .50 or Five .30	37-369	1
268	—	3,000	34,000	Two .30 and Three .50	38-211 — 38-223 38-258 — 38-270 38-583 — 38-584 38-610 39-001 — 39-010	39
300	227	3,400	36,000	Six .50 and One .30	40-2042 — 40-2079	38
318 @ 25,000	—	2,540	37,800	Six .50 and One .30	40-3059 — 40-3100	42
318	226	3,300	35,000	Eight .50 and One .30	41-2393 — 41-2699 41-9011 — 41-9245	512
325	160	4,420	37,000	Nine .50 and One .30	41-24340 — 41-24639 42-5050 — 42-5484 42-29467 — 42-31031	2,300
					Douglas Aircraft: 42-2964 — 42-3562 42-37714 — 42-37715 42-37717 — 42-37720	605
					Vega (Lockheed): 42-5705 — 42-6204	500
302	160	3,750	35,000	Thirteen .50	42-31032 — 42-32116 42-97058 — 42-97407 42-102379 — 42-102978 43-37509 — 43-39508	4,035
					Douglas Aircraft: 42-3563 42-37716 42-37721 — 42-38213 42-106984 — 42-107233 44-6001 — 44-7000 44-83236 — 44-83885	2,395
					Vega (Lockheed): 42-39758 — 42-40057 42-97436 — 42-98035 44-8001 — 44-9000 44-85492 — 44-85841	2,250

DESIGN ANALYSIS OF THE B-17

The Boeing B-17 was designed to be utilized as an Air Force bombardment aircraft capable of carrying heavy bomb loads over great distances and bombing from high altitude. To meet these requirements the Boeing Company designed a four-engined aircraft with a wingspan of 103′ 9.38″ and an over-all fuselage length, in the final "G" model, of 74′ 8.90″.

In designing this aircraft the Boeing engineers not only had to keep in mind its flying and fighting characteristics, but also its possibilities as a mass-produced aircraft which would benefit from interchangeability of parts. Service and repair under wartime conditions, too, were factors in the design. Therefore a sturdy plane of more or less conservative design was conceived enabling modification as circumstances demanded.

Although the B-17 underwent literally thousands of modifications, the basic design was never changed. The wing, in fact, was exactly the same on every model. The major modification was to affect the fuselage which was lengthened to accommodate the installation of the tail-gunner's station. This contributed to the addition of the dorsal fin which not only served to strengthen the rear of the plane but also increased its stability.

The circular cross section of the fuselage was selected because of its efficient strength/weight ratio as well as the fact that it was easier to manufacture. The fuselage of the B-17 was an all-metal, semi-monocoque structure with a maximum cross-section height of 103 inches and a maximum width of 90 inches. Structural strength was evenly distributed through the entire length so that damage to important structural members would not weaken the integrity of the airplane.

The fuselage was constructed of bulkheads and circumferential stiffeners joined throughout the length of the fuselage by longerons and longitudinal stiffeners aft to station 11 (that is, to the tail-gun compartment). Laid over this framework was the "skin" of 24ST Alclad fastened with aluminum alloy rivets. Skin thickness depended upon the section of the plane it covered; heavier Alclad was laid over those sections carrying the heaviest loads.

312

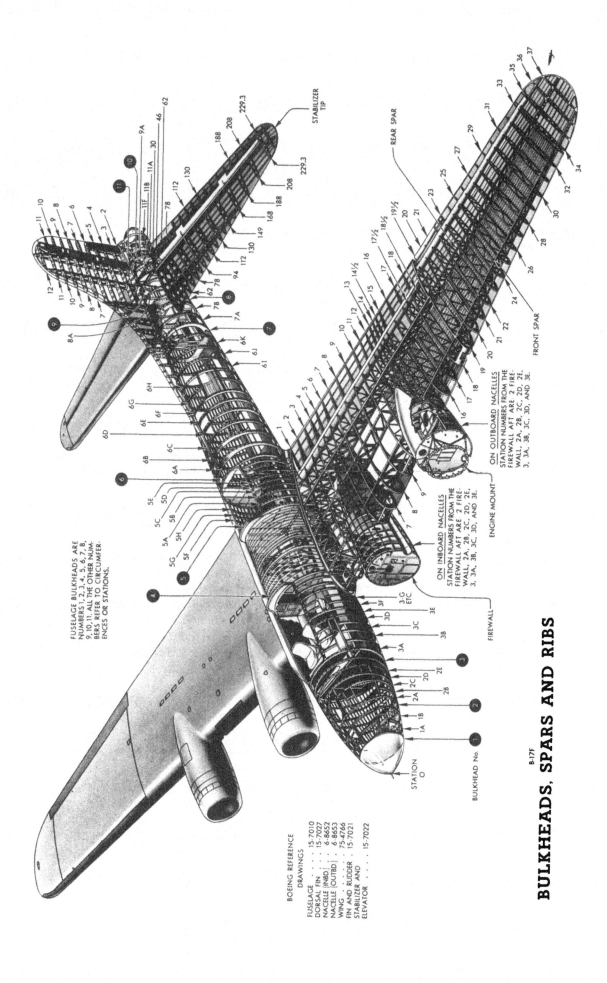

FUSELAGE BULKHEADS ARE
NUMBERS 1, 2, 3, 4, 5, 6, 7, 8,
9, 10, 11. ALL THE OTHER NUM-
BERS REFER TO CIRCUMFER-
ENCES OR STATIONS.

ON INBOARD NACELLES
STATION NUMBERS FROM THE
FIREWALL AFT ARE 2 FIRE-
WALL, 2A, 2B, 2C, 2D, 2E,
3, 3A, 3B, 3C, 3D, AND 3E.

ON OUTBOARD NACELLES
STATION NUMBERS FROM THE
FIREWALL AFT ARE 2 FIRE-
WALL, 2A, 2B, 2C, 2D, 2E,
3, 3A, 3B, 3C, 3D, AND 3E.

ENGINE MOUNT

FIREWALL

REAR SPAR

FRONT SPAR

STABILIZER
TIP

STATION O

BULKHEAD No.

BOEING REFERENCE
DRAWINGS

FUSELAGE 15-7010
DORSAL FIN 15-7027
NACELLE (INBD.) . . 6-8652
NACELLE (OUTBD.) . 6-8653
WING 75-4766
FIN AND RUDDER . . 15-7021
STABILIZER AND
ELEVATOR 15-7022

B-17F

BULKHEADS, SPARS AND RIBS

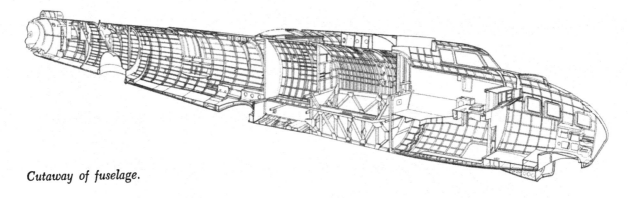

Cutaway of fuselage.

The fuselage was constructed in four sections: the forward section, which contained the bombardier-navigator and pilots' compartments, extended from the nose to the bulkhead directly aft of the pilots' cabin; the center section housing the bomb bay; the rear half and the tail section. These sections were assembled on jigs and later assembled on a production line.

The departures from the circular cross section occurred at the pilot's cabin, the curvature of the bomb-bay doors and in the tail section where the gunner's emplacement was installed. The middle section of the wing was incorporated into the fuselage.

The wing, like the fuselage, was of semi-monocoque construction utilizing two main spars of truss (bridge-like) design. The airfoil section combined the NACA 0018 at the root with the NACA 0010 at the tip. Wing area was 1420 square feet. Chord at root was 228 inches.

The front spar was located at 15 per cent of chord and joined the fuselage at an angle 6° off (rearward) a 90° angle from the airplane's center line. The wing was constructed in six sections: right and left inboard (which carried the engines and landing gear), right and left outboard (in which the ailerons were set) and the tips. The two main spars were built up truss type; the trusses were aluminum tubes riveted together into a single unit. The spars were tied together with ribs, spaced 15 inches to 18 inches apart. Over this was placed a layer of corrugated aluminum stiffeners riveted to the ribs. This was then covered with Alclad sheet aluminum. Control surfaces were fabric covered. A trim tab was placed only in the aileron of the left wing. De-icer strips were installed in the leading edges of the outer wing panels and between the engines. Flaps were of the split type; span was 24' 4 15/16". These were raised and lowered electrically, but could also be manually operated if necessary.

The inboard wing sections carried the engine nacelles which were connected to the wing by bulkheads at the front spar. The inboard nacelles housed the main landing gear, which retracted into a wheel well reinforced by heavy formed channels that connected with heavy steel landing gear support forgings and securely attached to the wing surface and compression ribs. Electrical retraction was controlled from the cockpit by a single switch which also actuated the tail wheel. Emergency manual provisions were made for each wheel.

Contained within the wings also were the fuel tanks, all self-sealing in later models. Three main tanks in each wing (inboard sections) and nine in the outboard sections made a possible fuel overload of 2780 gallons and with the addition of bomb-bay tanks, 3600 gallons.

314

The familiar dorsal fin, introduced in the model "E," was actually an integral part of the fuselage; it was assembled separately and joined to the fuselage as a completed assembly. The fin proper was of a two spar, web-type construction. The rudder, of metal framework, was covered with a specially processed fabric which served to provide minimal flutter due to dynamic air pressure. A trim tab was installed in the lower trailing edge of the rudder.

Horizontal tail surfaces, which in the later Fortresses spanned 43 feet and had an area of 331.1 square feet, consisted of the front stabilizer assembly and the elevator. Construction was similar to that of the fin and rudder; the stabilizer having two spar, web-type construction. The stabilizer was covered with Alclad. The metal frame of the elevators was covered with doped fabric; both elevators were equipped with trim tabs in the trailing edge near the fuselage/elevator joint.

A complexity of systems were responsible for the flight efficiency of the B-17. Flight controls, of course, controlled the aircraft and would include the aileron, rudder, elevator, tabs and the wing flaps. The flight controls were manually operated except when Automatic Flight Control Equipment (AFCE) was in use. Most systems were electrically actuated; the hydraulic system operated the cowl flaps on the engines, the wheel brakes and emergency brakes. The communications system on the B-17 was extremely complicated for not only were the members of the crew in communication with each other, but the pilot was in touch with the formation and with the base. Transmission by voice and Morse code was possible as well as receiving.

The electrical system furnished the power to operate the turrets, landing gear, wing flaps, bomb door, instruments, and other miscellaneous equipment.

Heat was provided by a heating unit, using Glycol fluid, located in the Number 2 engine nacelle. Heated by the exhaust, the Glycol was circulated through the heating system through the plane. At the usual operational altitude heated flying suits were necessary.

At this high altitude also, turbosuperchargers—one per each engine—were employed to provide sea-level air pressure. The outside air was drawn into the supercharger through intercooler air intakes in the wing's leading edge and compressed to the proper pressure before being fed into the engine's carburetor.

Oxygen was supplied through four independent systems through sixteen outlets throughout the plane (walk-around bottles were also installed). The system was supplied by eighteen bottles, each containing about a four hour supply of oxygen for one man at 30,000 feet. Most of these were stored in the pilots' compartment.

Armor plate was installed to protect the crew as much as possible. The pilots were protected by the backs of their seats and armor placed on bulkhead No. 3 (just in front of their windshield) and bulkhead No. 4 (leading into the bomb bay); this also gave some protection to the top-turret gunner. All other stations were similarly shielded, the ball turret gunner having the least, with a small patch upon which he sat.

Bomb-bay racks were fitted to carry a wide variety of bombs, ranging from 100-pound to 2000 pound bombs. External bomb racks were installed under the wings, but were not used with any frequency. Maximum bomb load restricted the B-17s range, so a careful balance was always struck between bomb load and fuel supply.

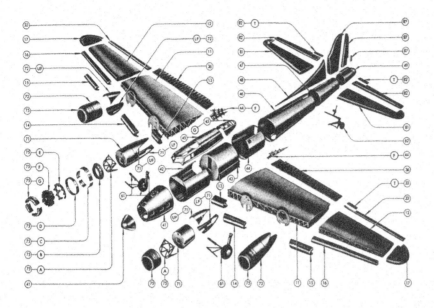

	LEGEND							
12	INBOARD WING ASSY.	L.H. OR R.H.	35-7975	61	LANDING GEAR AND BRAKES INST.	L.H. OR R.H.	75-4601
12	OUTBOARD WING ASSY.	L.H. OR R.H.	85-4772	62	TAS GEAR INST.		55-7470
13	WING NOSE INST. - WING STA. 1 TO 3	L.H. OR R.H.	74-1831	71	INBOARD NACELLE ASSY. AND INST.	L.H. OR R.H.	85-4805
14	WING NOSE INST. - WING STA. 7 TO 11	L.H. OR R.H.	35-7483	71UF	UPPER FAIRING INST. - INBOARD NACELLE		15-6333
15	WING NOSE INST. - WING STA. 15 TO 19	L.H. OR R.H.	13-7476	71LF	LOWER FAIRING INST. - INBOARD NACELLE		55-5929
16	WING NOSE INST. - WING STA. 19 1/2 TO 33	L.H. OR R.H.	13-7475	72	OUTBOARD NACELLE ASSY. AND INST.	L.H. OR R.H.	85-4806
17	WING TIP ASSY.	L.H. OR R.H.	75-3590	72UF	UPPER FAIRING INST. - OUTBOARD NACELLE		55-5962
33	AILERON ASSY.	L.H. OR R.H.	58-784	72LF	LOWER FAIRING INST. - OUTBOARD NACELLE		65-6007
33T	AILERON TRIM TAB	L.H. ONLY	58-784	75	ENGINE INSTALLATION ASSY.	ALL ALIKE	65-7359
36	WING FLAP ASSY.	L.H. OR R.H.	75-5127	75A	ENGINE MOUNT		55-6185
41N	FUSELAGE NOSE INST.		13-7991	75B	INNER COWLING - FIXED		13-7666
41	FUSELAGE ASSY. - FWD. SECTION - STA. 1 TO 3		55-7330	75C	OUTER COWLING - REMOVABLE		13-7667
42	FUSELAGE ASSY. - FWD. SECTION - STA. 3 TO 4		55-7330	75D	COWL FLAPS		55-7655
43	FUSELAGE ASSY. - FWD. SECTION - STA. 4 TO 5		55-7330	75E	EXHAUST COLLECTOR RING		55-6194
44	FUSELAGE ASSY. - FWD. SECTION - STA. 5 TO 6		55-7330	75F	ENGINE		------
44F	FAIRING INST. - REAR WING FILLET	L.H. OR R.H.	95-3684	75G	COWL RING INST.		65-7616
45	PILOT'S COMPT. - ENCLOSURE		15-8785	81	HORIZONTAL STABILIZER ASSY.	L.H. OR R.H.	15-7025
45G	TOP GUN EMPLACEMENT FAIRING		55-6612	82	ELEVATOR ASSY.	L.H. OR R.H.	15-7026
46	FUSELAGE ASSY. - REAR SECTION - STA. 6 TO 7		65-7331	82T	ELEVATOR TRIM TAB	L.H. OR R.H.	15-7073
47	FUSELAGE ASSY. - REAR SECTION - STA. 7 TO 11		55-7331	85	VERTICAL FIN ASSY.		15-7023
48	DORSAL FIN INST.		15-7027	87	RUDDER ASSY.		15-7024
49	TAIL GUN ENCLOSURE		15-7360	87T	RUDDER TRIM TAB		14-7043

Sub assembly breakdown.

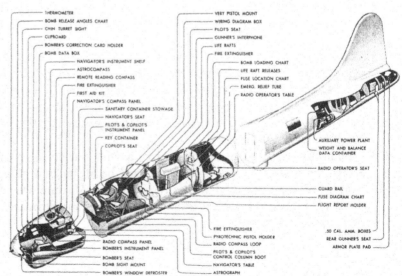

Equipment diagram.

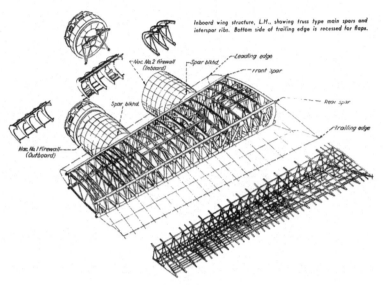

Inboard wing structure, L.H., showing truss type main spars and interspar ribs. Bottom side of trailing edge is recessed for flaps.

Nac.No.2 firewall (Inboard)

Spar blkhd.

Leading edge

Front spar

Spar blkhd.

Rear spar

Trailing edge

Nac. No. 1 firewall (Outboard)

Wing construction.

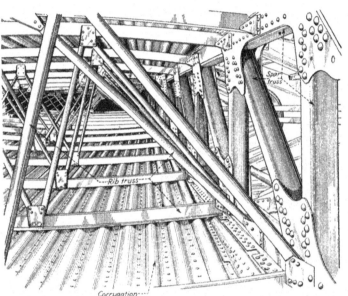

Spar truss

Rib truss

Corrugation

Close-up of internal wing structure.

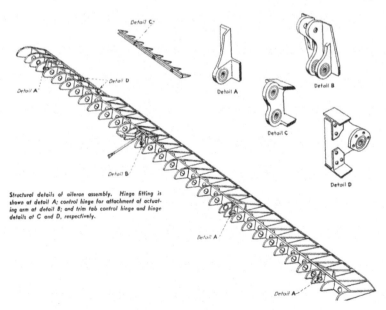

Detail C

Detail D

Detail A

Detail B

Detail A

Detail B

Detail C

Detail D

Structural details of aileron assembly. Hinge fitting is shown at detail A; control hinge for attachment of actuating arm at detail B; and trim tab control hinge and hinge details at C and D, respectively.

Detail A

Detail A

Structural details of aileron assembly.

317

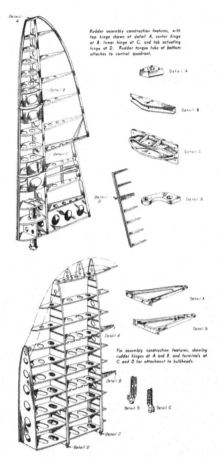

Rudder assembly construction features, with top hinge shown at detail A, center hinge at B, lower hinge at C, and tab actuating hinge at D. Rudder torque tube at bottom attaches to control quadrant.

Detail A

Detail B

Detail C

Detail D

Fin assembly construction features, showing rudder hinges at A and B, and terminals at C and D for attachment to bulkheads.

Rudder assembly construction.

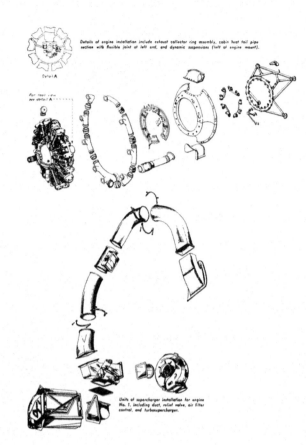

Details of engine installation include exhaust collector ring assembly, cabin heat tail pipe section with flexible joint at left end, and dynamic suspensions (left at engine mount).

Detail A

For rear view see detail A

Units of supercharger installation for engine No. 1, including duct, relief valve, air filter control, and turbosupercharger.

Engine installation details.

Stabilizer assembly. Note that front spar does not extend to tip end. Leading edge and rear spar take over as shear-carrying structure from end of front spar to tip (8 ft.). Stabilizer terminals at fuselage are shown at details A and B and elevator hinges at C and D,

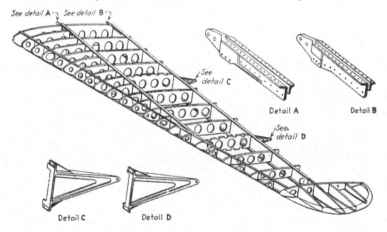

See detail A   See detail B

See detail C

Detail A   Detail B

See detail D

Detail C   Detail D

Stabilizer assembly.

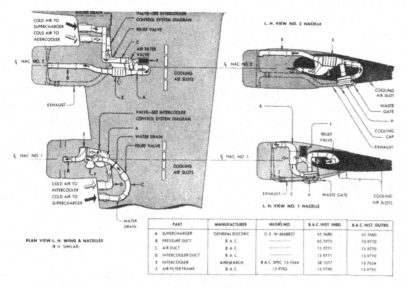

Supercharger installation diagram.

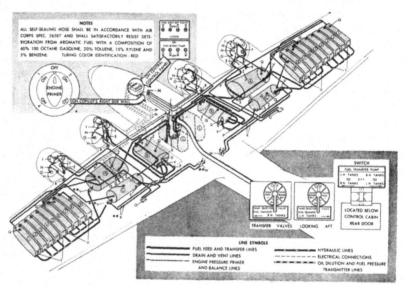

Fuel system diagram.

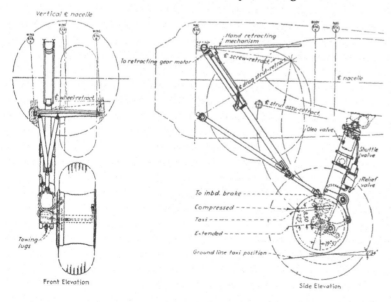

319

Landing gear diagram.

Top-turret gunner Harry Goldstein of the Bronx, New York. Top gunner was also B-17's crew chief, responsible for proper functioning of the aircraft from the engines to armament.

Waist-gun positions, with gunners dressed for high-altitude flight. Suits were electrically heated and oxygen was supplied through face masks. Side windows are open so that the waist gunners may command all lateral approaches to their plane. Temperatures in this position were at high altitudes as low as 40-degrees below zero.

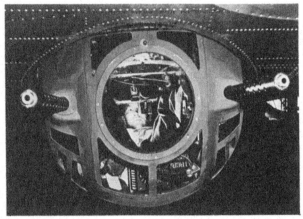

A ball-turret gunner (who was, of necessity, not a large man) in a position curled up inside the belly turret. With his left eye peering through the sight he controlled the movement of the guns by hand and by foot pedals.

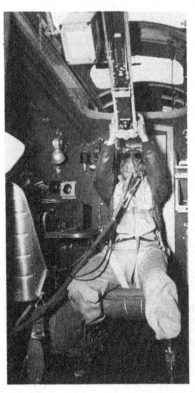

Radio operator's gun position, interior view.

The radio operator's gun position. Plexiglas cover protected the gunner from the cold and wind.

The B-17G, showing the new "chin" turret and details of the new all-Plexiglas nose and the bombardier's station. The famous "Blue Ox," the Norden bombsight, is under cover. The short slender object protruding from the nose is a thermometer for reading outside temperature. Large pear-shaped panel is the bombsight panel.

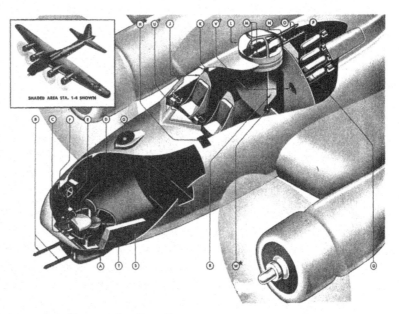

Armament diagram—front section.

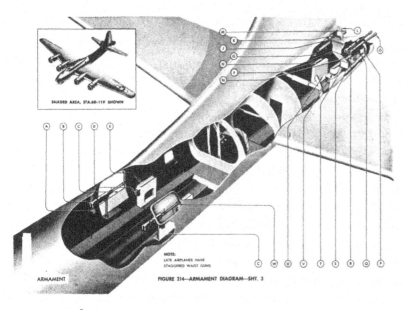

FIGURE 214—ARMAMENT DIAGRAM—SHT. 3

321

Armament diagram—rear section.

The Norden bombsight, very accurate and highly secret during World War II. Developed by Carl L. Norden and Captain Frederick I. Entwistle, assistant research chief of the Navy Bureau of Ordnance, the Norden sight, as it became known, speedily calculated a series of events. This precision instrument compensated for the plane's forward motion, drift, movement of the target; it computed automatically what would have taken a man many minutes.

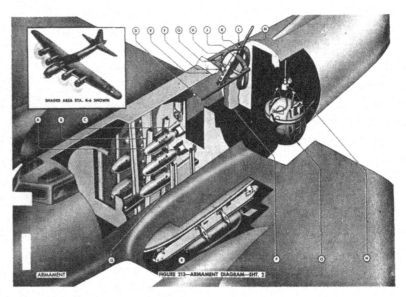

Armament diagram—mid section.

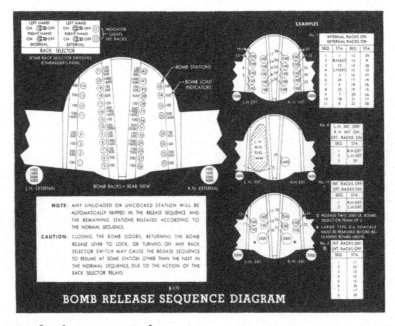

Bomb release sequence diagram.

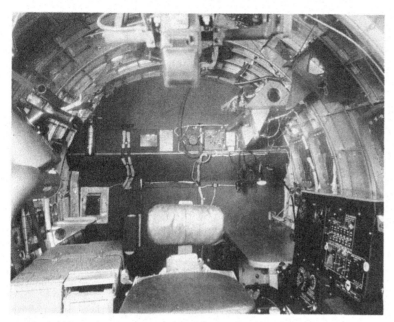

Interior view of bombardier's compartment, looking aft. Bombardier's control panel is on the right.

Radio compartment of the B-17G, looking forward. Bomb bay is on the other side of the bulkhead.

The final, modified, tail-gun position installed on the later B-17Gs.

EXCERPTS FROM THE PILOT TRAINING MANUAL FOR THE FLYING FORTRESS

THE AIRPLANE COMMANDER

Your assignment to the B-17 airplane means that you are no longer just a pilot. You are now an airplane commander, charged with all the duties and responsibilities of a command post.

You are now flying a 10-man weapon. It is your airplane, and your crew. You are responsible for the safety and efficiency of the crew at all times—not just when you are flying and fighting, but for the full 24 hours of every day while you are in command.

Your crew is made up of specialists. Each man—whether he is the navigator, bombardier, engineer, radio operator, or one of the gunners—is an expert in his line. But how well he does his job, and how efficiently he plays his part as a member of your combat team, will depend to a great extent on how well you play your own part as the airplane commander.

Get to know each member of your crew as an individual. Know his personal idiosyncrasies, his capabilities, his shortcomings. Take a personal interest in his problems, his ambitions, his need for specific training.

See that your men are properly quartered, clothed, and fed. There will be many times, when your airplane and crew are away from the home base, when you may even have to carry your interest to the extent of financing them yourself. Remember always that you are the commanding officer of a miniature army—a specialized army; and that morale is one of the biggest problems for the commander of any army, large or small.

Crew Discipline

Your success as the airplane commander will depend in a large measure on the respect, confidence, and trust which the crew feels for you. It will depend also on how well you maintain crew discipline.

Your position commands obedience and respect. This does not mean that you have to be stiff-necked, overbearing, or aloof. Such characteristics most certainly will defeat your purpose.

Be friendly, understanding, but firm. Know your job; and, by the way you perform your duties daily, impress upon the crew that you do know your job. Keep close to your men, and let them realize that their interests are uppermost in your mind. Make fair decisions, after due consideration of all the facts involved; but make them in such a way as to impress upon your crew that your decisions are to stick.

Crew discipline is vitally important, but it need not be as difficult a problem as it sounds. Good discipline in an air crew breeds comradeship and high morale, and the combination is unbeatable.

You can be a good CO, and still be a regular guy. You can command respect from your men, and still be one of them.

"To associate discipline with informality, comradeship, a leveling of rank, and at times a shift in actual command away from the leader, may seem paradoxical," says a brigadier general, formerly a Group commander in the VIII Bomber Command. "Certainly, it isn't down the military groove. But it is discipline just the same—and the kind of discipline that brings success in the air."

Crew Training

Train your crew as a team. Keep abreast of their training. It won't be possible for you to follow each man's courses of instruction, but you can keep a close check on his record and progress.

Get to know each man's duties and problems. Know his job, and try to devise ways and means of helping him to perform it more efficiently.

Each crew member naturally feels great pride in the importance of his particular specialty. You can help him to develop his pride to include the manner in which he performs that duty. To do that you must possess and maintain a thorough knowledge of each man's job and the problems he has to deal with in the performance of his duties.

THE COPILOT

The copilot is the executive officer—your chief assistant, understudy, and strong right arm. He must be familiar enough with every one of your duties—both as pilot and as airplane commander—to be able to take over and act in your place at any time.

He must be able to fly the airplane under all conditions as well as you would fly it yourself.

He must be extremely proficient in engine operation, and know instinctively what to do to keep the airplane flying smoothly even though he is not handling the controls.

He must have a thorough knowledge of cruising control data, and know how to apply it at the proper time.

He is also the engineering officer aboard the airplane, and maintains a complete log of performance data.

He must be a qualified instrument pilot.

He must be able to fly good formation in any assigned position, day or night.

He must be qualified to navigate by day or at night by pilotage, dead reckoning, and by use of radio aids.

He must be proficient in the operation of all radio equipment located in the pilot's compartment.

In formation flying, he must be able to make engine adjustments almost automatically.

He must be prepared to take over on instruments when the formation is climbing through

an overcast, thus enabling you to watch the rest of the formation.

Always remember that the copilot is a fully trained, rated pilot just like yourself. He is subordinate to you only by virtue of your position as the airplane commander. The B-17 is a lot of airplane; more airplane than any one pilot can handle alone over a long period of time. Therefore, you have been provided with a second pilot who will share the duties of flight operation.

Treat your copilot as a brother pilot. Remember that the more proficient he is as a pilot, the more efficiently he will be able to perform the duties of the vital post he holds as your second in command.

Be sure that he is allowed to do his share of the flying, in the pilot's seat, on takeoffs, landings, and on instruments.

The importance of the copilot is eloquently testified by airplane commanders overseas. There have been many cases in which the pilot has been disabled or killed in flight and the copilot has taken full command of both airplane and crew, completed the mission, and returned safely to the home base. Usually, the copilots who have distinguished themselves under such conditions have been copilots who have been respected and trained by the airplane commander as pilots.

Bear in mind that the pilot in the right-hand seat of your airplane is preparing himself for an airplane commander's post too. Allow him every chance to develop his ability and to profit by your experience.

THE NAVIGATOR

The navigator's job is to direct your flight from departure to destination and return. He must know the exact position of the airplane at all times.

Navigation is the art of determining geographic positions by means of (a) pilotage, (b) dead reckoning, (c) radio, or (d) celestial navigation, or any combination of these 4 methods. By any one or combination of methods the navigator determines the position of the airplane in relation to the earth.

Pilotage

Pilotage is the method of determining the airplane's position by visual reference to the ground. The importance of accurate pilotage cannot be over-emphasized. In combat navigation, all bombing targets are approached by pilotage, and in many theaters the route is maintained by pilotage. This requires not merely the vicinity type, but pin-point pilotage. The exact position of the airplane must be known not within 5 miles but within ¼ of a mile.

The navigator does this by constant reference to groundspeeds and ETA's established for points ahead, the ground, and to his maps and charts. During the mission, so long as he can maintain visual contact with the ground, the navigator can establish these pin-point positions so that the exact track of the airplane will be known when the mission is completed.

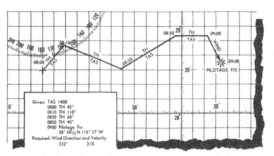

08:00
08:10
08:30
08:50
09:00
TH
TAS
WIND
09:00
PILOTAGE FIX
30'
29'
28'
Given: TAS 140K
0800 TH 45°
0810 TH 110°
0830 TH 60°
0850 TH 90°
0900 Pilotage Fix
28° 35½ N 115° 27' W
Required: Wind Direction and Velocity
332° 21K

Dead Reckoning

Dead reckoning is the basis of all other types of navigation. For instance, if the navigator is doing pilotage and computes ETA's for points ahead, he is using dead reckoning.

Dead reckoning determines the position of the airplane at any given time by keeping an account of the track and distance flown over the earth's surface from the point of departure or the last known position.

Dead reckoning can be subdivided into two classes:

1. **Dead reckoning as a result of a series of known positions obtained by some other means of navigation.** For example, you, as pilot, start on a mission from London to Berlin at 25,000 feet. For the first hour your navigator keeps track by pilotage; at the same time recording the heading and airspeed which you are holding. According to plan, at the end of the first hour the airplane goes above the clouds, thus losing contact with the ground. By means of dead reckoning from his last pilotage point, the navigator is able to tell the position of the aircraft at any time. The first hour's travel has given him the wind prevalent at altitude, and the track and groundspeed being made. By computing track and distance from the last pilotage point, he can always tell the position of the airplane. When your airplane comes out of the clouds near Berlin, the navigator will have a very close approximation of his exact position, and will be able to pick up pilotage points quickly.

2. **Dead reckoning as a result of visual references other than pilotage.** When flying over water, desert, or barren land, where no reliable pilotage points are available, accurate DR navigation still can be performed. By means of the drift meter the navigator is able to determine drift, the angle between the heading of the airplane and its track over the ground. The true heading of the airplane is obtained by application of compass error to the compass reading. The true heading plus or minus the drift (as read on the drift meter) gives the track of the airplane. At a constant airspeed, drift on 2 or more headings will give the navigator information necessary to obtain the wind by use of his computer. Groundspeed is computed easily once the wind, heading, and airspeed are known. So, by constant recording of true heading, true airspeed, drift, and groundspeed, the navigator is able to determine accurately the position of the airplane at any given time. For greatest accuracy, the pilot must maintain constant courses and airspeeds. If course or airspeed is changed, notify the navigator so he can record these changes.

Radio

Radio navigation makes use of various radio aids to determine position. The development of many new radio devices has increased the use of radio in combat zones. However, the ease with which radio aids can be jammed, or bent, limits the use of radio to that of a check on DR and pilotage. The navigator, in conjunction with the radio man, is responsible for all radio procedures, approaches, etc., that are in effect in the theater.

Celestial

Celestial navigation is the science of determining position by reference to 2 or more celestial bodies. The navigator uses a sextant, accurate time, and many tables to obtain what he calls a line of position. Actually this line is part of a circle on which the altitude of the particular body is constant for that instant of time. An intersection of 2 or more of these lines gives the navigator a fix. These fixes can be relied on as being accurate within approximately 10 miles. One reason for inaccuracy is the instability of the airplane as it moves through space, causing acceleration of the sextant bubble (a level denoting the horizontal). Because of this acceleration, the navigator takes observations over a period of time so that the acceleration error will cancel out to some extent. If the navigator tells the pilot when he wishes to take an observation, extremely careful flying on the part of the pilot during the few minutes it takes to make the observation will result in much greater accuracy. Generally speaking, the only celestial navigation used by a combat crew is during the delivering flight to the theater. But in all cases celestial navigation is used as a check on dead reckoning and pilotage except where celestial is the only method available, such as on long over-water flights, etc.

Instrument Calibration

Instrument calibration is an important duty of the navigator. All navigation depends directly on the accuracy of his instruments. Correct calibration requires close cooperation and extremely careful flying by the pilot. Instruments to be calibrated include the altimeter, all compasses, airspeed indicators, alignment of the astrocompass, astrograph, and drift meter, and check on the navigator's sextant and watch.

Pilot-Navigator Preflight Planning

1. Pilot and navigator must study flight plan of the route to be flown and select alternate airfields.

2. Study the weather with the navigator. Know what weather you are likely to encounter. Decide what action is to be taken. Know the weather conditions at the alternate airfields.

3. Inform your navigator at what airspeed and altitude you wish to fly so that he can prepare his flight plan.

4. Learn what type of navigation the navigator intends to use: pilotage, dead reckoning, radio, celestial, or a combination of all methods.

5. Determine check points; plan to make radio fixes.

6. Work out an effective communication method with your navigator to be used in flight.

7. Synchronize your watch with your navigator's.

Pilot-Navigator in Flight

1. **Constant course**—For accurate navigation, the pilot—you—must fly a constant course. The navigator has many computations and entries to make in his log. Constantly changing course makes his job more difficult. A good navigator is supposed to be able to follow the pilot, but he cannot be taking compass readings all the time.

2. **Constant airspeed** must be held as nearly as possible. This is as important to the navigator as is a constant course in determining position.

3. **Precision flying** by the pilot greatly affects the accuracy of the navigator's instrument readings, particularly celestial readings. A slight error in celestial reading can cause considerable error in determining positions. You can help the navigator by providing as steady a platform as possible from which he can take readings. The navigator should notify you when he intends to take readings so that the airplane can be leveled off and flown as smoothly as possible, preferably by using the automatic pilot.

Do not allow your navigator to be disturbed while he is taking celestial readings.

4. **Notify the navigator of any change in flight,** such as change in altitude, course, or airspeed. If change in flight plan is to be made, consult the navigator. Talk over the proposed change so that he can plan the flight and advise you about it.

5. If there is doubt about the position of the airplane, pilot and navigator should get together, refer to the navigator's flight log, talk the problem over and decide together the best course of action to take.

6. Check your compasses at intervals with those of the navigator, noting any deviation.

7. Require your navigator to give position reports at intervals.

8. You are ultimately responsible for getting the airplane to its destination. Therefore, it is your duty to know your position at all times.

9. Encourage your navigator to use as many navigation methods as possible as a means of double-checking.

Post-flight Critique

After every flight, get together with the navigator and discuss the flight and compare notes. Go over the navigator's log. If there have been serious navigational errors, discuss them with the navigator and determine their cause. If the navigator has been at fault, caution him that it is his job to see that the same mistake does not occur again. If the error has been caused by faulty instruments, see that they are corrected before another navigation mission is attempted. If your flying has contributed to inaccuracy in navigation, try to fly a better course next time.

Miscellaneous Duties

The navigator's primary duty is navigating your airplane with a high degree of accuracy. But as a member of the team, he must also have a general knowledge of the entire operation of the airplane.

He has a .50-cal. machine gun at his station, and he must be able to use it skillfully and to service it in emergencies.

He must be familiar with the oxygen system, know how to operate the turrets, radio equipment, and fuel transfer system.

He must know the location of all fuses and spare fuses, lights and spare lights, affecting navigation.

He must be familiar with emergency procedures, such as the manual operation of landing gear, bomb bay doors, and flaps, and the proper procedures for crash landings, ditching, bailout, etc.

THE BOMBARDIER

Accurate and effective bombing is the ultimate purpose of your entire airplane and crew. Every other function is preparatory to hitting and destroying the target.

That's your bombardier's job. The success or failure of the mission depends upon what he accomplishes in that short interval of the bombing run.

When the bombardier takes over the airplane for the run on the target, he is in absolute command. He will tell you what he wants done, and until he tells you "Bombs away," his word is law.

A great deal, therefore, depends on the understanding between bombardier and pilot. You expect your bombardier to know his job when he takes over. He expects you to understand the problems involved in his job, and to give him full cooperation. Teamwork between pilot and bombardier is essential.

Under any given set of conditions—groundspeed, altitude, direction, etc.—there is only one point in space where a bomb may be released from the airplane to hit a predetermined object on the ground.

There are many things with which a bombardier must be thoroughly familiar in order to release his bombs at the right point to hit this predetermined target.

He must know and understand his bombsight, what it does, and how it does it.

He must thoroughly understand the operation and upkeep of his bombing instruments and equipment.

He must know that his racks, switches, controls, releases, doors, linkage, etc., are in first-class operating condition.

DRIFT
WIND
TRAIL

He must understand the automatic pilot as it pertains to bombing.

He must know how to set it up, make any adjustments and minor repairs while in flight.

He must know how to operate all gun positions in the airplane.

He must know how to load and clear simple stoppages and jams of machine guns while in flight.

He must be able to load and fuse his own bombs.

He must understand the destructive power of bombs and must know the vulnerable spots on various types of targets.

He must understand the bombing problem, bombing probabilities, bombing errors, etc.

He must be thoroughly versed in target identification and in aircraft identification.

The bombardier should be familiar with the duties of all members of the crew and should be able to assist the navigator in case the navigator becomes incapacitated.

For the bombardier to be able to do his job, the pilot of the aircraft must place the aircraft in the proper position to arrive at a point on a circle about the target from which the bombs can be released to hit the target.

Consider the following conditions which affect the bomb dropped from an airplane:—

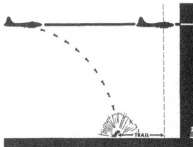

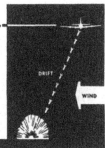

1. **ALTITUDE:** Controlled by the pilot. Determines the length of time the bomb is sustained in flight and affected by atmospheric conditions, thus affecting the range (forward travel of the bomb) and deflection (distance the bomb drifts in a crosswind with respect to airplane's ground track).

2. **TRUE AIRSPEED:** Controlled by the pilot. The measure of the speed of the airplane through the air. It is this speed which is imparted to the bomb and which gives the bomb its initial forward velocity and, therefore, affects the trail of the bomb, or the distance the bomb lags behind the airplane at the instant of impact.

3. **BOMB BALLISTICS:** Size, shape and density of the bomb, which determines its air resistance. Bombardier uses bomb ballistics tables to account for type of bomb.

4. **TRAIL:** Horizontal distance the bomb is behind the airplane at the instant of impact. This value, obtained from bombing tables, is set in the sight by the bombardier. Trail is affected by altitude, airspeed, bomb ballistics and air density, the first 2 factors being controlled by the pilot.

5. **ACTUAL TIME OF FALL:** Length of time the bomb is sustained in air from instant of release to instant of impact. Affected by alti-

tude, type of bomb and air density. Pilot controls altitude to obtain a definite actual time of fall.

6. **GROUNDSPEED:** The speed of the airplane in relation to the earth's surface. Groundspeed affects the range of the bomb and varies with the airspeed, controlled by the pilot.

Bombardier enters groundspeed in the bombsight through synchronization on the target. During this process the pilot must maintain the correct altitude and constant airspeed.

7. **DRIFT:** Determined by the direction and velocity of the wind, which determines the distance the bomb will travel downwind from the airplane from the instant the bomb is released to its instant of impact. Drift is set on the bombsight by the bombardier during the process of synchronization and setting up course.

The above conditions indicate that the pilot plays an important part in determining the proper point of release of the bomb. Moreover, throughout the course of the run, as explained below, there are certain preliminaries and techniques which the pilot must understand to insure accuracy and minimum loss of time.

Prior to takeoff the pilot must ascertain that the airplane's flight instruments have been checked and found accurate. These are the altimeter, airspeed indicator, free air temperature gauge and all gyro instruments. These instruments must be used to determine accurately the airplane's attitude.

The Pilot's Preliminaries

The autopilot and PDI should be checked for proper operation. It is very important that PDI and autopilot function perfectly in the air; otherwise it will be impossible for the bombardier to set up an accurate course on the bombing run. The pilot should thoroughly familiarize himself with the function of both the C-1 autopilot and PDI.

If the run is to be made on the autopilot, the pilot must carefully adjust the autopilot before reaching the target area. The autopilot must be adjusted under the same conditions that will exist on the bombing run over the target. For this reason the following factors should be taken into consideration and duplicated for initial adjustment.

1. Speed, altitude and power settings at which run is to be made.

2. Airplane trimmed at this speed to fly hands off with bomb bay doors opened.

The same condition will exist during the actual run, except that changes in load will occur before reaching the target area because of gas consumption. The pilot will continue making adjustments to correct for this by disengaging the autopilot elevator control and re-trimming the airplane, then re-engaging and adjusting the autopilot trim of the elevator.

Setting Up the Autopilot

One of the most important items in setting up the autopilot (see pp. 185-188) for bomb approach is to adjust the turn compensation knobs so that a turn made by the bombardier will be coordinated and at constant altitude. Failure to make this adjustment will involve difficulty and delay for the bombardier in establishing an accurate course during the run—with the possibility that the bombardier may not be able to establish a proper course in time, the result being considerably large deflection errors in point of impact.

Uncoordinated turns by the autopilot on the run cause erratic lateral motion of the course hair of the bombsight when sighting on target. The bombardier in setting up course must eliminate any lateral motion of the fore-and-aft hair in relation to the target before he has the proper course set up. Therefore, any erratic motion of the course hair requires an additional correction by the bombardier, which would not be necessary if autopilot was adjusted to make coordinated turns.

USE OF THE PDI: The same is true if PDI is used on the bomb run. Again, coordinated smooth turns by the pilot become an essential part of the bomb run. In addition to added course corrections necessitated by uncoordinated turns, skidding and slipping introduce small changes in airspeed affecting synchronization of the bombsight on the target. To help the pilot flying the run on PDI, the airplane should be trimmed to fly practically hands off.

Assume that you are approaching the target area with autopilot properly adjusted. Before

reaching the initial point (beginning of bomb run) there is evasive action to be considered. Many different types of evasive tactics are employed, but from experience it has been recommended that the method of evasive action be left up to the bombardier, since the entire antiaircraft pattern is fully visible to the bombardier in the nose.

EVASIVE ACTION: Changes in altitude necessary for evasive action can be coordinated with the bombardier's changes in direction at specific intervals. This procedure is helpful to the bombardier since he must select the initial point at which he will direct the airplane onto the briefed heading for the beginning of the bomb run.

Should the pilot be flying the evasive action on PDI (at the direction of the bombardier) he must know the exact position of the initial point for beginning the run, so that he can fly the airplane to that point and be on the briefed heading. Otherwise, there is a possibility of beginning to run too soon, which increases the airplane's vulnerability, or beginning the run too late, which will affect the accuracy of the bombing. For best results the approach should be planned so the airplane arrives at the initial point on the briefed heading, and at the assigned bombing altitude and airspeed.

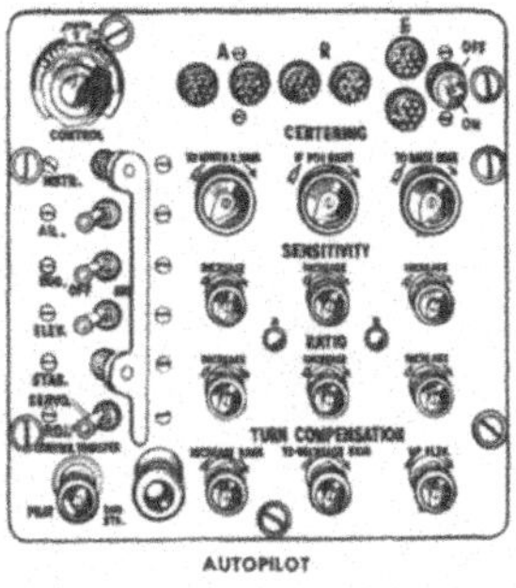

AUTOPILOT

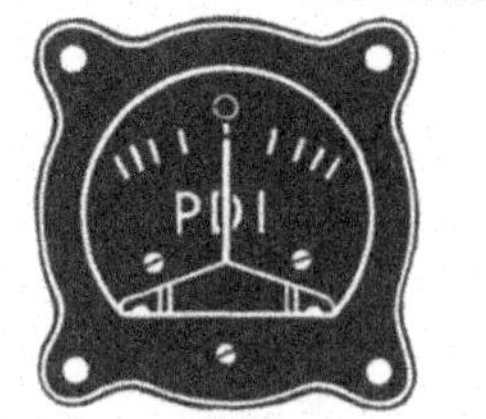

PDI

At this point the bombardier and pilot as a team should exert an extra effort to solve the problem at hand. It is now the bombardier's responsibility to take over the direction of flight, and give directions to the pilot for the operations to follow. The pilot must be able to follow the bombardier's directions with accuracy and minimum loss of time, since the longest possible bomb run seldom exceeds 3 minutes. Wavering and indecision at this moment are disastrous to the success of any mission, and during the crucial portion of the run, flak and fighter opposition must be ignored if bombs are to hit the target. The pilot and bombardier should keep each other informed of anything which may affect the successful completion of the run.

HOLDING A LEVEL: Either before or during the run, the bombardier will ask the pilot for a level. This means that the pilot must accurately level his airplane with his instruments (ignoring the PDI). There should be no acceleration of the airplane in any direction, such as an increase or decrease in airspeed, skidding or slipping, gaining or losing altitude.

For the level the pilot should keep a close check on his instruments, not by feel or watching the horizon. Any acceleration of the airplane during this moment will affect the bubbles (through centrifugal force) on the bombsight gyro, and the bombardier will not be able to establish an accurate level.

For example, assume that an acceleration occurred during the moment the bombardier was accomplishing a level on the gyro. A small

increase in airspeed or a small skid, hardly perceptible, is sufficient to shift the gyro bubble liquid 1° or more. An erroneous tilt of 1° on the gyro will cause an error of approximately 440 feet in the point of impact of a bomb dropped from 20,000 feet, the direction of error depending on direction of tilt of gyro caused by the erroneous bubble reading.

HOLDING ALTITUDE AND AIRSPEED: As the bombardier proceeds to set up his course (synchronize), it is absolutely essential that the pilot maintain the selected altitude and airspeed within the closest possible limits. For every additional 100 feet above the assumed 20,000-foot bombing altitude, the bombing error will increase approximately 30 feet, the direction of error being over. For erroneous airspeed, which creates difficulty in synchronization on the target, the bombing error will be approximately 170 feet for a 10 mph change in airspeed. Assuming the airspeed was 10 mph in excess, from 20,000 feet, the bomb impact would be short 170 feet.

The pilot's responsibility to provide a level and to maintain a selected altitude and airspeed within the closest limits cannot be over-emphasized.

If the pilot is using PDI (at the direction of the bombardier) instead of autopilot, he must be thoroughly familiar with the corrections demanded by the bombardier. Too large a correction or too small a correction, too soon or too late, is as bad as no correction at all. Only through prodigious practice flying with the PDI can the pilot become proficient to a point where he can actually perform a coordinated turn, the amount and speed necessary to balance the bombardier's signal from the bombsight.

Erratic airspeeds, varying altitudes, and poorly coordinated turns make the job of establishing course and synchronizing doubly difficult for both pilot and bombardier, because of the necessary added corrections required. The resulting bomb impact will be far from satisfactory.

After releasing the bombs, the pilot or bombardier may continue evasive action—usually the pilot, so that the bombardier may man his guns.

The pilot using the turn control may continue to fly the airplane on autopilot, or fly it manually, with the autopilot in a position to be engaged by merely flipping the lock switches. This would provide potential control of the airplane in case of emergency.

REDUCING CIRCULAR ERROR: One of the greatest assets towards reducing the circular error of a bombing squadron lies in the pilot's ability to adjust the autopilot properly, fly the PDI, and maintain the designated altitude and airspeeds during the bombing run. Reducing the circular error of a bombing squadron reduces the total number of aircraft required to destroy a particular target. For this reason both pilot and bombardier should work together until they have developed a complete understanding and confidence in each other.

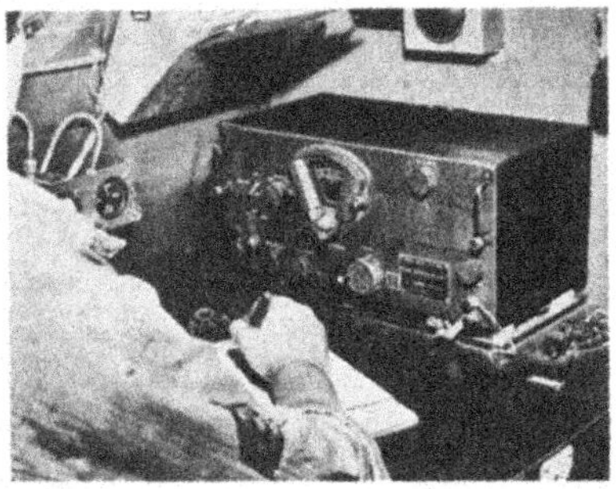

THE RADIO OPERATOR

There is a lot of radio equipment in today's B-17's. There is one man in particular who is supposed to know all there is to know about this equipment. Sometimes he does, but often he doesn't. And when the radio operator's deficiencies do not become apparent until the crew is in the combat zone, it is then too late. Too often the lives of pilots and crew are lost because the radio operator has accepted his responsibility indifferently.

Radio is a subject that cannot be learned in a day. It cannot be mastered in 6 weeks, but sufficient knowledge can be imparted to the radio man during his period of training in the United States if he is willing to study. It is imperative that you check your radio operator's ability to handle his job before taking him overseas as part of your crew. To do this you may have to check the various departments to find any weakness in the radio operator's training and proficiency and to aid the instructors in overcoming such weaknesses.

Training in the various phases of the heavy bomber program is designed to fit each member of the crew for the handling of his jobs. The radio operator will be required to:

1. Render position reports every 30 minutes.
2. Assist the navigator in taking fixes.
3. Keep the liaison and command sets properly tuned and in good operating order.
4. Understand from an operational point of view:
   - (a) Instrument landing
   - (b) IFF
   - (c) VHF

and other navigational aids equipment in the airplane.

5. Maintain a log.

In addition to being a radio operator, the radio man is also a gunner. During periods of combat he will be required to leave his watch at the radio and take up his guns. He is often required to learn photography. Some of the best pictures taken in the Southwest Pacific were taken by radio operators. The radio operator who cannot perform his job properly may be the weakest member of your crew—and the crew is no stronger than its weakest member.

THE ENGINEER

Size up the man who is to be your engineer. This man is supposed to know more about the airplane you are to fly than any other member of the crew.

He has been trained in the Air Forces' highly specialized technical schools. Probably he has served some time as a crew chief. Nevertheless, there may be some inevitable blank spots in his training which you, as a pilot and airplane commander, may be able to fill in.

Think back on your own training. In many courses of instruction, you had a lot of things thrown at you from right and left. You had to concentrate on how to fly; and where your equipment was concerned you learned to rely more and more on the enlisted personnel, particularly the crew chief and the engineer, to advise you about things that were not taught to you because of lack of time and the arrangement of the training program.

Both pilot and engineer have a responsibility to work closely together to supplement and fill in the blank spots in each other's education.

To be a qualified combat engineer a man must know his airplane, his engines, and his armament equipment thoroughly. This is a big responsibility: the lives of the entire crew, the safety of the equipment, the success of the mission depend upon it squarely.

He must work closely with the copilot, checking engine operation, fuel consumption, and the operation of all equipment.

He must be able to work with the bombardier, and know how to cock, lock, and load the bomb racks. It is up to you, the airplane commander, to see that he is familiar with these duties, and, if he is hazy concerning them, to have the bombardier give him special help and instruction.

He must be thoroughly familiar with the armament equipment, and know how to strip, clean, and re-assemble the guns.

He should have a general knowledge of radio equipment, and be able to assist in tuning transmitters and receivers.

Your engineer should be your chief source of information concerning the airplane. He should know more about the equipment than any other crew member—yourself included.

You, in turn, are his source of information concerning flying. Bear this in mind in all your discussions with the engineer. The more complete you can make his knowledge of the reasons behind every function of the equipment, the more valuable he will be as a member of the crew. Who knows? Someday that little bit of extra knowledge in the engineer's mind may save the day in some emergency.

Generally, in emergencies, the engineer will be the man to whom you turn first. Build up his pride, his confidence, his knowledge. Know him personally; check on the extent of his knowledge. Make him a man upon whom you can rely.

THE GUNNERS

The B-17 is a most effective gun platform, but its effectiveness can be either applied or defeated by the way the gunners in your crew perform their duties in action.

Your gunners belong to one of two distinct categories: turret gunners and flexible gunners.

The power turret gunners require many mental and physical qualities similar to what we know as inherent flying ability, since the operation of the power turret and gunsight are much like that of airplane flight operation.

While the flexible gunners do not require the same delicate touch as the turret gunner, they must have a fine sense of timing and be familiar with the rudiments of exterior ballistics.

All gunners should be familiar with the coverage area of all gun positions, and be prepared to bring the proper gun to bear as the conditions may warrant.

They should be experts in aircraft identification. Where the Sperry turret is used, failure to set the target dimension dial properly on the K-type sight will result in miscalculation of range.

They must be thoroughly familiar with the Browning aircraft machine gun. They should know how to maintain the guns, how to clear jams and stoppages, and how to harmonize the sights with the guns.

While participating in training flights, the gunners should be operating their turrets constantly, tracking with the flexible guns even when actual firing is not practical. Other airplanes flying in the vicinity offer excellent tracking targets, as do automobiles, houses, and other ground objects during low altitude flights.

The importance of teamwork cannot be over-emphasized. One poorly trained gunner, or one man not on the alert, can be the weak link as a result of which the entire crew may be lost.

Keep the interest of your gunners alive at all times. Any form of competition among the gunners themselves should stimulate interest to a high degree.

Finally, each gunner should fire the guns at each station to familiarize himself with the other man's position and to insure knowledge of operation in the event of an emergency.

PILOT'S OPERATIONAL EQUIPMENT

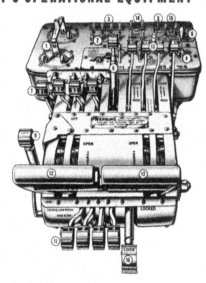

CONTROL PANEL AND PEDESTAL

1. Ignition switches
2. Fuel boost pump switches
3. Fuel shut-off valve switches
4. Cowl flap control valves
5. Landing gear switch
6. Wing flap switch
7. Turbo-supercharger controls (B-17F)
8. Turbo and mixture control lock
9. Throttle control lock
10. Propeller control lock
11. Propeller controls
12. Throttle controls
13. Mixture controls
14. Recognition light switches
15. Landing light switches

ABOVE WINDSHIELD

1. Clock
2. Compass
3. De-icer pressure gage
4. Compass card

LOWER CONTROL PEDESTAL

1. Elevator trim tab control
2. Automatic flight control panel
3. Rudder tab control
4. Elevator and rudder lock
5. Tailwheel lock

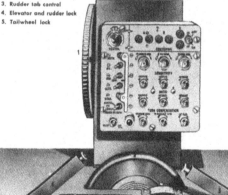

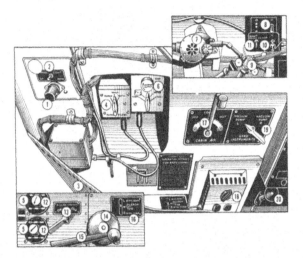

CONTROLS AT PILOT'S LEFT

1. Panel light
2. Panel light switch
3. Pilot's seat
4. Filter selector switch
5. Propeller anti-icer switch
6. Interphone jackbox
7. Oxygen regulator
8. Windshield wiper controls
9. Portable oxygen unit recharger
10. Windshield anti-icer switch

11. Windshield anti-icer flow control
12. Propeller anti-icer rheostats
13. Surface de-icer control
14. Aileron trim tab control
15. Pilot's seat adjustment lever
16. Aileron trim tab indicator
17. Cabin air control
18. Suit heater outlet
19. Vacuum selector valve
20. Emergency bomb release

36

PILOT'S CONTROL PANEL

1. Passing light switch
2. Running lights switch
3. Ammeters
4. Generator switches
5. Voltmeter
6. Battery switches
7. Alarm bell switch
8. Hydraulic pump servicing switch
9. Landing gear warning horn switch

10. Position lights switch
11. Voltmeter selector switch
12. Panel lights
13. Panel lights switch
14. Pitot heater switch
15. Interphone call light switch
16. Bomber call light switch
17. Inverter switch

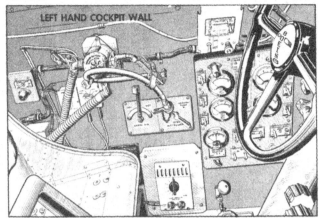

LEFT HAND COCKPIT WALL

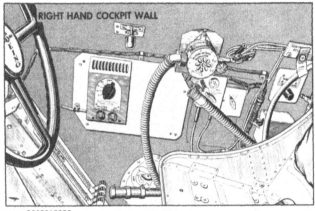

RIGHT HAND COCKPIT WALL

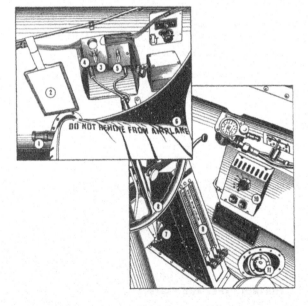

CONTROLS AT COPILOT'S RIGHT

1. Hydraulic hand pump
2. Checklist
3. Interphone selector switch
4. Interphone jackbox
5. Filter selector switch
6. Copilot's seat

7. Rudder pedal adjustment
8. Copilot's control wheel
9. Intercooler controls
10. Suit heater outlet
11. Engine primer

RESTRICTED   RESTRICTED

B-17 INSTRUMENT PANEL

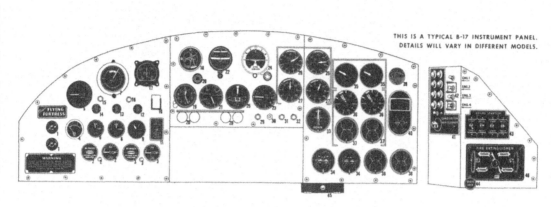

THIS IS A TYPICAL B-17 INSTRUMENT PANEL.
DETAILS WILL VARY IN DIFFERENT MODELS.

1. Fluorescent light switches
2. Pilot's oxygen flow indicator, warning light and pressure gage
3. Copilot's oxygen flow indicator, warning light and pressure gage
4. Voltmeter (AC)
5. Radio compass
6. Emergency oil pressure gage (Not on G)
7. Flux gate compass
8. Hydraulic oil pressure gage
9. Suction gage
10. Altimeter correction card

11. Airspeed alternate source switch
12. Vacuum warning light
13. Main system hydraulic oil warning light
14. Emergency system hydraulic oil warning light (Not on G)
15. Bomb door position light (Not on G)
16. Bomb release light
17. Pilot's directional indicator
18. Pilot's localizer indicator
19. Altimeter
20. Propeller feathering switches
21. Airspeed indicator

22. Directional gyro
23. Rate-of-climb indicator
24. Flight indicator
25. Turn-and-bank indicator
26. Manifold pressure gages
27. Tachometers
28. Marker beacon light
29. Globe test button
30. Bomber call light
31. Landing gear warning light
32. Tailwheel lock light
33. Flap position indicator
34. Cylinder-head temperature gages

35. Fuel pressure gages
36. Oil pressure gages
37. Oil temperature gages
38. Carburetor air temperature gages
39. Free air temperature gage
40. Fuel quantity gage
41. Carburetor air filter switch
42. Oil dilution switches
43. Starting switches
44. Parking brake control
45. Spare fuse box
46. Engine fire extinguisher controls (on some airplanes)

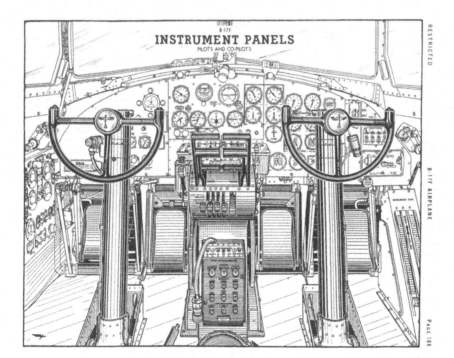

INSTRUMENT PANELS
PILOT'S AND CO-PILOT'S

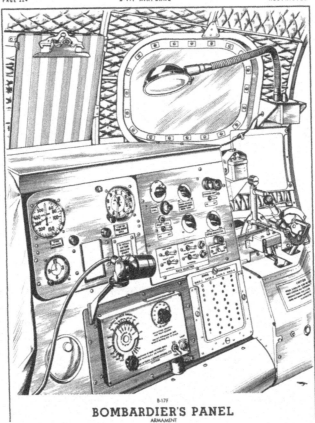

B-17F
BOMBARDIER'S PANEL
ARMAMENT

OFFICIAL A.A.F. PILOT'S CHECK LIST
B-17F AND B-17G AIRPLANES
For detailed instructions see Pilot's Handbook AN 01-20EF-1 or AN 01-20EG-1 in data case.

PILOT

BEFORE STARTING
1. Pilot's Pre-flight—Complete.
2. Form 1A, Form F, Weight and Balance—Checked.
3. Controls and Seats—Checked. Checked.
4. Fuel Transfer Valves and Switch—Off.
5. Intercoolers—Cold.
6. Gyros—Uncaged.
7. Fuel Shut-off Switches—Open.
8. Gear Switch—Neutral.
9. Cowl Flaps—Open Right—Open Left—Locked.
10. Turbos—Off.
11. Mixture Control—Checked.
12. Throttles—Closed.
13. High RPM—Checked.
14. Auto Pilot—Off.
15. De-icers and Anti-icers Wing and Prop.—Off.
16. Cabin Heat—Off.
17. Generators—Off.

STARTING ENGINES
1. Alarm Bell—Checked.
2. Wheel Chocks—In Place.
3. Fire Guard and Call Clear—Left—Right.
4. Master Switches—On.
5. Battery Switches and Inverters—On and Checked.
6. Parking Brakes—Hydraulic Check—On—Checked.
7. Booster Pumps—Pressure — On and Checked.
8. Carburetor Filters—Open.
9. Fuel Quantity—Gallons per tank.
10. Start Engines
   a. Fire Extinguisher Engine Selector—Checked.
   b. Prime—As Necessary.

CO-PILOT

BEFORE TAKE OFF
1. Tail Wheel—Locked.
2. Gyro—Set.
3. Generators—On.

AFTER TAKE OFF
1. Wheels—Pilot's Signal.
2. Power Reduction.
3. Cowl Flaps.
4. Wheel Check—OK Right. OK Left.

BEFORE LANDING
1. Radio Call Altimeter—Set.
2. Crew Positions—OK.
3. Ball Turret—Stowed.
4. Auto Pilot—Off.
5. Booster Pumps—On.
6. Mixture Controls—Auto Rich.
7. Intercooler—Set.
8. Carburetor Filters—Open.
9. Wing De-icers—Off.
10. Cabin Heat—Off.
11. Landing Gear
   a. Visual—Down right Down left Tail wheel Down, Antenna In
   b. Light—OK
   c. Switch—Neutral
   d. Manual Check.
12. Hydraulic Pressure—OK. Valves closed.
13. RPM 2300—Set.
14. Turbos—Set.
15. Flaps 1/3 — 1/3 Down.

FINAL APPROACH
1. Flaps—Pilot's Signal.
2. High RPM—Pilot's Signal.

30 January 1945
This list supersedes pilot's check lists of previous dates.

PILOT
   c. Energize
   d. Mesh
   e. Both Magnetos ON after one revolution.
11. Flight Indicator and Vacuum Pressures—Checked.
12. Radio—On.
13. Check Instruments—Checked.
14. Crew Report.
15. Radio Call and Altimeter—Set.

ENGINE RUN UP
1. Brakes—Locked.
2. Trim Tabs—Set.
3. Exercise Turbos (Hydraulic Regulators Only) and Props.
4. Check Generators—Checked and Off.
5. Run Up Engines.

AFTER LANDING
1. Hydraulic Pressure—OK.
2. Cowl Flaps—Open and Locked.
3. Turbos—Off.
4. Booster Pumps—Off.
5. Wing Flaps—Up.
6. Tail Wheel—Unlocked.
7. Generators—Off.

END OF MISSION
1. Dilute Engine Oil—When Necessary.
2. Engines—Cut.
3. Radio—On ramp.
4. Switches—Off.
5. Chocks.
6. Controls—Locked.
7. Form 1.

GO AROUND
1. High RPM and Power — High RPM.
2. Wing Flaps—Coming Up.
3. Power Reduction.
4. Wheel Check—OK Right—OK Left.

RUNNING TAKE OFF
1. Wing Flaps—Coming Up.
2. Power.
3. Wheel Check—OK Right—OK Left.

CO-PILOT

SUBSEQUENT TAKE OFF
1. Trim Tabs—Set.
2. Wing Flaps—Up.
3. Cowl Flaps—Open Right, Open Left.
4. High RPM—Checked.
5. Fuel—Gallons per tank.
6. Booster Pumps—On.
7. Turbos—Set.
8. Flight Controls—Unlocked.
9. Radio Call.

SUBSEQUENT LANDING
1. Landing Gear
   a. Visual—Down Right Down Left Tail Wheel Down
   b. Light—On.
   c. Switch—Neutral.
   d. Manual Check.
2. Hydraulic Pressure—OK.
3. RPM 2300—Set.
4. Turbo Controls—Set.
5. Wing Flaps 1/3 — 1/3 Down.
6. Radio Call.

FINAL APPROACH
1. Flaps—Pilot's Signal.
2. High RPM—Pilot's Signal.

(Items not underlined co-pilot answers.)

330

TAXIING

There is only one reason for a taxiing accident: carelessness. The pilot who taxies slowly and observes the few basic rules will never have the inexcusable experience of damaging an airplane in simple ground operation.

The pilot experienced on heavier types of aircraft should understand the reasons for taxiing slowly. Primarily they are safety considerations, and the mechanical limitations of the brakes.

Safety considerations are so obvious that they need little explanation. The pilot who taxies slowly **always has control of the airplane** and can stop whenever and wherever he chooses.

The mechanical limitations of brakes make slow taxiing mandatory. You can't stop 50,000 lb. of fast-moving airplane in a short space. It takes tremendous frictional energy to slow down and stop this large mass. Moreover, frequent application of brakes, which is necessary when the airplane is not taxied slowly, causes excessively high brake temperature and eventual brake failure.

1. Before wheel chocks are removed, check hydraulic pressure: it should be 600 to 800 lb.
2. Taxi from the parking area **with all 4 engines running**, using the outboard engines for turning. Keep your inboard engines idling at not less than 500 rpm, with just enough friction lock applied to prevent the throttles from creeping. Don't lock the throttles of the inboard engines tightly; you may need them in an emergency.
3. Never taxi faster than a ground crew man can walk.
4. Use brakes only to slow down or stop the airplane, or to aid in making turns, when necessary. At all other times, keep your feet off the brake pedals with your heels on the floor. Even slight pressure will result in brake heating. When it becomes necessary to use brakes, slide your feet up on the pedals until the balls of the feet are squarely on the brake controls. Apply brakes smoothly and firmly. (Don't pat the brakes.) As soon as the airplane is under control, release brakes and return heels to floor.
5. For all straight ahead taxiing—even for a short distance—keep the tailwheel locked.
6. Before making a turn, have the copilot unlock the tailwheel. Make turn by using the throttles, with as little brakes as possible.
7. Always make turns with the inside wheel rolling. Pivoting on the inside wheel causes excessive wear on the tire and places a heavy torque strain on the gear.

Use Brakes Sparingly

RIGHT ➡

⬅ **WRONG**
NEVER PIVOT

UNLOCK TAILWHEEL
AND REDIRECT
USING OUTBOARD
ENGINE

WIND

8. If a side wind blows the airplane off a straight line, wait until you reach the other side of the runway, then unlock the tailwheel and redirect the airplane, crabbing away from the windward side of the runway in a series of arcs or S's. (See cut.) Use the outboard engine on the side from which the wind is blowing to decrease the rapidity of your drift toward the windward side of the runway.
9. Hold the aileron and elevator controls in a neutral position, so that these control surfaces will be streamlined with wing surfaces and elevator stabilizers respectively. Don't try to taxi an airplane by steering with the control wheel as you would drive a car.
10. Take particular care never to allow the inboard engines to idle slowly enough to load up. During any one period of parking, don't permit them to idle at less than 1000 rpm. If you have to taxi over a long distance, stop and run up the engines high enough and often enough to keep them clear.
11. Don't try to taxi if hydraulic pressure is low and will not build up. (You will only lose what little pressure you have.) Have the airplane towed back to the line.
12. Have your auxiliary power unit turned on for all ground operations. This insures operation of the electrically operated hydraulic pump.

Remember that cold weather and low rpm do not work together. Therefore, when the temperature is low clear the engines oftener than usual. Naturally, this will require an increased use of brakes.

TAKEOFF TECHNIQUE

Taxi to run-up area, park into the wind when possible, and call for engine run-up check. Copilot responds: "Brakes set." Make sure that the throttles are set at not less than 1000 rpm.

Trim Tabs

Set the trim tabs for takeoff. Check to see that all 3 tabs are at the "0" (zero) setting. Incorrect setting of any trim tab on takeoff can cause a serious accident, especially if the airplane is heavily loaded.

Exercise Turbos and Propellers

Advance throttles to 1500 rpm, and run the turbo controls through their range several times. Still maintaining 1500 rpm, and with turbo controls "OFF," run the propellers through to "LOW RPM," then back to full "HIGH RPM."

Allow ample time for the propellers to change pitch. Watch carefully for the drop in rpm (approximately 300-400 rpm) indicated by the tachometers.

When rpm decreases to approximately 1100, return the propeller controls to "HIGH RPM." At the same time, return turbo controls to the "OFF" position.

Repeat these turbo and propeller exercises three or four times, or more if the outside air temperature is below 0°C.

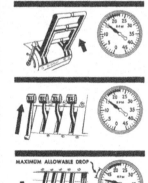

MAXIMUM ALLOWABLE DROP

Check Generators

Check the generators while the engines are operating at 1500 rpm. Check them for ample output; and, by using the voltmeter selectors, check for voltage output.

With all generators on, check the pitot heaters by watching for a rise in the ammeter reading. Then turn the pitot heater off.

Turn generators "OFF." Idle engines at not less than 1000 rpm.

Run Up Engines

Run up engines one at a time and in sequence. Open throttle to 28" manifold pressure. Then turn to left magneto, back to both, then to right magneto, then back to both. Do not operate on one magneto for more than 5 seconds at a time.

The copilot watches for roughness of engine operation by observing any drop in rpm. The pilot keeps an eye on the engine nacelle and cowling for visible indications of engine roughness. While the visual check of the nacelles and cowling is more reliable than the tachometer indication, utilize **both** methods as a double check. If much roughness is noticed on either magneto, run the engine up to full throttle **with turbo off** for about 10 seconds; then return to 28" manifold pressure, and check again.

During the pilot's ignition check, the copilot will check the following items:

Fuel pressure

DESIRED ....12 TO 16 LB. SQ. IN.
MAXIMUM ....16 LB. SQ. IN.
MINIMUM ....12 LB. SQ. IN.

Oil pressure

DESIRED ....75 LB. SQ. IN.
MAXIMUM ....80 LB. SQ. IN.
MINIMUM ....70 LB. SQ. IN.

Oil temperature

DESIRED ....70°C.
MAXIMUM ....88°C.
MINIMUM ....60°C.

Cylinder head temperature

MAXIMUM ....205°C.

Run-up Procedure

1. After checking magnetos, hold at 28" Hg., and move turbo control full forward against the stop.
2. Wait for increased manifold pressure (usually about 5-8" Hg. surge). This indicates that turbo wheel is turning up to speed.
3. Run throttle forward, and adjust turbo to give desired takeoff setting.

Remember that because of direct linkage control, the waste gate will open immediately when turbo control is moved toward closed position, and will lag when moved forward. Therefore, care should be exercised in adjusting control so that excessive full throttle operation is avoided on the ground.

Check rpm. Normally, for ground operation, rpm can vary between 2400 and 2500 maximum.

Reduce throttle to 1000 rpm.

Repeat the foregoing run-up procedure on engines No. 2, No. 3 and No. 4 in sequence.

Throttle Technique

The most comfortable and effective way to handle the throttles of the B-17 for operation of all 4 engines is to hold the **right hand palm upward,** thus grasping all 4 throttle handles firmly within the palm and fingers. (See cut.)

Holding them in this manner permits an easy wrist movement for **progressively** leading and controlling the throttles, and tends to favor the inboard throttles.

Progressively leading the throttles means alternately advancing right and left engines—in other words, **walking the throttles** steadily forward.

Adjustment of the throttle friction lock should be just enough to prevent the throttles from creeping. Don't jam the lock lever hard forward; you'll only have to struggle to loosen the lock each time you want to change throttle settings. Friction should be such that (1) throttle creeping is prevented, and (2) the throttle can be moved without too much pressure in case of emergency.

Before Takeoff

After engine run-up has been completed, make your radio call to the tower and request permission to taxi to takeoff position. Do not taxi on the runway until this radio contact has been completed. Bear in mind that it may be necessary for the tower to respond by using a red or green Aldis light.

Pilot and copilot should check visually to be sure the runway is clear and that no aircraft are landing. The tower is not infallible.

When cleared by the tower, instruct the copilot to unlock brakes. Then, with engines idling at not less than 800-1000 rpm, taxi on to the runway. Take a position that will allow use of the full runway. See that all windows are closed and locked. Cowl flaps must be left open on takeoff. Call for takeoff check.

See that the airplane is lined up properly with the runway. Instruct the copilot to "Lock tailwheel." The copilot will lock the tailwheel as the airplane is slowly rolling forward, and will inform you: "Tailwheel locked; light out—Gyros."

Check the gyros. Set the directional gyro to correspond with the magnetic compass. When lined up for takeoff, check your compass reading with the runway heading. Pilot responds: "Gyros set."

Copilot calls: "Generators" as throttles are advanced for takeoff. When 1500 rpm is reached, pilot turns on generators with left hand.

TAKEOFF

Duties of the pilot, copilot, and flight engineer on takeoff are well defined. Each has specific duties to perform, and it is important that all three should have an over-all understanding of the takeoff procedure.

1. Apply power gradually, **progressively leading the throttles.** (See p. 69.) Avoid **over-control,** which will require reduction of power on either side.
2. Keep your right hand on the throttles.
3. During the takeoff run, maintain directional control with rudder and throttles. **Keep ailerons neutral.**
4. Always take off from a 2-point, tail-low attitude. (The 3-point takeoff should never be attempted except in an emergency.) Don't attempt to pull the airplane into the air. Normally when you have attained an airspeed of approximately 110-115 mph, moderate back pressure on the control column will enable the airplane to fly itself off the ground.
5. The copilot follows through on the throttles, keeping his left hand in position to make adjustments for variations in manifold pressure, and prepared to take immediate action in such emergencies as runway propellers or overspeeding turbos.
6. The copilot's principal duty on takeoff is to watch the engine instruments, particularly manifold pressure, rpm, pressure gages, and temperature gages. He must divide his attention between engine instruments and the actual progress of the takeoff.

7. Takeoff distances for various field conditions and airplane loading are stated specifically on the seat-back operating instructions and in AN 01-20EF-1 and AN 01-20EG-1.
8. After the airplane has left the ground, and you are positive that you have sufficient flying speed and that everything is under control, signal to the copilot to raise the landing gear. The copilot will apply brakes gently to stop the rotation of the wheels, and raise the gear. Both pilot and copilot make a visual check, and acknowledge the retraction of the main wheels (Pilot: "Landing gear up left." Copilot: "Landing gear up right." The flight engineer checks and reports "Tailwheel up.") The copilot places the landing gear switch in the neutral position.
9. The B-17 is so constructed that very little change in trim will be required after takeoff.
10. Depending upon elevation and gross load, signal the copilot either to reduce or shut off the turbos.
11. Reduce power upon attaining an airspeed of 140 mph. To obtain normal climb attitude, the pilot reduces the throttles to a manifold pressure between 32″ and 35″ Hg. in the transition type B-17, and 35″ Hg. in the normally operated tactical airplane. Then the copilot reduces rpm to 2300.
12. The copilot will make the necessary adjustments of cowl flaps to regulate cylinder-head temperature during the climb. They should be closed whenever possible.

AT 110-115 MPH APPLY
MODERATE BACK PRESSURE
ON CONTROL COLUMN

2 POINT WITH
TAIL LOW

PLANE WILL FLY
ITSELF OFF THE GROUND

RUNNING TAKEOFF

This type of takeoff does not vary much in basic technique from the normal takeoff.
1. Make a normal 3-point landing.
2. When the airplane has settled into the landing roll, inform the copilot: "Running takeoff."
3. The copilot immediately checks propeller controls for "HIGH RPM," and places the flap switch in the "UP" position.
4. Now apply power, walking up throttles steadily and smoothly. Avoid abrupt throttle movement.

5. Use rudder for directional control. The airplane still has most of its landing speed when power is applied. If directional control is difficult before full power is attained, use coordinated throttle and rudder.

From this point forward, the operation is the same as a normal takeoff. Complete the usual after-takeoff check: (1) Signal copilot for "Wheels up" if leaving traffic; (2) reduce power; (3) adjust cowl flaps; (4) make check of "Wheels up right." "Wheels up left." Engineer: "Tailwheel up."

CROSSWIND TAKEOFF

The crosswind takeoff requires **use of more rudder** and more **differential throttling** than the normal takeoff.

Most modern airfields are so constructed that there is seldom any occasion for taking off in an extreme crosswind. However, because the large vertical surfaces of the airplane are exposed to any wind from the side the airplane will tend to veer **into** the wind. Therefore, the technique of the crosswind takeoff is extremely important and frequently useful.

Remember that the important elements in the crosswind takeoff control, in order of importance, are: (1) rudder, (2) differential throttling, and (3) the downwind brake **only as a last resort.**

Use rudder to keep the airplane straight as long as possible. However, in a strong crosswind, if use of rudder is not sufficient to keep the airplane straight, apply more power to the upwind engines. Remember that progressive application of power (on all 4 engines) is necessary to attain takeoff speed as quickly as possible.

If the upwind engines have been used all the way to the stop and the rudder still will not straighten the airplane, **only then apply slight reduction of power on the downwind engines.** Under most crosswind conditions, this should not be necessary.

Don't attempt to use the downwind brake except as a last resort.

CORRECT WITH RUDDER
AND UPWIND ENGINES

WIND

CLIMBING AND CRUISING

The rate at which an airplane will climb is obtained directly from the difference between the **power required for level flight** and the **power available** from the engines. This difference is the **reserve power** which can be used for climbing.

Climbing the B-17

Flight tests have shown that for B-17's of all weights, the difference between **power required** for level flight and **power available** reaches a maximum at approximately 135 mph IAS. For stability purposes, another 5 mph is added as a

safety margin. Therefore, **make your climb at 140 mph IAS,** except on instruments.

Climbing on Instruments

On instruments below 20,000 feet, climb at 150 mph IAS. Here again an allowance has been made in the recommended airspeed for a safety margin.

Power Settings for Climbing

Power settings for the normal climbing conditions are as follows:

GRADE 100 FUEL	RPM	MANIFOLD PRESS.	MIXTURE
Maximum climb	2300	38″ Hg.	Auto-Rich
Desired climb	2300	35″ Hg.	Auto-Rich
GRADE 91 FUEL			
Maximum climb	2300	37″ Hg.	Auto-Rich
Desired climb	2300	35″ Hg.	Auto-Rich
Desired climb (light transition planes)	2300	32–35″ Hg.	Auto-Rich

FLIGHT CHARACTERISTICS

The B-17F possesses many outstanding flight characteristics, chief among which are: (1) directional stability; (2) strong aileron effect in turns; (3) ability to go around without change in elevator trim; (4) exceptionally satisfactory stalling characteristics; and (5) extremely effective elevator control in takeoff and landing.

Trim Tabs

The airplane will go around without changes in elevator trim tab settings. However, trim must be changed with adjustment of cowl flaps and power settings, for these reasons:

1. Increased power on the inboard engines causes the airplane to become slightly tail-heavy. (Power change on the outboard engines has no appreciable effect on trim.)

2. Closing the cowl flaps on the inboard engines also causes tail-heaviness. (The effect of cowl flaps on the outboards is negligible.)

With the airplane properly trimmed for a power-off, flaps-down landing, you can take off and go around again by applying power and putting the flap switch "UP" with no change in trim. The flaps will retract at a satisfactorily slow rate.

Turns

Because of the inherent directional stability of the B-17, dropping one wing will produce a noticeable turning effect. Very little rudder and aileron will enable you to roll in and out of turns easily. Carefully avoid uncoordinated use of aileron.

In shallow turns the load factors are negligible. But in steeper turns proportionately more back pressure is required, thereby increasing the load factor.

In banks from 10° to 70° the load factor increases from 1.5 to 3.0. Obviously, steep turns of a heavily loaded airplane may place sufficient stress on the wings to cause structural failure.

If the airplane tends to slip out of turns, recover smoothly without attempting to hold bank. Decrease the bank. Use proper coordination of rudder and aileron.

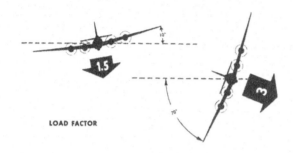

LOAD FACTOR

RECOVER FROM STALL SMOOTHLY

Stall Recovery

For the B-17F the procedure for recovering from a stall is normal.

1. Regain airspeed for normal flight by smooth operation of the elevators. This may require a dive up to 30°.

2. While regaining airspeed, use rudder to maintain laterally level flight. After airspeed is regained, use ailerons also for lateral control—but not until airspeed is regained.

The important thing is to **recover from the dive smoothly**. Penalty for failure to make a smooth recovery may be a secondary stall or structural damage to the airplane, both because of excessive load factors. Rough or abrupt use of elevators to regain normal flying

speed may cause the dive to become excessively steep.

The additional airspeed necessary to regain normal flight need not be more than 20 mph. This means that excessive diving to regain airspeed is absolutely unnecessary.

Remember these additional facts about stalls:
1. Stalls with wheels down will increase the stalling speed about 5 mph.
2. Stalls with wheels and flaps down will decrease the stalling speed about 10 mph.
3. Stalls with de-icer boots operating will increase the stalling speed 10-15 mph. In recovering from stalls with de-icer boots operating, regain slightly more than the usual 20 mph needed for recovery. Such stalls are apt to be more abrupt, with a greater tendency to roll.

Rough Air Operation

In rough air, use both rudder and ailerons without worrying about excessive loads. Both aileron and rudder forces vary with changes in airspeed in such manner that it is almost im-

possible to damage the system without deliberately trying to do so. Necessary control pressures are small enough, and the responses large enough, to maintain ample control of the airplane.

However, in the case of the elevators, exercise great care, both in rough air and in recovery from dives, to assure smooth operation. In thunder storms, squalls, and in or near turbulent cumulus clouds, it is possible to develop excessive load factors by means of the elevators unless they are used properly. This does not mean that there is any greater tendency to exceed allowable load factors in the B-17 than in other heavy bombardment or transport airplanes. It means that **the larger the airplane, the greater the time and distance required to complete any maneuver.** In operation, you **must** allow more distance and time in proportion to the size of the airplane.

Generally, in rough air, hold constant airspeed by means of the elevator, but do it smoothly. Remember that recovery to the desired airspeed may take time.

Avoid hurried recovery from dives, climbs or changes in airspeed. Never dive the airplane through a cloud layer or through rough air at maximum diving speed. Don't attempt high-speed flight in rough air.

Spins

Accidental spinning of the B-17 is extremely unlikely. The directional stability and damping are great, and it is probable that even a deliberate spin would be difficult. However, remember that **the airplane was not designed for spinning, and deliberate spins are forbidden.**

Dives

The maximum permissible diving speed in the B-17F (flaps and wheels up) with modified elevators is 270 mph IAS; without elevator modifications, the maximum diving speed is 220 mph.

The structural factors limiting the diving speed of the B-17F are the engine ring cowl strength, the wing leading-edge de-icer boot

MAXIMUM DIVING SPEED WITHOUT ELEVATOR MODIFICATIONS IS 220 MPH.

Stalls

The stall characteristics of the B-17 are highly satisfactory. The tendency to roll—commonly caused by lack of symmetry in the stalling of either wing–is minimized by the large vertical tail. Under all conditions a stall warning at several mph above stalling speed is indicated by buffeting of the elevators.

If airspeed is reduced rapidly near the stall, the speed at which the stall will occur will be lower than when the stall is approached gradually. The stall will also be more violent because the wing's angle of attack will be considerably above the stalling attitude.

The stalling speed of the B-17F, like that of any other airplane, depends upon: (a) the gross weight, (b) the load factor (number of Gs), (c) the wing flap setting, (d) the power, (e) de-icer operation and ice formation.

The effect of gross weight upon stalling speed is obvious: the heavier the load, the higher the stalling speed.

The effect of the load factor is simply to increase the effective gross weight in proportion to the load factor.

The greater the flap angle the lower the stalling speed. The greater the power, the lower the stalling speed. Full flaps reduce the stalling speed about 15 mph for gross weights of 40,000 to 45,000 lb., and a load factor of 1.0; but full military power for the same loading conditions may reduce the stalling speed another 15 mph.

Any yawing, accidental or otherwise, will increase the stalling speed and any tendency to roll at the stall. This is obvious, since the normal procedure in deliberately making a spin is to yaw the airplane as it stalls. For example, if the left wing drops at the stall and you apply right aileron to raise the left wing, the ailerons will have a tendency to overbalance and reverse effectiveness, because of the drag induced by the aileron. The result will be increased dropping of the left wing. The aileron procedure in recovering from a stall, therefore, is to **hold ailerons neutral and refrain from their use until coming out of the dive in the final phase of recovery.**

strength, the cockpit windshield and canopy strength, and the critical flutter speed. The engine ring cowl has been designed to withstand 420 mph. The windshield and cockpit canopy have ample margin at 305 mph. The wing leading-edge de-icer boots begin to raise slightly from the wing at 305 mph, and any additional speed would be likely to lift the upper part of the boot above the wing surface, possibly causing structural failure. The mass balance of the control surface is so essentially complete both statically and dynamically that, basically, the critical flutter speed depends entirely on the wing-bending torsion critical speed, which is approximately 375 mph.

Therefore, it is obvious that simply diving the airplane (with modified elevators) to 270 mph involves no danger whatsoever. The only danger that must be considered is in recovery. Recovery must be smooth and gradual. Normally, a load factor of 2 will not be exceeded. At the gross weight of 50,000 lb., the initial-yield point factor is slightly less than 3, making the ultimate load factor slightly over 4. Obviously, at that gross weight the load factor 3 should never be reached; the load factor 2 normally will not be exceeded.

Heavy Loads

The B-17 is stable longitudinally with heavy loads as long as the center of gravity is forward of 32% of the Mean Aerodynamic Chord (87 inches aft of the leading edge of the center section).

For all normal loading the CG must be kept forward of 32% of the MAC. If an excessive load is placed in the rear, the airplane will have neutral or negative stability. It is possible to trim the airplane with an unstable load, but it will be difficult to fly, especially on instruments. It is also much easier to stall inadvertently when flying an unstable airplane on instruments.

Loading for the forward CG positions is preferred because, in addition to being easier to fly, it gives a smooth increase in elevator forces required to pull out of dives, and eliminates the necessity of using excessive elevator trim to hold the tail up.

LANDINGS

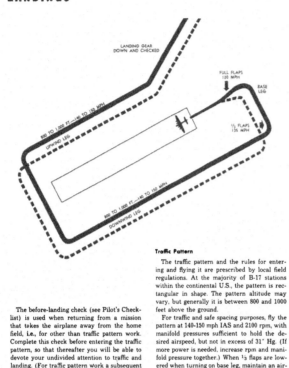

LANDING GEAR
DOWN AND CHECKED

FULL FLAPS
120 MPH

BASE
LEG

800 TO 1,000 FT.—140 TO 150 MPH

UPWIND LEG

½ FLAPS
135 MPH

800 TO 1,000 FT.—140 TO 150 MPH

DOWNWIND LEG

Traffic Pattern

The traffic pattern and the rules for entering and flying it are prescribed by local field regulations. At the majority of B-17 stations within the continental U.S., the pattern is rectangular in shape. The pattern altitude may vary, but generally it is between 800 and 1000 feet above the ground.

For traffic and safe spacing purposes, fly the pattern at 140-150 mph IAS and 2100 rpm, with manifold pressures sufficient to hold the desired airspeed, but not in excess of 31" Hg. (If more power is needed, increase rpm and manifold pressure together.) When ⅓ flaps are lowered when turning on base leg, maintain an airspeed of 135 mph.

The before-landing check (see Pilot's Checklist) is used when returning from a mission that takes the airplane away from the home field, i.e., for other than traffic pattern work. Complete this check before entering the traffic pattern, so that thereafter you will be able to devote your undivided attention to traffic and landing. (For traffic pattern work a subsequent landing check is provided. See pp. 55-56.)

92

BEFORE-LANDING CHECK

Radio Call, Altimeter Setting

Radio call to the tower is made by pilot or copilot (see **Pilot's Information File**). Obtain altimeter setting for the field and landing instructions. Repeat the altimeter setting to the tower to insure correctness. (Final radio call will be made while in traffic.)

Crew Positions

Have the engineer check the crew to see that all members are in proper positions for landing.

The radio operator will check the trailing antenna and see that it is retracted.

Gunners will check their guns and make sure they are in proper position for landing.

Automatic Pilot

See that the automatic pilot is "OFF." All switches must be turned "OFF" to eliminate any possibility of accidental engagement.

Booster Pumps

Check the booster pumps "ON."

Intercoolers

Be sure the intercoolers are in the "OFF" or "COLD" position for landing. Intercoolers "ON" will cause detonation and loss of power if emergency power is needed on the landing.

When freezing precipitation is present during the approach glide to the runway, and there is danger of carburetor icing, turn the intercoolers "ON," but be sure to notify the copilot and all persons on the flight deck. This will serve as a reminder to all that, in any emergency, the intercoolers must be turned "OFF" immediately.

Carburetor Filters

Place the carburetor filters in the "ON" (or "OPEN") position for landing. With filters off, or closed, a rise in available manifold pressure takes place. If left off or closed for landing, dangerous manifold pressures will develop

should emergency power or full throttle be used.

Wing De-icer Boots

Check the wing de-icer boots: controls should be in the "OFF" position except when testing or actually in use.

Make a visual check to be sure the de-icer boots are deflated before the final approach. Remember that action of the wing de-icer boots disturbs the flow of air over the lifting surfaces and materially increases the stalling speed.

Check propeller anti-icers: "OFF." The rheostats of the propeller anti-icers usually are set at a predetermined rate of flow. Their adjustment should not be changed.

Landing Gear

Instruct the copilot to put the landing gear switch in the "DOWN" position. Make a visual check from the left-hand window, and report aloud: "Down left." The copilot will make a similar check on his side and will report, "Down right." From the rear of the airplane, the engineer will check the tailwheel and report: "Tailwheel down." At the same time, the engineer will visually check the condition of the tailwheel assembly (no worn threads or gear, etc.), and see that the trailing antenna is retracted. Engineer will check the ball turret.

Check Landing Gear Warning Lights

Copilot returns switch to neutral position and checks warning light: green light on.

Hydraulic Pressure

With landing gear down, check the hydraulic pressure gages: normal pressure is 800 lb.

Service the accumulators, if necessary.

Be sure the cowl flap controls are in the "LOCKED" or neutral position to prevent any loss of oil supply through leaks in the actuating mechanism.

If in doubt about hydraulic pressure, instruct the copilot to stand by on the hand pump, awaiting your signal.

93

Increase RPM

In the traffic pattern, signal the copilot to increase rpm to 2100.

Turbos

Decrease manifold pressure to about 23", then signal the copilot to place the turbo controls full "ON," readjust manifold pressure to desired value. Be extremely careful that allowable manifold pressures are not exceeded with the turbos in the full "ON" position. This is important in case an emergency takeoff or go-around is necessary after an attempt landing. Normally, full takeoff manifold pressure will not be needed in such an emergency, since the airplane still will be at or near flying speed and no original inertia has to be overcome.

Flaps

Lower ½ flaps when turning on base leg, after airspeed has been reduced below 147 mph.

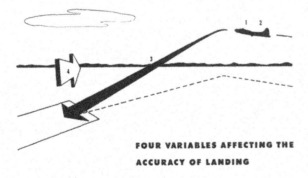

FOUR VARIABLES AFFECTING THE ACCURACY OF LANDING

94

FINAL APPROACH

Flaps

For normal landings, place the wing flaps in the full down position on the final approach. However, in heavy winds or heavy crosswinds partial flaps produce better results.

In the event of an emergency takeoff or go-around after an attempted landing, do not retract flaps until full power has been applied.

High RPM

While fully retarding throttle, signal the copilot to move propeller controls to full "HIGH RPM."

Power-off Approach

The power-off approach can be executed successfully on normal empty-weight B-17's, and is taught in transition schools.

The important factors in making a successful power-off approach are: (1) setting the proper base leg—not more than 3 miles out; (2)

maintaining constant altitude on the base leg; (3) maintaining constant airspeed and angle of glide; and (4) the wind.

These are the 4 variables. The first 3 are under your control; the fourth—the wind—can be taken care of by proper application of the first 3 factors.

Usually, a good approach means a good landing. The best approach can be made by setting the base leg approximately 2 miles from the field, never more than 3 miles.

Maintain altitude throughout the turn on the approach.

The third and most important consideration in the successful approach and landing is to maintain a constant glide. Roll out of the turn on the approach, lower flaps, maintain altitude, and reduce power at the proper point. Smoothly blend power reduction to the change to gliding attitude.

A good or bad landing of a 4-engine airplane usually is determined by the way it has descended to 300 feet. By that time the pilot should have established constant glide, constant airspeed, constant rate of descent, and made an accurate judgment of distance. If he has accomplished these things, the landing is in the bag.

Proper altitude for breaking a power-off glide is approximately 150 feet with a medium load. The flatter the glide, the lower the glide may be broken.

Level off for landing smoothly and gradually. In the B-17 an abrupt change of attitude from the vertical to the horizontal plane will increase the wing loading, thereby increasing the stalling speed. There is no danger of this if you level off smoothly and gradually.

Power Approach

The same 4 variables—setting the base leg, maintaining altitude on the base leg, holding constant airspeed and angle of glide, and reckoning with the wind, govern the success or failure of the power approach.

The power approach does **not** mean flying the airplane in at excessive speed and skimming over half the runway's length. Nor does it mean bringing the airplane in at such a low

speed that it is virtually hanging on the prop to stall in as soon as throttles are cut.

The power approach is a **controlled glide** in which power is used to obtain accuracy in landing on a selected spot, and greater control of the airplane.

Put down flaps and reduce power on the approach. Continue to reduce power **gradually** until the desired airspeed and rate of descent have been established. (Approximately 15" Hg. on the B-17E, and approximately 20" Hg. on the B-17F and B-17G). Hold a desired manifold pressure until you are ready to close throttles when nearing the runway. This eliminates any need for jockeying throttles back and forth, and makes for a smooth, precise landing.

Normally, the gliding speed should be maintained at 120 mph; but this will vary with the gross weight and CG location, rigging, angle of descent, wind conditions, and pilot technique. Correct glide usually results from bringing these factors into harmonious relationship. Proper gliding speed is approximately 20% above stalling speed for a B-17 with a medium load.

Strong Winds

When landing in strong winds, the use of full flaps often is inadvisable. Use your discretion as to the amount of flaps to use. However, never use less than ½ flaps.

Crosswinds

When turning on the approach in a crosswind, be careful to prevent the wind from forcing you off your approach to a degree where it is impossible to align with the runway.

There are 3 possible ways of making a crosswind approach and landing: (1) holding the airplane straight toward the runway, dropping one wing into the wind with just enough top rudder to counteract drift; (2) heading the airplane into the wind (crabbing) just enough to keep a straight ground path; and (3) a combination of the first two methods.

The last combination of methods is preferred, because it eliminates the possibility of dropping the wing too low, or of crabbing too much. It also prevents crossing controls and

95

CROSSWIND LANDING TECHNIQUES

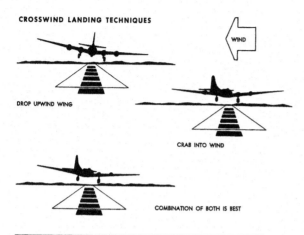

DROP UPWIND WING

CRAB INTO WIND

COMBINATION OF BOTH IS BEST

WIND

decreases the amount of correction needed to straighten out and level off during the round-out.

If the airplane drifts after leveling off, nose just a little downwind. This will eliminate some of the sideload that may be placed on the wheels. However, the necessity for nosing downwind can be eliminated by gliding in with slightly less speed.

Make a 3-point landing, gliding at 120 mph with full flaps, or at 125 mph with ½ flaps.

Watch Brakes

On all landings, take particular care to avoid holding brakes while using rudder on the approach. Landing with brakes, or applying

brakes before the full weight of the airplane settles, will cause blown tires and possible damage to the landing gear without the pilot ever knowing what is happening.

Caution

NEVER LAND WITH BRAKES.

NEVER APPLY BRAKES

BEFORE FULL WEIGHT OF

PLANE SETTLES.

96   RESTRICTED

FORMATION

When you get into combat you will learn that your best assurance of becoming a veteran of World War II is the good, well-planned, and well-executed formation.

Formation flying is the first requisite of successful operation of the heavy bomber in combat. Groups that are noted for their proficiency in formation flying are usually the groups with the lowest casualty rates. Proper formation provides: controlled and concentrated firepower, maneuverability, cross-cover, precise bombing pattern, better fighter protection.

Heavy Bomber Formations

Formation flying in 4-engine airplanes presents greater problems than formation flying in smaller aircraft. The problems increase in almost direct proportion to the airplane's size and weight. In the B-17, relatively slower response to power and control changes require a much higher degree of **anticipation** on the

part of the pilot. Therefore you must allow a greater factor of safety.

Violent maneuvers are unnecessary and seldom encountered. Close flying becomes an added hazard which accomplishes no purpose and is not even an indication of a good formation. Bear in mind that it is much more difficult to maintain position when flying with proper spacing between airplanes than with wings overlapping.

Safety first is a prerequisite of a good formation because a greater number of lives and a larger amount of equipment is in the hands of the responsible pilot in a large 4-engine airplane.

Clearance

In flying the Vee formation, aircraft will not be flown closer to one another than 50 feet from nose to tail and wingtip to wingtip. Maintain this horizontal clearance whenever vertical clearance is less than 50 feet, thus providing a minimum of 50 feet clearance between wingtips as well as the line of nose and tail under all formation flying conditions.

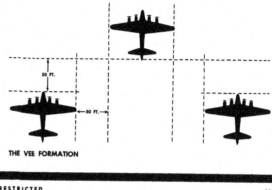

50 FT.

50 FT.

THE VEE FORMATION

RESTRICTED   119

FORMATION TAKEOFFS

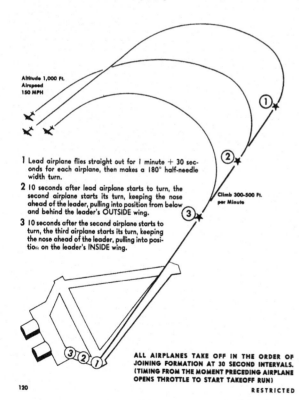

Altitude 1,000 Ft.
Airspeed
150 MPH

Climb 300-500 Ft.
per Minute

1 Lead airplane flies straight out for 1 minute + 30 seconds for each airplane, then makes a 180° half-needle width turn.

2 10 seconds after lead airplane starts to turn, the second airplane starts its turn, keeping the nose ahead of the leader, pulling into position from below and behind the leader's OUTSIDE wing.

3 10 seconds after the second airplane starts to turn, the third airplane starts its turn, keeping the nose ahead of the leader, pulling into position on the leader's INSIDE wing.

ALL AIRPLANES TAKE OFF IN THE ORDER OF JOINING FORMATION AT 30 SECOND INTERVALS. (TIMING FROM THE MOMENT PRECEDING AIRPLANE OPENS THROTTLE TO START TAKEOFF RUN)

120   RESTRICTED

Taxiing Out

At H hour, all ships start engines and stand by on interphone frequency. The formation leader checks with all planes in his formation. After this he calls the tower and clears his formation for taxi and takeoff instructions. As he taxies out No. 2 man follows, then No. 3, etc., each airplane taking the same place respectively on the ground that it is assigned in the air. As soon as the leader parks at an angle near the end of the takeoff strip, the other aircraft do likewise. At this point all aircraft run up engines and get ready for takeoff. The leader makes certain that everyone is ready to go before he pulls out on takeoff strip.

Takeoff

Formation takeoffs should be cleared from an airdrome in a rapid and efficient manner. Individual takeoffs will be made. Therefore, the following method is suggested.

The leader goes into takeoff position and takes off at H hour. No. 2 man starts pulling into position as soon as the leader starts rolling. When the leader's wheel leaves the runway, No. 2 starts taking off. (The time lapse is about 30 seconds.) The leader flies straight ahead at 150 mph, 300-500 feet per minute ascent, for one minute plus 30 seconds for each airplane in the formation. He levels off at 1000 feet above the terrain to prevent high rates of climb for succeeding aircraft. (Cruise at 150 mph.)

As soon as the leader has flown out his exact time, he makes a 180° half-needle-width turn to the left. The second airplane in formation assumes the outside or No. 2 position, while the third airplane assumes the inside or No. 3 position. The leader of the second element assumes position on the outside of the formation and his elements assemble on him in the same manner.

3-Airplane Vee

The 3-airplane Vee is the standard formation and the basic one from which other formations are developed. Variations of the Vee offer a concentration of firepower for defense under

RESTRICTED

close control with sufficient maneuverability for all normal missions, and afford a bombing pattern which is most effective.

Flight of 6

A formation of 6 aircraft is known as a flight or squadron which is composed of two 3-airplane Vees. At least 50 feet vertical clearance will be maintained between elements in a flight and at least 50 feet horizontal clearance between the leader of the second element and wingmen of the first element.

From this basic squadron formation of 6 aircraft, the group, made up of 12 to 18 aircraft, is formed. Second or third flights will be echeloned right or left, up or down, with a vertical clearance of 150 feet and a horizontal clearance of 100 feet.

The high squadron flies 150 feet above and 100 feet behind the lead squadron with its second element stacked down and echeloned to the outside of the formation.

The low squadron flies 150 feet below and 100 feet behind the lead squadron with its sec-

TOP VIEW

Element of Six

FRONT VIEW

RESTRICTED   121

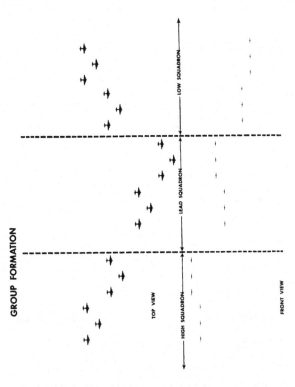

GROUP FORMATION

LOW SQUADRON

LEAD SQUADRON

HIGH SQUADRON

TOP VIEW

FRONT VIEW

ond element stacked down and echeloned to the outside of the formation.

Flights may be placed in the high or low positions, as desired by the leader, by order over radio and receipt of acknowledgment. The flights simply go up or down in their respective positions. In this formation the positions of individual airplanes in each element will be those always flown in the 3-airplane Vee.

With but small variations, this basic formation can be changed to the combat formations used overseas. It is the job of training to teach a basic formation which can be readily understood and flown by students and easily adapted to tactical use.

Spacing of Wing Positions

It is particularly important for the leader to avoid violent maneuvers or improper positions which will cause undue difficulty for the wingmen.

The spacing of the wing positions in Vee formation is:

1. Vertically: On the level of the lead airplane.

2. Laterally: Far enough to the side to insure 50 feet clearance between the wingtips of the lead airplane and the wing airplane.

3. Longitudinally: Far enough to the rear to insure 50 feet clearance between the tail of the lead airplane and the nose of the wing airplane.

Turns in Vee formation will maintain the relative position of all airplanes in the element. In other words, the wing airplanes will keep their wings parallel to the wings of the lead airplane and on the same plane.

Trail

A formation is in Trail when all airplanes are in the same line and slightly below the airplane ahead. The distance between airplanes will be such that the nose of each succeeding airplane is slightly to the rear of the tail of the airplane ahead. If this distance is too great the propeller wash of the airplane ahead will cause difficulty in maintaining position. This forma-

tion will be used only when there are from 3 to 6 aircraft involved for changing the lead, for changing wingmen, and for peel-off for landing (optional).

Changing Wing Position

When changing from Vee to Trail, the wingman into whom a turn is made while in Vee assumes the No. 2 position in Trail, while the outside man is in the No. 3 position in the Trail. When returning from Trail to Vee, the No. 3 man in Trail assumes the inside position of the Vee. Remember this, for it is the procedure for changing from Vee to Trail and from Trail to Vee. Also, it provides a method for changing wing positions in a Vee formation.

It is often desirable for a leader to change the wing position of his formation, i.e., to reverse the right and left positions. If this maneuver is not executed properly in accordance with a pre-arranged plan, there is danger of collision. A safe plan is for the leader to announce on the radio that the formation will go into Trail on his first turn. If the turn is executed to the right, it will result in the inside man, or No. 2 wingman, being No. 2 in the Trail, and the outside man, or No. 3 wingman, being No. 3 in the Trail when the turn is completed. The leader will then announce that the formation will re-form in Vee when the Trail executes a turn to the right. This second turn to the right will re-form the Vee with wingmen reversed.

As stated above, this will result in the No. 2 man of the Trail assuming the outside position of the Vee, and the No. 3 man of the Trail assuming the inside position of the Vee. It is desirable for the leader to designate the ultimate position each wingman will assume prior to each turn in order to insure complete understanding.

Changing Lead

Formation will go into Trail from the usual 90° turn to the right or left. The leader of the formation will make a 45° turn to the left and fly that heading for approximately 20 seconds or until such time as a turn back will place him in the rear of the formation. When the

---

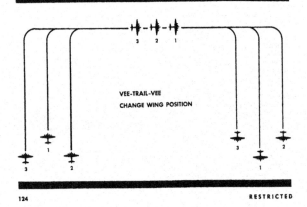

VEE-TRAIL-VEE

NO CHANGE IN WING POSITION

VEE-TRAIL-VEE

CHANGE WING POSITION

No. 1 airplane starts his 45° turn, the No. 2 plane in the Trail immediately becomes the leader of the formation and continues to fly straight ahead. At the end of 20 seconds, or thereabouts, the original leader turns back and takes up the No. 3 position in his element, or No. 6 position if in a flight of 6, and notifies the new leader that the maneuver is complete.

Landing

The formation will approach the field at an altitude of 1500 feet above the terrain in Vee in such a direction that two 90° turns either right or left can be made to bring the formation heading upwind in line with the runway on which the landing is to be made. The formation will go into Trail, stepped down, on the first 90° turn and the leader will order gears down as soon as the Trail has been formed, at which time the checklist may be started. The leader will then fly up to the runway and peel off to the left when he is directly over the spot on which he intends to land. Each succeeding plane will peel off without interval spacing achieved on first turn. The leader will put down ½ flaps, retard throttles, and make a continuous power let-down with just enough base leg to enable him to make a straight-away approach rather than a landing out of a turn, other ships in the formation spacing themselves and accomplishing the same approximate pattern of let-down and approach as their leader. There will be no more than 3 ships on the runway at the same time (one turning off, one midway, and one just landing).

Landing from Vee

The formation will approach the airdrome at an altitude of 1500 feet above the terrain into the wind up the landing runway, at which time the wheels will be ordered down by the leader and checklist accomplished. The second element will maintain assigned position echeloned to the right. The leader will call No. 3, when over the edge of the landing runway, to peel off, No. 3 acknowledging by peeling off. No. 1 follows; No. 2 following No. 1; No. 6 following No. 2 and so on. Approach and landing accomplished as outlined.

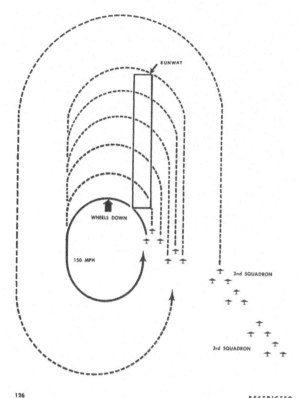

RUNWAY

WHEELS DOWN

150 MPH

2nd SQUADRON

3rd SQUADRON

A Group Landing from Vee

The group will approach the airfield in an echelon of flights to the right. This echelon of flights will be accomplished by order of the leader by radio and acknowledged by the leader of flight indicated. The leader will have the formation with high squadron (flight) in second position, low squadron in third position still stacked down in low position, relative to leader's flight, but maintaining position on high squadron. Each flight will land individually, the lead flight landing first as previously outlined. The high and low flights will complete a 360° turn and land in turn as shown by diagram.

Conclusion

In conclusion, it should be stated that a good formation is a safe formation. An air collision is the result of carelessness or lack of clear understanding between members of the formation. If the simple rules, as outlined, are followed explicitly, there is no excuse for mistakes in the air. A mistake in formation flying may result in costly, irreparable loss of lives and equipment.

It should be reiterated that it is not a display of skill to fly too close; it is a display of bad judgment and lack of common sense.

TIPS ON FORMATION FLYING

1. Set rpm to minimum allowable for the maximum manifold pressure you expect to use.

2. At altitudes where superchargers are needed, set superchargers to give about 5" more manifold pressure than the average being used.

3. Use throttles to increase and decrease power to maintain position. But when far out of position, or when catching up with a formation, increase rpm to maintain proper manifold pressure and rpm relationships.

4. When under attack, use all available power required to stay in formation.

5. In cross-over turns, keep a sharp watch out for your side of the airplane and have the copilot do the same on his side. The pilot or copilot (whichever can see the airplane below) should automatically take over the controls. If neither pilot nor copilot can see airplane below, then bombardier should give instructions by interphone.

6. In changing leads in practice formations or in Trail positions, avoid closing to proper formation position too rapidly. This can be dangerous.

7. In moving about in position, move the airplane in a direction that will not interfere with or endanger any other aircraft in the formation. In route formation, aircraft should be spread in width rather than depth in order to resume tight formation quickly.

8. At high altitudes, remember that rate of closure will be much more rapid than at low altitudes. It may be difficult to slow down quickly enough. Therefore, you will have to begin stopping the closure much sooner. On the other hand, acceleration is slower, so anticipation of change in position must be more acute.

9. Learn to anticipate changes in position so that only slight corrections need be made. Large corrections and constant fighting of the controls quickly wear out even a strong pilot.

10. Trim the ship properly. An improperly trimmed ship is difficult to hold in position.

11. Do not lock inboards and use outboards to maintain position. Use all 4 engines.

12. Whenever possible enter formation **from below** or on the level with the formation, never from above.

EMERGENCY PROCEDURES

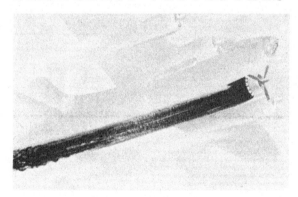

FIRES IN FLIGHT

No emergency in an airplane is more serious than fire. Combat crews must always be conscious of the hazards involved in fire. They must be constantly on the alert for possible fire while in flight. They must be thoroughly familiar with methods of fire prevention and fire extinguishing.

Fires in flight can be prevented by more thorough preflight checks. Although most fires usually develop internally, many are caused by defects that could have been detected by visual inspection while on the ground. When making your visual inspection, look carefully for cracked or split exhaust stacks, excessive oil leakage, leaky primers, and gasoline fumes in the bomb bay or cockpit. All these are possible causes of fire in flight.

Be strict in forbidding smoking by crew members while transferring fuel in flight, and particularly when any gasoline fumes are detectable in the airplane.

Be careful in your checking procedure to see that the proper number of extinguishers are on board, and that the seals are not broken.

General Precautions

In case of fire during flight:

1. Warn all crew members to have parachutes attached in readiness for possible emergency use, and to stand by for orders.

2. If flying low, climb to safe altitude for possible bailout.

3. Determine whether airplane can be landed, or make plans for bailout.

Fire Inside the Airplane

1. Close all windows and ventilators.

2. If an electrical fire, cut electrical power to affected part.

3. If fuel line is leaking, cut fuel flow to affected line.

4. Make immediate use of either carbon dioxide or carbon tetrachloride extinguisher—preferably carbon dioxide, if available.

5. If necessary to use carbon tetrachloride, stand as far as possible from the fire. The effective range of this extinguisher is 20-30 feet. Remember that carbon tetrachloride produces a poisonous gas—phosgene. Do not use in a confined area, and do not stand near the fire when using it. A very small concentration of phosgene may prove fatal. After extinguishing a fire with carbon tetrachloride, open windows and ventilators.

Engine Fire in Flight

1. Alert the crew.

2. Cut fuel at tank by use of fuel cut-off switch.

3. Place propeller control in "HIGH RPM."

4. Apply full throttle to quickly scavenge engine and line of gasoline. With high rpm fuel pressure will drop almost before the pilot's hand can travel from the throttle to the feathering button. But if fuel pressure fails to drop (i.e., if the fuel shut-off valve has failed since

the preflight), don't wait for a drop in fuel pressure.

5. Feather to cut the oil pressure.

6. Cut the generator and pull the voltage regulator to eliminate possibility of aggravating the fire if it happens to be an electrical fire.

7. Set selector and pull CO_2 charges (if installed).

8. Complete after-feathering procedure (see p. 143).

If it is a gasoline fire, cut off the source of fuel by using the fuel shut-off switch.

If it is an oil fire, cut the source of fuel by feathering.

If it is an electrical fire, remove the cause by cutting generator and pulling voltage regulator.

Engine Fire on the Ground

1. Close fuel shut-off switch.

2. Place propeller control in "HIGH RPM."

3. Apply full throttle.

4. Feather the engine.

5. When propeller stops turning, cut off master switch.

Be sure that cowl flaps are open so that the fire guard can effectively use external extinguisher.

If necessary, set and pull the engine fire extinguisher.

The next move is to get out of the airplane.

FEATHERING PROPELLERS

Feathering mechanism is incorporated in propellers for two reasons: (1) to reduce drag when the airplane must continue flight with only 3 or 2 engines operating; (2) to eliminate vibration of a damaged engine that might otherwise weaken the airplane's structure.

To Feather or Not to Feather?

Feathering is an important and valuable procedure—when needed. When you're satisfied that feathering is indicated, and you're sure you know what you're doing, don't be afraid to feather the engine. But don't be too hasty in hitting that feathering button. Be sure you know when to feather. Be sure you clearly understand the advantages to be gained by feathering. **Be sure you feather the proper engine.**

When to Feather

When confronted with engine trouble, and the question of whether or not to feather the damaged engine, follow these rules.

1. Be calm, think clearly, move slowly. Your problem is to decide whether or not to feather;

and, if feathering is indicated, to feather the proper engine.

2. Generally, an engine losing power should not be feathered so long as it is still producing power and is not vibrating excessively. If you are not sure the engine is still operating, engage the turbo. A rise in manifold pressure will indicate whether the engine is still putting out some power. In a possible emergency, don't throw away usable power.

3. If an engine is running rough, try a change of power setting. Try a change of mixture control position; also check intercooler control position. These checks will sometimes produce smoother operation.

4. Be sure that the real trouble lies in the engine, not in your engine instruments. If oil pressure drops, for instance, check your oil temperature gage: oil temperature will rise if anything is radically wrong (unless you're out of oil). If your oil pressure drops to about 30 lb., however, feather the propeller while you still have oil, and ask questions later.

5. Before deciding that you have a runaway propeller, set a definite rpm at which you will

feather (2760 rpm maximum). Unless rpm reaches that danger point, continue to operate the engine with reduced manifold pressure, especially on takeoff.

6. Once you have decided to feather, be sure that you feather the damaged engine and not one of your good engines by mistake. In addition to checking manifold pressure, rpm, oil pressure, and oil temperature, look for the other signs which indicate the location of the faulty engine.

7. Tendency to turn will indicate whether the faulty engine is on the left or right side.

8. Noticeable vibration often will identify the faulty engine.

If there is no reserve supply, and oil pressure falls to 30 lb., feather the engine at once. If a reserve supply is available, watch for a rise in oil temperature before feathering: this will indicate whether oil pressure is really low.

How to Feather in an Emergency

When you have decided to feather, and you're sure that you're feathering the proper engine, your immediate procedure is as follows:

1. Close the propeller feathering switch.

2. Turn turbo supercharger control "OFF."

3. Close throttle.

4. Move mixture control to "IDLE CUT-OFF."

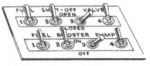

5. Switch fuel shut-off valve "CLOSED," booster pump "OFF."

6. After propeller has stopped, turn ignition switch "OFF."

When these immediate steps have been taken, continue with this clean-up procedure.

1. Turn generator "OFF."

2. If landing gear is down, retract it unless you can land immediately.

3. Have copilot adjust mixture controls on the other engines, and increase rpm as required. Increase manifold pressure.

4. Trim the airplane.

5. Change vacuum selector position, if necessary.

6. Close cowl flaps on the dead engine. Adjust cowl flaps on the other 3 engines to maintain cylinder-head temperatures within safe limit.

7. Transfer fuel from the dead-engine tank, if needed.

Emergency Measures

1. Tune the radio compass to nearest stations, so that you can use the radio compass needle for making turns and if instruments fail through loss of vacuum, you can maintain direction by homing from one station to another.

2. If vacuum is out and you have to fly on instruments, turn the automatic pilot "ON." Refer to tell-tale lights to maintain level flight attitude. **Don't turn on rudder, elevator or aileron switches.** This is used only as an additional aid. Otherwise use airspeed, ball, and compass.

Normally the feathering switch is released by hydraulic pressure built up in the system after the propeller has reached the full feathered position. Sometimes viscous oil in the propeller system builds up this trip-out pressure prematurely, preventing full feathering. If this happens, hold the feathering switch down until the propeller is fully feathered.

Accidental Unfeathering

In some cases hydromatic propellers have begun to unfeather almost immediately after reaching the full feathered position. This is because the switch failed to cut out automatically when the feathered position was reached.

Should this condition occur, pull out the feathering switch button as soon as the propellers begin to unfeather. Leave it out for 2 or 3 seconds, then close the switch again. When the full feathered position has been reached (indicated by the cessation of windmilling) pull the feathering switch button out again. This will prevent further unfeathering.

Failure of Feathering System

Total loss of engine oil in combat, or line failure in the engine oil system, will make feathering impossible (unless auxiliary supply is available). If normal feathering is impossible, try to make the propeller windmill at the lowest possible rpm. Since windmilling is proportional to airspeed, it can be reduced to a minimum by reducing airspeed to 20-30 mph above stalling speed (i.e., to approximately 120-130 mph IAS).

1. Place propeller control in "LOW RPM."

2. Place mixture control in "IDLE CUT-OFF."

3. Turn ignition switch to "OFF" position.

4. Set throttle to fully closed position.

5. Fuel shut-off switch: "OFF."

Vibration can be reduced or minimized by flying at the absolute minimum airspeed.

Engine Seizure

Frequently loss of oil for lubrication will cause the engine to seize and stop suddenly. In some cases of engine seizure the reduction gear housing will break, allowing the propeller, propeller shaft, and reduction gearing to fall off. In other cases, only the reduction gears will be stripped. This relieves the propeller of engine drag and permits it to windmill.

Emergency Unfeathering

Never unfeather a propeller of a faulty engine unless it is needed for landing or continued flight. If the propeller was feathered because of engine damage, remember that unfeathering may result in still further damage.

Be especially careful in starting and warming up a cold engine. Oil drains into the bottom cylinder of a dead engine, and structural damage may result from re-starting the engine.

When practicing feathering, don't allow the propeller to remain in the feathered position for more than 5 minutes. Under cold weather conditions, unfeather the propeller at once.

How to Unfeather

1. With throttle closed, turn ignition switch "ON." (Except in B-17G.)

2. Switch fuel shut-off valve "OPEN," booster pump "ON."

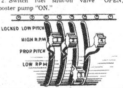

3. Set propeller control to "LOW RPM."

4. Close feathering control switch, and keep it closed until tachometer reads 800 rpm. Then pull out propeller control switch.

5. Place mixture control in "AUTO-RICH" position.

6. Allow engine to operate at 800 rpm, until 100° cylinder-head temperature is obtained. Then operate throttle gradually until engine speeds up to minimum rpm, or speed at which governor is set.

7. Adjust mixture, rpm and throttle to desired settings, and synchronize propellers.

HOW TO DITCH THE B-17

Ditching drill is the responsibility of the pilot. Duties should be studied, altered if necessary to agree with any modifications, memorized, and practiced until each member of the crew performs them instinctively.

The pilot's warning to prepare for ditching should be acknowledged by the crew in the order given here—copilot, navigator, bombardier, flight engineer, radio operator, ball turret gunner, right waist gunner, left waist gunner, and tail gunner, i.e., "Copilot ditching," "Navigator ditching," etc.

Upon acknowledgment, crew members remove parachutes, loosen shirt collars and remove ties and oxygen masks unless above 12,000 feet. When preparations for ditching are begun above 12,000 feet, main oxygen supply or emergency oxygen bottle is used until notification by the pilot. All crew members wearing winter flying boots should remove them. No other clothing should be removed.

Releases on life rafts should not be pulled until the plane comes to rest.

Beware of puncturing rafts on wing and horizontal surfaces after launching. The dinghies should be tied together as soon as possible.

Injured men should get first consideration when leaving the airplane.

Life vests should not be inflated inside the plane unless the crew member is certain that the escape hatch through which he will exit is large enough to accommodate him with the vest inflated.

When personnel are in dinghy, stock of rations and equipment should be taken by the airplane commander (or copilot). Strict rationing must be maintained. Flares should be used sparingly and only if there is a reasonable chance that they will be seen by ships or aircraft. Don't forget the Very pistol.

Lash the life rafts together.

Landing crosswind is recommended unless the wind exceeds about 30 mph, in which case and into the wind. In executing the crosswind landing, the pilot will line up with the lines of the crests, at any convenient altitude, adjust flaps, power settings, trim, and make the approach with a minimum rate of descent, with a minimum forward speed. Land on a crest parallel to the line of crests or troughs. Crabbing will be necessary to remain over the crest while making the approach.

DUTIES OF THE CREW

Airplane Commander

(1) Give "Prepare for ditching" warning over interphone; give altitude; sound ditching bell signal of six short rings.

(2) Fasten safety harness.

(3) Open and close window to insure freedom of movement. Place ax handy for use in case of possible jamming.

(4) Order radio operator to ditching post.

(5) Order tail gunner to lower the tailwheel by cranking about 10 turns.

(6) 20 seconds before impact, order the crew to "brace for ditching." Give long ring on signal bell.

(7) Release safety harness and parachute straps. Exit through side window when airplane comes to rest. Inflate life vest.

(8) Proceed to left dinghy, cut tie ropes. Take command.

Copilot

(1) Assists pilot to fasten safety harness.

(2) Fastens own safety harness, opens and closes right window to insure freedom of movement.

(3) Releases safety harness, parachute straps, exits through right window when plane comes to rest. Inflates life vest.

(4) Proceeds to right dinghy, cuts ropes. Takes command.

Navigator

(1) Calculates position, course, speed, giving this information to the radio operator. De-

stroys secret papers. Gathers maps and celestial equipment. Gives wind and direction to the pilot.

(2) Proceeds to radio compartment. Closes radio compartment door.

(3) Attaches rope on emergency radio equipment and signal set (if radio is stored in radio compartment).

(4) Assumes ditching position.

(5) Hands the following items in the order given to the bombardier, who is already out: signal set and emergency radio, ration kits, navigation kits, parachutes.

(6) Exits through radio hatch and goes to left dinghy.

Bombardier

(1) Jettisons bombs, closes bomb bay doors, destroys bombsight, goes to radio compartment, closing compartment door. Takes first-aid kits to radio compartment.

(2) Takes position, partially inflates life vest by pulling cord on one side.

(3) Directs and assists exit of men through radio hatch. Stands above and forward of hatch and receives equipment from navigator and hands it to crew members as follows: signal set and radio to radio operator; ration kit No. 1 to tail gunner; ration kit No. 2 to right waist gunner; navigation kit to ball turret gunner; pigeon crate to left waist gunner. Assists flight engineer in making exit.

(4) Goes to right dinghy.

Flight Engineer

(1) Jettisons ammunition and loose equipment, turns top turret guns to depressed position pointing forward.

(2) Goes to radio compartment. Lowers the radio hatch and moves it to the rear of the plane, jettisons loose equipment in radio compartment, and slides back top gun.

(3) Stands with back to aft door of radio compartment and assists other members out by boosting them.

(4) Last man to leave radio compartment, with bombardier's help. Goes to left dinghy.

Radio Operator

(1) Switches on liaison transmitter (tuned to MFDF) sends SOS, position and call sign continuously, turns IFF to distress, remains on intercom, transmits all information given by navigator.

(2) Obtains MFDF fix, continues SOS, remains on intercom.

(3) On pilot's order clamps key, takes ditching position, inflating life vest partially, remains on intercom, repeating pilot's "Brace for ditching" to crew.

(4) Receives signal kit and emergency radio from bombardier.

(5) Assists with dinghy inflation and inspects for leaks.

(6) Goes to right dinghy.

Ball Turret Gunner

(1) Turns turret guns aft, closes turret tightly, goes to radio compartment with first-aid kits and ration kits.

(2) Pulls both dinghy releases as aircraft comes to rest.

(3) Goes to left dinghy.

Right Waist Gunner

(1) Jettisons his gun, ammunition, all loose equipment.

(2) Closes right waist window tightly, goes to radio compartment, collecting emergency radio and signal box in fuselage (if radio is stored elsewhere than in radio compartment).

(3) Takes position, partially inflates vest.

(4) Assists in inflating right dinghy, inspects for leaks, applying stoppers if necessary.

Left Waist Gunner

(1) Jettisons his gun, ammunition, loose equipment, closes left waist window, goes to radio compartment.

(2) Partially inflates vest.

(3) Receives pigeon crate from bombardier.

(4) Goes to right dinghy.

Tail Gunner

(1) Jettisons ammunition; goes forward, cranks down tailwheel about 10 turns; collects

emergency ration pack (stowed in fuselage); is last to enter radio compartment.

(2) Takes position, partially inflates life vest.

(3) Carrying ration pack, goes to left dinghy, assists with dinghy inflation, inspects for leaks.

CREW POSITIONS FOR DITCHING

The positions illustrated should best enable crew members to withstand the impact of crash landings on either land or water. On water 2 impacts will be felt, the first a mild jolt when the tail strikes, the second a severe shock when the nose strikes the water. Positions should be maintained until the aircraft comes to rest. Study them carefully.

Emergency equipment for use in the dinghy should be carried to crash positions. Any equipment carried free must be held securely during ditching to prevent injury.

Parachute pads, seat cushions, etc., should be used to protect the face, head, and back.

1. Jettison bombs, ammunition, guns and all loose equipment and secure that equipment which might cause injury. Close bomb bay doors and lower hatches. If there is not enough time to release bombs or depth charges place them on "SAFE." Retain enough fuel to make a power landing.

2. Navigator calculates position, course, and speed and passes data to radio operator. Latter tunes liaison transmitter to MFDF and sends SOS, position and call sign continuously. Radio operator also turns IFF to distress and remains on intercom; clamps down key on order to take ditching post.

3. These tips will help you determine wind direction and speed: (a) waves in open sea move downwind; (b) direction of spray indicates wind direction; (c) wind lanes—a series of lines or alternate strips of light and shade—also show direction; (d) approach on waves should be made into wind at right angles to them; (e) approach on swells should be made along top, parallel to swell, and may be executed in winds not over 10 mph.

JETTISON LOAD....

SOS... AND ASSUME POSITIONS

BRACE FOR DITCHING

How to Determine Wind Speed

A FEW WHITE CRESTS	10 to 20 mph
MANY WHITE CRESTS	20 to 30 mph
FOAM STREAKS ON WATER	30 to 40 mph
SPRAY FROM CRESTS	40 to 50 mph

ACKNOWLEDGMENTS

A work of this nature owes a good deal to a great number of people who generously gave of their time and knowledge to help make the author's work lighter if not less complex. Over a period of more than a year I researched through old archives, through memories and histories to attempt to put together the story of the B-17. All along the way I encountered only very cooperative and helpful people, most of whom I now count among my friends.

In addition to the hundreds with whom I spoke over this long stretch of time, there were also dozens with whom I corresponded and from whom I received authentication of unique stories, unusual photographs and, not the least, encouragement.

From the very beginning I received understanding aid from General Ira C. Eaker who not only replied to my queries with warming promptness, but also granted me an interview which helped to confirm some of my opinions and views. Throughout General Eaker remained accessible to help me over some rough spots and to offer suggestions and aid.

My editor, Harold Kuebler, has revealed a Job-like patience and a willingness to share my own enthusiasm, not to mention the ability to refrain from reminding me that the book was due in, which combined to make life simpler for an author whose life is hardly simple. Our association is also one of the nice things that has come from the writing of this book.

I should mention, too, the comforting presence of Kenneth McCormick, a presence which has influenced all my past books and will likewise influence those of the future. Former Sergeant McCormick, no longer

with the Air Force's Office of Flying Safety but a friend of long-standing, was one of those responsible for the remarkable series of Air Force manuals produced during the Second World War, including one pertaining to the B-17 which served to impress the ever more youthful pilot trainees that they held a potentially "lethal instrument" in their hands almost completely devoid of the margin of safety of the family Chevrolet.

Mark E. Nevils of Boeing's New York office has contributed much more than I had a right to demand. Requests for photographs, information and what must have seemed a disconnected and random supply of B-17 material were always greeted without the blinking of an eye. And even more importantly, without a frown. In addition, every request was filled. Over this long haul Nevils and I have become friends rather than associates in a shared venture.

My wife, Edith, who still doesn't know what makes an airplane fly, has since however picked up quite a lot of information on the B-17 if not the science of flight. She has patiently put up with me through stress and storm (some prolonged absences, too) and, worse, carefully read the entire manuscript in a no doubt vain attempt to clear up my grammar and correct my wayward spelling. Besides this she had to attend to the household chores (I *did* do the evening dishes) and saw to it that the muse was not interrupted by such as Emily, Carla, and David. They are wonderful and welcome interruptions but display a sweet disregard for deadlines and such. David, who is ten, has actually been an assistant in the research on this book and a very good one; he has been a great help in identifying the various models and types of aircraft in addition to having a humanistic attitude toward our former enemies. He is also a fine historian.

I should mention those members of the 100th Bombardment Group, most of whom I talked with at length and who furnished me with the material for the section devoted to their unit. Those I was actually able to see were John M. Bennett, Jr. (Major General, USAF, Res.), who was quite surprised to learn that many felt he was most responsible for the resurgence of the 100th; Marvin S. Bowman, who supplied so many photographs as well as insights and the introduction to the story of Robert Rosenthal; Harry H. Crosby of Boston University helped with stories, flashingly brilliant ideas and the use of his home on a memorable occasion when several 100th Group (and one 95th) members met to talk about another time. Robert Rosenthal, now living quietly in Harrison, New York, and practicing law in New York City, is still reticent and not given over to

discussing his war exploits. His story was pieced together from other sources and only then was I able to get corroboration. Also present at the meeting in Boston were former 100th members, Stanley Russell and Horace Varian, whose recollections taken down on tape added so much to the story. Lieutenant Colonel Everett E. Blakely and Owen D. Roane, the former at Notre Dame University, and the latter a principal of a Texas high school, answered my letters with courtesy and genuine interest.

I might add that none of these men had any conception of how I would use their material in this book.

Of the Air Force I've received continual aid from Lieutenant Colonel Gene Guerny, Director of the USAF Book Program, Washington, D.C. Also from Royal D. Frey, Chief, Research Division at the Air Force Museum, Wright-Patterson Air Force Base, Ohio. Both men went out of their way to help make this book as complete and as accurate as possible. I only hope I've done them justice.

Others who assisted in this project are:

General S. E. Anderson, USAF (Ret).

James N. Bannister, Sperry Gyroscope Company.

John F. Bartel, Bay City, Michigan.

Harald P. Bauer of the Associated Press, formerly of the *Luftwaffe*.

Roger F. Besecker, American Aviation Historical Society.

Stephen Birdsall, Sydney, Australia.

Henry Blankfort of the Blankfort Group.

Joseph Bonem, Bay City, Michigan.

Elizabeth Brown, Institute of Aerospace Sciences, New York.

Mrs. Helen Burnard, Department of the Air Force, for many kindnesses not the least of which was arranging over a period of several days my interview with General Curtis E. LeMay.

Louis S. Casey of the staff of the National Air Museum who drove David and I out to the Storage and Restoration Facilities of the Museum where I was able to go through several files on the B-17 and where we saw several veterans of the Second World War, including a Zero and *The Swoose*.

Constance Cowley, the Boeing Company.

John V. Crisp, Essendon, Hertsfordshire, England, for the story of the Phantom Fortress.

Walter Cronkite of CBS, who was one of the correspondents who returned from Wilhelmshaven.

Paul M. Davis, Chief, Historical Division, Air Force Logistics Command, Wright-Patterson Air Force Base, Ohio.

James H. Doolittle, Space Technology Laboratories, Inc.

General Dwight D. Eisenhower, for a reply to my letter in reference to the bombing of Dresden.

Ray Ellsworth, formerly of the 15th AF, now of Brooklyn.

Joseph H. Filian, USAF.

Mrs. Virginia G. Fincik, USAF Book Program, Washington, D.C.

John G. Fitzgerald, Norden Division, United Aircraft Corp.

Marie L. Gericke, German Information Center.

Lieutenant Colonel C. V. Glines, Office of the Assistant Secretary of Defense, for aid from the very beginning of this project and particularly for some much appreciated last-minute help.

Gordon F. Gray, North American Aviation, Inc.

Marvin G. Gregory, former B-17 and B-29 instructor.

Staff Sergeant Norman E. Harvey, USAF.

Randolph Hawthorne, formerly of "Pinetree."

Philip S. Hopkins, director, National Air Museum, Smithsonian Institution.

Lieutenant Colonel Raymond E. Houseman, USAF, for any number of things, including laughs.

Sergeant James Hutchenson, USAF.

Edward Hymoff, co-author, with Martin Caidin, of *The Mission*.

Mr. and Mrs. William Jablonski, my parents, who found some B-17 crew members for me.

R. E. Johnson, Curtiss-Wright Corp.

Carlyle H. Jones, Sperry Gyroscope Co.

Stanley J. Kavan of Columbia Records, formerly 15th AF.

Thomas T. Keasbey, a former guest of the Third Reich.

Marguerite K. Kennedy, Chief, Archives Division, Air University, Alabama.

George C. Kenney, Major General, USAF (Ret).

Beirne Lay, Jr., for *Twelve O'Clock High*, among other things.

General Curtis E. LeMay, USAF, for a memorable interview.

Thomas F. Lohr, Muhlenberg College, Pennsylvania.

Airman First Class Earl W. McCaughey, USAF.

R. D. McGrath, World War I Aero Book Shop.

Lieutenant Colonel Ped G. Magness, USAF.

R. H. Maltby, Chief, Public Information Division, Aeronautical Systems Division, Wright-Patterson Air Force Base, Ohio.

Alice R. Martin, USAF Book Program, Washington, D.C.

David Massover, for help with certain difficult photographs.

Maurer Maurer, Chief, Historical Studies Branch, Air University, Maxwell Air Force Base, Alabama.

Crosby Maynard, Douglas Aircraft Co.

N. L. Mead, Curtiss-Wright Corp.

Erik Miller, Lockheed-California Co.

Robert K. Morgan of the *Memphis Belle* and *Dauntless Dottie*.

Allie Moszyk, Bay City, Michigan: 97th Bomb Group.

James Murray, the Boeing Co., Washington, D.C.

John H. Newland, the Boeing Company, Seattle, Washington.

Richard Paine of the 95th Bomb Group.

Technical Sergeant C. P. Piatek, USAF.

Lewis Pinkussohn, former navigator-bombardier.

Caroline Piven, of Doubleday, bless her.

Joel K. Rubenstein, Revell, Inc. for the *Memphis Belle* kit.

Major Francis N. Satterlee, Pictorial Branch, USAF Book Program, Washington, D.C.

Sergeant William H. Schiffer, for background on the Pacific air war.

Leon Schloss, Republic Aviation Corp.

Joseph A. Skiera, USAF Book Program, Washington, D.C.

General Carl A. Spaatz, USAF (Ret), for one of the most stimulating afternoons spent on this book.

Captain James C. Sparks, USAF, for assists from beginning to end.

Chief Master Sergeant Frederick Spielmann, formerly of the 305th Bomb Group.

Oliver O. Turnheim, New York, who translated from German texts.

Joseph Wackerly, Bay City, Michigan.

Edward C. Wells, the Boeing Company, and chief designer of the B-17.

W. L. White, for *Queens Die Proudly*, and for his graciously worded permission to quote from this valuable book which so beautifully captured the mood of the early months of the Second World War.

Sergeant George Zimmerman, USAF.

Thanks also to: *The Airman*, Official Journal of the Air Force, for printing my letter which led to many interesting stories and photographs.

Aviation Week and Space Technology, Robert B. Hotz, editor, graciously granted me permission to quote from its Design Analysis of the B-17 written by Wellwood E. Beall and published in *Aviation* magazine.

Thanks to Holt, Rinehart and Winston for permission to quote from Ernie Pyle's *Here Is Your War*.

BIBLIOGRAPHY

Arnold, Henry H., *Global Mission*, New York, Harper & Brothers, 1949.

Baumbach, Werner, *The Life and Death of the Luftwaffe*, New York, Coward-McCann, 1960.

Bennett, John M. Jr., *Letters from England*, Privately printed, San Antonio, 1945.

Brereton, Lewis H., *The Brereton Diaries*, New York, William Morrow and Co., 1946.

Buchanan, A. R., ed., *The Navy's Air War*, New York, Harper & Brothers, 1946.

Caidin, Martin, *Black Thursday*, New York, E. P. Dutton & Co., 1960.

Churchill, Winston S., *The Second World War*, Vols. I–VI, Boston, Houghton Mifflin Co., 1948–1953.

Craven, W. F. and Cate, J. L., *The Army Air Forces in World War II*, Vol. I–VI, Chicago, the University of Chicago Press, 1948.

Drake, Francis Vivian, *Vertical Warfare*, New York, Doubleday, Doran & Co., 1943.

Edmonds, Walter D., *They Fought With What They Had*, Boston, Little, Brown & Co., 1951.

Eisenhower, Dwight D., *Crusade in Europe*, New York, Doubleday & Co., 1948.

Emme, Eugene M., *The Impact of Air Power*, Princeton, D. Van Nostrand Co., 1959.

Familiarization Manual for Maintenance of Model B-17F Bombardment Airplane, Seattle, The Boeing Co., 1942.

Familiarization Manual for Operation of Model B-17F Bombardment Airplane, Seattle, The Boeing Co., 1942.

Galland, Adolf, *The First and the Last*, New York, Henry Holt & Co., 1954.

Gurney, Gene, *Journey of the Giants*, New York, Coward-McCann, Inc., 1961.

——, *War in the Air, The*, New York, Crown Publishers, Inc., 1962.

Hinton, Harold B., *Air Victory:* The Men and the Machines, New York, Harper & Brothers, 1948.

Howard, Clive and Whitley, Joe, *One Damned Island After Another*, Chapel Hill, University of North Carolina Press, 1946.

Howarth, David, *D-Day*, New York, McGraw-Hill Book Co., 1959.

Inoguchi, Rikihei and Nakajima, Tadashi (with Roger Pineau), *The Divine Wind*, Annapolis, U. S. Naval Institute, 1958.

Irving, David, *The Destruction of Dresden*, New York, Holt, Rinehart & Winston, 1963.

Kenney, George C., *General Kenney Reports*, New York, Duell, Sloan & Pearce, 1949.

Lord, Walter, *Day of Infamy*, New York, Henry Holt & Co., 1957.

Majdalany, Fred, *Cassino, Portrait of a Battle*, London, Longmans, Green & Co., 1957.

Mansfield, Harold, *Vision*, New York, Duell, Sloan & Pearce, 1956.

Maurer, Maurer, *Air Force Combat Units in World War II*, New York, Franklin Watts, 1963.

Morrison, Wilbur H., *The Incredible 305th*, New York, Duell, Sloan & Pearce, 1962.

Nilsson, John R., *The Story of the Century*, Beverly Hills, John R. Nilsson, 1946.

Okumiya, Masatake and Horikoshi, Jiro (with Martin Caidin), *Zero!*, New York, E. P. Dutton & Co., 1956.

Rumpf, Hans, *The Bombing of Germany*, New York, Holt, Rinehart & Winston, 1963.

Ryan, Cornelius, *The Longest Day*, New York, Simon and Schuster, 1959.

Sakai, Saburo (with Martin Caidin & Fred Saito), *Samurai*, New York, E. P. Dutton & Co., 1957.

Saundby, Robert, *Air Bombardment*, New York, Harper & Row, 1961.

Shirer, William L., *The Rise and Fall of the Third Reich*, New York, Simon and Schuster, 1960.

Toland, John, *But Not in Shame*, New York, Random House, Inc., 1961.

Tuleja, Thaddeus, *Climax at Midway*, New York, W. W. Norton & Co., 1960.

USAAF, *Pilot's Flight Operating Instructions For Army Model B-17F*, Patterson Field, 1944.

——, *Pilot Training Manual for the Flying Fortress*, Washington, 1944.

——, *Target Germany*, New York, Simon and Schuster, 1943.

White, W. L., *Queens Die Proudly*, New York, Harcourt, Brace & Co., 1943.

Ziegler, Mano, *Rocket Fighter*, New York, Doubleday & Co., 1963.

344

A NOTE ABOUT THE ILLUSTRATIONS

The bulk of the photographs come from two major sources, the United States Air Force Documentary Photo Library and the Archives of the Boeing Company. Accrediting each and every photograph, diagram or drawing would have been repetitious and cluttering. Every combat photo, every shot of Air Force men in action or at work are Air Force photographs; technical and structural detail illustrations were supplied by Boeing.

Illustrative materials were also contributed by the Air Force Museum, Curtiss-Wright Corp., German Information Center, Lockheed Aircraft Corp., the National Archives, Norden Division-United Aircraft Corp., North American Aviation Corp., Republic Aviation Corp. and Sperry Gyroscope Company.

Personal photographs were loaned from the private collections of Major General John M. Bennett, Jr., USAF (Res.), Roger F. Besecker, American Aviation Historical Society, Stephen P. Birdsall, Lieutenant Colonel Everett E. Blakely, Joseph Bonem, Marvin S. Bowman, Martin Caidin, Dr. Harry Crosby, Lieutenant General Ira C. Eaker, USAF (Ret.), Royal D. Frey, Marvin Gregory, Randolph Hawthorne, Edward Hymoff, Stanley J. Kavan, Thomas T. Keasbey, General George C. Kenney, USAF (Ret.), Thomas F. Lohr, Allie Moszyk, Mark E. Nevils, T/Sergeant Casimer P. Piatek, USAF, Lewis Pinkussohn, Owen D. Roane, Robert Rosenthal, Stanley Russell, William Schiffer, Frederick Spielman, Horace Varian and Joseph Wackerly.

Mrs. Virginia G. Fincik, Air Force Photo Center, Washington, D.C. helped me find practically every AF photograph in the book. She also found the beautiful color shot which appears on the jacket showing a B-17 in England returning from a bombing mission.

INDEX

349

Davis, Thomas J., 106
DB-1, 9
D-Day, France, 131, 141, 148–49, 156–60, 261; "Bloody 100th," and, 214–15
Death camps, 293
DeBlasio, W. J., 201; photo of, 199
DeBolt, Harold R., 164–67
Debrecen (Hungary), 237, 241
De-icer boots, xxii, 314
Delao, P., 182, 184
Del Carmen, 51
Delehanty, William J., 55
Del Monte (Mindanao), 49 ff, 56–58 ff, 66, 67; Japanese attack, 59
Dempsey, T. A., 151
Desert Air Force (RAF), 233
"Destroyer School I," 130
"Devastators," 71
Devers, Jacob L., 234; photo, 124
Dieppe, 94, 108
Diss (England), 171, 175
Distinguished Flying Cross, 111, 118, 177, 207
Distinguished Service Cross, 184, 225
Distinguished Unit Citations, 79
Ditching instructions, 339
Dobodura (New Guinea), 76
Donkey, as pet, 182
Doolittle, James H., 69, 106, 108, 141, 147, 214, 225; commands 8th Air Force, 234; commands 15th Air Force, 233; and North African campaign, 231; photos of, 162, 207; Spaatz message to, 267–68; on "Torch" assault, 108
Dopko, Bernard M., xi–xii
Dorsal fins, B-17, 312, 313, 315
Douglas Aircraft Company, 6, 34, 308, 309
Douglas B-18, 11
Douglas C-47, 257
Douglas DB-1, 9
Douglas TBD-1 Devastators, 71
Douglass, James R., 178, 180, 188, 190, 192–93

Dowding, Sir Hugh, photo of, 27
Dresden, bombings of, 162, 224, 291, 292; photos of, 286
Duchess, The (B-17), 118–20
Dudecz, W., 228
Dümmer Lake, 210
Dutch, the. *See* Netherlands and the Dutch
Dutch Harbor (Aleutians), 271

"Eager Beavers, The," 75–78
Eaker, Ira C., xiv, 80, 85–89, 91, 92, 93–94, 98, 100, 129; against sub-pen raids, 146; Churchill congratulates, 137; commands Mediterranean AAF, 141–42, 234, 237; leaves 8th Air Force, 141–43; on Marienburg bombing, 136, 137; and mission selection, 299; photos of, 86, 124; on Regensburg-Schweinfurt bombing, 130–31; with Russian shuttle mission, 237–42; and "Snuffy" Smith, 123 and strategic bombing, 112, 113–14, 118
East Anglia, 86, 92, 112, 131
East Indies, 52, 64–65
East Prussia, 135
Edburn, H. E., 182–84
Eden, Anthony, photo of, 111
Egan, John C. ("Bucky"), 173, 175, 197, 199, 200; photo of, 199
Egtvedt, Clairmont, L., xvii, xviii, xix, xxii, 4, 6, 9; photos of, xx, 27
Egypt, 129
Eighth Air Force, 83, 86–228, 237 (*see also* specific actions, planes, units, etc.); casualties, 293; Churchill congratulates, 118, 137; fighter protection for, 256–68 (*see also* Fighters: Allied; specific actions planes); first B-17Es to, 34; mission described in photos, 299–

307; Samford Chief of Staff, 18
Eighth Army, British, 108
Eighth Bomber Command, 85, 86–89 ff, 110–11, 115 ff (*see also* specific actions, planes, units, etc.); mission described in photos, 299–307
Eighth Fighter Command, 162
Eisenhower, Dwight D., 85, 148, 233, 284; and African operation, 105–6
El Alamein, 108
Electrical systems, B-17, 315
Eleventh Air Force, 78, 271
Eleventh Bombardment Group, 73
Elizabeth, Queen Consort of George VI, photo of, 162
Elliot, George, Jr., 41, 45
Elton, Albert M., 226
Emden, 134, 186, 256
Emergency procedures, B-17, manual instructions for, 337
Emery, E. G., 5
Emmons, Delos C., 19
Engel, R., 182–84
Engineer, B-17, 327
Engine installation details, B-17, 318
Engine nacelles, B-17, 313, 314
England. *See* Great Britain
English Channel, 85, 92, 97, 134, 184; on D-Day, 156
Enola Gay (B-29), 105, 284–85; photo of, 281
Enterprise, U.S.S., 71, 72
Entwistle, Frederick I., 322
Equipment diagram, B-17, 316
Erkner ball-bearing plant, bombing of, 209, 221
Ernst, John, 221–22
Erps-Querps, 162
Essen (Germany), 291
Eubank, Eugene L., 48, 50
European theater, 78, 83–228 ff
Evans, Henry W., 80
Evans, Vincent R., 123
Extermination camps, 293

267; to Berlin, 152, 209, 210; to Bremen, 186; to Münster, 198; photos of, 258, 304

P-51 Mustang, 143, 146, 210, 238, 257, 259, 267; to Berlin, 152, 259; in Pacific area, 277, 279; photos of, 144, 258, 280; photos from gun-cameras of, 265

Pacific theater, xii, 43–80; B-29s and, 271–85

Paine, Joseph, 204

Panama, 4, 18

Panama Canal, 18

Pan American Airways, 18

Pantelleria, 233

Parachuting instructions, 246

Para-frag bomb, 74

Paris, 130, 161, 182, 228

Parsel, E. L., 53, 59

Partridge, Earle E., 219

Pathfinders, 134, 184, 247

PB-1, 38, 39

PB-1 W, 38

PBY, 65

Pearl Harbor, xii, 43–51, 68

Pease, Harl, Jr., 67, 73–74, 79; photo of, 67

Peel, Robert, 204

Peenemünde, 161

Perrin, Edwin S., 61

Pershing, John J., xvii–xviii

Petrich, Oran B., 173, 177

"Phantom Fortress," 162–67

Philippine Islands, 45, 46, 48–51, 52–58, 66 ff; Mac-Arthur returns to, 272, 281

Phillips (crew member), 117–18

Piatek, Casimer P., 116–18, 119, 245; photo of, 117

"Piggy-back" bombings, 267

Pilot, B-17, training manual instructions for, 324–39

"Pinetree" (High Wycombe), 86, 142

Pinkussohn, Lewis, 248, 255

Piryatin (Russia), 218

Ploesti oil fields, attacks on: by 8th Air Force, 129, 154, 156; by 15th Air Force, 234–36

Poetry, POW, 250

"Pointblank," 141

Poland, 25, 135, 215, 234, 291; Air Force of, 287; blitzkrieg warfare against, 286–87; Rosenthal in, 223–24; Warsaw uprising, 242

Polebrook, 92

Politz, 155

Poltava mission, 216–18, 224, 237

Portal, Sir Charles, 118

Port Moresby, 69, 70, 73, 74

Portsmouth (England), 291

Portugal, 106

Post, Robert B., 116

Potts, Ramsey, 299, 300

POWs. See Prisoners of war

Pratt & Whitney engines, xx, 6, 11

Presidential citations, 207

Presque Isle (Maine), 89

Prestwick (England), 89

Prince of Wales, H.M.S., 52

Prinz Eugen (battleship), 85

Prisoners of war, 227–28, 245–55

"Project A" (for Model 299), 4–14, 19

Propellers, instructions for feathering, 338

Prussia, East, 135

Pugh, "Pudge," 76–78

Purple Heart awards, 121, 207, 226

Putt, Donald, 9–11

PWs. See Prisoners of war

Pyle, Ernie, vii

Quinian, John P., 121, 123

Rabaul (New Guinea), 66, 69, 73, 272

Rabo, F. A., 154

Radar, 84, 134–35

Radio-jamming devices, 135

Radio-operator's station, B-17, 34, 320, 323, 326

RAF, 83–84 ff, 91, 112–14, 128, 140, 146, 147, 152, 167, 288–96 (see also specific actions, planes); Bomber Command, 37, 267 (see also specific actions); Coastal Command, 29, 34, 37, 146;

Cologne raid, 143; on D-Day, 156; Desert Air Force, 233; at Dresden, 162; and Fortress I, 27–31; and Fortress IIA, 34; and Fortress III, 37; in Mediterranean Allied Air Forces, 141; No. 90 Squadron, 28, 29; No. 205 Group, 234; relief missions, 242

"Rainbow 5" plan, 49

"Rainbow" Infantry Division, 139

Raley, James, 242

Red Cross, 249, 252

Red Gremlin (B-17), 106

Reeder, Sumner, 182–84, 225; photos of, 183, 215, 225

Reeve, Delbert D., 227

Reeves, Joseph M., xvii, xviii

Regensburg, bombing raids on, 129–33, 147, 236, 237, 242, 257; "Bloody 100th" and, 132, 178–80

Reigel, Don, 225

Relief missions, 227, 242, 244; to French Maquis, 219, 220, 221

Republic P-47. See P-47 Thunderbolt

Repulse, H.M.S., 52

Rex (Italian liner), 20–21

Rhine River, 226

Richards, Robert, 47, 49

Ridgewell (Essex County), 88

Rio de Janeiro, 19

Rjukan (Norway), 203

Roane, Owen D. ("Cowboy"), 181 ff, 201, 203, 204, 341; photo of, 183

Roberts, Sergeant, 117

Robins, Donald D., 56

Robinson, R. H., photo of, 199

Rocket bombs, 161, 296

Rocket fighters, German, 264–66; photos of, 266

Rolls-Royce engines, 93

Rommel, Erwin, 85, 108, 233

Rooney, Andy, 182

Roosevelt, Franklin D., 19, 22, 24, 80, 293; and daylight bombing, 113, 114; on Lend-Lease, 26–27

CPSIA information can be obtained
at www.ICGtesting.com
Printed in the USA
BVOW04s2300240817

492853BV00001B/14/P

9 781626 549043